macromedia®
FLASH® MX
ACTIONSCRIPTING
ADVANCED
TRAINING FROM THE SOURCE

Derek Franklin
Jobe Makar

macromedia®
PRESS

Macromedia Flash MX ActionScripting: Advanced Training from the Source

 Published by Macromedia Press, in association with Peachpit Press,
a division of Pearson Education.

Macromedia Press
1249 Eighth Street
Berkeley, CA 94710
510/524-2178
510/524-2221 (fax)
Find us on the World Wide Web at:
http://www.peachpit.com
http://www.macromedia.com

Printed and bound in the United States of America

ISBN 0-201-77022-9

9 8 7 6 5 4

CREDITS

Production Coordinator

Myrna Vladic, Bad Dog Graphics

Compositors

Rick Gordon, Emerald Valley Graphics

Debbie Roberti, Espresso Graphics

Editors

Jill Marts Lodwig, Wendy Sharp, Jill Simonsen

Indexer

Emily Glossbrenner

Tech Reviewers

Bentley Wolfe, Senior Support Engineer, Macromedia

I'm so very thankful to the people in my life that support me in so many ways. To Kathy and Ashlie, your understanding and long-suffering have not gone unnoticed. I love you both. Jobe, I can't think of anyone I would have rather have had by my side. You have a mastery of ActionScript that is pure genius. Jill Marts Lodwig, I'm so very happy that we got to work together again. Jill Simonsen, your thoroughness and intelligent suggestions and input have made a marked improvement in this book. Wendy Sharp, I'm sorry I ever doubted your wisdom about the book. I'm continually grateful to Marjorie Baer. To all the other folks at Peachpit Press that make this book something to be very proud of, I want to say thank you! And big thank you's to Justin Bratton, Edeltraud Rothmeier, and Sue Stailey (they're all my biggest fans), and my dear ol' dad, Roy Franklin, who died unexpectedly last year. I miss and love him so much!

—Derek

This book would not have been possible without the constant help and support from many people. To my beautiful wife Kelly, your infinite support and constructive comments have earned you the title of Biggest Supporter! Derek, this book's artwork is sheer wizardry and your writing is brilliant! It has been a pleasure working with you from concept to design. Jill Marts Lodwig, it's been a long and bumpy road. Thank you so much for your masterful editing, great advice, and constant understanding. Thanks also to Wendy Sharp and Jill Simonsen for making my sentences coherent. The files in this book requiring server-side integration would not have been possible without the help of Mike Grundvig of www.electrotank.com. Thanks Mike! Thanks also to Branden Hall of figleaf.com for letting us use AquaServer, an open-source socket server. And finally, Free, you are still my fluffiest supporter. Thanks for keeping my feet warm!

—Jobe

table of contents

INTRODUCTION   1

LESSON 1 INTRODUCING ACTIONSCRIPT   6

Why Learn ActionScript?
ActionScript Elements
The Planning Process
Writing Your First Script
Testing Your First Script

LESSON 2 USING EVENT HANDLERS   32

What Event Handlers Do
Choosing the Right Event Handler
Using Mouse Events
Making the Most of Attaching Mouse Events to Movie Clips
Using Frame Events
Using Clip Events
Orchestrating Multiple Events
Understanding Event Handler Methods
Using Event Handler Methods
Using 'Listeners'

LESSON 3 UNDERSTANDING TARGET PATHS 84

Understanding Multiple Timelines
Targeting the Current Movie
Targeting the Main Movie
Targeting a Parent Movie
Targeting Movie Clip Instances
Targeting Movies on Levels
Targeting Movie Clip Instances on Levels
Understanding Multiple Identities
Creating and Referencing Global Elements

LESSON 4 UNDERSTANDING AND USING OBJECTS 122

What Objects Are and Why They're Useful
Object Types
Using the Color Object
Using the Key Object to Add Interactivity
Working with String and Selection Objects

LESSON 5 USING FUNCTIONS 150

Creating Functions
Adding Parameters to Functions
Using Local Variables and Creating Functions that Return Results

LESSON 6 CUSTOMIZING OBJECTS 172

Understanding Object Mechanics
Defining a Custom Class and Creating Instances of that Class
Genetically Programming an Object by Customizing Its Prototype
Instance-Level Properties
Creating Subclasses
Creating Custom Methods for Custom Classes
Watching Properties
Enhancing Existing Object Methods
Defining Custom Methods for Prebuilt Objects
Registering Classes

LESSON 7 USING DYNAMIC DATA   236

Creating Variables
Creating Arrays
Creating Dynamic Text Fields and Retrieving Information
Retrieving the Data

LESSON 8 MANIPULATING DATA   264

Data Types
Building Expressions
Operators
Manipulating Numerical Data Using Math
Manipulating Strings

LESSON 9 USING CONDITIONAL LOGIC   282

Controlling a Script's Flow
Determining Conditions
Reacting to Multiple Conditions
Defining a Boundary
Turning Power On/Off
Reacting to User Interaction
Detecting Collisions

LESSON 10 AUTOMATING SCRIPTS WITH LOOPS   310

Why Loops Are Used
Types of Loops
Writing and Understanding Loop Conditions
Nested Loops
Loop Exceptions

LESSON 11 GETTING DATA IN AND OUT OF FLASH   336

Understanding Data Sources and Data Formats
Get vs. Post
Using the loadVars Object
Using Shared Objects

LESSON 12 USING XML WITH FLASH   366

Learning XML Basics
Using the XML Object
Introducing Socket Servers
Using the XMLSocket Object

LESSON 13 VALIDATING AND FORMATTING DATA   396

The Logic Behind Validating Data
Using Validation Routines
Handling Errors
Validating Strings
Validating Sequences
Validating Against a List of Choices
Validating Numbers
Dynamic Text Formatting with HTML
Creating and Controlling Text Fields with ActionScript
Using textFormat Objects

LESSON 14 CONTROLLING MOVIE CLIPS DYNAMICALLY   448

Creating Movie Clip Instances Dynamically
Using attachMovie()
Building Continuous-Feedback Buttons
Using ActionScript to Dynamically Draw Lines
Using the Draw Methods
Creating Filled Shapes Dynamically
z-Sorting Movie Clip Instances
Dragging and Dropping Movie Clip Instances
Removing Dynamically Created Content

LESSON 15 TIME- AND FRAME-BASED DYNAMISM   494

The Use of Time in Flash
Determining Current Date and Time
Determining the Passage of Time
Controlling the Playback Speed and Direction of a Timeline
Tracking Playback and Downloading Progression

LESSON 16 SCRIPTING FOR SOUND 524

Controlling Sound with ActionScript
Creating a Sound Object
Dragging a Movie Clip Instance Within a Boundary
Controlling Volume
Controlling Panning
Attaching Sounds and Controlling Sound Playback

LESSON 17 LOADING EXTERNAL ASSETS 556

The Ins and Outs of Loading External Assets
Loading Movies into a Target
Loading JPGs Dynamically
Creating an Interactive Placeholder
Loading Movies into a Level
Controlling a Movie on a Level
Loading MP3s Dynamically
Reacting to Dynamically Loaded MP3s

APPENDIX A RESOURCES 594

INDEX 596

introduction

ActionScript is the programming language that enables you to use Macromedia Flash to create highly interactive, multimedia-based Web sites, product demos, teaching materials, and more. If you're familiar with the logic behind other programming languages (especially JavaScript), you'll find ActionScript familiar. If, however, you're new to scripting, you'll probably wish you'd started earlier—especially once you begin to understand the language itself and what you can do with it. By the time you reach the end of this book, you'll be armed with a thorough knowledge of ActionScript— knowledge that will allow you to express yourself in ways you never before imagined!

This "Advanced Training from the Source" book introduces you to ActionScripting by guiding you, step by step, through projects that explain not only what's happening but *why* and *how*. Because the focus of each project is to teach you ActionScript, you'll find that any graphical elements and objects that aren't directly related to the task are already set up for you (though we'll always tell you why we're including them and, if necessary, what they do). The curriculum of this course should take you 20 to 25 hours to complete and includes the following lessons:

Lesson 1: Introducing ActionScript
Lesson 2: Using Event Handlers
Lesson 3: Understanding Target Paths
Lesson 4: Understanding and Using Objects
Lesson 5: Using Functions
Lesson 6: Customizing Objects
Lesson 7: Using Dynamic Data
Lesson 8: Manipulating Data
Lesson 9: Using Conditional Logic

Lesson 10: Automating Scripts with Loops
Lesson 11: Getting Data In and Out of Flash
Lesson 12: Using XML with Flash
Lesson 13: Validating and Formatting Data
Lesson 14: Controlling Movie Clips Dynamically
Lesson 15: Time- and Frame-Based Dynamism
Lesson 16: Scripting for Sound
Lesson 17: Loading External Content

Each lesson begins with an overview of the lesson's content and learning objectives, and is divided into tasks that teach you how to use aspects of the scripting language that relate to the theme of the lesson. What distinguishes this *Advanced* Training from the Source book from a standard Training from the Source course is that it offers *more:* more conceptual information, more in-depth material, and more explanations— plus special features, including:

Tips. These offer shortcuts for carrying out common tasks as well as ways to use the skills you're learning to solve common problems.

Notes. Additional information pertaining to the task at hand.

In addition, Appendix A contains a list of Flash resources pertaining to many aspects of using Flash, including scripting, design, animation, usability and more.

This course is designed so that you build your skills as you work through each lesson. By the time you've completed the entire course, you should understand ActionScript's syntax, capabilities, and the logic that drives it—and thus be able to create your own dynamic, highly interactive Flash content!

The enclosed CD contains all of the files necessary to complete each lesson. Files for each lesson appear in their own folders, titled with the lesson name. Each lesson folder contains two subfolders: Assets and Completed. The Assets folder contains any media files needed for the lesson, as well as the initial Flash file for the lesson. The files you will need are identified at the beginning of each lesson. The Completed folder contains completed files so that you can compare your work or see where you're headed.

We suggest that you create a folder on your hard drive and transfer all lesson files to that folder before beginning the course. The reason for this is that you will need to test your work using Flash's Test Movie command, which creates a temporary test file in the same directory as the currently opened .fla. Thus, if the authoring file was opened from the CD, Flash will attempt to create the temporary test movie on the CD, which is almost always impossible and will result in an error.

The lessons in this book assume the following:

- You know how to use menus, open and save files, and so on for either the Windows or Macintosh operating system.

- Flash MX is already installed on your machine, and your computer meets the system requirements listed below.

- You're familiar with Flash's interface as well as authoring movies, creating and using movie elements, using the timeline, using basic actions, and (especially) employing the Actions panel. If not, you might want to begin by working your way through *Macromedia Flash MX: Training from the Source*, an introductory book from Macromedia Press.

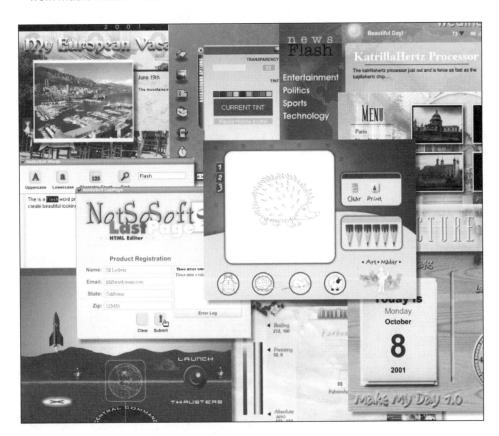

A collage of some of the many projects you will script in this course.

WHAT YOU WILL LEARN

By the end of this course, you will be able to:

- Plan an interactive project
- Understand ActionScript syntax and how it works
- Use the numerous event handlers to create a variety of interactivity
- Target movies using relative and absolute paths
- Use and understand built-in objects, properties, and methods
- Use functions to centralize your code
- Create custom objects and methods
- Manipulate text and numbers dynamically to perform specific tasks
- Use conditional logic to enable your movie to make decisions and react to varying circumstances
- Use loops to automate scripting tasks
- Move data in and out of Flash using text files and XML
- Connect to a socket server for real-time data transfer
- Validate and format all types of data
- Dynamically control movies via scripting (as opposed to the timeline)
- Load and unload media assets
- Script sounds
- Employ date, time, and frame-based interactivity
- Use time-tested methodologies for creating dynamically driven Flash applications

MINIMUM SYSTEM REQUIREMENTS

Windows

- 200 MHz Intel Pentium processor
- Windows 98 SE, Windows Me, Windows NT4, Windows 2000, or Windows XP
- 64 MB of free available system RAM (128 MB recommended)
- 85 MB of available disk space
- 1024 × 768, 16-bit (thousands of colors) color display or better
- CD-ROM drive

Macintosh

- Mac OS 9.1 and higher, or OS X 10.1 and higher
- 64 MB of free available system RAM (128 MB recommended)
- 85 MB of available disk space
- 1024 × 768, 16-bit (thousands of colors) color display or better
- CD-ROM drive

NOTE *To complete the exercises in Lesson 12, Using XML with Flash, you will need access to a Windows server. In addition, users of Macintosh OS 9.1, Windows Me, and Windows NT4 will not be able to complete the exercises* Introducing Socket Servers *and* Using the XMLSocket Object, *also in Lesson 12.*

introducing ActionScript

Introductions form the start of any great relationship. Get ready, then, to be introduced to your new best friend: ActionScript! We believe you'll find ActionScript a satisfying companion—especially as you delve deeper into the relationship. Although you may not necessarily think of scripting as a creative endeavor, a working knowledge of ActionScript can spark all kinds of ideas—ones that will enable you to create dynamic content that can interact with your users on myriad levels. Best of all, you'll get the satisfaction of watching your ideas grow into working models that fulfill your projects' objectives.

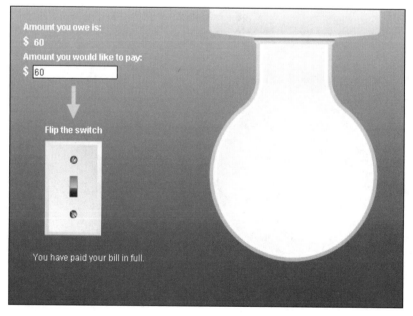

We'll plan, create, and test a highly interactive electric bill payment system.

In this chapter, we'll show you some compelling reasons for learning ActionScripting, as well as what makes it tick. And if you're feeling a little shy, sometimes the best thing to do is jump right in—which is exactly what you'll do here as you create and test a complete interactive project before chapter's end.

WHAT YOU WILL LEARN

In this lesson, you will:

- Discover the benefits of ActionScript

- Learn about script elements

- Plan a project

- Write your first script

- Test your script

APPROXIMATE TIME

This lesson takes approximately 1 hour to complete.

LESSON FILES

Media files:

None

Starting File:

Lesson01/Assets/electricbill1.fla

Completed Projects:

electricbill2.fla

electricbill3.fla

7

WHY LEARN ACTIONSCRIPT?

In its early days, Macromedia Flash was considered primarily an animation tool. However, as people began to comprehend the awe-inspiring things they could accomplish with the program, Flash sites began to pop up everywhere. Macromedia responded by delivering more powerful tools for creating Web content, and Flash quickly went from being a simple animation program to a powerful application development tool. Now, Web site visitors expected not just eye-popping animations but mind-blowing interactivity as well. Everyone from individuals to Fortune 500 corporations began to see the potential of interactive content. However, even though a number of technologies (including JavaScript) existed to help facilitate this interactivity, none was as elegant or easy as Flash. Once people began to realize they didn't need a computer science degree to use the program, Flash's popularity exploded.

Today, if you're a Flash developer, one thing is certain: Animation skills, no matter how phenomenal, are no longer enough. A firm grasp of ActionScript is essential because without it, only the most elementary interactivity is possible. By acquiring an in-depth knowledge of ActionScript, you can:

- Provide a personalized user experience
- Achieve greater control over movie clips and their properties
- Animate elements in your movie programmatically—that is, without using the timeline
- Get data in and out of Flash to create forms, chat programs, and more
- Create dynamic projects that respond to the passage of time or the current date
- Dynamically control sound volume and panning
- Much more

Add to these benefits the fact that viewing and interacting with Flash content can be more than just a Web experience. Flash can create self-running applications or mini-programs that operate independently of the browser—a capability more and more people are putting to use to create games, learning applications, and more. If you want to do this, too, you need at least an intermediate knowledge of ActionScript.

ACTIONSCRIPT ELEMENTS

ActionScript is a language that bridges the gap between what you understand and what Flash understands. As such, it allows you to provide both action-oriented instructions (*do this*) and logic-oriented instructions (*analyze this before doing that*) to your Flash project. Like all languages, ActionScript contains many different elements, such as words, punctuation, and structure—all of which you must employ properly to get your Flash project to behave the way you want it to. If you don't employ ActionScript correctly, you'll find that interactivity either won't occur or won't work the way you intended. Many of these elements, as well as several other more logical elements such as logical statements and expressions, will be dealt with in much more detail throughout the book.

To begin to understand how ActionScript works, take a look at the following script, which contains many of the essential elements that make up a typical script. Following the script is a discussion of these elements and their role in the script's execution. We can assume that this script is attached to a button:

```
on (release) {
  //set the cost of the mug
  mugCost = 5.00;
  //set the local sales tax percentage
  taxPercent = .06;
  //determine the dollar amount of tax
  totalTax = mugCost * taxPercent;
  //determine the total amount of the transaction
  totalCost = mugCost + totalTax;
  //display a custom message
  myTextBox.text = "The total cost of your transaction is " + totalTax;
  //send the cashRegister movie clip instance to frame 50
  cashRegister.gotoAndPlay (50);
}
```

Although at first glance this may look like Latin, once you become acquainted with some of its elements, you shouldn't find it too difficult to understand.

NOTE *There are additional script elements (for example, objects, functions, loops, properties, and methods), which we will discuss in greater detail throughout the book.*

EVENTS

These are things that occur, during the playback of a movie, which trigger the execution of a particular script. In our sample script above, the event that triggers the script is `on (release)`. This signifies that when the button to which this script is attached is released, the script will execute. Every script is triggered by an event, and your movie can contain numerous events—everything from a button being pressed to text changing in a text field to a sound completing its playback, and more.

ACTIONS

These form the heart of your script and are usually considered to be any line that instructs Flash to do, set, create, change, load, or delete something.

The following are a couple of examples of actions from the sample script above:

```
mugCost = 5.00;
cashRegister.gotoAndPlay (50);
```

Generally speaking, actions comprise most of the lines in a script that are within curly braces ({}) and usually separated by semicolons (see below).

OPERATORS

These include a number of symbols (=, <, >, +, -, *, &&, etc.) and are used to connect two elements in a script in various ways. Take a look at the following examples:

`taxPercent = .06;` assigns a value of .06 to the variable named `taxPercent`

`amountA < amountB` asks if `amountA` is less than `amountB`

`value1 * 500` multiplies `value1` times 500

KEYWORDS

These are words reserved for specific purposes within ActionScript syntax. As such, they cannot be used as variable, function, or label names. For example, the word `on` is a keyword and can only be used in a script to denote an event that triggers a script, such as `on(press)`, `on(rollOver)`, `on(rollOut)`, and so on. Attempting to use keywords in your scripts for anything other than their intended purpose will result in errors. (Other keywords include `break`, `case`, `continue`, `delete`, `do`, `else`, `for`, `function`, `if`, `in`, `instanceOf`, `new`, `return`, `switch`, `this`, `typeOf`, `var`, `void`, `while`, and `with`.)

DATA

A dynamic script almost always creates, uses, or updates various pieces of data during its execution. Variables are the most common pieces of dynamic data found in scripts and represent pieces of data that have been given unique names. Once a variable has been created and assigned a value, its value can be accessed anywhere in the script simply by inserting its name.

In our sample script above, we gave a variable name of `mugCost` to the value of 5.00. Later in the script, the name of that variable is used to refer to the value it contains.

CURLY BRACES

Generally speaking, anything that falls between opening and closing curly braces signifies an action or actions the script needs to perform when triggered. Think of curly braces as being used to say, "As a result of this – {do this}." For example:

```
on (release) {
  //set the cost of the mug
  mugCost = 5.00;
  //set the local sales tax percentage
  taxPercent = .06;
}
```

SEMICOLONS

Appearing at the end of most lines of scripts (within curly braces), semicolons are used to separate multiple actions that may need to be executed as the result of a single event (similar to the way commas are used to separate thoughts in a single sentence). The following example denotes six separate actions, separated by semicolons:

```
mugCost = 5.00;
taxPercent = .06;
totalTax = mugCost * taxPercent;
totalCost = mugCost + totalTax;
myTextBox = "The total cost of your transaction is " + totalTax;
cashRegister.gotoAndPlay (50);
```

DOT SYNTAX

Dots (.) are used within scripts in a couple of ways: One is to denote the target path to a specific timeline. For example, _root.usa.indiana.bloomington points to a movie clip on the main (_root) timeline named "usa," which contains a movie clip named "indiana," which contains a movie clip named "bloomington."

Because ActionScript is an object-oriented language, most interactive tasks are accomplished by changing a characteristic (property) of an object or by telling an object to do something (invoking a method). When changing a property or when invoking a method, dots are used to separate the object's name from the property or method being worked with. For example, movie clips are objects; thus to set the rotation property of a movie clip instance named **wheel**, you would use the following syntax:

```
wheel._rotation = 90;
```

Notice how a dot separates the name of the object from the property being set.

To tell the same movie clip instance to play (invoking the `play()` method), you would use the following syntax:

```
wheel.play()
```

Once again, a dot separates the name of the object from the method invoked.

PARENTHESES

These are used in various ways in ActionScript. For the most part, scripts employ them to set a specific amount that an action will use during its execution. Look at the last line of our sample script that tells the **cashRegister** movie clip instance to go to and play Frame 50:

```
cashRegister.gotoAndPlay (50);
```

If the value within parentheses is changed from 50 to 20, the action still performs the same basic task (moving the timeline to a specified frame number); it just does so according to the new value. Parentheses are a way of telling an action to work based on what's specified in between them.

QUOTATION MARKS

These are used to denote textual data in the script. Because text is used to create the script, quotation marks provide the only means for a script to distinguish between instructions (pieces of data) and actual words. For example, Derek (without quotes) signifies the name of a piece of data. "Derek," on the other hand, signifies the actual word *Derek*.

COMMENTS

These are lines in the script preceded by two forward-slash marks (//). When executing a script, Flash ignores lines containing comments. Instead, these are provided as a means to insert descriptive notes about what the script is doing at this point in its execution. By using comments, you can review a script months after it was written and still get a clear idea of its underlying logic.

INDENTATION/SPACING

Although not absolutely necessary, it's a good idea to indent and space the syntax in your code. For example:

```
on(release) {
mugCost = 5.00;
}
```

Will execute the same as:

```
on(release) {
  mugCost = 5.00;
}
```

However, by indenting code, you make it easier to read. A good rule of thumb is to indent anything within curly braces to indicate that the code within those braces represent a *code block*, or chunk of code, that is to be executed at the same time. (Flash MX's autoformat feature takes care of most of this for you.) You can nest code blocks within other code blocks—a concept that will become clearer as you work through the exercises.

For the most part, white space is ignored within a script. Take a look at the following line of script:

```
totalCost = mugCost + totalTax ;
```

This will execute in the same way as:

```
totalCost=mugCost+totalTax;
```

While some programmers feel that extra white space makes their code easier to read, others believe it slows them down to insert spaces. For the most part, the choice is yours. There are, however, a couple of exceptions to be aware of: Variable names cannot contain spaces, nor can you put a space between an object name and an associated property/method. Thus, although the following is acceptable:

```
myObject.propertyName
```

This is not:

```
myObject. propertyName
```

THE PLANNING PROCESS

When creating a project that will contain a generous amount of ActionScript, it's wise to do some planning up front. Dealing with problems in the idea stage makes a lot more sense than dealing with them in the development stage, where they often require a great deal of time and frustration to fix. We guarantee you'll save time in the long run.

Many issues must be addressed before you even open Flash and start scripting. A good way to go about this is to ask yourself a series of questions.

WHAT DO YOU WANT TO OCCUR?

This is most important question in the script-planning process. Be as clear, informative, and visual as possible in your answer, but avoid going into too much detail.

For the project we'll create in this exercise, we want to create a scene that acts as a front end for paying your electric bill. We want the amount of the bill to be loaded into the movie from an external source, a text file. We then want to allow the user to enter an amount to pay into a text box. When a button is *pressed*, the amount the user paid will be compared to the amount he or she owed, and a visual and textual representation (a custom message) of the result—overpaid, underpaid, or paid in full—will be presented. When the user *releases* that button, we want the visual and textual elements in the scene to return to their original state. The script that accomplishes this will be the main script in the project.

WHAT PIECES OF DATA DO YOU NEED TO TRACK?

In other words, what numbers or values in the application are integral to its function? In our case, that data is the amount of the electric bill—$60. We will also need to keep track of the difference between what the user owes and what he or she has paid, so that we can display that value in custom messages.

WHAT NEEDS TO HAPPEN IN THE MOVIE PRIOR TO A SCRIPT BEING TRIGGERED?

In our project, the amount of the electric bill must be established in the movie before anything else can happen. Since the primary goal of our project is to compare the amount of the electric bill with the amount the user chooses to pay, if the amount of the electric bill isn't established when the movie first plays, there will be nothing to compare when the script is executed. Creating and setting data prior to a script being executed, or when a movie first plays, is known as initializing the data—a common practice in scripting and something that's usually transparent to the user.

At this point, you need to start thinking about how the data—the amount of the electric bill—will get into the movie. You can place it within the movie when you author it, or you can have it loaded from an external source (for example, a server or text file) when the movie plays. For our project, we're going to opt for the latter: We'll use a simple script to load a text file containing the amount of the electric bill ($60) into the movie. This text file that's loaded into the movie to provide data is known as a *data source*.

WHAT EVENT WILL TRIGGER THE MAIN SCRIPT?

In our case, the answer is obvious: a button press. However, all kinds of events can trigger a script in Flash, so it's important to give some thought to this question. Does something need to happen when a user moves, presses down, or releases the mouse, or when he or she presses a key? How about when a movie clip first appears in the scene? Or does the event need to happen continuously (the whole time the movie is playing)? We'll discuss such events in detail in your next lesson.

ARE THERE DECISIONS TO BE MADE WHEN THE MAIN SCRIPT IS TRIGGERED?

When the main script in our movie is triggered, the amount the user enters to pay needs to be compared with the amount he or she owes to determine whether the payment amount is too much, too little, or right on target. The answers to these questions will determine what custom message will be displayed as well as what is visible on the screen.

WHAT ELEMENTS MAKE UP THE SCENE? HOW DO THEY FUNCTION?

Our scene will be made up of a number of elements, some of which we need to name so that ActionScript can use, control, and/or interact with them. Our scene will need a button to trigger the script, which in light of the project (pun intended), we'll make appear as a light switch flipping on and off as it's pressed and released.

We'll also need a dynamic text field to display the amount of the bill; we'll name this text field **owed**. In addition, we'll need an input text field where the user can enter the amount he or she wishes to pay; we'll name this text field **paid**. We'll also need a dynamic text field to display the custom message generated by the script; we'll name this text field **message**. Lastly, for visual purposes, we'll add a big light bulb to the scene. Initially, and if the user has not paid enough, it will appear off. The bulb will light if the user pays the exact amount, and it will glow if the user overpays. This light bulb will be a movie clip instance named simply **light**.

WHAT WILL YOUR SCENE LOOK LIKE?

Use whatever means you want—an illustration program or even a napkin—to create a rough graphical representation of your scene (both its appearance and the action that will take place). Include all of the information you've gathered up to this point. This important part of the planning process is often referred to as storyboarding.

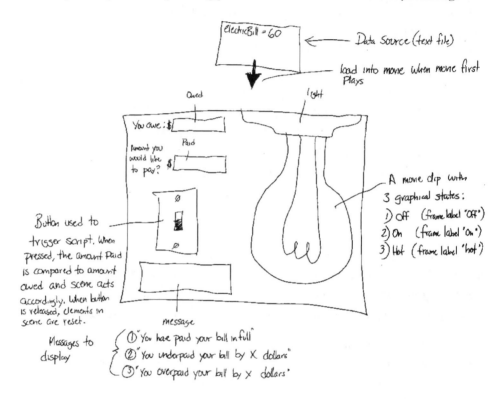

As you grow more proficient at ActionScript and develop additional projects, you'll soon be able to ask (and answer) these questions intuitively. However, no matter what your skill level, storyboarding remains an essential part of the planning process.

WRITING YOUR FIRST SCRIPT

Now that we have all the information we need as well as a rough storyboard for our project, let's begin assembling it.

1) Open Windows Notepad or Apple Simple Text to create a new text file, and type the following: *&electricBill=60.*

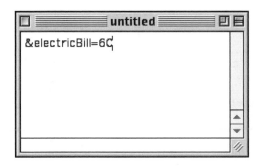

In the first part of this exercise we'll create the source for the data to be loaded into our movie when it plays. For our project, this data source contains a value representing the amount of the electric bill. When Flash loads this text file, it interprets this line of text and creates within the movie a piece of data (called a *variable)* named **electricBill** and assigns it a value of 60. The value of this variable will be used several ways in our project.

NOTE *Loading data into Flash from external sources is discussed in detail in Lesson 11, Getting Data In and Out of Flash. Variables are discussed in detail in Lesson 7, Using Dynamic Data.*

2) Name the text file Electric_Bill.txt and save it in the folder that contains the files for this lesson, then open electricbill1.fla in the Lesson01/Assets folder.
Because the focus of this book is ActionScript, *not* how to use Flash, you'll find that with the exception of setting up scripts, our project elements are largely in place.

Our project's main timeline contains five layers, each of which are 10 frames long. The layers will be named in such a way that their content is evident. Currently, the Actions layer is empty.

3) Open the Property inspector, then select the text field in the upper left corner of the scene, just under the text that reads "Amount you owe is:". In the Property inspector, give this text field an instance name of *owed*.

Since this text field will be used to display the amount of the electric bill, we've named it **owed**.

In Flash 5, giving text fields variable names was the preferred way of identifying them for use in ActionScript. In Flash MX, however, text fields are now instances of the new Text Field object. As such, they are now identified using instance names. Although you can still assign variable names to text fields, some of the new functionality afforded Text Field objects will not be available if you do so. Thus, it's better to use instance names to identify text fields.

4) With the Property inspector still open, select the text field under the text that reads, "Amount you would like to pay is:". In the Property inspector, give this text field an instance name of *paid*.

Looking at the Property inspector, you'll notice that this is an Input Text field. It will be used to accept input from the user, specifically the amount he or she wants to pay toward the electric bill. We've entered zero (0) in this text field, so that's the amount that will appear initially when our movie plays.

5) With the Property inspector still open, select the text field at the bottom of the scene, under the Switch button. In the Property inspector, give this text field an instance name of *message*.

This text field will be used to display a custom message to our user, depending on how much he or she chooses to pay.

6) Select the lightbulb movie clip instance and name it *light*.

Since our script will affect this movie clip instance, we must give the movie clip instance a name so that we can tell the script what to do with it. This movie clip instance has three frame labels (Off, On, and Hot) on its timeline that represent how it will look under various conditions. Initially, it will appear as Off.

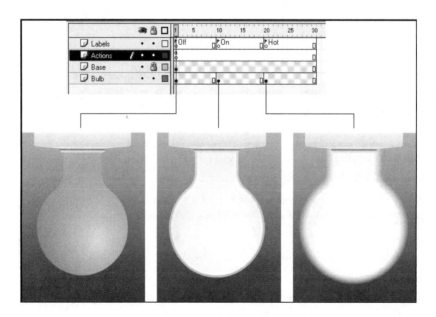

In our script (which we'll set up in a moment), we want the movie clip to remain at this label if the user pays less than what he or she owes—that is, the light won't come on because the user hasn't paid enough. If the user pays the exact amount, we want to send the clip's timeline to the frame label On—that is, we want the light to come on. If the user pays too much, we want the clip's timeline to go to the frame labeled Hot so that the light appears to be getting more juice than it needs.

Now that all of our scene elements are named, we're ready to begin scripting; we'll begin by instructing our movie to load the data from our external text file.

7) With the Actions panel open (and set to Expert Mode), select Frame 1 of the Actions layer, and enter the following script:

```
loadVariablesNum ("Electric_Bill.txt", 0);
```

NOTE *We suggest you leave the Actions panel in Expert Mode because it represents the easiest way to enter most of the scripts discussed in this book.*

This line of script does one thing: It loads the variables from the Electric_Bill.txt file (which we created earlier) into Level 0, which is the movie file we're working on now. The Electric_Bill.txt file contains a single variable named `electricBill` with a value of 60. Thus, after this line of script has executed, our movie will contain an `electricBill` variable with a value of 60. This process simply transfers the variables from our text file into our movie.

`loadVariablesNum()` is an action. We make it work a specific way by placing unique parameter values inside the parentheses. This particular action has two parameter settings, separated by a comma. The first setting is used to indicate the source containing the external data; the second is used to indicate the timeline into which to load the data. You'll find that many ActionScript elements can accept multiple parameter settings in a similar fashion.

We've placed this script on Frame 1 of our movie so that it will be executed as soon as the movie begins playing—important since our movie needs the `electricBill` value in order for the script that we'll be adding to the Light Switch button to work.

8) Add a keyframe to Frame 10 of the Actions layer. Then, with the Actions panel open, enter the following script on that keyframe:

```
owed.text = electricBill;
stop ();
```

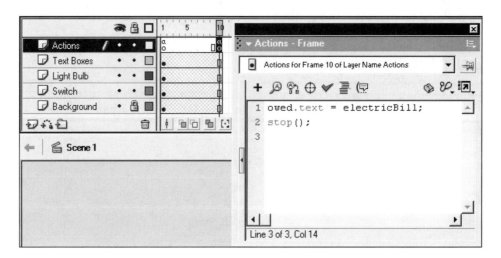

As set up in the last step, Frame 1 contains an action that will load the variables in the Electric_Bill.txt file. The movie's timeline continues to play as the text file loads; then, when it reaches Frame 10, the above actions are executed.

The first action will set the value displayed in the **owed** text field instance to equal the value of `electricBill`. You'll remember that **owed** is the instance name we assigned to the text field in the upper-left corner of our project, and that `electricBill` is the variable loaded in from our text file with a value of 60. Thus, this line of script will cause the number 60 to appear in the **owed** text field.

As mentioned earlier, text fields are now considered objects in Flash MX. As such, they also have numerous properties. One of the new properties of a text field instance is its `text` property. This property is used to designate the text displayed in an instance. The above script demonstrates how this property is used to set the text displayed in the text field instance named **owed.** Notice how a dot (.) separates the object name from the name of its property. In ActionScript, this is how you specify that you want to work with something specific concerning the object—in this case, one of its properties.

The first line also demonstrates the use of an operator between two elements, an object property and a variable (and its value). Here, the equals sign (=) is used to tell the script to assign the value of the `electricBill` variable to the text property of the **owed** text field instance.

The last action in the script simply stops the timeline from playing. Because this action does not require any unique parameter values, the parentheses are left empty.

TIP *You'll notice that there's a span of several frames between the frame containing the action to load the variables from the text file and the Frame 10 action that actually uses the `electricBill` variable that's been loaded. This allows time for the text file to actually load. If we tried to use the `electricBill` variable before the text file had finished loading, we would encounter problems. In fact, our movie might act as if the text files had never loaded. A frame cushion, as we've created here, is one way to prevent problems. We'll discuss other ways in later lessons.*

Now it's time to set up the script for our Light Switch button.

9) With the Actions panel open, select the Light Switch button and enter the following script:

```
on (press) {
  amountPaid = Number(paid.text);
  amountOwed = Number(owed.text);
}
```

The first thing to notice about this script is that it executes when the button it's attached to is pressed. Following this event is an opening curly brace ({), a couple lines of script, then a closing curly brace (}). These curly braces are used to say, "Do these two things as the result of the button being pressed."

The above script accomplishes two things: First, a variable named `amountPaid` is created and its value is set to equal that displayed in the **paid** text field instance—though with a twist. Normally, anything entered in a text field is considered text. Thus, even if a value of 100 appears in the text field as numerals, it's considered text (consisting of the characters 1, 0, and 0, or "100" with quotes) rather than the number 100 (without quotes).

You can think of the `Number()` function as a specialized tool that allows you to convert a text value to a numerical value in such a way that ActionScript recognizes it as a number instead. You need to place the text that you want to convert between the parentheses of the function. For example:

```
myNumber = Number("945");
```

This will convert the text "945" to the number 945 (no quotes) and assign that number value to the variable named `myNumber`. In the above script, we used the `Number()` function and placed a reference to the text value to be converted between the parentheses of the function. Thus, if the user types "54" (text initially) into the **paid** field, the `Number` function causes `amountPaid` to be given a value of 54 (no quotes, thus the number 54) as well.

The next line in the script does essentially the same thing, only the value of `amountOwed` is set to equal the converted-to-a-number value displayed in the **owed** text field instance. You'll remember that this text field instance displays the amount of the electric bill, or "60". Thus, after the conversion takes place, `amountOwed` is given a value of 60.

The reason for converting the values in the text fields in this way is that most of the rest of the script will be using them to make mathematical evaluations/calculations—which means it needs to see them as numbers, not text, in order for them to work.

In summary, when the button is pressed, the text values displayed in the **paid** and **owed** text fields are converted to numbers. These number values are assigned to the variables named `amountPaid` and `amountOwed`, respectively. These variable values will be used in the remainder of the script.

10) With the Actions panel still open, add the following lines of script to the script created in the previous step. Add them within the curly braces ({}), just below where it says `amountOwed = Number(owed.text);`**:**

```
if (amountPaid < amountOwed) {
  difference = amountOwed - amountPaid;
  light.gotoAndStop ("Off");
  message.text = "You underpaid your bill by " + difference + " dollars.";
} else if (amountPaid > amountOwed) {
  difference = amountOwed - amountPaid;
  light.gotoAndStop ("Hot");
  message.text = "You overpaid your bill by " + difference + " dollars.";
} else {
  light.gotoAndStop ("On");
  message.text = "You have paid your bill in full.";
}
```

Since we added these lines of script *within* the curly braces of the `on(press)` event, they are also executed when the button is pressed.

This part of the script is essentially broken into three parts, identified by the following lines:

```
if (amountPaid < amountOwed)
else if (amountPaid > amountOwed)
else
```

```
4     if (amountPaid < amountOwed) {
5         difference = amountOwed - amountPaid;
6         light.gotoAndStop ("Off");
7         message.text = "You underpaid your bill by " + difference + " dollars.";
8     } else if (amountPaid > amountOwed) {
9         difference = amountOwed - amountPaid;
10        light.gotoAndStop ("Hot");
11        message.text = "You overpaid your bill by " + difference + " dollars.";
12    } else {
13        light.gotoAndStop ("On");
14        message.text = "You have paid your bill in full.";
15    }
```

These three lines represent a series of conditions the script will analyze when executed. The condition to be analyzed is specified between the parentheses. Underneath each of these lines in the script (between additional curly braces) are several lines of indented script, which represent the actions that will be executed if that particular condition proves true. Here's how it works:

When our Light Switch button is pressed, we want our script to determine whether the amount the user enters to pay is more, less, or equal to the amount owed. That's what the three conditions our script analyzes are all about. Let's review the first condition, which looks like this:

```
if (amountPaid < amountOwed) {
  difference = amountOwed - amountPaid;
  light.gotoAndStop ("Off");
  message.text = "You underpaid your bill by " + difference + " dollars.";
}
```

The first line is a less-than operator (<) used to compare the value of one variable to another. It basically states, "If the amount the user enters to pay (amountPaid) is *less* than the amount he or she owes (amountOwed), take the actions below." These actions are only executed if this condition is true. And if they are executed, it's as a group, which is why they're placed within their own set of curly braces. The first action creates a variable named difference and assigns it a value of amountOwed minus amountPaid. If the user has entered 40 as the amount to pay, difference would have a value of 20 (amountOwed – amountPaid, or 60 – 40). It's important to note that any equation to the right of the equals sign is calculated prior to assigning the calculated value to the item to the left. The next line tells the **light** movie clip instance to go to and stop at the frame labeled Off. Since this action is only executed if the user underpays his or her bill, it's appropriate that the light stays off. The last line will generate a custom message to be displayed in the **message** text field.

We call this a *custom* message because of the way the message is constructed within the script. Note the use of the difference variable in this line: The value of difference is inserted in the middle of this message between the two sections of quoted text and the plus signs. If difference has a value of 20 (as described above), this message would read:

"You underpaid your bill by 20 dollars."

Remember that anything within quotes is considered plain text. Because difference is not enclosed in quotes, ActionScript knows that it references a variable's name and thus will insert that variable's value there. The plus sign (+) is used to concatenate (join) everything to create a single message. The equals sign is used to assign the final, concatenated value to the text property of the **message** text field.

If the amount the user enters to pay is the same as what's owed, or more, this part of the script is ignored and the next part of the script is analyzed. It reads as follows:

```
else if (amountPaid > amountOwed) {
  difference = amountOwed - amountPaid;
  light.gotoAndStop ("Hot");
  message.text = "You overpaid your bill by " + difference + " dollars.";
}
```

The first line here states, "If the amount the user enters to pay is *more* than the amount he or she owes, take the actions below." The actions executed here are just variations on the ones discussed above—with a couple of minor differences: The first difference is that the **light** movie clip instance is sent to the frame labeled Hot, which displays a light bulb getting too much energy to signify that the user has overpaid. The second difference comes in the wording of the custom message. Instead of saying *underpaid*, here it says *overpaid*. The actions in this section are only executed if the user pays more than what's owed. If that's not the case, these actions are ignored and the last part of the script is analyzed. It reads as follows:

```
else {
  light.gotoAndStop ("On");
  message.text = "You have paid your bill in full.";
}
```

You'll notice that here the script doesn't begin by asking if amountPaid is more or less than amountOwed (as did the first two sections). This is because the script wouldn't be carrying out this analysis if the user had entered the exact amount owed—that is, this part of the script will only execute if neither of the first sections do.

In the end, when the button is pressed, only one of these three actions will execute. As a result, the **light** movie clip instance will appear a certain way and a custom message will appear in the **message** text field.

When the Light Switch button is released, we want to reset the elements in our scene so that they appear as they did when the movie first played. Let's add that functionality.

11) With the Actions panel open and the Light Switch button still selected, enter the following script at the end of the current script:

```
on (release) {
  light.gotoAndStop ("Off");
  message.text = "";
}
```

This script is triggered when the button is released. It will send the **light** movie clip instance to the frame labeled Off and empty the **message** text field, returning these scene elements to their original state.

12) Save this file as electricBill2.fla.

We'll use this file in the next exercise in this lesson.

TESTING YOUR FIRST SCRIPT

It would be pure fantasy to believe ActionScripts always work exactly as planned. Just as it's easy to forget a comma or to misspell a word when writing a letter, it's easy to make mistakes when writing scripts—regardless of how familiar you are with ActionScript. However, unlike your letter recipients, Flash is unforgiving when it comes to script errors. In scripting, errors mean bugs, and bugs mean your script either won't work at all or won't work as planned. Luckily, Flash provides some handy ways to test scripts and stamp out bugs.

1) If electricBill2.fla isn't already open, open it now.

This is the file we set up in the last exercise. In this exercise, we'll test the project's functionality from within Flash's testing environment.

2) From Flash's menu bar, choose Control > Test Movie.

This command creates a temporary, fully functional version of your exported movie and displays it in Flash's testing environment. Although there are all kinds of ways you can test your movie in this environment (determining overall file size, streaming capability, and appearance), we're interested in testing its interactive features—which means doing everything we can to mess it up.

TIP *Enlist as many friends and colleagues as possible to help you test your project. This way you have a greater chance of testing every possible scenario and thus finding all of the potential bugs.*

3) Enter various amounts in the "Amount you would like to pay:" text field, then press the Light Switch button.

- **Enter an amount *less* than 60.** If you enter 35 in this text field, a message should appear that says, "You underpaid your bill by 25 dollars," and the **light** movie clip instance should remain off.

- **Enter an amount *more* than 60.** If you enter 98 in this text field, a message should appear that says, "You have overpaid your bill by 38 dollars," and the **light** movie clip instance should appear hot (its visual state at the frame labeled Hot). As we said, though, this is what *should* happen. What really happens is that the message shows an overpayment of –38 dollars, not 38 dollars! We'll log this bug as an error and continue testing.

- **Enter the exact amount of 60.** If you enter 60 into this text field, a message should appear stating, "You have paid your bill in full," and the **light** movie clip instance should appear to be on.

- **Erase everything in this field.** If you do this and press the Light Switch button, you get a message stating, "You have paid your bill in full" and the **light** movie clip instance will appear on. Obviously, this is wrong: We will log this as an error and continue testing.

- **Enter some text.** If you enter anything beginning with a letter and then press the Light Switch button, you'll get a message reading, "You have paid your bill in full" and the **light** movie clip instance will turn on—another obvious mistake, which we'll log as an error.

> **TIP** *When you find bugs while testing a complex project, it's sometimes best to stop testing and begin the bug-stomping process immediately (as opposed to logging several bugs first, then attempting to fix them all at once). The reason for this is that when attempting to eliminate a bug, you may unwittingly introduce a new one. Thus, fixing several bugs at once could result in several new bugs—obviously not what you want. By fixing bugs one at a time, you can better concentrate your bug-squashing efforts and avoid a lot of needless backtracking.*

As you learned from the above, our project contains the following three bugs:

- If a user overpays his or her bill, the overage is shown as a negative number in the custom message that is displayed.

- If a user chooses not to pay anything, our project functions incorrectly.

- If a user enters text rather than a numeric value, our project functions incorrectly.

Now let's think about why these bugs are occurring: In the case of the first bug, we know that the numeric value that appears in this dynamic message is based on the value of difference when the script is executed. In addition, we know that the problem only occurs if the user pays *more* than the amount of the bill. Thus, the problem lies in the way difference is calculated when the user overpays his or her bill. We'll review that part of our script.

As for the other two bugs, our script is set up to act various ways when executed, depending on what amount the user enters to pay. However, we forgot to account for the possibility that the user might not enter anything, or that he or she might enter text, both of which cause our project to act funny. We'll make a slight addition to our script to account for this.

4) Close the testing environment and return to the authoring environment. Select the Light Switch button and modify Line 9 of the script, which currently reads:

difference = amountOwed - amountPaid; **to read** difference = amountPaid — amountOwed;

```
   ┌─────────────────────────────────────────────────────────────────────[×]─┐
   │ ⋮ ▼ Actions - Button                                                  ≣  │
   ├──────────────────────────────────────────────────────────────────────────┤
   │ 🔄 Actions for [No instance name assigned] (Light_Switch)         ▼  ⤝│ │
   │ + 🔎 🎞 ⊕ ✔ ≣ ⊡                                          ◈ 🐾 ▦⤢ │
   │  1 on (press) {                                                        ▲│
   │  2      amountPaid = Number(paid.text);                                 │
   │  3      amountOwed = Number(owed.text);                                 │
   │  4      if (amountPaid < amountOwed) {                                  │
   │  5          difference = amountOwed - amountPaid;                       │
   │  6          light.gotoAndStop ("Off");                                  │
   │  7          message.text = "You underpaid your bill by " + difference + " dollars.";│
   │  8      } else if (amountPaid > amountOwed) {                           │
   │  9          difference = amountPaid - amountOwed;                       │
   │ 10          light.gotoAndStop ("Hot");                                  │
   │ 11          message.text = "You overpaid your bill by " + difference + " dollars.";│
   │ 12      } else {                                                        │
   │ 13          light.gotoAndStop ("On");                                   │
   │ 14          message.text = "You have paid your bill in full.";          │
   │ 15      }                                                               │
   │ 16 }                                                                    │
   │ 17 on (release) {                                                       │
   │ 18      light.gotoAndStop ("Off");                                      │
   │ 19      message.text = "";                                              │
   │ 20 }                                                                    │
   │ 21                                                                      ▼│
   │ ◀                                                                    ▶   │
   │ Line 9 of 21, Col 1                                                      │
   └──────────────────────────────────────────────────────────────────────────┘
```

In reviewing the section of the script that determines what happens when amountPaid exceeds amountOwed, we discover that difference is being calculated by subtracting amountOwed by amountPaid. How is this a problem? If the user pays 84 dollars, the difference being calculated is 60 – 84 (or amountOwed minus amountPaid). Subtracting a larger number from a smaller number resulted in a negative number. To fix the problem, we simply switched the position of amountOwed and amountPaid in the line of script that sets the value of difference. Now, the smaller number is subtracted from the larger one, resulting in a positive number.

NOTE *You don't need to modify the other area in the script where the value of difference is set because that area is only executed when the user pays less than he or she owes, in which case the value will be calculated properly.*

5) With the Light Switch button still selected and the Actions panels still open, make the following addition and modification to the `if` statement:

Addition:

```
if (isNaN (amountPaid)) {
  message.text = "What you entered is not a proper dollar amount. Please try
again.";
}
```

Modification to what used to be the initial if statement:

```
} else if (amountPaid < amountOwed) {
  difference = amountOwed - amountPaid;
  light.gotoAndStop ("Off");
  message.text = "You underpaid your bill by " + difference + " dollars.";
}
```

You'll notice that with this addition and modification, what used to be the first condition that was analyzed has now been delegated to the second condition. Modifying the script in this way will cause this new condition to be analyzed first.

ADDITION

MODIFICATION

This addition allows the script to deal with the contingency that the user enters nothing or enters text as the amount to pay. It says that when the Light Switch button is pressed, if the value of `amountPaid` is not a number (or `isNaN`), do nothing in the scene but display a message that asks the user to enter a proper dollar amount. If the amount entered cannot be converted to a numerical value (for example, "frog") or if the field is left blank, this part of the script executes. The `isNan()` function is another special tool that ActionScript provides to take care of simple yet critical tasks. Notice that instead of inserting a literal value between the parentheses of this function (such as "cat", or 57), we've placed a reference to a variable's name. This causes the value that the variable holds to be analyzed.

NOTE *The* `isNaN()` *function is covered in greater detail later in the book.*

We made this the first condition to look for because it's the most logical thing to check when the script is first executed. If the user enters a numeric value, this part of the script is ignored and the rest of the script continues to work as previously described.

5) From Flash's menu bar choose Control › Test Movie. In the exported test file, enter various amounts in the "Amount you would like to pay:" text field, then press the Light Switch button.

At this point our movie should work properly under all circumstances.

6) Close the testing environment and return to the authoring environment. Save this file as electricBill3.fla.

Congratulations: You've completed your first lesson!

WHAT YOU HAVE LEARNED

In this lesson, you have:

- Familiarized yourself with the various elements that make up a script (pages 8–13)
- Planned and developed an ActionScript project (pages 13–16)
- Written the project script (pages 16–26)
- Tested the script, searching for bugs (pages 26–28)
- Fixed bugs to complete the project (pages 29–31)

using event handlers

LESSON 2

It's common knowledge that for every action there is a reaction. In the physical world, things happen around us all the time—usually as the result of a specific action. We push buttons, we push people, we even push people's buttons, all with a single purpose: to solicit a response. The Macromedia Flash way of saying this is that for every *event* there is an action.

In a Flash environment, the responses that come from pushing, holding, moving, entering, leaving, and so on are triggered by *event handlers*. They represent the first step in getting your movie to do anything interactive—which is why a thorough understanding of them is vital.

We'll create several projects in this lesson, including this self-running presentation that uses frame events to provide the user with a hands-free experience.

WHAT YOU WILL LEARN

In this lesson, you will:

- Learn how event handlers are used in scripts

- Determine the best event handler for the job

- Use mouse/button events to control interactivity

- Add keyboard control to a project

- Create a self-running presentation using frame events

- Use clip events to create an interactive project

- Orchestrate multiple events to accomplish a task

- Define and use event handler methods

- Learn about listeners and how to use them

APPROXIMATE TIME

This lesson takes approximately
2 hours to complete.

LESSON FILES

Media Files:

None

Starting Files:

Lesson02/Assets/MouseEvents1.fla

Lesson02/Assets/FrameEvents1.fla

Lesson02/Assets/ClipEvents1.fla

Lesson02/Assets/OrchestratingEvents1.fla

Lesson02/Assets/CarParts1.fla

Completed Projects:

MouseEvents2.fla

FrameEvents2.fla

ClipEvents2.fla

OrchestratingEvents2.fla

CarParts2.fla

WHAT EVENT HANDLERS DO

Event handlers orchestrate your movies' interactivity by controlling when scripts are triggered. They provide a "when" to a script so that it executes only when something specific occurs. Every script in your movie is triggered by an event—a user rolling over a button or pressing a key, your movie's timeline reaching a certain frame, and so on.

In ActionScript, event handlers (with the exception of frame events) usually represent the first lines in any script. For example:

```
When this happens (eventHandler) {
  do this;
  do this;
}
```

Frame events occur when the timeline reaches a frame that contains a script. When placing a script on a frame, you don't need to identify a frame event to trigger that script because the timeline reaching the frame is enough to cause it to execute. Thus, if placed in a frame, the above script would look like this:

```
  do this;
  do this;
```

The better you understand event handlers, the more control you'll have over your user's experience. By using event handlers properly, you can create immersive environments the user will feel a part of.

Many computer programs allow users to accomplish tasks by letting them drag and drop items on the screen, resize windows, make adjustments with sliders, and create artistic masterpieces using "virtual" art tools—all modes of interaction determined by the way the software has been programmed to deal with various events (mouse presses, mouse movements, keyboard input, and so on).

CHOOSING THE RIGHT EVENT HANDLER

Using event handlers properly presents one of the biggest challenges for ActionScript users—perhaps because most of us haven't given much thought to how things happen around us, and thus how to translate that knowledge into creating interactive environments. Understanding and being mindful of how things and people interact in the real world, however, can go a long way toward helping you re-create such interactions in your Flash movies.

As we introduce you to Flash's many event handlers, we'll examine some of the ways their use can be translated into real-world events. As you review these events, remember what you learned at the beginning of this lesson: In Flash, for every event, there is an action (or reaction).

NOTE *Later in the lesson we'll discuss event handler methods, which are an extension of the standard event handlers.*

USING MOUSE EVENTS

Mouse events control the execution of scripts when the mouse interacts with a button or movie clip instance. You use them to emulate things you might do with your hands.

NOTE *If you're familiar with Flash 5's implementation of mouse events, you know that you can only use them with buttons. In Flash MX, however, you can attach mouse events to movie clip instances as well (which we'll discuss in detail later in the exercise).*

Making contact: `on (press)`

When you touch or press something—say a person or an ice cube—in the physical world, you expect a reaction: The person responds; the ice cube begins to melt; and so on. The `on(press)` event handler works great for emulating touching, grabbing, or just plain pushing (as well as the results of any of these actions). You can use this event handler to trigger a script when the cursor is above a button or movie clip instance and the mouse button is pressed.

Letting go: `on (release)`

When you release something or cease to make contact with it, you're usually finished interacting with it and ready to move on. This event handler—which emulates letting go of something (or dropping it)—is the most direct way of allowing the user to make your movie take action. It's often used on buttons or movie clip instances to trigger actions. You can use it to trigger a script when the mouse button is depressed (if it was first pressed while over a button or movie clip instance).

Pulling, snapping: on (releaseOutside)

Imagine a deck of cards sitting on a table: You push down on the top card with your finger, drag it away from the deck, and then let your finger up. In Flash, this deck of cards could represent a button that the user presses, drags away from, then releases. You can use this event handler to trigger a script when your user has pressed a movie button or movie clip instance but released the mouse away from it, making it useful for emulating pulling or snapping.

Keyboard control: on (keyPress)

You can use this event to program your movie to trigger a script when a user presses a letter, number, punctuation mark, symbol, arrow, or the Backspace, Insert, Home, End, Page Up, or Page Down keys.

Over but not touching: on (rollOver)

You can place your hand over a hot stove and feel the heat without actually touching the stove. Consider using this event handler to emulate the way objects are affected by other objects that radiate heat, cold, light, air, and so on—with the radiation source being the button or movie clip instance. You can also use this event handler to display information about what a button or movie clip instance does before it's pressed (similar to a ToolTip or an HTML hotspot graphic). You employ this event handler to trigger a script when the user places his or her mouse over a button or movie clip instance.

No longer on top of: on (rollOut)

Obviously, when you move your hand away from that stove, you cease to feel the heat it's radiating and your hand cools down. That's what this event handler emulates. You can use this event handler to trigger a script when the user moves his or her hand away from a button or movie clip instance it was formally over.

Grooves, bumps, rubbing: `on (dragOver)`

The act of rubbing entails a back-and-forth motion across an area. When a shoe is being shined (cloth dragged over it), for example, it gets slicker with each pass (action). This event lets you emulate this type of activity in your movie by triggering a script each time the mouse passes over the same movie button or movie clip instance while the mouse button remains pressed.

Oops: `on (dragOut)`

This event allows you to emulate what can happen when you press or touch something but then pull away—such as if you were to touch somebody by accident, then pull your hand away. You can use this event handler to trigger a script when the user places the pointer over a movie button or movie clip instance, presses the mouse button, and drags it away from the movie button or movie clip instance (while still pressing the mouse button).

In the following exercise, we'll create a fingerprint scanner that interacts with the user in various ways. In the process, you'll learn several creative uses for these event handlers, enabling you to emulate rubbing, snapping, and more.

1) Open MouseEvents1.fla in the Lesson02/Assets folder. Open the Scene panel and Property inspector.

Since we're focusing on the ActionScript that makes this project work, most of the elements are already in place. Let's get acquainted with what's on the stage.

The Scene panel shows that our project contains two scenes, Scan and Playroom. We'll begin our work in the Scan scene, which contains five layers that are named according to their content.

If you select the box in the bottom middle of the screen, you'll see in the Property inspector that this is a Dynamic Text field with an instance name of **message**.

If you select the hand graphic, you'll notice on the Property inspector that this is a movie clip instance named **hand**. The black box in the middle of the screen is also a movie clip instance, this one named **scanner**. On top of this movie clip instance is a button that appears to be a square piece of glass. Soon we'll attach several scripts to this button.

2) Lock the Scanner button layer, and then double-click the scanner movie clip instance in the middle of the stage to edit it in place.

You are now looking at this movie clip's timeline. The overall functionality of this movie clip is not important (though feel free to move the playhead to see how it appears visually at various points). It is, however, important to be aware of the six frame labels on its timeline. One of the functions of the several scripts we'll attach to our Glass button (on the main timeline) will be to move this movie clip's timeline to these various labels whenever a particular mouse event occurs.

3) Return to the main timeline. With the Actions panel open, select Frame 1 of the Actions layer and add the following script:

```
stop ();
Mouse.hide();
startDrag ("hand", true);
message.text = "Please place your finger on the scanner and press down.
Release after 2 seconds.";
```

The first action prevents the movie from moving past this scene until we instruct it to.

The next action hides the mouse cursor because we will be using the **hand** movie clip instance as a custom cursor. The next instructs Flash to drag this instance and move it around the screen as if it were the normal mouse cursor.

The last action places the initial text in the text field named **message**.

Since these actions are on Frame 1 of the first scene, they occur as soon as the movie begins to play.

4) With the Actions panel still open, unlock the Scanner button layer and select the button that is on that layer (which appears as a square sheet of glass) and add the following script:

```
on (rollOver) {
  scanner.gotoAndPlay ("Active");
  message.text = "Please press on the screen to continue.";
}
```

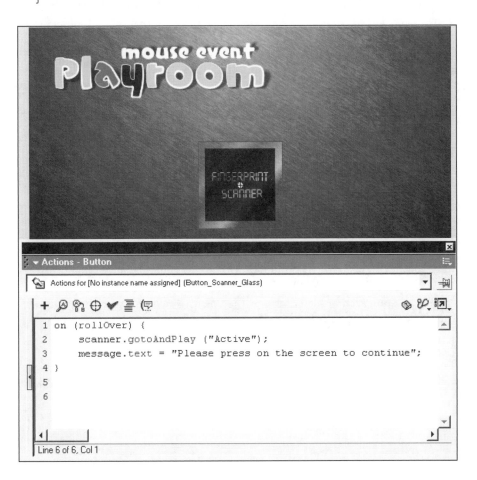

When the hand moves over the Glass button, we want to give the impression that it's being "sensed" by the scanner. The `rollOver` event lets us do that by triggering an action when the hand first hovers over the button. This event handler triggers two actions: It sends the **scanner** movie clip instance to the Active frame, where a short animation provides a visual cue that the scanner is active and ready to be pressed. It then changes the text being displayed in the **message** text field.

5) Add the following script just below the current script:

```
on (rollOut) {
  scanner.gotoAndPlay ("Inactive");
  message.text = "Please place your finger on the scanner and press down.
Release after 2 seconds.";
}
```

As you can see from this addition, a single button can respond to multiple events.

This script (and the `rollOut` event that triggers it) addresses what happens when the mouse moves away from the button without pressing it. In this case, the **scanner** movie clip instance is sent to the Inactive frame, where a short animation provides a visual cue that the scanner is resetting.

The next action in this script changes the text displayed in the **message** text field. This is the same text that appears when the movie is first played, once again giving the impression that the scanner has been reset.

5) Add the following script just below the current script:

```
on (press) {
  scanner.gotoAndPlay ("Scan");
  message.text = "Now scanning...";
}
```

When the user presses the button and holds it down, this script is triggered. The first action sends the **scanner** movie clip instance to the frame labeled Scan, where a short, repeating animation of scan lines moving up and down on a scanner provides a visual cue that a scan is taking place.

The next action in this script changes the text displayed in the **message** text field.

6) Add the following script just below the current script:

```
on (dragOut) {
  scanner.gotoAndPlay ("Error");
  message.text = "An error has occurred. You have removed your finger prior to
processing. Please try again.";
}
```

This script, and the dragOut event that triggers it, addresses what happens when the mouse button is pressed while over the button but then dragged away from it while remaining pressed. The thinking here is that the user pressed the button to start the scanning process but then pulled away, abruptly ending the scan. As a result, the **scanner** movie clip instance is sent to the frame labeled Error, where a short animation provides a visual cue that there was an error in the scan.

The next action in this script changes the text displayed in the **message** text field.

7) Add the following script just below the current script:

```
on (release) {
  scanner.gotoAndPlay ("Process");
  message.text = "Processing your scan...";
}
```

When the user presses the button then releases it, this script is triggered. The first action sends the **scanner** movie clip instance to the frame labeled Process, where a short animation indicates that something is being processed and then cleared. At the end of this animation, a frame action instructs the main timeline to go to the Room frame and stop. This frame label is actually on Frame 1 of the Playroom scene, the next scene in our project. This functionality allows an action on the movie clip's timeline to move the main timeline between scenes.

The next action in this script changes the text displayed in the **message** text field.

You've now finished setting up this scene. During playback, with proper user interaction, our project should progress to the Playroom scene. Let's next begin our work there.

8) With the Scene panel open, click the scene named Playroom.

This scene contains seven layers, named according to their contents.

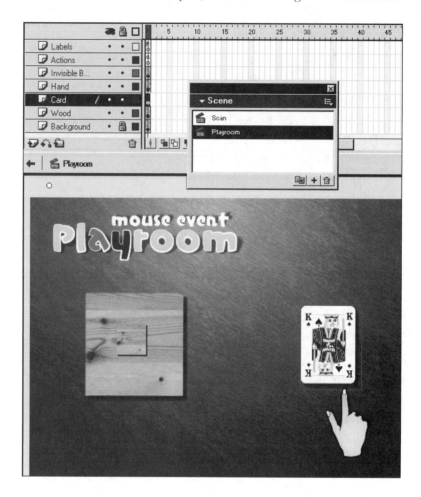

In this scene, we'll attach mouse events to movie clip instances to facilitate interactivity—and in so doing demonstrate how you can employ mouse events in almost the same fashion as buttons and movie clip instances. In the top-left portion of the work area, just above the stage, you'll see a small circle that represents an empty movie clip instance (no graphical content). We'll attach a couple of mouse events to this instance. In the middle of the square piece of wood is a smaller piece of wood, which is a movie clip instance named **bump**. We'll place a mouse event on this instance that allows us to emulate sanding this bump away. The card on the right side of the stage is a movie clip instance. We'll script this instance to "snap" into place when it's clicked and dragged.

42

9) With the Actions panel open, select Frame 1 of the Actions layer and add the following script:

```
startDrag ("hand", true);
```

This action is the same as the one in the previous scene that enabled the **hand** movie clip instance to be dragged around the stage. Although the mouse remains hidden when the timeline moves from one scene to another (as our project is set up to do), dragging of objects needs to be reinitiated whenever a scene changes, which is what this action does.

10) With the Actions panel still open, select the small piece of wood (with an instance name of *bump*) and add the following script:

```
on (dragOver) {
  this._alpha = this._alpha - 10;
}
```

If the user presses and holds down the mouse button while moving the cursor back and forth over this instance, its opacity will decrease by 10 percent with each pass (dragOver). After 10 passes, the bump will be invisible, producing the effect of rubbing the bump away.

The way this script works is simple: With each dragOut event, we're setting the movie clip instance's alpha property (transparency) to equal its current value minus 10. The term this is a contextual reference to the object to which the script is attached.

NOTE *For more information about the term this, as well as other target paths, see Lesson 3, Understanding Target Paths.*

11) With the Actions panel still open, select the *card* movie clip instance and add the following script:

```
on (releaseOutside) {
  this._x = _root._xmouse;
  this._y = _root._ymouse;
}
```

If the mouse is placed on top of the instance, pressed, moved away from the instance (while remaining pressed down), and then released, this script will be executed. The script will move the **card** movie clip instance's x and y position to match the x and y position at the time the event occurs. In other words, suppose the **card** movie clip instance is on the left side of the stage: If the user places his or her mouse over the instance, presses and holds down the mouse button, drags the cursor away from the instance (say to the right side of the stage), and then releases the mouse button, the **card** instance's position will snap to the right side of the stage—the cursor's location on release of the mouse button.

12) With the Actions panel open, select the empty movie clip instance just above the stage and add the following script:

```
on (keyPress "<Space>") {
  _root.bump._alpha = 100;
}
on (keyPress "<Left>") {
  _root.gotoAndStop (1);
}
```

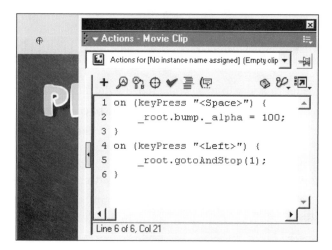

Here we've added two keyPress events to this movie clip instance. Note that you don't need to place the instance on a visible portion of the stage because the actions attached to it are triggered by keyboard presses rather than cursor interaction.

The first keyPress event is triggered when the user presses the space bar. When this occurs, the transparency of the **bump** movie clip instance is reset to 100, making it fully visible again (in case it had been rubbed away).

The second keyPress event is triggered when the user presses the left arrow key. When this occurs, the main timeline (_root) is sent back to Frame 1, which contains the Scan scene where the user must scan his or her fingerprint again to return to the playroom.

This completes the scripting for our project.

13) From the menu choose Control › Test Movie to see the movie in action.

Interact with the scanner and then with elements in the playroom to solidify your understanding of how these events work.

14) Close the test movie to return to the authoring environment. Save your project as MouseEvents2.fla.

This completes the exercise. You should now have a thorough understanding of mouse events and the ways you can use them to enhance your projects.

MAKING THE MOST OF ATTACHING MOUSE EVENTS TO MOVIE CLIPS

In Flash 5 and earlier versions, only button instances were able to have mouse events attached to them. With Flash MX, however, movie clip instances can also have attached mouse events (as shown in the above exercise). To make the most of this powerful new capability, you need to be aware of a few things—especially if you're familiar with Flash's earlier implementation of button instances and mouse events:

- To cause a movie clip to be treated as a button, simply attach a mouse event to it. Under most circumstances, you cannot attach both mouse events and clip events to a single instance; however, you can use event handler methods (discussed later in this lesson) to set a movie clip instance to react to both mouse and clip events.

- When a movie clip instance is assigned mouse events so that Flash recognizes it as a button, it retains all of its movie clip functionality.

- When a movie clip instance is assigned mouse events so that Flash recognizes it as a button, a hand cursor will appear when the user places his or her mouse over it. If you want a movie clip instance to act like a button but don't want the hand cursor to appear, set the `useHandCursor` property of the instance to `false` with a `rollOver` event, as follows:

  ```
  on(rollOver){
    this.useHandCursor = false;
  }
  ```

  The `useHandCursor` property can be set for button instances as well (see below).

- Although you can place mouse events on movie clip instances, you cannot place clip events on button instances (as we'll discuss later in this lesson).

- Button instances can now be assigned instance names, and they have properties similar to movie clip instances (for example, `_alpha`, `_rotation`, `_y`, and so on). Thus, if you give a button an instance name of **myButton**, you can change its transparency using `myButton._alpha = 50`.

- Although you can assign instance names to buttons (and they're treated similarly to movie clip instances, now employing properties and methods) buttons aren't independent timelines (as movie clips are)—an important thing to remember when using the term `this` as a target path. For example, if you were to place the following script on a movie clip instance, the instance itself would rotate:

```
on(press){
  this._rotation = 30;
}
```

However, if you were to place the same script on a button, the button's parent will rotate. Think of it this way: Movie clip instances *are* timelines, even when attaching mouse events so that Flash recognizes them as buttons. Even though buttons can now be given instance names as well as have properties and methods, they are still *part* of a timeline, not timelines themselves.

You may now be asking, Since movie clips can now be treated as buttons while still maintaining all of their powerful movie clip instance capabilities, why use standard buttons at all anymore? Well, primarily because a button's up, over, and down states are still much easier to re-create and implement using an actual button. So, for quick and easy button functionality, use button instances. For highly sophisticated button functionality, use movie clip instances with mouse events attached to them.

- If you use a movie clip instance as a button, you can place three special frame labels (_up, _over, _down) on a movie clip's timeline to easily facilitate the movie clip button's appearance when the mouse interacts with it (though you aren't *required* to do this in order to use a movie clip instance as a button).

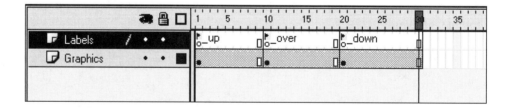

- By default, the hit area of a movie clip button will be the shape and area of any graphical content it contains, but you can change the hit area at any time by defining its `hitArea` property. For example, the following will set a movie clip instance as the hitArea of a movie clip button.

```
myClipButton.hitArea = "_root.myHitClip";
```

This property is only available to movie clip buttons, not standard buttons.

USING FRAME EVENTS

Frame events are probably the easiest events to understand. When you attach a series of actions to a keyframe on the timeline, Flash executes those actions when the movie reaches that frame during playback. Frame events are great for triggering actions based on the passage of time or actions that need to be somehow synchronized with elements currently visible on the stage.

TIP *Many dynamically based projects need to have a number of things set in place as soon as they begin to play. Known as* initializing, *this process usually involves creating data or establishing certain aspects of the movie's functionality. For this reason, many developers place a number of actions on Frame 1 of the main timeline to implement this initialization process. These actions are then used to create variables and arrays as well as to define functions—all of which may be needed soon after the movie begins to play.*

In the following exercise, we'll create a simple self-running presentation that displays pictures and related text sequentially using frame events.

1) Open FrameEvents1.fla in the Lesson02/Assets folder; then open the Property inspector.

First, let's get acquainted with what's on the stage.

This 200-frame scene contains six layers (named according to their content), five text fields, three buttons, and two movie clip instances. The movie will begin playing at Frame 1, displaying a picture and associated text on the screen. We will be placing actions on Frame 200 to advance the picture as well as send this timeline back to Frame 1 to begin the process all over again. Because our movie is set to play at 20 frames per second, each picture (and the information it contains) will be visible for 10 seconds (200 frames divided by 20 frames a second) before moving on. If you select the picture in the middle left portion of the stage, you'll notice on the Property inspector that this is a movie clip instance named **picture,** which itself contains several pictures: These form the basis of our slide show. Soon, we'll add frame events to this clip's timeline. The other movie clip instance, **indicator,** appears as a small white circle in the bottom right corner of the stage. This instance contains a short animation that alerts the user that the picture is about to change (in case he or she wants to pause the presentation).

There are three text fields to the right of the **picture** movie clip instance: These fields have instance names of (in clockwise order) **date**, **country,** and **caption**. Using frame events, these will be filled with information related to the currently displayed picture. Two other text fields appear above and to the left of our control (Play, Stop, and Rewind) buttons. The text field above these buttons is named **warning** because this is where text will be displayed indicating that the picture is about to change. To the left of the control buttons is a text field named **balloon**. When the user rolls over one of the control buttons, the function of that button will be shown here.

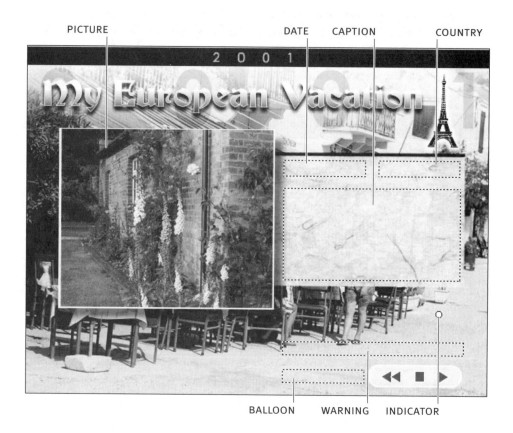

2) Double-click the *picture* movie clip instance in the middle of the stage to edit it in place.

You're now looking at this movie clip's timeline. It contains two layers labeled Pix and Actions. The Pix layer contains five keyframes, each of which contains a different picture. (You can move the playhead to view these pictures, if you wish.) The Actions layer contains six blank, or empty, keyframes. (We'll explain shortly why this layer has one more keyframe than the Pix layer.)

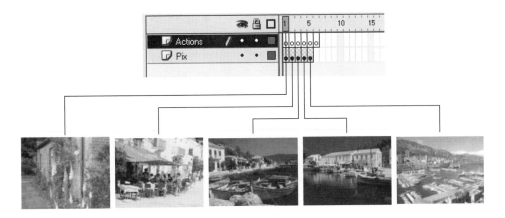

Now let's fill these empty keyframes with scripts.

3) With the Actions panel open, select Frame 1 on the Actions layer and add this script:

```
stop ();
_root.date.text = "June 15th";
_root.country.text = "Scotland";
_root.caption.text = "Isn't this a beautiful place?";
```

The first action will prevent this movie clip from playing beyond Frame 1 until we instruct it to.

The next three actions place text into the appropriate text fields on the main timeline. This textual information relates to the graphic that appears on Frame 1 of the Pix layer on this timeline. In other words, whenever this timeline is on this frame, the visible picture and the text displayed in the text fields will coincide with one another.

3) With the Actions panel open, select Frame 2 on the Actions layer and add this script:

```
_root.date.text = "June 16th";
_root.country.text = "Italy";
_root.caption.text = "The food was excellent!";
```

When this movie's timeline is moved to Frame 2, these three actions will update the respective text in the appropriate text fields on the main timeline. This textual information relates to the graphic that appears on Frame 2 of the Pix layer on this timeline.

4) With the Actions panel open, select Frames 3, 4, and 5 on the Actions layer and add the following scripts, respectively:

Place on frame 3:

```
_root.date.text = "June 17th";
_root.country.text = "Greece";
_root.caption.text = "We went for a boat ride.";
```

Place on frame 4:

```
_root.date.text = "June 18th";
_root.country.text = "France";
_root.caption.text = "We took another boat ride.";
```

Place on frame 5:

```
_root.date.text = "June 19th";
_root.country.text = "Monaco";
_root.caption.text = "The mountains were amazing!";
```

Each of these sets of actions has the same effect as the previous two sets; the only difference is that these are triggered when this movie's timeline is moved to Frames 3, 4, and 5, respectively.

5) With the Actions panel open, select Frame 6 on the Actions layer and add this script:

```
gotoAndStop (1);
```

As you'll soon see, we'll advance through the frames in this movie clip dynamically by telling Flash to simply go to the next frame in the timeline—we won't use frame numbers or labels. Since we run out of pictures after Frame 5, this script is triggered when the movie clip is advanced to the next frame (Frame 6)—immediately sending the timeline back to Frame 1, and the first picture. Thus, our demonstration loops through these five graphics until the presentation is stopped or the user exits it.

The way this is set up, it should be easy to add additional pictures and text to the presentation.

Now let's set up the functionality that advances our presentation through these graphics.

6) Return to the main timeline. With the Actions panel open, select the keyframe on Frame 140 and add the following script:

```
warning.text = "The picture will change in 3 seconds.";
indicator.gotoAndPlay ("On");
```

Eventually, Frame 200 will contain a script to advance the picture being displayed. Since our movie is set to play at 20 frames per second, placing this script on Frame 140 will cause it to be executed three seconds (200 frames minus 140 frames equals 60 frames, or 3 seconds) prior to the picture change.

The first action displays a warning message in the **warning** text field instance indicating that the picture will change in three seconds. The next action sends the **indicator** movie clip instance to the frame labeled On, where a short animation acts as a visual cue that the picture is about to change.

6) With the Actions panel open, select the keyframe on Frame 160 and add the following script:

```
warning.text = "The picture will change in 2 seconds.";
```

This action simply updates the message in the **warning** text field to indicate that the picture will be changing in two seconds.

7) With the Actions panel open, select the keyframe on Frame 180 and add the following script:

```
warning.text = "The picture will change in 1 second.";
```

This action simply updates the message in the **warning** text field to indicate that the picture will be changing in one second.

8) With the Actions panel open, select the keyframe on Frame 200 and add the following script:

```
pictures.nextFrame();
warning.text = "";
gotoAndPlay (1);
```

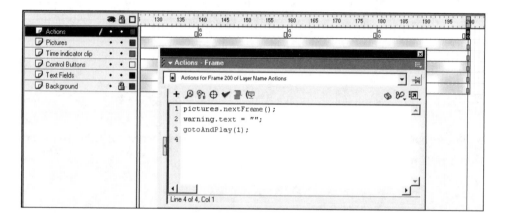

This set of actions represents the foundation that makes our presentation work. If the act of displaying a picture and its associated text for 10 seconds were called a cycle, these actions would be executed at the end of each cycle.

The first action advances the **pictures** movie clip instance to the next frame of its timeline. Doing so will cause the next picture to be displayed and the frame actions on that frame to be triggered. This will cause the text info for that picture to be displayed as well.

The next action clears all text from the **warning** text field since the warning phase is complete—at least for several seconds.

The last action sends the main timeline back to Frame 1, which continues to play, and the entire process is repeated.

Since we want to let the user control the presentation's playback, that will be our focus in the next few steps.

52

9) With the Actions panel open, select the triangular button on the control panel and add the following script:

```
on (release) {
  play ();
}
on (rollOver) {
  balloon.text = "Play";
}
on (rollOut) {
  balloon.text = "";
}
```

Here you can see that this button will respond to three events: When it's pressed and released, the main timeline will play (though obviously only if the presentation was stopped in the first place); when it's rolled over, the word *Play* will appear in the **balloon** text field (providing the user with a visual cue as to what the button does); and when it's rolled away from, the **balloon** text field will be cleared.

10) With the Actions panel open, select the square button on the control panel and add the following script:

```
on (release) {
  stop ();
}
on (rollOver) {
  balloon.text = "Stop";
}
on (rollOut) {
  balloon.text = "";
}
```

This button is also set up to respond to three mouse events: When the button is pressed and released, the main timeline will stop (though only if it was playing in the first place); when it's rolled over, the word *Stop* will be displayed in the **balloon** text field (to cue the user as to what the button does); and when the user moves away from the button, the **balloon** text field is cleared.

11) With the Actions panel open, select the double-triangular button on the control panel and add the following script:

```
on (release) {
  gotoAndPlay (1);
  pictures.gotoAndStop (1);
  warning.text = "";
}

on (rollOver) {
  balloon.text = "Rewind";
}

on (rollOut) {
  balloon.text = "";
}
```

When this button is pressed and released, the main timeline and the **picture** movie clip instance are sent back to Frame 1. This resets the presentation to its original state, regardless of how it's progressed. The next action will display the word *Rewind* in the **balloon** text field when the button is rolled over (to cue the user as to what the button does). The rollOut event empties the **balloon** text field when the user moves away from the button.

12) From the menu choose Control › Test Movie to see the movie in action.

View the presentation from start to finish to get a feel for how it works. Use the control buttons to control playback.

13) Close the test movie to return to the authoring environment. Save your work as FrameEvents2.fla.

You have now completed this exercise. As you can see, by using frame events properly, you can create highly interactive presentations that you can add to easily.

USING CLIP EVENTS

When a movie clip instance with attached scripts enters a scene, that scene can take on a new look, feel, and function through the use of clip events. These events allow actions to be triggered when an instance enters or leaves a scene, when the mouse moves around in the scene, as well as several other ways.

The following describes the various clip events as well as provides real-world analogies for their uses. Note that you can only use clip events with scripts attached to movie clip instances.

Presence: `onClipEvent (load)`

When someone or something enters a room or an area, there can be all kinds of ripple effects: People's demeanors can change; the environment can be affected in some way; even the person (or thing) entering the room can change as a result of what's going on inside. This event handler provokes a similar response by triggering a script when a movie clip instance enters a scene—useful for initializing the movie clip, for having it be affected by the environment it's entering, or for having it affect the environment.

Absence: `onClipEvent (unLoad)`

If a movie clip instance can affect a scene when it enters, it can also affect the scene when it leaves (sometimes in the opposite way). You can use this event handler to trigger a script when a movie clip instance exits a scene.

Power, energy: `onClipEvent (enterFrame)`

When an object is given energy or power, it usually signifies that it is taking action on a continual basis. Look at a clock; without power it sits motionless and useless. If you provide power to it, it begins ticking, the hands on the face begin moving and you're able to use it to tell time. This event handler is used to trigger a script continually, at the same rate your movie plays. If your movie's frame rate is set to 20 frames per second, the scripts this event handler triggers are executed 20 times a second. There are many powerful applications for this event handler, as you'll learn throughout this book.

Movement: `onClipEvent (mouseMove)`

Think of this event as a motion detector within your movie. If a movie clip instance is present in the scene to which this clip event is attached, a set of actions can be executed each time the user moves the mouse (even just a pixel). This allows you to create motion-related interactivity—for example, the ability to detect movement direction (right, left, up, and down), current mouse position, and more.

Computer-based interaction: `onClipEvent (mouseDown)`, `onClipEvent (mouseUp)`, `onClipEvent (keyDown)`, `onClipEvent (keyUp)`

Because the mouse and keyboard are designed to interact with computers, these clip events don't really have real-world equivalents. They do, however, provide a means of executing scripts when specific keys or the mouse button are pressed (or released). Although these events may seem similar to the `press`, `release`, and `keyPress` mouse events described earlier in this lesson, they're actually a bit more powerful. Using the `keyUp` and `keyDown` clip events, you can create key combinations, or keyboard shortcuts, in your application so that action is taken when a sequence of keys are pressed. In contrast, the `keyPress` mouse event allows for only a single key to initiate action. The `mouseUp` and `mouseDown` clip events are different than the `press` and `release` mouse events because while the latter only triggers scripts when the user interacts directly with a button, the `mouseDown` and `mouseUp` events trigger scripts when the mouse is pressed or released *anywhere* on the stage.

55

Receiving instructions: `onClipEvent (data)`

In real life, incomplete instructions can lead to all sorts of problems. The same holds true in Flash. Because Flash lets you load various types of data (variables, external SWFs, JPGs) from external sources into movie clip instances, this event handler plays a vital role in that it triggers a script, attached to an instance, only after this data has been *completely* loaded into it from the source. In so doing, it prevents you from receiving the type of errors that result from incomplete instructions. You can use this event to re-execute actions (refresh) if data is loaded into the clip more than once.

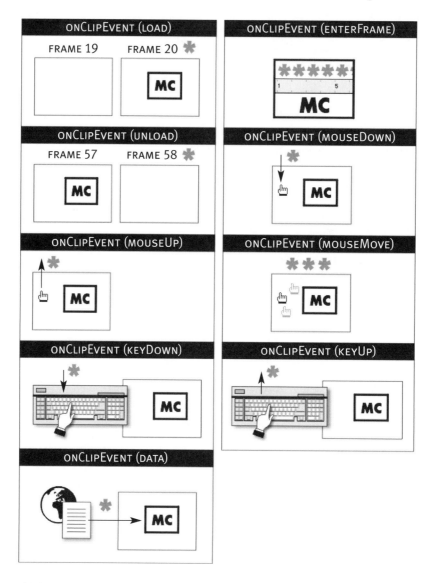

This is a visual representation of how clip events are triggered. The down arrow represents the mouse button being pressed down; the up arrow represents it being released. The asterisk represents an occurrence of the event.

In the following exercise, we'll create a project that simulates a burglar being caught in the act. The burglar's presence (or absence) will determine how the scene plays, and the burglar himself will be programmed to respond to the environment in various ways using clip events.

1) Open ClipEvents1.fla in the Lesson02/Assets folder. Open the Property inspector.

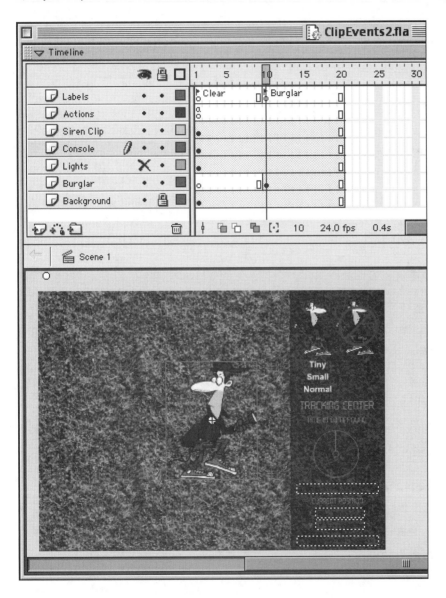

This project contains a single scene that includes seven layers, which are named according to their content. Take special note of the two frames with labels: The one labeled Clear represents the scene without the burglar, and the one labeled Burglar introduces the burglar into the scene. (Move the playhead between these frames to get a handle on this concept since it will be critical to the success of our project.) The burglar graphic is actually a movie clip instance named **burglar**, which will contain most of the scripts that control our movie's interactivity. (More on that in a bit.) The **burglar** movie clip instance is the only movie element that appears and disappears when navigating between these two frame labels; all other elements are constantly present. Let's look at those.

At the top right of the stage are four buttons. The one that depicts the burglar with the international sign of No (red circle with a line through it) on top will eventually be set up to move the scene to the Clear frame, thus "removing" the burglar from the scene. The other three buttons—Tiny, Small, and Normal—will be used to dictate our burglar's size.

Below these buttons is a light-green circle graphic. This is a movie clip instance named **timer**. We will program **timer** to spin when the burglar is in the scene, giving the sense that it's tracking time.

Below the **timer** movie clip instance is a text field named **timeAmount**. Here, we will be incrementing a number as long as the burglar is present—once again to give the sense that we're tracking time.

Below this text field are two more text fields, one with an X beside it, the other with a Y. Since we'll be programming our burglar to follow the mouse as it moves around, these text fields—named **mouseXPosition** and **mouseYPosition,** respectively—will be used to display the current X and Y coordinates of the **burglar** movie clip instance as it moves.

Below these text fields is our last text field. Named **message,** it will provide the current status of our environment ("All Clear," "ALERT!!" and so on).

Our scene contains only two other elements—both movie clip instances that need to be examined in depth to be understood.

2) Double-click the small circle in the top left of the work area, just above the stage, to edit this movie clip in place.

This movie clip has an instance name of **siren**. With its timeline visible, you can see that it's made up of three layers and two frame labels. At the frame labeled On there's a siren sound on the timeline. When this movie's timeline is sent to that frame label, the sound will play. This will be used to simulate an alarm being turned on. The other frame label on this timeline, Off, contains no sound; thus, when the timeline is sent to that frame, the alarm will cease playing.

3) Return to the main timeline. On the Lights layer, press the Show Layer button (red X) to reveal a big black box that covers the entire stage. Double-click it to edit this movie clip in place.

This movie clip has an instance name of **lights**. With its timeline visible, you can see that it's made up of four layers and five frame labels. This movie clip is used to simulate various light angles in the movie. We'll be scripting our project so that when the burglar moves to a particular area of the screen, the appropriate light will come on. For example, if he moves left, the left "light" will come on (frame labeled "left"). On the Sound layer, we've placed a sound at each one of the frame labels that gives the audio effect of a big switch being toggled (the light is turning on).

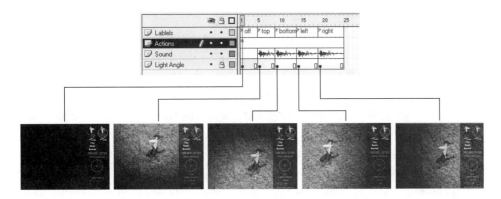

Now that the introductions are complete, it's time to start scripting!

4) Return to the main timeline. On the Lights layer, press the Hide Layer button to hide the big black area that is the *lights* movie clip instance. With the Actions panel open, select Frame 1 on the Actions layer and attach the following script:

```
message.text = "All Clear";
stop ();
```

The first action places the text "All Clear" in the **message** text field as soon as the movie plays. Also, whenever the timeline is sent back to this frame label, this action will executed again. Knowing this, we can deduce that whenever "All Clear" appears in the **message** text field, the main timeline is at Frame 1 and the burglar is not present. An understanding of this functionality will prove important in a moment.

The next action stops the timeline from moving past this frame until we instruct it to.

5) With the Actions panel open, select the Tiny button and attach the following script:

```
on (release) {
  if (message.text == "All Clear") {
    size = 50;
    gotoAndStop ("Burglar");
  } else {
    burglar._xscale = 50;
    burglar._yscale = 50;
  }
}
```

When this button is pressed then released, it will take one of two sets of actions, depending on whether the main timeline is on the frame labeled Clear (no burglar) or the one labeled Burglar (burglar is present.) In essence, this script says that if the **message** text field contains the text "All Clear" (which it will whenever the main timeline is on Frame 1 and the burglar is not present), set the value of the size variable to 50 and move the main timeline to the frame labeled Burglar. At this frame the burglar will be present. The size variable will eventually be used to set the size of the burglar when he first appears in the scene. If **message** does not contain "All Clear," these actions are ignored and the ones below them are executed instead. This will also mean that the main timeline is currently at the frame labeled Burglar and the **burglar** movie clip instance is present in the scene. If this is the case, these actions will scale the vertical and horizontal size of the **burglar** movie clip instance to 50 percent of its original size.

6) With the Actions panel open, select the Small button and attach the following script:

```
on (release) {
  if (message.text == "All Clear") {
    size = 75;
    gotoAndStop ("Burglar");
  } else {
    burglar._xscale = 75;
    burglar._yscale = 75;
  }
}
```

This is just a variation of the script attached to the button in the preceding step. The only difference is that size is given a value of 75 and the two actions that scale the **burglar** movie clip instance (if present in the scene) scale it to 75 percent.

7) With the Actions panel open, select the Normal button and attach the following script:

```
on (release) {
  if (message.text == "All Clear") {
    size = 100;
    gotoAndStop ("Burglar");
  } else {
    burglar._xscale = 100;
    burglar._yscale = 100;
  }
}
```

Once again, this is just a variation of the script attached to the button in the previous step. The only difference is that `size` is given a value of 100 and the **burglar** movie clip instance (if present) is scaled to 100 percent, or its original size.

8) With the Actions panel open, select the No Burglar button and attach the following script:

```
on (release) {
  gotoAndStop ("Clear");
}
```

This button does one thing: moves the main timeline to the frame labeled Clear—where, as you'll remember, the **burglar** movie clip instance does not exist. When the timeline is moved back to Frame 1, the actions we set up in Step 4 will be executed again.

In summary, the Tiny, Small, and Normal buttons are used to make the burglar appear or to resize it. The button we just configured makes the burglar disappear.

The rest of the scripting for our project will be placed on the **burglar** movie clip instance itself.

9) With the Actions panel open and the main timeline at the frame labeled Burglar, select the *burglar* movie clip instance and attach the following script:

```
onClipEvent (load) {
  startDrag (this, true);
  this._xscale = _root.size;
  this._yscale = _root.size;
  _root.lights.gotoAndStop("bottom");
  _root.mouseXPosition.text = _root._xmouse;
  _root.mouseYPosition.text = _root._ymouse;
  _root.message.text = "ALERT!";
}
```

This set of actions is triggered when this movie clip first appears (loads), or when it reappears in the scene as a result of the timeline being moved to this frame. The first action causes the **burglar** movie clip itself (`this`) to become draggable. The next two actions scale the movie clip's horizontal and vertical size based on the current value of the `size` variable (which exists on the root, or main, timeline). You'll remember that we set this variable with one of our three buttons (Tiny, Small, Normal). Thus, when one of the buttons is pressed, the following will happen: The `size` variable is set to a value of 50, 75, or 100 (depending on which button was pressed); the main timeline is sent to the frame containing this movie clip instance; and on loading, the value of the `size` variable is used to set the size of the burglar.

The next action tells the **lights** movie clip instance to move to the frame labeled bottom. At this label it appears that light is shining from the bottom of the screen. This is just a default setting. We'll make the **light** movie clip instance a bit more dynamic in a moment.

The next two actions display the mouse's current X and Y positions in the text fields on the root timeline (**mouseXPosition** and **mouseYPosition**, respectively).

The last action displays the text "ALERT!" in the **message** text field on the root timeline to indicate that the burglar is now present.

10) Add this script just below where the current one ends:

```
onClipEvent (enterFrame) {
  _root.time++;
  _root.timeAmount.text = _root.time;
  _root.timer._rotation = _root.timer._rotation + 1;
}
```

Here, the `enterFrame` event is used to execute three actions—which are executed 24 times a second because this type of event executes actions at the same rate that the movie plays.

The first action uses a variable named `time` to hold the value of an incrementing number. Using the `++` operator, each time the `enterFrame` event occurs (24 times a second), the value of this variable is incremented by 1. This syntax is the same as writing the following:

```
_root.time = _root.time + 1;
```

The next action is used to display the incrementing value of the `time` variable in the **timeAmount** text field.

The last action rotates the **timer** movie clip instance by 1 degree 24 times a second. This will produce the effect of the timer being turned on while the burglar is present.

NOTE *Since this script exists on the **burglar** movie clip instance, it will only execute while that instance is present in the scene.*

11) Add this script just below where the current one ends:

```
onClipEvent (mouseMove) {
  if (_root._xmouse > Number(_root.mouseXPosition.text) + 10) {
    _root.lights.gotoAndStop("right");
    _root.message.text = "Intruder is moving East";
  } else if (_root._xmouse < Number(_root.mouseXPosition.text) - 10) {
    _root.lights.gotoAndStop("left");
    _root.message.text = "Intruder is moving West";
  } else if (_root._ymouse > Number(_root.mouseYPosition.text) + 10) {
    _root.lights.gotoAndStop("bottom");
    _root.message.text = "Intruder is moving South";
  } else if (_root._ymouse < Number(_root.mouseYPosition.text) - 10) {
    _root.lights.gotoAndStop("top");
    _root.message.text = "Intruder is moving North";
  }
  _root.mouseXPosition.text = _root._xmouse;
  _root.mouseYPosition.text = _root._ymouse;
}
```

The actions in this script are triggered every time the mouse is moved. An `if/else if` statement compares the mouse's current position with its last known position, then acts accordingly. We'll examine the first comparison in the statement; having done that, the rest should be self-explanatory. Before we begin, it's important to note that the `load` event we set up a few steps ago contained two actions that set the text displayed in the `mouseXPosition` and `mouseYPosition` text fields based on the X and Y positions of the mouse when the **burglar** movie clip is loaded. We will now use those text values in the comparisons made in this script. Since the information displayed in the fields will be used in mathematical comparisons in our `if/else if` statement, their values have to converted to numbers using the `Number()` function mentioned in Lesson 1. Thus, the script sees them as numeric values rather than text values.

The first part of this script states that if the *current* horizontal position of the mouse (`_root._xmouse`) is greater than the value of `mouseXPosition` plus 10, two actions will be executed. By checking the mouse's current position against its last recorded position, we can determine which direction it's moving. For example, if the current horizontal position of the mouse (`_root._xmouse`) is 300 and the previously recorded position (as displayed in the **_root.mouseXPosition** text field) was 200, we know the mouse has moved to the right. This is because 300 is further to the right than its last recorded position of 200. In this case, our script would trigger two actions: one to move the **light** movie clip instance to the frame labeled right (where the light appears to come from the right part of the stage) and one to display the message "The intruder is moving right" in the **message** text field. The `if` statement uses four comparisons to determine whether the mouse has moved right, left, up, or down.

NOTE *Keep in mind that although the mouse can move in two directions simultaneously (for example, up and right in a diagonal direction), our script gives single-direction movement precedence. This means that right-left movements are of higher priority than up-down movements. Thus, if the mouse moves both left and down, the script will detect only the left movement. The reason for this is that the `if` statement first looks to see if the mouse has moved right. If it has, the two actions for dealing with this are executed, but no other part of the `if` statement is executed. If the mouse hasn't moved right, that part of the `if` statement is ignored, and our script checks whether the mouse has moved left. If it has, the two actions for dealing with this are executed, but no other part of the `if` statement is executed. This same process continues when checking for down and up movements. In essence, once a movement in any single direction has been detected, the rest of the script is ignored. Since the `if` statement looks for right, left, down, and up movement in that order, if it detects right and left movements first, down and up movements won't matter.*

On a side note, you'll notice that in each comparison we add or subtract 10 from the value of `mouseXPosition` or `mouseYPosition` (whatever the case may be) so that the mouse must move at least 10 pixels from its last recorded position before *any* action will occur. If we didn't do this, the mouse's movement on screen would look like firecrackers going off—that is, visually too intense!

The last two actions of this script (placed just before the last curly brace in the script) record the current X and Y positions of the mouse so that the next time this script is executed (that is, when the mouse is moved), these values can be used in the comparison process of the `if` statement again. Since these values are placed in the **mouseXPosition** and **mouseYPosition** text fields, each time the mouse is moved and these values are updated, the changes are displayed in those fields as well.

In essence, this script compares the current position of the mouse against its previously recorded position; takes appropriate action based on whether the mouse has moved left, right, up, or down; and records the mouse's current position for the next time the mouse is moved.

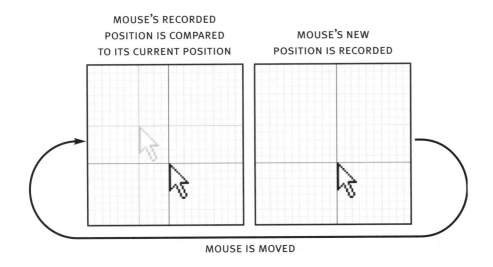

MOUSE'S RECORDED
POSITION IS COMPARED
TO ITS CURRENT POSITION

MOUSE'S NEW
POSITION IS RECORDED

MOUSE IS MOVED

12) Add this script just below where the current one ends:

```
onClipEvent (unload) {
  _root.time = 0;
  _root.timeAmount = _root.time;
  _root.timer._rotation = 0;
  _root.message.text = "All Clear";
  _root.mouseXPosition.text = "";
  _root.mouseYPosition.text = "" ;
  _root.lights.gotoAndStop ("Off");
}
```

This script dictates what happens when this movie clip instance (**burglar**) is unloaded, or no longer in the scene (as a result of the main timeline moving to a frame where it doesn't exist). This occurs when the No Burglar button is clicked and the main timeline is moved to the Clear frame, which is actually Frame 1.

The above actions restore the elements to their original state (that is, before the burglar appeared in the scene): The first one resets the `time` variable to 0; the next action sets what is displayed in the **timeAmount** text field to the value of `time` (making it 0 as well); the next action resets the rotation property of the **timer** movie clip instance to 0; the action after that displays "All Clear" in the **message** text field; the subsequent two actions clear the **mouseXPosition** and **mouseYPosition** text fields; and the last action moves the **lights** movie clip instance to the frame labeled Off. This turns the scene black again.

13) Add this script just below where the current one ends:

```
onClipEvent (mouseDown) {
  this.gotoAndStop("right");
  _root.message.text = "Intruder is confused";
}
```

When the mouse button is pressed anywhere on screen, these two actions are executed. The first sends the **burglar** movie clip instance (**this**) to the frame labeled right. At this label the intruder appears to be looking to his right. In addition, a short audio clip plays of him saying, "Oh, no!" The second action causes the **message** text field to display "Intruder is confused."

14) Add this script just below where the current one ends:

```
onClipEvent (mouseUp) {
  this.gotoAndStop("left");
  _root.message.text = "Intruder is running";
}
```

When the mouse button is released anywhere on screen, these two actions are executed. The first sends the **burglar** movie clip instance (**this**) to the frame labeled left. At this label the intruder appears to be looking to his left. The second action causes the **message** text field to display "Intruder is running."

15) Add this script just below where the current one ends:

```
onClipEvent (keyDown) {
  _root.siren.gotoAndStop("on");
  _root.message.text = "Backup has been called";
}
```

When any key is pressed, these two actions are executed. The first sends the **siren** movie clip instance to the frame labeled on, causing a siren to be heard. The second action causes the **message** text field to display "Backup has been called."

16) Add this script just below where the current one ends:

```
onClipEvent (keyUp) {
  stopAllSounds ();
  _root.siren.gotoAndStop("off");
  _root.message.text = "Silent alarm activated";
}
```

When any key is released, these three actions are executed. The first stops all sounds, including the currently playing siren. The second action sends the **siren** movie clip instance to the frame labeled off (causing the siren to be turned off). And the last action causes the **message** text field to display "Silent alarm activated."

NOTE *Since the mouseDown/mouseUp and keyDown/keyUp clip events are attached to the* **burglar** *movie clip instance, none has any affect until that instance appears in the scene.*

The scripting of our project is now complete.

17) Choose Control › Test Movie to test the functionality of our project.
Press one of the buttons on the top right corner of the stage to make the burglar appear. When he appears, notice how the environment changes. Move him around to see what changes his movement provokes. Press the button to remove him and notice what happens. When the burglar is in the scene, press the mouse or the space bar on the keyboard. Most of our movie's interactivity depends on the **burglar** instance being present in the scene, showing how introducing a single instance into the scene can change its dynamics completely.

18) Close the test movie and save your work as ClipEvents2.fla.
This completes the exercise.

ORCHESTRATING MULTIPLE EVENTS

As you've no doubt figured out by now, different events can occur simultaneously in your movie. For example, the user can have the mouse button pressed down (triggering a press mouse event) while moving the mouse around the screen (triggering a mouseMove clip event). By writing scripts that work in harmony while multiple events are occurring, you can add powerful interactivity to your projects.

In this exercise, you'll orchestrate several events to simulate a cue ball being hit with a pool stick. Although there are some quite sophisticated ways of doing this, we'll take an intermediate approach.

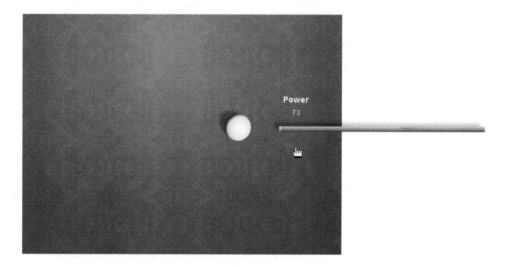

1) Open OrchestrateEvents1.fla in the Lesson02/Assets folder.

This project contains a single scene with five layers that are named according to their contents.

The white cue ball is a movie clip instance named **ball**. We'll soon be attaching some scripts to this clip. To the right of this instance is a transparent-blue rectangle—an invisible button that will contain some scripts, which when used in tandem with those on the **ball** movie clip instance will facilitate the interactivity we seek. To the right of this button is a graphic of a pool stick. This is a movie clip instance named **stick**. The timeline of this movie clip contains two frame labels, Starting and PullBack. At the Starting label, the stick appears as it does now, up against the ball. At the PullBack label, the stick is animated so that it appears as if it's being pulled to the right, in anticipation of hitting the ball. Lastly, just above the pool stick is a text field instance named **powerAmount**, which will display the power at which the ball is hit, based on how far the stick has been "pulled" to the right.

We're going to set up our project so that when the invisible button is pressed, pulled away from, then released, the distance between the point where it was first pressed and where it was released will be calculated. That amount will be used to move the ball to the left. The greater the distance, the further the ball will move to the left.

Let's begin the scripting process.

2) With the Actions panel open, select the invisible button and add this script:

```
on (press) {
  ball._x = 360;
  ball._y = 180;
  power = 0;
  powerAmount.text = power;
  hitAmount = 0;
  trackMouse = true;
  mouseStart = _root._xmouse;
}
```

The first thing to be aware of about this button is its location. It's placed at the tip of the pool stick, just between it and the ball—a logical spot since, as the point of impact, it's also the best place to "pull back" from.

Most of the actions in this script have an initializing effect in our project and are triggered when the mouse button is first pressed. Since we know the user may want to hit the ball more than once, the first two actions are necessary in order to move the ball back to its initial horizontal (x) and vertical (y) positions, essentially resetting it for the next hit. The next action sets the value of power to 0. This variable's value—which will be used to determine how hard the ball is hit—will change as the pool cue is pulled back. Thus, it will need to be reset to 0 at the beginning of each hit. The next action simply displays the current value of the power variable in the **powerAmount** text field.

A script placed on the **ball** movie clip instance will use the value of hitAmount to determine the distance the ball should move. We'll set up that script in a moment. For now, the next action in the above script sets the value of hitAmount to 0. Since this variable's value will change after the ball is hit, this action is used to reset its value when the button is pressed.

The next action sets the value of trackMouse to true. All you need to understand at this point is that this variable's value acts like a switch for turning on a script that will be attached to the **ball** movie clip instance.

The last action records the current horizontal position of the mouse when the button is pressed and places that value in the variable named mouseStart. Shortly, this value will be used to determine the force (hitAmount) at which the ball is hit.

3) With the Actions panel open, add the following to the end of the current script:

```
on (dragOut) {
  stick.gotoandPlay ("PullBack");
}
```

When the user moves away from the invisible button (with the mouse still pressed), this action is executed (the **dragOut** event occurs), moving the **stick** movie clip instance to the PullBack frame. Here the stick appears to pull back—a nice visual cue to emulate the action occurring on screen.

4) With the Actions panel open, add the following to the end of the current script:

```
on (releaseOutside) {
  stick.gotoandStop ("Starting");
  mouseEnd = _root._xmouse;
  hitAmount = mouseEnd - mouseStart;
  trackMouse = false;
}
```

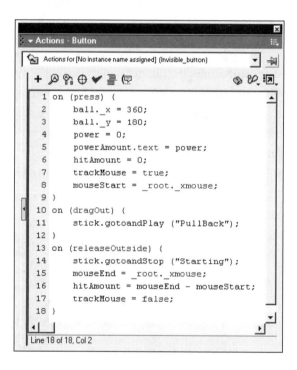

When the invisible button is pressed, moved away from (with the mouse still pressed), then released (the **releaseOutside** event occurs), these actions are executed. Since the act of pressing, dragging, then letting go is similar to what you would employ when using a sling shot, here we'll use it to emulate the pool stick hitting the ball.

The first action moves the **stick** movie clip instance to the frame labeled Starting. Here, the stick appears in its starting position, against the ball. This, along with the ball being set in motion (which we'll discuss in a moment), gives the appearance of the ball being hit and then moved.

The next action records the mouse's horizontal position at the time it's released. We now have the mouse's horizontal position when the invisible button was first pressed (mouseStart) as well as when it was released (mouseEnd). Now let's take a look at how the next action uses these two values.

The value of hitAmount is determined by subtracting mouseEnd from mouseStart. If mouseStart equals 200 and mouseEnd equals 300, hitAmount is assigned a value of 100. This represents the distance the mouse moved from the time the button was first pressed to the time it was released—in other words, the "force" with which our ball was hit, and thus how far it will move to the left.

The last action sets the value of trackMouse to false. All you need to understand here is that this value acts like a switch for turning off a script that will be attached to the **ball** movie clip instance. You'll remember that when the button is pressed, this value is set to true, turning the script on. Thus, this script is turned on when the button is pressed and turned off when it's released outside. (We'll explain the script we're turning on and off here in a couple of steps.)

The only thing left to do is attach a couple of scripts to the **ball** movie clip instance. One will move the ball; the other will use the trackMouse variable we've been discussing.

5) With the Actions panel open, select the *ball* movie clip instance and add this script:

```
onClipEvent (enterFrame) {
  if (_root.hitAmount > 5) {
    this._x = this._x - 10;
    _root.hitAmount = _root.hitAmount - 2;
  }
}
```

This script uses an enterFrame event handler to execute. It contains an if statement that looks at the value of hitAmount on the root timeline before taking action. (You'll remember that the value of hitAmount is set by the functionality on our invisible button and is used to determine how hard the ball will be hit.)

The script states that if the value of hitAmount is more than 5, move the **ball** movie clip instance (this) to its current x position minus 10 (this moves it left) as well as deduct 2 from the value of hitAmount. This means that as long as hitAmount is more than 5, these actions will be executed 24 times per second because we've used the enterFrame event. As a result, the **ball** movie clip instance will move 10 pixels to the left 24 times a second. Since the second action subtracts 2 from the value of hitAmount each time it's executed, the value of this variable will eventually drop below 5, which will cause this script to stop executing. It will only begin executing again when hitAmount is assigned a value greater than 5, which, once again, is what the functionality we set up on our button provides. This is a perfect example of orchestrating several events to accomplish a single interactive goal.

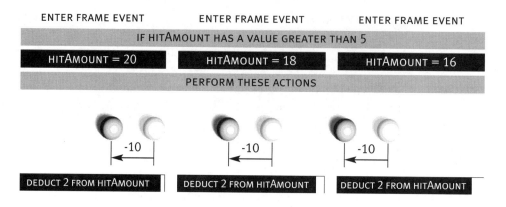

6) **Add this script at the end of the current one:**

```
onClipEvent (mouseMove) {
  if (_root.trackMouse == true) {
    _root.power = _root._xmouse - _root.mouseStart;
    _root.powerAmount.text = _root.power;
  }
}
```

This script uses a mouseMove event handler to execute. It also contains an if statement that looks at the value of trackMouse on the root timeline before taking action. You'll remember that the value of this variable is set to true when the invisible button is pressed but false when it's released. Since this script only takes action if its value is true, alternating the value of this variable—as we do with various mouse events—has the effect of turning the script on and off.

The script states that if the value of trackMouse is true, set the value of the variable named power to equal the difference between the mouse's current horizontal position minus the value of mouseStart. You'll remember that mouseStart is the recorded horizontal position of the mouse the moment the invisible button is pressed. The next action is used to display the value of power in the **powerAmount** text field. Since these actions are executed whenever the mouse is moved (and trackMouse has a value of true), it provides a real-time display of the power used to hit the ball.

In the end, the value displayed in the **powerAmount** *text field is the same as that assigned to the variable* hitAmount, *which determines how far the ball moves when hit.*

The concept you need to grasp here is the idea of turning clip event-based scripts on and off using scripts triggered by mouse events—a capability that gives you a great deal of control in an interactive environment. You'll see many more examples of this throughout this book.

7) Choose Control > Test Movie.

Press the mouse on the tip of the pool stick and move your mouse to the right. You'll notice the interaction. Release the mouse after pulling a distance and notice how the pull stick hits the ball and the ball moves to the left, based on the amount of power applied. After completing the process, try it again. Each time the ball is hit with a different amount of power, it moves accordingly.

8) Close the test movie to return to the authoring environment and save your work as OrchestratingEvents2.fla.

This completes the exercise.

UNDERSTANDING EVENT HANDLER METHODS

Although we've discussed a number of events thus far, we've really just scratched the surface of the things Flash can react to. You already know that scripts react to all kinds of triggers: interaction with the mouse, the timeline reaching a specific frame, movie clip instances entering a scene. But did you also know that by using event handler methods, you can make your scripts execute when sounds finish playing, when the stage is resized, or when the text in a text field changes? You can even use event handler methods to extend the functionality of the events we've already used in this lesson.

Although event handler methods and standard event handlers are used for the same basic purpose (that is, executing a script when something happens in your movie), you must implement them a bit differently.

By now, you know how to set up a script to be executed as the result of an event. For example, the following script is attached to a movie clip instance named **myMovieClip** and is executed whenever the mouse is pressed down while the instance is present in the scene:

```
onClipEvent(mouseDown) {
  _rotation = 45;
}
```

This script will rotate that instance by 45 degrees when the mouse is pressed down.

Using an event handler method, the following script would be placed on a frame of the timeline to accomplish the same purpose, rotating **myMovieClip** whenever the mouse is pressed down.

```
myMovieClip.onMouseDown = function() {
  myMovieClip._rotation = 45;
}
```

Instead of using `onClipEvent` to define the event handler (as shown in the first script), here we use a dot (.) to separate the name of the object (in this case **myMovieClip**) from the event to which it needs to react. And to reiterate, we've placed this script on a frame rather than attach it to the instance.

Don't worry about the use of `function()` in the above script. We'll provide an in-depth discussion of functions in Chapter 5. All you need to know about this use of `function()` is that it's a necessary part of the syntax for implementing the event handler method, as shown.

TIP *Once you become familiar with functions, if you would like a particular one to be executed when defining an event handler method, you would change the above syntax in the following manner:* `myMovieClip.onMouseDown = nameOfFunction;`

The actions in the second line of the script (between curly braces) define what needs to happen when the event occurs.

NOTE *You'll notice that in the first script, no target path is defined (`_rotation = 45`), but that in the second a target path is defined (`myMovieClip._rotation = 45`). Since the first script is attached to myMovieClip, no target path is necessary—that is, the target is understood to be the movie clip itself. However, because the second script is on a frame, you need a path to identify the object to be rotated. When using event handler methods as described here, you need to be aware of the target paths in the triggered actions. For more on target paths, see Lesson 3, Understanding Target Paths.*

Since this script describes how the **myMovieClip** instance reacts to the `onMouseDown` event, that instance must exist in the scene at the time the event handler method is defined. This will attach the defined functionality to the instance. By the same token, event handler methods assigned to objects are removed when the object leaves the scene (or is otherwise removed). If the object appears in the scene again, any event handler methods will need to be defined again.

At first glance, you may be wondering how event handler methods are much different than the regular events, and if there are any advantages of using one over the other. That's what we'll discuss next.

74

Event handler methods play a large role in the way custom objects are set up to react to events. For more information, see Lesson 6, Customizing Objects.

USING EVENT HANDLER METHODS

All standard event handlers have equivalent event handler methods, as demonstrated by the following:

`on(press)` is `buttonName.onPress` or `movieClipName.onPress`

`on(release)` is `buttonName.onRelease` or `movieClipName.onRelease`

`on(enterFrame)` is `movieClipName.onEnterFrame`

In addition, the following event handler methods exist but have no standard event equivalents:

Buttons/Movie Clips

```
nameOfClipOrButton.onKillFocus
nameOfClipOrButton.onSetFocus
```

Sound

```
nameOfSoundObject.onLoad
nameOfSoundObject.onSoundComplete
```

Text Fields

```
nameOfTextField.onChanged
nameOfTextField.onKillFocus
nameOfTextField.onScroller
nameOfTextField.onSetFocus
```

LoadVars Object

```
nameOfLoadVarsObject.onLoad
```

XML

```
nameOfXMLObject.onData
nameOfXMLObject.onLoad
```

XML Socket

```
nameOfXMLSocketObject.onClose
nameOfXMLSocketObject.onConnect
nameOfXMLSocketObject.onData
nameOfXMLSocketObject.onXML
```

As you can see, you can use numerous events to trigger a script. Since some of these objects are intangible (for example, Sound, LoadVars, XML, and so on), defining event handler methods (on a keyframe of the timeline) is the only way to execute a script when an event occurs in relation to that object (in contrast to buttons and movie clip instances, which you can select on the stage and attach scripts directly to).

NOTE *We will discuss and use many of these event handler methods throughout this book. For more information about each, see the ActionScript dictionary.*

By attaching a script to a button or movie clip instance using a regular event handler, you pretty much lock down not only what happens when an event occurs but also the events that actually trigger a script to be executed. Take a look at the following script:

```
on(press){
  gotoAndPlay(5);
}
```

If you were to attach this script to a button, the button would react *only* to the press event, performing a single action when that event occurred. To give you an idea of the power and flexibility of event handler methods, assume there's a button instance on the stage named **myButton**. By placing the following script on Frame 1 of the main timeline (assuming the button exists at that frame), you define how that button will react to certain events:

```
myButton.onPress = function() {
  stopAllSounds();
}
myButton.onRelease = function() {
  myMovieClip._xscale = 50;
}
```

When pressed, the button will halt all sounds; when released, it will scale **myMovieClip** to 50 percent of its original size.

However, by moving that timeline to Frame 2—which contains the following script (assuming the button exists at Frame 2)—you would change the button's function completely:

```
myButton.onPress = null
myButton.onRelease = null
myButton.onRollOver = function() {
  stopAllSounds();
}
myButton.onRollOut = function() {
  myMovieClip._xscale = 50;
}
```

76

By using `null`, you prevent the button from continuing to react to an `onPress` or `onRelease` event—and instead instruct it to react to the two newly defined events.

As you can see, by using event handler methods, we can change the button's functionality and the events it reacts to—a powerful capability!

Event handler methods also come in handy for dynamically created objects. Since the act of dynamically creating an object involves putting an object in your movie that wasn't there when the movie was authored, you can't set the object up to react to an event by selecting it. (It hasn't been created yet!) This is where event handler methods become really useful. Take a look at the following sample script to see how you could implement this:

```
_root.createEmptyMovieClip("newClip", 1);
_root.newClip.onEnterFrame = function(){
  myVariable++;
}
_root.newClip.onMouseMove = function(){
  myCursorClip._x = _root._xmouse;
  myCursorClip._y = _root._ymouse;
}
```

As you can see, after creating a movie clip instance named **newClip**, we immediately use event handler methods to define what that instance will do when certain events occur.

In the following exercise, we'll place event handler methods on Frame 1 of our movie to define the way scene elements react to various events. The idea behind this project is that when the user selects a particular text field (or types text into a field), elements in the scene will react and other elements will be dynamically configured to react to various mouse and clip events.

1) Open CarParts1.fla in the Lesson02/Assets folder.

This project contains a single scene with eight layers that are named according to their contents.

The Background layer contains the main background graphic. The CarClip layer contains the red car at the top left of the stage—a movie clip instance named **car**. That movie clip's timeline contains a couple of movie clip instances, **wheel1** and **wheel2**, which represent the wheels of the car. The next layer, Text Fields, contains three text fields: **text1**, **text2**, and **text3**. As you will see, the way the user interacts with these text fields will dictate how the project functions. The next layer, Arrows, contains three small arrow movie clip instances: **arrow1**, **arrow2**, and **arrow3**. These arrows appear below each text field and will be set up to move horizontally along the bottom of the text field as text is entered and removed from a field. The next layer, Wheel, contains the movie clip **wheelClip**, which will be dynamically scripted to react to the onEnterFrame event *only* when the **text1** text field has been selected. The layer above that, Speedometer, contains a movie clip instance named **speedClip** whose timeline contains a short animation of a needle rotating in the gauge as well as a revving sound. When the clip is played, these things make the clip appear to operate like the real thing. This instance will be dynamically scripted to play when the onPress event occurs—but only after the **text2** text field has been selected. The next layer, Fan, contains a movie clip instance named **fanClip**, which will be set up to react to the onEnterFrame event *only* when **text3** has been selected. Finally, Frame 1 of the Actions layer will contain most of the script for our project.

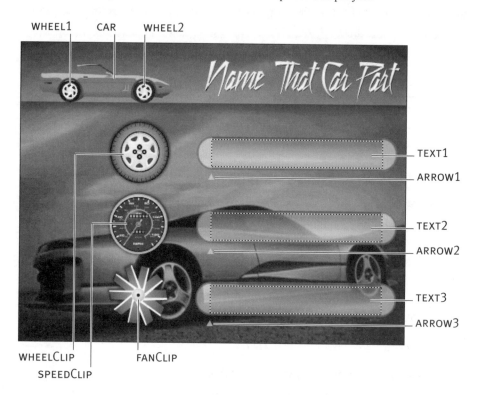

2) With the Actions panel open, select Frame 1 and add this script:

```
text1.onChanged = function(){
  car._x += 2;
  car.wheel1._rotation += 10;
  car.wheel2._rotation += 10;
  arrow1._x = text1._x + text1.textWidth;
}
```

This script defines what happens when the text in the **text1** text field is changed, added to, or deleted.

The first action is used to horizontally move the **car** instance 2 pixels to the right by adding *2* to its current *x* property. The next two actions will rotate the **wheel1** and **wheel2** movie clip instances (which are in the **car** instance) by adding 10 degrees to their current rotation values. This will cause them to appear to spin as the car moves right.

NOTE *As shown in an earlier script, using += in the script is the same as saying, "Add the value on the right of the equals sign to the current value of what is identified on the left"— which in this case is the rotation value of the* **wheel1** *and* **wheel2** *movie clip instances.*

The last action is used to move **arrow1** horizontally so that it appears just below the last letter in the **text1** text field. It does this by adding the horizontal location of **text1** (its *x* property) to the width of the text in the field. The sum of this amount will position **arrow1** appropriately. Every time text is changed (**onChanged**) in **text1**, these actions will be triggered.

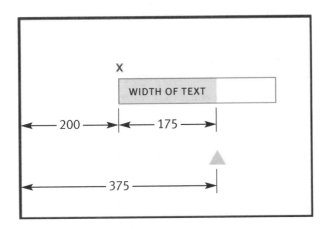

3) With the Actions panel open, add the following script just below the script you just added:

```
text1.onSetFocus = function(){
  wheelClip.onEnterFrame = function(){
    wheelClip._rotation += 30;
  }
  speedClip.onPress = null;
  fanClip.onEnterFrame = null;
}
```

This script defines what happens when the **text1** text field has been given focus or clicked on. (To "focus" on a field means to make it the active field, into which the user can immediately enter information.)

79

When this event handler method is triggered it does an interesting thing: It configures three other event handler methods. Yes, they are that flexible! First, the **wheelClip** is set up to react to the `onEnterFrame` event, so that it will spin by an additional 30 degrees each time the event is triggered (24 times a second). This will cause it to spin as soon as **text1** is selected. Since we will be adding script in the next couple of steps that will enable **speedClip** and **fanClip** to react to `onPress` and `onEnterFrame` events respectively, the next two actions are used to remove that functionality when **text1** is selected.

The following additions to the script are just a variation on what has been added so far.

4) With the Actions panel open, add the following script just below the script you just added:

```
text2.onChanged = function(){
  car._x += 2;
  car.wheel1._rotation += 10;
  car.wheel2._rotation += 10;
  arrow2._x = text2._x + text2.textWidth;
}
```

Syntactically and functionally, this script is the same as the script shown in Step 2—with two exceptions: First, it's executed when the text in the **text2** text field changes. Also, the last action is used to move **arrow2** horizontally so that it appears just below the last letter in the **text2** text field.

5) With the Actions panel open, add the following script just below the script you just added:

```
text2.onSetFocus = function(){
  wheelClip.onEnterFrame = null;
  speedClip.onPress = function(){
    speedClip.play();
  }
  fanClip.onEnterFrame = null;
}
```

Once again, this script is a variation of that included in Step 3. It dictates what occurs when **text2** is given focus (or selected). You'll notice that the **speedClip** instance is set up to react to an `onPress` event. Thus, pressing the **speedClip** instance once **text2** has been given focus will cause that instance to play. The other actions prevent the **wheelClip** and **fanClip** instances from reacting to the `onEnterFrame` event, that other parts of the script define. As you may have realized, the idea behind this functionality is to enable the instance to the left of a text field to react to an event when the field is given focus but prevent it from reacting to that event when another field is given focus.

6) With the Actions panel open, add the following script just below the script you just added:

```
text3.onChanged = function(){
  car._x += 2;
  car.wheel1._rotation += 10;
  car.wheel2._rotation += 10;
  arrow3._x = text3._x + text3.textWidth;
}
text3.onSetFocus = function(){
  wheelClip.onEnterFrame = null;
  speedClip.onPress = null;
  fanClip.onEnterFrame = function(){
    fanClip._rotation += 20;
  }
}
```

Once again, this script is a variation of those presented in previous steps. It dictates what occurs when **text3** is given focus or when text within that field changes.

7) Choose Control › Test Movie.

Click the top text field (**text1**): That text field will be given focus, and thus the **wheelClip** instance will begin spinning. As you type text into the field, two things will occur: The **car** movie clip instance will move to the right, with its wheels spinning, and the arrow underneath the field will continue to appear just below the last character in the field. Try pressing the **speedClip,** and you'll notice that nothing happens. Click **text2**, and that changes: The **wheelClip** instance will quit spinning, and pressing on the **speedClip** instance will make that instance play. Clicking **text3** will cause the **speedClip** instance to become inactive again, but the **fanClip** instance will begin spinning.

8) Close the test movie to return to the authoring environment and save your work as CarParts2.fla.

This completes the exercise.

USING 'LISTENERS'

Just as a single transmitter broadcasts radio waves to thousands of radio receivers, events can be "broadcast" to any number of objects so that they respond accordingly. You do this by employing what are known as *listeners*— events that can be broadcast to objects that have been "registered" to listen for them (listening objects).

Suppose you wanted an object (sound, movie clip, text field, array, custom) to react to a certain event being triggered in your movie. You would first create an event handler method for that object:

```
myTextField.onMouseDown = function(){
  myTextField.text="";
}
```

Here we've set up a text field named **myTextfield** to react when the mouse is pressed down. The onMouseDown event is not a standard event that a text field can react to, and at this point it still won't. In order for the text field to react to this event, you must register the text field as a listener for the event. You can do that by adding the following code:

```
Mouse.addListener("myTextField");
```

Here the text field is registered with the Mouse object, since the onMouseDown event is a listener of that object. Now, whenever the mouse is pressed down, the event handler method we created earlier will execute. You can set up any number of objects to a single listener event as long as the object has been given an event handler method to deal with the event, and it has been registered to listen for that event. If you no longer want an object to listen for an event, you can unregister it using the following syntax:

```
Mouse.removeListener("myTextField");
```

Listeners just give you a bit more flexibility for scripting your projects to react to various events.

NOTE *Not all events can be treated as listeners. With this in mind, be aware of which events are listed as listeners in the Actions toolbox. If an event is not listed as a listener, other objects can not be set up to listen to it.*

WHAT YOU HAVE LEARNED

In this lesson, you have:

- Learned how event handlers are used in scripts (pages 32–34)

- Determined the best event handlers for specific types of jobs (pages 35–37, 54–56)

- Used mouse/button events to control interactivity (pages 37–46)

- Added keyboard control to a project (page 44)

- Created a self-running presentation using frame events (pages 47–54)

- Used clip events to create an interactive project (pages 57–67)

- Orchestrated various events to create a highly interactive environment (pages 68–73)

- Used event handler methods to dynamically set how an object reacts to an event (pages 73–81)

- Learned what listeners do and how to use them (page 82)

understanding target paths

LESSON 3

Communication is an important part of our everyday lives. We communicate via phones, e-mail, regular mail, and so on. Since nearly everyone in the world communicates in a similar fashion, without a system of individual identification, it would be impossible to route those communications from one person to another. We all have unique phone numbers, e-mail addresses, and street addresses—all of which ensure that the communications intended for us actually reach us.

Just as phone numbers, e-mail addresses, and street addresses lead communications to their intended recipients, Macromedia Flash *target paths* lead one timeline to another, allowing them to communicate. In this lesson, we'll take a look at the various target paths used in typical Flash projects as well as show you how to use Flash's

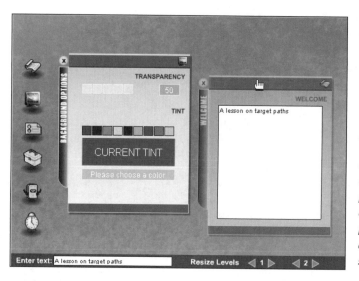

A thorough understanding of target paths and how to use them will allow you to create sophisticated applications where independent timelines can work together to perform tasks. The above "windowed" Flash application (which we'll create in this lesson) will provide an excellent example of the way target paths can be used to give a project more depth and sophistication.

powerful ability to have timelines talk to each other—a capability you'll use to give your projects more depth and sophistication.

WHAT YOU WILL LEARN

In this lesson, you will:

- Gain an understanding of the hierarchy of timelines in Flash movies
- Learn about absolute and relative target paths
- Learn how movies communicate with one another
- Control specific timelines within a single project
- Control movies loaded into levels
- Use the parent-child relationship in movies to create an "effect" clip
- Learn how to make global references to various ActionScript elements

APPROXIMATE TIME

This lesson takes approximately 1 ½ hours to complete.

LESSON FILES

Media Files:

None

Starting File:

Lesson03/Assets/currentTarget1.fla
Lesson03/Assets/rootTarget1.fla
Lesson03/Assets/parentTarget1.fla
Lesson03/Assets/movieclipTarget1.fla
Lesson03/Assets/backgroundControl1.fla
Lesson03/Assets/textBox1.fla
Lesson03/Assets/levelTarget1.fla
Lesson03/Assets/levelTarget2.fla
Lesson03/Assets/backgroundControl2.fla
Lesson03/Assets/levelTarget.swf

Completed Project:

currentTarget2.fla
rootTarget2.fla
parentTarget2.fla.
movieclipTarget2.fla.
textBox2.fla
levelTarget3.fla
backgroundControl3.fla

UNDERSTANDING MULTIPLE TIMELINES

Every project includes a main timeline. But projects also include movie clip instances that have timelines of their own. And you can use the `loadMovie ()` action to add external SWFs to a project, thereby adding even more timelines. A single project can therefore have many separate timelines, all of which can act independently of one another, with their own variables, properties, objects, and function.

However, these timelines can also work together; one timeline can control another. In fact, any timeline present in a scene can tell another present timeline to do something. (Timelines are considered *present* as long as they exist in the Player movie window. Thus, if a movie clip instance appears in your movie for 40 frames, it's only considered present—and targetable—during those 40 frames.)

The communication lines for these movie elements are provided by target paths—addresses to objects (for example, movie clip instances) that begin by describing the overall area in which the object exists and then narrow that area with each subsequent level. To better understand this concept, take a look at the following example. The target path to one of your authors (!) would look something like the following:

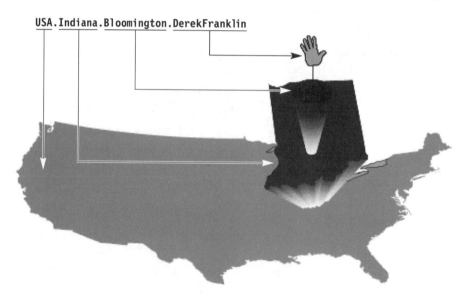

This target path contains four levels—separated by dots—with each subsequent level smaller in size and scope, until you reach the target: Derek Franklin! This is what's known as an *absolute path*—the complete and absolute location of Derek Franklin here on Earth. There are also *relative target paths*—the paths you would provide to people who also live in Bloomington. To locate him, these people don't need all of the information included in the absolute path; thus, we could simply provide them with the following *relative path:*

A relative path—as you can see from the above—targets an object in relation to the object trying to locate it. Thus, if the entire city of Bloomington (Derek Franklin included) were to relocate to Paris, those people could still locate Derek Franklin using `DerekFranklin`. This is because even though the absolute path has changed to `France.Paris.DerekFranklin`, Derek Franklin's relative position (to the ex-citizens on Bloomington) remains the same.

USA.Indiana.Bloomington.DerekFranklin

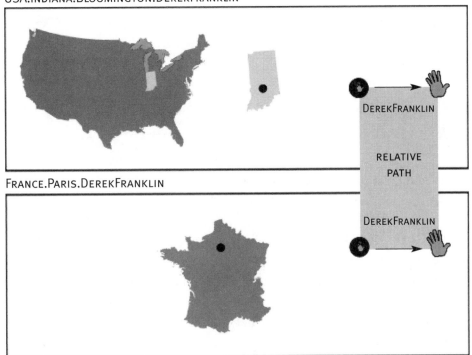

Relative paths are extremely powerful because they enable you to script a "chunk" of timelines to work together, in a unique way, based on their relationship to one another. As long as these timelines' relative relationship to one another remains the same, they'll continue to work together—even if you move them to another location in your project, or to another project altogether.

You can think of a Flash project as a hierarchy of movies (where timelines can exist within other timelines), with the main, or *root*, movie serving as the starting point (see "Targeting the Main Movie"). When timelines exist in a hierarchical structure (as they do in Flash projects), it becomes critical that you understand how to address, or *target*, a timeline using target paths.

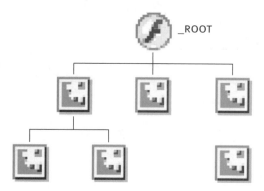

You will use target paths not only to alter timelines but to access their variable data, functions, objects, and so on.

TARGETING THE CURRENT MOVIE

Whenever a script is placed in a timeline, such as on a frame or on a button, and the target for those actions is that same timeline, it can be said that the target for the actions in that script is the current movie. This is sort of like telling yourself to do something: For example, if you were to tell yourself to stand up, that action could be said to be targeting the "current" person—you—since you gave *and* responded to the command. (That is, you're both the commander *and* the person taking orders!) If you were to script this action, it would look something like the following:

```
standUp();
```

Note that the action doesn't include a target path: This is because it targets the current movie. After all, if you were to tell yourself to stand up, you wouldn't normally address yourself prior to giving the command. In much the same way, Flash understands that when an action doesn't include a target path, it's meant to affect the timeline where the script resides.

Another way to address the current movie in a script is by preceding an action with the term `this`, as in the following:

```
this.standUp();
```

In essence, you're saying, "With 'this' timeline, take the following action." We'll go into greater detail about this later in the book, but for the time being just remember that in all cases, the following are interchangeable when addressing the current movie:

```
action ();
this.action ();
```

Keep in mind that your project may contain many scripts on various timelines that don't contain target paths. When this is the case, each script affects its own timeline, or the current movie.

In the following exercise, we'll target the current movie for several timelines using no target path and the term this interchangeably. We use both because we want you to grow accustomed with the use of this as well as how it relates to the current referenced object because you will have opportunities to use it in more advanced ways later.

1) Open currentTarget1.fla in the Lesson03/Assets folder.

This project consists of a single scene with four layers, each named according to its content. The Background layer contains four keyframes: At each of these keyframes the background is a different color. (Moving the playhead back and forth will reveal this.) In the middle of the stage is a movie clip instance of a very rounded fellow.

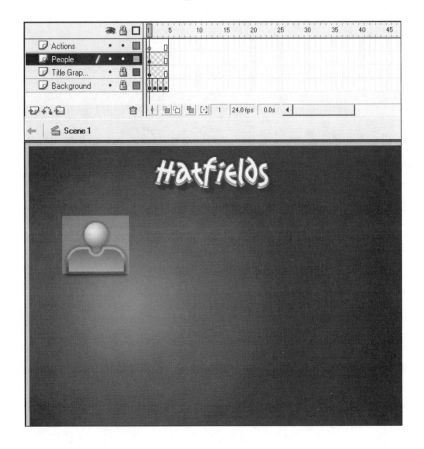

In our first scripting task, we'll instruct the main timeline to move to a random frame when it begins playing, causing a random background color to appear. After that, we'll work with the movie clip instance in the middle of the stage, script it to do something, add a few family members, and then script them to do something as well.

2) Select Frame 1 of the main timeline and add the following script:

```
startingColor = random (4) + 1;
this.gotoAndStop (this.startingColor);
```

The first thing to be aware of is that the keyframe on Frame 1 of the main timeline is currently selected—which means the main timeline is the current movie in the context of this script. Thus, any actions you enter in the Actions panel without a target path (or that use `this`) will affect this timeline.

The first action generates a random number between 1 and 4, and assigns it to `startingColor`. By using `random (4)` we're asking Flash to generate a random number with four possible values, which always begin with zero—that is, 0, 1, 2, or 3. By adding 1, as we have, the possible values generated become 1, 2, 3, or 4—necessary because that number will be used next to tell the current movie to go to and stop at a frame number based on the value of `startingColor` (and timelines don't have a Frame 0). This will result in the random display of one of the background colors when the movie begins playing.

Notice also that no target path is used in assigning the value of `startingColor`; however, `this` is used with the variable in the next action: They mean the same thing and are thus interchangeable.

3) Double-click the movie clip instance in the middle of the stage to edit it in place.
Since you'll need a solid understanding of this movie clip's timeline to complete several of the exercises in this lesson, let's take a minute now to get acquainted with it.

This timeline has two frame labels: Quiet and Speak. At the Speak label a text balloon appears that includes a text field named **balloon**. We will soon create a script that displays text within this text field whenever the timeline is moved to the Speak label.

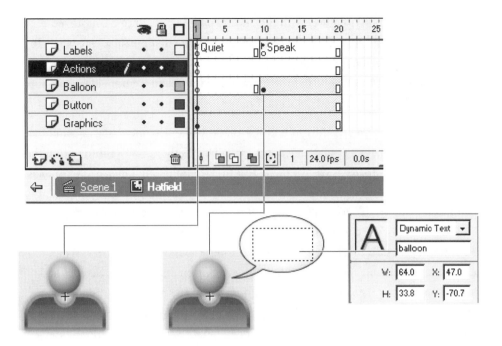

The Button layer of this timeline consists of an invisible button that's placed on top of all of the graphics on this timeline. We will script this button in the next step.

Finally, Frame 1 of this timeline's Actions layer contains a `stop()` action to prevent the timeline from moving past this frame until we instruct it to.

4) With the Actions panel open, select the invisible button and add this script:

```
on (press) {
  startDrag (this);
  gotoAndStop ("Speak");
  balloon.text = words;
}
on (release) {
  stopDrag ();
  this.gotoAndStop ("Quiet");
}
```

The first set of actions is executed when this button is pressed, causing the movie clip instance to become draggable. Next, the same timeline is sent to the frame labeled Speak. In addition, we set the text to be displayed in the **balloon** text field to the value of words—the name of a variable that will contain a string of text. We will define this variable shortly.

As the script shows, when the button is released, dragging stops and the timeline is sent to the frame labeled Quiet.

5) Return to the main timeline. With the Library panel open, drag a couple more instances of the Hatfield movie clip onto the stage. Choose Control > Test Movie to test what you've done so far.

The first thing you'll notice is that the main timeline goes to a random frame to display one of the background colors on Frames 1 through 4.

Press any of the instances, and you'll notice that they've become draggable and that their text balloons appear. The concept to grasp here is that the invisible button that enables this functionality is part of the *master* movie clip itself. Thus, each instance of the clip contains this button as well as the script that makes it work. The script on the button is set up to make the timeline it is part of (the current movie) draggable. Since each instance is considered a separate timeline, only the instance that contains the currently pressed button will be dragged when the button is pressed. When actions are placed on a movie clip's timeline or a button *inside* the movie clip, and those actions target its own timeline, each instance of the movie clip inherits that scripted functionality. Think of this as genetically programming instances that are based on the same master movie clip so they all have a fundamental function.

Using clip event handlers, we can give each instance its own personality, on top of what it is "genetically" programmed to do. Let's look at that next.

6) Close the test window to return to the authoring environment. With the Actions panel open, select one of the three instances on the stage and add this script:

```
onClipEvent (load) {
  words = "My name is Derek";
  this._xscale = 75;
  _yscale = 75;
}
```

As you learned in the previous lesson, clip events (load, enterFrame, mouseMove, and so on) are event handlers attached to movie clip instances. As such, they allow you to script actions that affect single movie clip instances (rather than every instance of a movie clip). Thus, you would use clip events—*outside* the movie clip's timeline—to script characteristics unique to specific movie clip instances, but you would script shared traits *inside* the movie clip's timeline (on a frame or button inside the clip) so that all instances of that movie clip would inherit those characteristics. Both sets of actions target the current timeline—but with a different scope.

92

If you were to extend this metaphor to people, you could think of shared traits (the things you script inside your movie clip's timeline) as humans' common capacity to think, feel, and move—things we all inherit. Unique characteristics (the things you script outside your movie clip's timeline), on the other hand, could include name, size, and location—things that are individual to each of us.

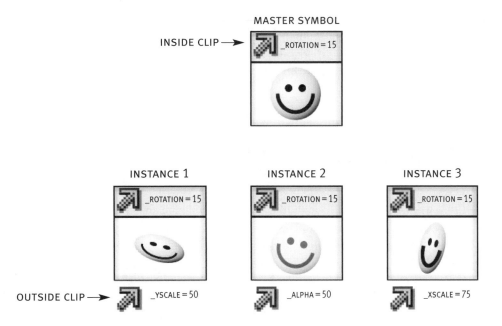

The script above is executed when the instance loads, or first appears in the movie. The first action assigns a text value to words. When this action is executed, both the name and value of this variable are stored in this instance. You'll also remember that the value of this variable is used to set the text that is displayed in the **balloon** text field mentioned in Step 4. The next two actions scale the instance by 75 percent.

7) With the Actions panel open, select one of the other two instances on the stage and add this script:

```
onClipEvent (load) {
  words = "My name is Ashlie";
  _x = 400;
  _y = 300;
}
```

This script is similar to the previous one except that it sets the value of words to "My name is Ashlie" and, on loading, moves this instance to a location 400 pixels horizontally from the left of the stage and 300 pixels vertically from the top of the stage.

8) With the Actions panel open, select the last instance on the stage and add this script:

```
onClipEvent (load) {
  words = "My name is Kathy";
}
onClipEvent (mouseMove) {
  this._rotation = this._rotation + .5;
}
```

When this instance is loaded, the first action will set the value of words to "My name is Kathy." A second clip event rotates the instance half a degree each time the mouse is moved.

9) Choose Control > Test Movie to see what we've done so far.

On loading, you'll see that our scripts have caused several things to occur: The first instance we scripted is now 75 percent smaller than the other two. The second instance we scripted can be seen at the X and Y coordinates we told it to go to on loading. And the third instance rotates as the mouse is moved. Press any of these movie clip instances, and you'll see that you can still drag as before but that the text balloon now includes text customized for each instance. Once again, remember that while scripts placed *inside* the movie clip they target will affect all instances of that clip, clip events (attached to individual instances) let you customize each instance.

10) Close the testing environment to return to the authoring environment. Save this file as currentTarget2.fla.

We will build on this file (with a few modifications) in the following exercise.

TARGETING THE MAIN MOVIE

The main, or root, movie represents the main timeline of a SWF. All of your project's other timelines exist, in some way, inside this one.

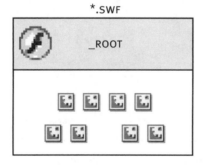

Targeting the main timeline is very simple. The syntax would be as follows:

```
_root.play();
```

You can place this script on any timeline—exactly as shown—and it will always cause the main timeline to play.

NOTE *A movie loaded into a level is also considered a root timeline. We'll explain how this affects your scripting in the section "Targeting Movies on Levels."*

1) Open rootTarget1.fla in the Lesson03/Assets folder.

This file is similar to the one we just finished working on except that two buttons appear in the lower-right portion of the stage. We will script these to resize the main timeline when clicked. We will then copy these buttons, place them inside of our movie clip instances, and—without modifying the target paths used in the script— demonstrate how you can use **_root** to target the main timeline from any other timeline in the SWF.

2) With the Actions panel open, select the button with the minus sign over it and add the following script:

```
on (release) {
  _root._xscale = _root._xscale - 10;
  _root._yscale = _root._yscale - 10;
}
```

When this button is pressed and released, the main timeline's size will be reduced by 10 percent. One thing to note: Since the button to which we're attaching this action resides on the main timeline—which is also the timeline affected by the button—this script doesn't really require a target path. We simply use an absolute target path here to demonstrate their universal effectiveness.

3) With the Actions panel open, select the button with the plus sign over it and add this script:

```
on (release) {
  _root._xscale = _root._xscale + 10;
  _root._yscale = _root._yscale + 10;
}
```

This script is similar to the last one except that this time when this button is pressed and released, the main timeline's size will *increase* by 10 percent.

4) Drag-select both buttons (as well as the text on top of the buttons) and copy them. Double-click one of the movie clip instances on the stage to edit it in place. Paste the buttons on the 'Change root buttons' layer on the movie clip's timeline and position them just below and center of the current graphics.

Although these copies of the buttons on the main timeline exist within this movie clip timeline, the actions attached to them still target the main timeline because a **_root** target path always refers to the main timeline of the movie (SWF).

5) Choose Control > Test movie to test the project.

The first thing you'll notice is that every instance of our movie clip includes the buttons. In addition, the buttons appear in their original placement—on the bottom-right portion of the stage. Click any of these buttons, and you get the same result: The main timeline is resized. As it resizes, however, something interesting occurs: All of the other timelines are resized as well. This is due to the parent-child relationship between the main timeline and the movie clip instances on it—something we'll discuss in more detail in the next exercise.

6) Close the testing environment to return to the authoring environment. Save the project as rootTarget2.fla.

We will build on this file (with a few modifications) in the following exercise.

TARGETING A PARENT MOVIE

Flash allows you to place one timeline inside of another—which is, in fact, what you're doing whenever you add a movie clip instance to the main timeline. However, even movie clip instances can contain other movie clip instances, many levels deep. Placing one timeline inside of another creates a parent-child relationship between the timelines. The parent is the timeline that *contains* the other movie; the child is the movie *contained* within the other timeline.

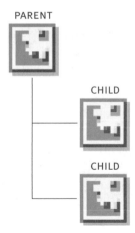

A child movie can easily tell its parent what to do (not so easy in real life!) by using the following syntax:

```
_parent.play();
```

To understand how this works, imagine placing a movie clip instance named **myMovieClip** on the main timeline and then placing another movie clip instance, this one named **myOtherMovieClip**, inside **myMovieClip**. The absolute target path of this movie structure would look like the following:

```
_root.myMovieClip.myOtherMovieClip
```

If you wanted an action on **myOtherMovieClip**'s timeline to cause **myMovieClip**'s timeline to go to Frame 50, you would use this syntax:

```
_parent.gotoAndPlay(50);
```

You could place this same syntax on **myMovieClip**'s timeline, and it would cause the main timeline to go to Frame 50, because the main timeline is that movie clip's parent.

In the following exercise, we'll place movie clips inside movie clips, creating parent-child relationships. Such a relationship can have all sorts of ramifications within a project, helping you make your movies more interactive. You will also create a simple "effect" clip that you can drag and drop into any timeline, causing that timeline to do something.

1) Open parentTarget1.fla in the Lesson03/Assets folder.
The only difference between this file and the file we worked on in the last exercise is that the buttons set up to scale the main timeline have been removed to avoid confusion.

2) Double-click one of the movie clip instances on the stage to edit it in place. With the Library panel open and the Child Clip layer selected, drag an instance of the Hatfield Child movie clip onto the stage, just to the right of the graphics in the current movie clip.
You've just placed one movie clip within another, creating a parent-child relationship: The movie clip instance you just dragged onto the stage is the child, and the timeline you dragged it to is the parent. The child's timeline is set up in the exact same way as the parent's timeline. It contains an invisible button that when pressed will drag the instance as well as display a text balloon. The text field in this balloon is also named **balloon**, just as it is in the parent movie.

3) With the Actions panel open, select the child movie clip instance and add this script:

```
onClipEvent (load) {
  this.words = _parent.words + "'s kid";
}
```

When this movie clip instance is loaded—which occurs at the same time the parent is loaded because it resides on Frame 1 of its parent timeline—data is transferred from the parent to the child. The above action can be translated as follows: "Make the value of the words in this timeline equal to words' value in the parent timeline plus 's kid.' " Thus, if words has a value of "I'm Derek" in the parent, then words will have a value of "I'm Derek's kid" in the child. Let's test it.

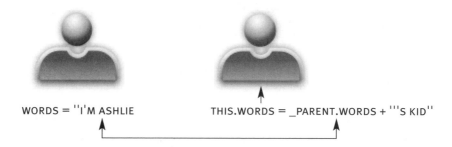

WORDS = ''I'M ASHLIE   THIS.WORDS = _PARENT.WORDS + '''S KID''

4) Choose Control > Test Movie to view the project up to this point.

The first thing you'll notice when the movie plays is that each of our instances now includes a child movie clip instance. If you press one of the child movie clip instances, not only does it become draggable but its text balloon appears with text indicating who its parent is. This is the functionality we set up in the last step.

98

Press and drag one of the parent movies and you'll notice that its child is dragged as well. The same thing occurs with the parent movie that rotates as the mouse moves: Its child movie rotates along with it. Datawise, a child movie clip is independent of its parent: Data in one timeline does not affect data in the other unless you program it to. Graphically, however, it's another story. Size, position, transparency, and other graphical changes made dynamically to a parent movie clip will automatically affect its children in the same way. However, changes to a child have no inherent affect on a parent; if you want child clips to affect parent clips, you must program them to do so. This means you can program groups of timelines to work together but remain separate from other groups in the project.

Let's look at another use of this parent-child relationship between timelines.

5) Close the testing environment to return to the authoring environment. With the Library panel open, double-click the Swirl Clip movie clip instance:

This places Flash in Symbol Editing mode with Swirl Clip's timeline visible. This clip contains no graphical data, just four empty keyframes to which we will add scripts next.

6) With the Actions panel open, select Frames 1, 2, 3, and 4 and add the following scripts, respectively:

Place on Frame 1:

```
_parent._x = _parent._x - 1;
_parent._xscale = _parent._xscale - 1;
```

Place on Frame 2:

```
_parent._y = _parent._y - 1;
_parent._yscale = _parent._yscale - 1;
```

Place on Frame 3:

```
_parent._x = _parent._x + 2;
_parent._xscale = _parent._xscale - 1;
```

Place on Frame 4:

```
_parent._y = _parent._y + 2;
_parent._yscale = _parent._yscale - 1;
```

At this point, these scripts' makeup isn't terribly important; what *is* important is that the actions all target the parent movie clip, and that when this movie is placed inside a timeline, its parent will appear to spiral away into nothingness. Let's demonstrate this.

7) Return to the main timeline. With the Library panel open and the Swirl Clip layer selected, drag a Swirl Clip instance onto the stage. Choose Control > Test Movie to test the project.

As soon as the movie begins to play, the main timeline begins to swirl away into nothingness—an effect achieved by the movie clip instance we dropped into it. You can apply this effect to any timeline just by placing that same movie clip instance inside it—which we'll do next.

8) Close the test window to return to the authoring environment. Select the Swirl Clip instance on the main timeline and choose Edit > Cut. Double-click one of the Hatfield movie clip instances to go to its timeline. With the Swirl Clip layer selected, choose Edit > Paste to paste Swirl Clip into this timeline. Choose Control > Test Movie to test the project.

When the movie plays, the main timeline no longer swirls away, but every instance of the Hatfield movie clip does instead. This is because once the Swirl Clip instance was moved, the main timeline ceased being its parent and the Hatfield movie clip became its parent instead. Getting a movie clip to swirl away is just the tip of the iceberg when it comes to exploiting this ability to create drag-and-drop behaviors.

You can also target many levels up, using the parent target path such as in the following:

```
_parent._parent._alpha = 50
```

This enables you to create even more sophisticated behaviors.

9) Close the test window to return to the authoring environment. Save your work as parentTarget2.fla.

This completes the exercise.

TARGETING MOVIE CLIP INSTANCES

When you drag a movie clip instance into a timeline and assign it an instance name, that name (as well as the clip's relationship to other timelines) determines its target path. Say, for example, you placed a movie clip instance on the main timeline and gave it an instance name of **alien**. That movie clip instance's absolute target path would be as follows:

```
_root.alien
```

As the movie's absolute target path, you can use the above in a script in any timeline of your project to communicate with this particular instance.

However, to target that instance from the main timeline, since it's a child movie of the main timeline, you could use the following relative path:

```
alien
```

If you were to place this same movie clip instance inside another movie clip instance named **spaceship**, which resided on the root timeline, the absolute target path would become the following:

```
_root.spaceship.alien
```

Since the relationship between the root timeline and the **alien** movie clip instance has changed, the root timeline must now use the following relative path to target it:

```
spaceship.alien
```

In addition, because the **spaceship** movie clip instance is now in the same position relative to the **alien** movie clip instance as the root timeline was before, the **spaceship** instance can now target the **alien** movie clip instance as follows:

```
alien
```

In the following exercise, you will target specific movie clips based on their names and positions relative to the timeline that contains the script.

1) Open movieclipTarget1.fla in the Lesson03/Assets folder.

This file picks up where we left off in the last exercise. We will name the various instances on the stage so that we can target them in a script.

2) With Property inspector open, select each instance on the stage and name it according to the value that the instance assigns to words when it loads.

For example, if the selected instance were to set the value of words to "I'm Derek" on loading, you would name this instance Derek. Do the same for the other instances on the stage.

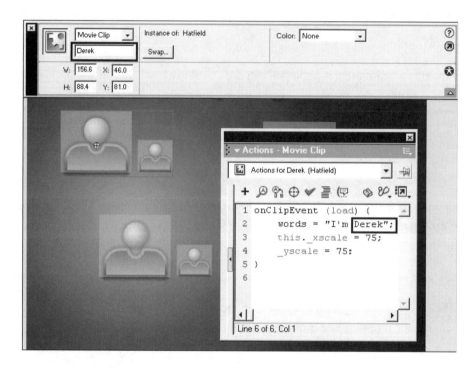

3) Double-click one of the instances to edit it in place. Inside this timeline is an instance of the Hatfield Child movie clip. With the Property inspector open, select the instance and name it *myKid*. Return to the main timeline.

There are now six movie clip instances that you can target from any other timeline. Their absolute target paths are as follows:

```
_root.Derek
_root.Derek.myKid
_root.Kathy
_root.Kathy.myKid
_root.Ashlie
_root.Ashlie.myKid
```

4) With the Actions panel open, select the instance named _Kathy_ and add the following script at the end of the current script (where it reads `this._rotation = this._rotation + .5;`**):**

```
myKid._rotation = myKid._rotation + 20;
_root.Derek.myKid._xscale = _root.Derek.myKid._xscale + .5;
_root.Derek.myKid._yscale = _root.Derek.myKid._yscale + .5;
_root.Ashlie.myKid._y = _root.Ashlie.myKid._y - .5;
```

The placement of these lines of script dictates that they be triggered with each mouse movement. Since this script is attached to the instance named **Kathy**, the first action uses a relative target path to target the **myKid** instance within itself. It sets the rotation property of this instance to its current value plus 20 every time the mouse is moved. The next two actions use absolute target paths to target the **myKid** instance inside the **Derek** instance. These actions will cause that instance to grow by .5 percent each time the mouse is moved. The last action uses an absolute target path to target the **myKid** instance inside the **Ashlie** instance. Each time the mouse is moved, the instance will move .5 pixels up from its current position.

5) Choose Control > Test Movie to test the project.
As you move the mouse, the **myKid** movie clip instances we targeted should perform the actions we scripted for them.

6) Close the test movie to return to the authoring environment. Save your file as movieclipTarget2.fla.
This completes this exercise as well as our use of this file in this lesson.

TARGETING MOVIES ON LEVELS

Using the `loadMovie()` action, Flash enables you to load more than one .swf file into the Flash player window simultaneously (something you'll learn how to do in the exercise that follows and that we discuss more in depth in Lesson 17, Loading External Content). SWFs exist in the player window in what are known as *levels*. Functionally, levels (for holding SWFs) are similar to layers (for holding content) on a timeline: They are a plane of existence, a depth, that puts a loaded SWF and all its content on top of or below other movies that have been loaded in the player window. You can load hundreds of external .swf files into various levels in the player window.

When you use the `loadMovie()` action to load a movie into a level, you must assign a level number to load the movie into. However, you don't need to load movies into sequential levels; you can assign arbitrary numbers, such as 46 or 731, if you'd rather. Once a movie has been loaded into a level, its target path to timelines on other levels is its level number. For example, if you were to load a movie into Level 37, movies on other levels would target that movie using the following target path:

```
_level37
```

To tell the main timeline on this level to stop, you would use the following syntax:

```
_level37.stop ();
```

NOTE *The first movie to appear in the player window automatically loads into Level 0.*

A level's target path is the key to controlling the SWF loaded there, including its main timeline and any movie clip instances it may contain.

Because you're loading multiple SWFs into the player window using the `loadMovie()` action, its important to note that each SWF's main timeline is considered the `_root` timeline in relation to other movies within that SWF. Thus, although a SWF loaded into a level might be addressed as `_level37` by movies on other levels, the main timeline of that SWF can be addressed as `_root` by movie clip instances within that same SWF. This means that if movies have been loaded into 15 levels, there are a total of 16 root movies (including the one on Level 0). Whenever a timeline targets another timeline on that same level, it can use a relative target path.

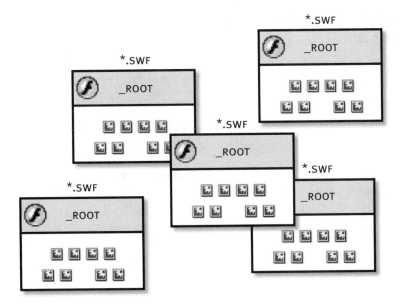

In the following exercise, we'll load movies into Levels 1 and 2, then control them from Level 0.

1) Open backgroundControl1.fla in the Lesson03/Assets folder.

This is the movie that will be loaded into Level 1. It looks like an operating system dialog box, and it contains a single scene made up of six layers, each of which is named according to its content.

In the next exercise we'll script the functionality of many of the buttons you see. For now, we'll simply make the window draggable as well as allow it to be closed.

2) With the Actions panel open, select Frame 1 on the main timeline and add the following script:

```
_visible = false;
```

Since this action targets the current movie, and this movie will be loaded into Level 1, the movie on Level 1 will be invisible when it's first loaded—giving the effect of a closed window when it is initially loaded. A script on Level 0 will be used to "open" it, or make it visible.

3) With the Actions panel open, select the round Exit button (with an X on it) and add the following script:

```
on (release) {
  _visible = false;
}
```

This button will be used to "close" the window if it has been made visible.

4) With the Actions panel open, select the rectangular invisible button at the top of the dialog box and add the following script:

```
on (press) {
  _alpha = 50;
  startDrag (this);
}
on (release) {
  _alpha = 100;
  stopDrag ();
}
```

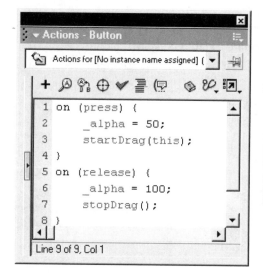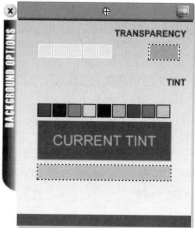

When this button is pressed, this movie will become 50 percent transparent as well as draggable. When the button is released, the movie will once again become 100 percent opaque and dragging will stop—thus emulating the effect of a draggable dialog box.

It's important to note that since we know this movie will be loaded into Level 1, the following syntax would work as well.

```
on (press) {
  _level1._alpha = 50;
  startDrag ();
}
on (release) {
  _level1._alpha = 100;
  stopDrag ();
}
```

Notice how the action that changes the movie's transparency now contains an absolute target path to Level 1. Although this will work, there's a major disadvantage to using absolute target paths to script actions that affect a movie's own timeline. Using the above example, we *know* this movie will be loaded into Level 1, so we can use an absolute target path to Level 1 in our script. But if our project were a bit more dynamic, it might allow this movie to be loaded into any level arbitrarily (say Level 82). In this case, the line of script that changes the alpha property will not work, since it targets the movie on Level 1, but this movie is actually loaded into Level 82. By using a relative path in these scripts (as the first script shown in this step), you ensure that the movie can be loaded into any level and that all of its scripts will continue to work properly.

5) Export this movie as backgroundControl.swf in the Lesson03/Assets folder.

This creates a SWF from our project, which will be loaded into Level 1.

Now let's set up the movie that will be loaded into Level 2.

6) Save your work as backgroundControl2.fla.

We'll work with this file again in the next exercise.

7) Open textBox1.fla in the Lesson03/Assets folder.

This movie will be loaded into Level 2. As with the last movie we worked on, this movie resembles an operating system dialog box. It contains a single scene made up of four layers, each of which is named according to its content.

All of the scripts we're adding to this file are the same, and they work just like those we added to the previous file. The only difference is that they affect *this* movie, which is loaded into Level 2.

8) With the Actions panel open, select Frame 1 on the main timeline and add the following script:

```
_visible = false;
```

Since this action targets the movie that will be loaded into Level 2, the movie on Level 2 will be made invisible on loading—with the same effect as described in Step 2.

9) With the Actions panel open, select the round Exit button (with an *X* on it) and add the following script:

```
on (release) {
  _visible = false;
}
```

This button will be used to "close" the window if it has been made visible.

10) With the Actions panel open, select the rectangular invisible button at the top of the dialog box and add the following script:

```
on (press) {
  _alpha = 50;
  startDrag (this);
}
on (release) {
  _alpha = 100;
  stopDrag ();
}
```

When this button is pressed, the movie in Level 2 will become 50 percent transparent as well as draggable. When the button is released, that movie will once again become 100 percent opaque and dragging will cease—with the same effect as that described in Step 4.

You're finished scripting this movie for the time being.

11) Export this movie as textBox.swf in the Lesson03/Assets folder.
This creates a SWF from our project, which will be loaded into Level 2.

12) Save your work as textBox2.fla.
We'll work with this file again in the next exercise.

13) Open levelTarget1.fla in the Lesson03/Assets folder.

This is the movie that will be loaded into the player initially (into Level 0, though we don't need to define this). We will add actions to this movie to load backgroundControl.swf into Level 1 and textBox.swf into Level 2. We will then add actions that enable us to control these movies from Level 0.

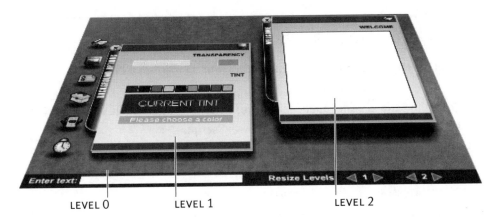

LEVEL 0   LEVEL 1   LEVEL 2

This file takes the appearance of an operating system desktop. It contains a single scene made up of four layers, each named according to its content.

14) With the Actions panel open, select Frame 1 and add the following script:

```
loadMovieNum ("backgroundControl.swf", 1);
loadMovieNum ("textBox.swf", 2);
```

The first action loads backgroundControl.swf into Level 1, and the second action loads textBox.swf into Level 2.

Remember that both of these movies are set up to become invisible on loading. To make them visible, we must script two of the buttons on our desktop—which we'll do next.

15) With the Actions panel open, select the button on the left of the stage that resembles a computer icon and add the following script:

```
on (release) {
  _level1._visible = true;
}
```

This action makes the movie loaded into Level 1 visible—emulating the effect of a dialog box opening. As you can see, targeting a movie loaded into a level is very straightforward.

16) With the Actions panel open, select the button on the left of the stage that resembles a paper scroll and add the following script:

```
on (release) {
  _level2._visible = true;
}
```

This has the same effect as the script on the last button, only this will make the movie loaded into Level 2 visible when pressed.

Next, let's set up the buttons that will be used to scale the movies on Levels 1 and 2.

17) With the Actions panel open, select the left-arrow button to the left of the *1*, at the bottom of the screen, and add the following script:

```
on (release) {
  _level1._xscale = _level1._xscale - 5;
  _level1._yscale = _level1._yscale - 5;
}
```

When this button is pressed then released, the horizontal and vertical proportions of the movie on Level 1 will be scaled down to their current values minus five.

18) With the Actions panel open, select the right-arrow button to the left of the *1* at the bottom of the screen, and add the following script:

```
on (release) {
  _level1._xscale = _level1._xscale + 5;
  _level1._yscale = _level1._yscale + 5;
}
```

These actions have the same effect as those discussed in the last step except that they *increase* the horizontal and vertical proportions of the movie on Level 1.

19) With the Actions panel open, place the following actions, respectively, on the two buttons on either side of the *2* at the bottom of the screen:

Place on left-pointing button:

```
on (release) {
  _level2._xscale = _level2._xscale - 5;
  _level2._yscale = _level2._yscale - 5;
}
```

Place on right-pointing button:

```
on (release) {
  _level2._xscale = _level2._xscale + 5;
  _level2._yscale = _level2._yscale + 5;
}
```

These actions have the same effect as those discussed in the last two steps except that they control the movie loaded into Level 2.

20) Choose Control > Test Movie to test the project's functionality.

When this project begins playing, backgroundControl.swf is loaded into Level 1 and textBox.swf is loaded into Level 2. However, you may remember that we set up these movies to be invisible on loading. Clicking either of the icon buttons on the desktop that we scripted will show the appropriate movie on that level. With the movies visible, press the scale buttons at the bottom of the screen to see how movies loaded into levels can be targeted. You can also drag these movies using the drag buttons we set up, or you can close one of these "dialog box" windows by pressing the Exit button on either.

21) Close the testing environment to return to the authoring environment and save your work as levelTarget2.fla.

We will use this file (with a small addition) in the next exercise.

TARGETING MOVIE CLIP INSTANCES ON LEVELS

Targeting a movie clip instance that exists within a SWF loaded into a level is a straightforward process: Simply input the level number of the SWF that holds it, followed by the instance name itself. An instance called **cuteDog** within a SWF loaded on Level 42, for example, would have the following target path (relative to movies on other levels):

```
_level42.cuteDog
```

If cuteDog itself contained a movie clip instance named **tail**, that instance's target path would be as follows:

```
_level42.cuteDog.tail
```

Although we've used absolute paths in the above (since we're targeting timelines on different levels), remember that you can use relative target paths to target timelines on the same level.

In this exercise we'll build on our operating system project by targeting movie clip instances in SWFs loaded into levels as well as show you how to use simple data from one level in another.

1) Open levelTarget2.fla in the Lesson03/Assets folder.

This is the same file that we added scripts to in the last exercise—with one addition: The timeline now includes a layer called Color Clip.

2) Press the Show Layer button (with the big red *X)* on the Colors Clip layer to reveal the content of this layer.

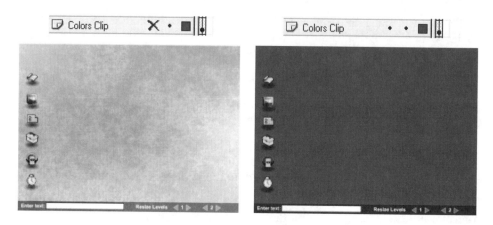

You should now see a purple box that covers the entire stage. This box is a movie clip instance named **colors**. This movie clip instance will act as a color layer above the multicolored textured background you see when this instance is not visible. Changing the color and transparency of this instance will make it seem as if the textured background on the desktop is changing. Soon we'll script the movie that's loaded into Level 1 (backgroundControl.swf) to change colors and control transparency of this instance.

3) Double-click the *colors* movie clip instance in order to edit it in place.

The timeline of the **colors** movie clip instance now appears. This timeline is made up of a single layer that contains several frame labels. At each of these frame labels, the colored box on stage is filled with the color associated with that frame label's name. We will control this clip's color by sending it to different labels on its timeline. Initially, the clip will be purple because this is the color at Frame 1, and that frame includes a `stop()` action to prevent the timeline from moving until we instruct it to.

4) Return to the main timeline. With the Property inspector open, select the text field in the lower left portion of the stage, next to where it says "Enter Text:"

Looking at the Property inspector, you'll notice that this is an Input text field named **inputText**. The user can enter any text he or she wishes here, and that text will be used in the movie loaded into Level 2 (textBox.swf). Next, we'll set up the script that creates this functionality.

5) With the Actions panel open, select the button on the desktop that resembles a scroll of paper and add the following line of script just below `_level2._visible = true;`**:**

```
_level2.inputText.text = _level0.inputText.text;
```

There is a text field in the movie that gets loaded into level 2 that is named **inputText**, which is the same name as the text field in this movie, as we discussed in the previous step. When this button is pressed, this action will set the value of the text field on Level 2 to the same value as the text field in this movie. This is a simple example of how data can be transferred between timelines.

6) With the Actions panel open, select Frame 1 of the main timeline and add the following line of script just below where it says `loadMovieNum ("textBox.swf", 2);`**:**

```
_level0.colors._alpha = 50;
```

This action will make the **colors** movie clip instance (which resides on the Colors Clip layer) 50 percent transparent when the movie begins to play. We used a target path of `level0` for this action—even though it's not required—to reinforce your understanding that the first movie to load (this movie) is automatically loaded into Level 0.

7) Export this file to a SWF and name it levelTarget.swf in the Lesson03/Assets folder.

We will play this file at the end of this exercise.

8) Save this file as levelTarget3.fla.

We're finished scripting this file.

9) Open backgroundControl2.fla in the Lesson03/Assets folder.

This is the same file we used in the last exercise—the one that gets loaded into Level 1 of our project. In the previous exercise we scripted it to become invisible on loading, to close when the Exit button is pressed, and to become draggable when the invisible button at the top of the box is pressed. Here, we'll enhance its functionality by enabling it to control the **colors** movie clip instance that resides on Level 0. We'll attach scripts to the many square buttons that you see.

Before we begin scripting, you need to familiarize yourself with several of the elements on the stage. On the left, just below the word **Transparency**, you'll see a dynamic text field named **alphaAmount**. You will use it in two ways: to display the current transparency of the **colors** movie clip instance on Level 0, and to display the amount of transparency that will be applied to that instance when any of the five Transparency buttons are rolled over. To the left of this text field are five square buttons that will be scripted to change the transparency of the **colors** movie clip instance. Below these buttons are nine additional buttons that resemble color swatches. These will be set up to send the **colors** movie clip (Level 0) to the various frame labels on its own timeline. Below these buttons is a movie clip instance named **currentColor**, which is essentially a smaller version of the **colors** movie clip instance. Its timeline has similar color boxes, as well a frame labels as the **colors** movie clip instance. This movie clip instance will be used to display the current color applied over the textured background on the desktop (Level 0). Below this movie clip instance is another text field, **colorName**, which displays the name of the color as the mouse rolls over the color swatches above it.

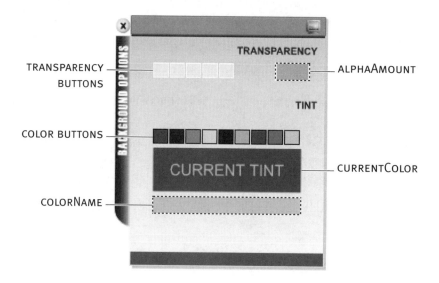

10) With the Actions panel open, select the square button farthest left from the
alphaAmount **text field and add this script:**

```
on (rollOver) {
  alphaAmount.text = 0;
}
on (release) {
  _level0.colors._alpha = 0;
}
on (release, rollOut) {
  alphaAmount.text = _level0.colors._alpha;
}
```

This button will be used to set the transparency of the **colors** movie clip instance on Level 0 to 0.

The first action will display 0 in the **alphaAmount** text field when the button is rolled over. This is simply to provide the user feedback about what amount of transparency this button will apply. With the next action, when the button is released, the alpha property of the **colors** movie clip instance is set to zero, which makes it transparent. (Note the simplicity of this target path: level number followed by instance name.) The next action will set the value displayed in the **alphaAmount** text field to the current transparency of the **colors** movie clip instance when the button is released or rolled away from.

You can attach the same script to the buttons to the right of this one and simply replace the 0 values with 25, 50, 75, and 100, respectively.

11) With the Actions panel open, select the purple Color Swatch button (the first one on the left) and add this script:

```
on (rollOver) {
  colorName.text = "Purple";
}
on (release) {
  currentColor.gotoAndStop ("Purple");
  _level0.colors.gotoAndStop ("Purple");
}
on (release, rollOut) {
  colorName.text = "Please choose a color";
}
```

This button will set the color of the **colors** movie clip instance on Level 0 by moving that timeline to the appropriate frame label.

The first action will display "Purple" in the **colorName** text field when the button is rolled over to tell the user what color tint this button will apply. When the button is released, two actions are executed: The first sends the **currentColor** movie clip instance to the frame labeled Purple. This will change the box below the Color Swatch buttons to purple, indicating that this is the current tint. The next action sends the **colors** movie clip instance on Level 0 to the frame labeled Purple, causing the textured background on Level 0 to take on a purple tint (depending on its current transparency). The last action will reset the text in the **colorName** text field to read "Please choose a color."

You can attach this same script to the buttons to the left of this one, simply replacing the three areas that have "Purple" values with "Maroon," "Lavender," "SkyBlue," "DeepBlue," "Orange," "GrassGreen," "SeaGreen," and "Pink," respectively.

ON (ROLLOVER)   ON (RELEASE)   ON (RELEASE, ROLLOUT)

12) Export this movie as backgroundControl.swf in the Lesson03/Assets folder.
This creates a SWF from our project, which will be loaded into Level 1, overwriting a previously saved version from the last exercise.

13) Save your work as backgroundControl3.fla.
We're now finished working with this file.

116

14) Locate the levelTarget.swf file that you created. Double-click it to open and play it.

As soon as this file begins to play, backgroundControl.swf is loaded into Level 1 and textBox.swf is loaded into Level 2—both of which are made invisible on loading. The **colors** movie clip instance that overlays the textured background is currently tinted purple and has a transparency of 50 percent.

Enter any text in the text field at the bottom of the screen, then press the button on the screen that resembles a scroll of text. This button was set up to make Level 2 visible as well as to feed this text to a text field on that level.

Now press the button resembling a computer monitor to make the movie on Level 1 visible. This movie controls the color and transparency of the **colors** movie clip instance on Level 0. Press the Transparency and Color buttons in this movie to see how they affect that movie clip instance.

◎ POWER TIP *As discussed at the beginning of this lesson, timelines can contain their own data, functions, and objects. While we haven't touched on these yet, it would still be prudent to briefly discuss a few points about how target paths relate to these dynamic elements, since most projects are set up so that a dynamic element on one timeline can be used by another.*

For example, a variable may be named myVariable. *If that variable exists in a movie clip instance named* **myMovieClip** *which itself is inside a movie loaded into level 74, then to use this variable in any of your scripts on any timeline, you would simply place the appropriate target path in front of the variable name, such as:*

```
_level27.displayText =_level74.myMovieClip.myVariable;
```

The same thing applies to function calls:

```
_root.anotherMovieClip.myFunction();
```

Or any type of object:

```
_parent.myObject
```

The importance of this will become more evident as we progress through the lessons in this book.

UNDERSTANDING MULTIPLE IDENTITIES

As you've learned in this chapter, you can target a single timeline in many ways, depending on its relationship to the timeline targeting it (not to mention your own needs and personal preferences). The following graphic shows the interchangeable target paths that can be used when one movie targets another.

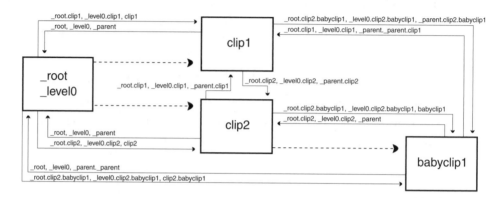

Solid lines and arrows represent one movie targeting another. Dotted lines and arrows represent child movies.

CREATING AND REFERENCING GLOBAL ELEMENTS

There's no denying that even with a thorough understanding of target paths, it's sometimes hard to keep track of them—especially when you have timelines within timelines within timelines. As you might imagine, target paths can become quite long. To help simplify things, ActionScript provides access to a global object. As a global element, this special Flash object exists apart from any specific timeline but is omnipotent in relation to your Flash project: You can reference it from any timeline *without* a target path and take advantage of its power to reference other timelines (and the variables, functions, and other dynamic elements they contain).

Let's first take a look at how you can create a global element, then we'll show you how you can convert an element with a target path into a global element.

Creating a global element, such as a variable, is as simple as the following:

```
_global.myVariable = "hello";
```

Because this variable is now a global element, you can reference it from any timeline simply by using its name:

```
_root.myMovieClip.favoriteGreeting = myVariable;
```

or

```
_root.favoriteGreeting = myVariable;
```

You can also use the global identifier to create global functions (see Lesson 6, Using Functions):

```
_global.myFunction = function(){
  //actions…
}
```

This function can now be called from any timeline simply by using the following:

```
myFunction();
```

The same is true when creating instances of objects (see Lesson 4, Understanding and Using Objects):

```
_global.myDateObject = new Date();
```

As mentioned above, you can easily convert an element with a target path (such as a movie clip instance) so that it can be referenced globally (that is, without a path). For example, suppose there was a movie clip instance in your project with a target path of `_root.car.engine.piston`. If you wanted to make it easier to reference this instance, you could give it a global address:

```
_global.myPiston = _root.car.engine.piston;
```

To control that instance, you would simply reference its global address from any timeline:

```
myPiston.play();
```

Is there a benefit to using a global element? Usually, it comes down to a matter of preference—as well as what a given project dictates. In general, though, any element that you use frequently or that's used by number of timelines is a good candidate for becoming a global element.

One thing to keep in mind, though, is that naming collisions can occur when you use global elements—that is, an element in a timeline (for example, a variable) may end up with the same name as a global element. For example, suppose you had a movie clip instance with a variable named `myVariable`: If you had a global variable with the same name, you wouldn't have a problem using the variable's absolute target path to reference it on the timeline:

```
_root.myMovieClip.myVariable
```

However, you would have a problem if **myMovieClip** attempted to reference the global variable named `myVariable` using the following:

```
myVariable
```

This is because this timeline has its own local variable named `myVariable`. If you use the above syntax (without a target path), Flash won't be able to tell whether you're referencing the local variable or the global one—a conflict it resolves by automatically referencing the closest variable to the timeline itself, which is the local one.

An easy way to avoid these naming collisions is to preface global element names with a small *g:*

```
gMyVariable
gFavoriteColor
```

Another thing to remember is that a global element uses memory that can only be freed up by deleting the global element. Therefore, using lots of global elements may not be an efficient use of memory.

WHAT YOU HAVE LEARNED

In this lesson, you have:

- Gained an understanding of the timeline hierarchy in Flash movies (pages 86–88)

- Learned about absolute and relative target paths (pages 86–88)

- Learned to control multiple clip instances (pages 88–94)

- Controlled the main timeline of a project (pages 94–96)

- Used the parent-child relationship in movies to create an "effect" clip (pages 96–100)

- Controlled specific timelines within a single project (pages 101–103)

- Controlled movies loaded into levels (pages 104–117)

- Learned how to create global references to various ActionScript elements (pages 118–120)

understanding and using objects

LESSON 4

Every day you use objects to perform any number of activities. You may have used Tupperware to store fresh cookies to prevent them from becoming stale, or the trashcan to store a fruitcake from your Aunt Sally. Objects are items designed to meet specific needs. You can use them to perform tasks of their own (for example, a VCR playing or recording a movie), or you can employ them as simple storage devices, like Tupperware.

Objects in Macromedia Flash are similar to real-world objects. Each of the many types of Flash objects meets specific needs in your Flash applications. In this chapter, we'll introduce you to Flash's objects and help you gain experience using them.

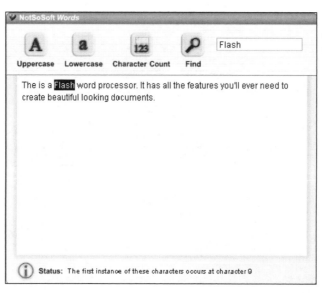

This Flash word processor is one of the projects you'll create in this lesson.

WHAT YOU WILL LEARN:

In this lesson, you will:

- Learn what objects are and why they are useful

- Get acquainted with the various objects available in ActionScript

- Use the Color object

- Create an interactive scene using the Key object

- Create a word processor using properties and methods of the String and Selection objects

APPROXIMATE TIME:

This lesson takes approximately 45 minutes to complete.

LESSON FILES:

Media Files:

None

Starting Files:

Lesson04/Clown1.fla

Lesson04/balloon1.fla

Lesson04/wordProcessor1.fla

Completed Projects:

Clown2.fla

balloon2.fla

wordProcessor2.fla

WHAT OBJECTS ARE AND WHY THEY'RE USEFUL

Imagine for a moment that you're a carpenter. As such, you use prefab objects to build houses for a living. To build a doorframe, you might use some two-by-fours, a hammer, and a bunch of nails—objects that have certain characteristics that allow you to do your job. Sometimes—as in the case of a cement mixer—you may not even know precisely how an object works: You simply give it one thing, and it spits out another.

You can conceptualize Flash objects in much the same way as these carpenter's objects—elements used in a specific way in order to build an application or perform a certain task. If you think of objects as tools and building materials for your project, you can begin to understand their benefits.

ActionScript provides a number of prebuilt objects for various purposes. However, if you can't find a premade object that fits your needs, you can create one of your own and program it to do just what you want it to do.

Objects are defined by two primary characteristics: *properties* and *methods*. Let's take an in-depth look at both.

PROPERTIES

Many, but not all, objects have properties—values that represent an object's characteristics. In the real world, a car has properties like color, make, model, horsepower, and so on. If that car was an ActionScript object, you might define it as follows:

```
car.color = "red";
car.make = "Volkswagen";
car.model = "Beetle";
car.horsepower = 200;
```

There are several objects in Flash that have properties. For example, the MovieClip object has property values that represent its transparency, visibility, horizontal position, vertical position, rotation, and more. Changing any of these properties affects the movie clip's appearance or functionality, just as giving a car a paint job or changing its engine would alter it. You can use property values of various objects in your scripts to set values elsewhere. Let's assume that a script in your project moves your car at a speed based on its horsepower. That line of script might look like the following:

```
speedFactor = car.horsepower;
```

Let's look at one more example of a property and how it's used in ActionScript.

The length of a string is a *property* of the String object. For instance, the length of "Flash" is 5, because it contains five characters. In ActionScript, this would be written as follows:

```
name = "Flash";
lengthOfName = name.length;
```

The first line of code above creates a variable called `name` whose value is the string `"Flash"`. The second line creates a variable called `lengthOfName` whose value is that of the `length` property of the name object (5). Although property names associated with movie clips are *usually* preceded by an underscore (`_alpha`, `_rotation`, and so on), not all object property names follow this convention. The reason for this is that the convention is a holdover from Flash 4 (when properties were introduced and ActionScript was much different than it is today).

NOTE *Objects can store arrays, variables, and even other objects—all of which are considered properties.*

METHODS

A method represents a task that an object can perform. If you think of a VCR as an object, its methods include the abilities to play, record, stop, rewind, fast forward, pause, and so forth. A method consists of its name followed by a set of parenthesis. The methods of our VCR object would look like this:

```
play();
rewind();
record();
```

To invoke a method of an object, you must first indicate the object (or the name of an instance of an object, which we'll explain in a moment), followed by a dot, then the name of the method:

```
myVCR.record();
```

This tells the object named myVCR to start recording.

The parentheses included with method sometimes allow you to invoke it in a unique way using a parameter or set of parameter values. Using our VCR example again, let's say you wanted to record a TV show on Channel 8 from 10 p.m. to 11 p.m. on September 9. The script required to perform this task might look like this:

```
myVCR.record(8, 10:00 pm, 11:00 pm, September 9);
```

As you can see, commas separate the different method parameters. Keep in mind that parameter values can be hard coded (as shown above), or they can be dynamic values such as variables. You can even use other methods as parameters.

Although many ActionScript objects have methods that accept parameters, not all do. Some simply perform tasks that don't require any special settings. For example, the stop() method of the MovieClip object simply causes the timeline to stop—nothing more, nothing less.

Each object has a unique set of methods—which makes sense because each object has a specific function.

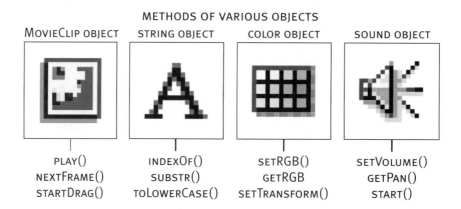

METHODS OF VARIOUS OBJECTS

MovieClip object	String object	Color object	Sound object
play()	indexOf()	setRGB()	setVolume()
nextFrame()	substr()	getRGB	getPan()
startDrag()	toLowerCase()	setTransform()	start()

Object methods in ActionScript perform all sorts of tasks, including the following:

- Getting and setting values (see below)
- Doing conversions (for example, converting a negative number to a positive)
- Indicating whether something is true or false
- Activating or deactivating something
- Manipulating something (such as text or numbers)

We'll demonstrate some of these tasks in this lesson and many more throughout the book.

NOTE *An object does not have to contain any properties or methods to be considered an object. However, a object with no properties or methods is of no use.*

OBJECT TYPES

Objects are organized in *classes*, which represent sets of objects that share the same properties and methods. In the real world, cars represent one class of objects; fish, books, and even people represent others. The 6 billion people on this planet can each be thought of as instances of the Person class. Although each of these people is unique, they share similar properties (name, age, hair color, height, and so on) and actions (breathing, walking, touching, seeing, and so on). Since each new movie clip instance that you create is an instance of the MovieClip object, it inherits all of the properties and methods available to that class of objects.

CLASSES OF OBJECTS

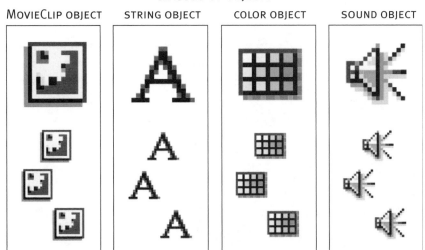

Most projects contain multiple instances of some classes of objects—for example, the MovieClip object we just discussed or the String object (since your project may comprise various strings, each considered an instance of the String object). In contrast, other objects are universal or global, meaning your project can contain only once instance of them. Take, for example, the Mouse object, which controls cursor visibility (among other things). Since you have just one cursor, you can't create instances of it; instead, you simply use the methods available to it to do various things with the mouse.

You can create object instances in one of two ways: To create a new instance of the MovieClip object, you simply drag it onto the stage. However, you can only create a few types of objects in this way. To create other object instances, you must use a *constructor*—a simple line of code that tells Flash to create an instance of a particular object. A constructor looks something like this:

```
nameOfInstance = new nameOfObject();
```

Thus, if you wanted to create an instance of the Sound object, the constructor would look like this:

```
nameOfSoundInstance = new Sound();
```

Whenever you create an object instance, you must give it a unique name. This allows you to change a property or invoke a method as it relates to that particular instance—as we'll demonstrate in the following examples. As you gain programming experience, you'll begin to understand when you should use constructors.

NOTE *Object names follow the same naming conventions as variables, which means they can't contain spaces, symbols, or a number as the first character.*

TIP *Flash allows you to attach a suffix to an object name in order to facilitate code-hinting in the Actions panel. For example, instead of naming a movie clip instance* **myMovieClip***, you could name it* **myMovieClip_mc***. Using this naming convention enables the Actions panel to determine when an object of a certain type is being scripted and thus quickly provide you with a drop-down list of appropriate properties and methods for that object. Consult the ActionScript dictionary for a complete list of these suffixes.*

In the Actions panel under the Objects book, you can access all of Flash's objects, each of which is contained in one of the following four objects' subbooks:

- **Core.** These objects deal with information storage and manipulation, not including information that's being moved into or out of Flash itself.
- **Movie.** These objects deal with visual content and system-related information such as movie clips, text fields, the stage and accessibility.

- **Client/Server.** These objects control how information is moved in and out of Flash.
- **Authoring.** These objects assist you in creating custom actions and custom components.

The following describes the many object classes available in ActionScript as well as where and how you might use them. We'll also indicate whether an object is global, or you must create individual instances.

ACCESSIBILITY OBJECT (GLOBAL)

This object contains read-only information about the user's computer's ability to use a screen reader:

```
Accessibility.isActive();
```

The above line of ActionScript returns a result of either true or false. If the result is true, the user's computer can employ a screen reader.

ARRAY OBJECT (INSTANCES)

An array is a storage device for multiple pieces of information. Arrays store information that can be set and referenced using a numbering system. For instance:

```
cakeType = new Array();
cakeType[0] = "Chocolate";
cakeType[1] = "Angel Food";
cakeType[2] = "Baked Alaska";
```

The first line of script above creates a new instance of the Array object called cakeType using the Array constructor. The next few lines place data inside that array.

The Array object contains many useful methods that will help you add, remove, and sort array items.

NOTE *For more on arrays, see Lesson 7, Working with Dynamic Data.*

BOOLEAN OBJECT (INSTANCES)

The Boolean object stores one of two values, true or false. You can create a Boolean object by using the Boolean constructor or by using the = assign operator. For instance:

```
toggle = new Boolean(false);
```

and

```
toggle = false;
```

create identical objects.

Button Object (Instances)

When you place a button on the stage, you create an instance of the Button object. Only the MovieClip and TextField objects are created in similar fashion—that is, by placing actual instances on the stage. The Button object contains properties and methods that allow you to control its appearance, tab order, functionality and more.

Capabilities Object (Global)

This object contains information about the user's computer, such as screen resolution and whether it can play sounds. The following line of ActionScript places the horizontal resolution of the user's computer into myVariable:

```
myVariable = System.capabilities.screenResolutionX;
```

TIP *Being able access this information allows you to create movies that automatically tailor themselves to the capabilities of your user's computer. For example, it can help you determine whether a handheld computer is accessing the movie—and if so, redirect the user to a page designed expressly for handheld devices.*

Color Object (Instances)

You use this object to change a movie clip's color dynamically. When you create a Color object, you point it at a particular movie clip. Then, using the Color object's methods, you can alter your movie clip's color. You create a Color object using the Color object constructor method, as follows:

```
myColor = new Color(pathToTimeline);
```

Later in this lesson you'll complete an exercise using the Color object.

Date Object (Instances)

With this object, you can access the current time as local time or Greenwich Mean Time, as well as easily determine the current day, week, month, or year. To create a new instance of the Date object, you would use the Date object constructor method. The following example demonstrates one use of the Date object:

```
now = new Date();
largeNumber = now.getTime();
```

This creates a variable called largeNumber whose value is the number of milliseconds since midnight January 1, 1970.

NOTE *We will use the Date object in Lesson 15, Time- and Frame-Based Dynamism.*

KEY OBJECT (GLOBAL)

You use the Key object to determine the state of the keys on the keyboard—for example, whether caps lock is toggled on, which key was pressed last, and which key or keys are currently pressed.

You will complete an exercise using this object later in this lesson.

LOADVARS OBJECT (INSTANCES)

Flash allows you to load data (for example, variables) into a movie from an external source. Using the LoadVars object, Flash can load in variables from a specified URL (which can be a static text file). For example:

```
myOb = new LoadVars();
myOb.load("http://www.mysite.com/myFiles/file.txt");
```

In the above example, all of the loaded variables become properties of `myOb`.

MATH OBJECT (GLOBAL)

With the Math object, you can perform many useful calculations and have the result returned. Here's one use of the Math object:

```
positiveNumber = Math.abs(-6);
```

The above script uses the absolute value method of the Math object to convert –6 to a positive number.

MOUSE OBJECT (GLOBAL)

The Mouse object controls cursor visibility, as well as allows you to set up *listeners* to track mouse activity. Here is an example use:

```
Mouse.hide();
```

The above line of script hides the mouse from view. The mouse is still active, just not visible.

MOVIECLIP OBJECT (INSTANCES)

You create instances of this most familiar object either in the authoring environment (by placing them on the stage) or with ActionScript actions such as `createEmptyMovieClip()` and `duplicateMovieClip()`—*not* by using the constructor method. Movie clips have many properties and methods that are used frequently in an interactive project. Here's an example use:

```
myClip.gotoAndStop("Menu");
```

With this script, a movie clip with an instance name of **myClip** will be sent to the frame labeled Menu.

NUMBER OBJECT (GLOBAL)

You can create a Number object instance by using its constructor method or by assigning a number as the value of a variable. For instance:

```
age = new Number(26);
```

is equivalent to:

```
age = 26;
```

The new `Number()` constructor method is rarely used, however, because creating a new number without the constructor is shorter and achieves the same result.

OBJECT OBJECT (INSTANCES)

No, it's not a typo: There is an Object object! You can use this generic object—which is also known as ActionScript's root object (meaning it's the highest object in the class hierarchy) in various ways: By employing the properties and methods available to it, you can affect and modify other object classes (such as those listed in this section). It also comes in handy for creating objects that hold information about the current user or that track chunks of related data (to name just a couple of uses).

The following is the syntax for creating a generic object:

```
names = new Object();
names.cat = "Hayes";
```

The first line of script creates a new object called `names`. The second line adds a variable to the object called `cat`. The variable is considered a property of this object.

In Lesson 6, Customizing Objects, we'll show you how to create your own custom objects (better than generic objects!) as well as how to create properties and methods for your custom object. Once you know how to do this, you can create objects that do precisely what you want.

SELECTION OBJECT (GLOBAL)

You use the Selection object to retrieve information or set characteristics relating to selected items in your movies, especially text in text fields. When the cursor is in an area of a text field, that field is said to be "in focus." You can employ the Selection object to set the focus to a specific text field, to find out which text field is currently in focus, or even to programmatically select specific chunks of text in a field so that it can be manipulated in some way. The following is an example of one use of the Selection object:

```
Selection.setFocus("firstName");
```

This script sets the input text field with the instance name of **firstName** into focus.

You'll complete an exercise using this object later in this lesson.

Sound Object (Instances)

You use the Sound object to control sounds—for example, setting volume and adjusting left and right speaker pan settings. To learn more about this object, see Lesson 16, Scripting for Sound.

String Object (Instances)

You use the String object to manipulate and get information about strings. You can create a new string by using the String object constructor method or by putting quotes around a value when setting a variable. For instance:

```
bird = new String("Robin");
```

is the same as:

```
bird = "Robin"
```

You'll use this object to complete an exercise later in this lesson.

Stage Object (Global)

With the Stage object, you can control and get information about characteristics of the stage, such as alignment. For instance:

```
Stage.height
```

The above line of ActionScript returns the height of the stage in pixels.

System Object (Global)

This object contains information about your user's computer's system, such as the operating system, the language being used, and all of the properties of the Capabilities object. One of the System object's properties is a string, called *serverString*, which contains a list of the system capabilities (concatenated into one string). You can then send this list to the server so that you can store or use the information it contains. To access the string, you would use the following:

```
System.capabilities.serverString
```

TextField Object (Instances)

Using this object, you can dynamically create a new text field and control most of its characteristics—for example setting the format of the text field or the scrolling of text. Instances of this object are created when a text field is placed on the stage or created dynamically using `createTextField()`. We'll use this object later in this lesson.

TextFormat Object (Instances)

TextFormat objects are used to change the format of text displayed in text fields. Once created, you *apply* the TextFormat object to a text field using the `setTextFormat()` or `setNewTextFormat()` method of the TextField object:

```
nameOfTextField.setTextFormat(nameOfFormatObject);
```

XML Object (Instances)

XML is one of the most popular standards for formatting data—no surprise when you consider that XML-formatted data lets all kinds of applications transfer information seamlessly. Using Flash, you can create an XML object to store an XML-formatted document (which can then be sent from or loaded into XML objects). Here's one use of the XML object:

```
myXML = new XML();
myXML.load("myFile.xml");
```

The above script creates a new XML object and loads an XML-formatted file into that object.

XMLSocket Object (Instances)

Flash also allows you to set up a persistent connection with a socket server—an application that runs on a Web server. The socket server waits for users to connect to it. Once connected, the socket server can transfer information between all connected users at very fast speeds—which is how most chat systems and multiplayer games are created. An XML socket is called such because it uses the XML format as the standard for transferred information. You can create an XMLSocket object instance by using its constructor method. The following is an example of one use of this type of object:

```
mySocket = new XMLSocket();
mySocket.connect("http://www.electrotank.com", 8080);
```

This script creates a new XMLSocket object and then opens up a connection with a socket server. See Lesson 12, Using XML with Flash, for a detailed description of socket servers and the XMLSocket object as well as an exercise in creating your own chat application.

It's beyond the scope of this book to cover every object in detail. However, during the course of this book, we'll use many of these objects in various ways, and provide detailed instructions about how and why we're using them. The following exercises will concentrate on just a few of these objects to give you a general idea of how you can use them.

USING THE COLOR OBJECT

To use a Color object, you must first create it using the Color object constructor. The following is the syntax for creating a new Color object:

```
myColor = new Color(shirt);
```

The above line of ActionScript creates a new instance of the Color object named `myColor` and associates it with a movie clip instance named **shirt**.

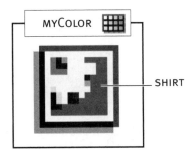

You can create the object anywhere, and the constructor accepts one parameter, the path to the movie clip it should modify. If you want to create a Color object with ActionScript from within a movie clip that will reference itself, you would use `this` as the path. Take, for example, the following:

```
myColor = new Color(this);
```

This creates a new instance of the Color object on the movie clip instance that contains this script.

> **NOTE** *As with any constructor-created object, you can create many different Color objects in a single project and associate them with various timelines, providing you with dynamic control over the color of many instances simultaneously.*

The most common Color object method is `setRGB()`, which changes the color of the movie clip instance specified as the parameter when the object was created. Here's an example of one use of `setRGB()`:

```
myColor = new Color(shirt);
myColor.setRGB(0xFF3300);
```

The above ActionScript creates a new Color object named `myColor` and then uses the `setRGB()` method to change the color of the **shirt** movie clip instance to red. This method accepts a parameter (`0x`) followed by the hex value for a color. The 0x parameter is a reserved character combination that tells Flash that what follows is a hexadecimal number.

135

The number system we're accustomed to using is called *base 10*, which means ten numbers are used for all values (zero through nine). In other words, all other numbers (28; 6,403; 496; 300, 439; and so on) can be described using a combination of these ten. Hexadecimal numbers, in contrast, are base 16, which means their values are expressed using numbers *and* letters: zero through nine, and *A* through *F*. Using these, you can create hexadecimal values of 00 to FF, with 00 being a base 10 value of 0 and FF a base 10 value of 255.

Base 10

10 numbers ——→ 0 1 2 3 4 5 6 7 8 9
before repeating ——→ 10 11 12 13 14 15 16 17 18 19

Base 16

16 numbers/letters ——→ 00 01 02 03 04 05 06 07 08 09 0A 0B 0C 0D 0E 0F
before repeating ——→ 10 11 12 13 14 15 16 17 18 19 1A 1B 1C 1D 1E 1F

However, you don't absolutely have to know hex values to describe certain colors when using the `setRGB()` method: Instead, if you know the RGB value of a color, you can convert it to a hexadecimal value dynamically using the Number object and the `parseInt()` function—which we'll show in the following exercise (though we won't cover it in detail).

In this exercise you'll create a simple interactive scene in which you'll be able to change the color of a clown's hair using several buttons.

1) Open Clown1.fla in the Lesson04/Assets folder.

The content has already been created and placed on the stage so that we can focus on the ActionScript involved in changing the color of a movie clip. There are three layers on the main timeline: Background, Clown Hair, and Buttons.

The Clown Hair layer contains a movie clip instance named **hair**. You will be changing the color of this instance with ActionScript.

The Buttons layer contains five circular, colored buttons. You'll be adding ActionScript to these buttons to change the color of the clown's hair.

2) With the Actions panel open, select the red button and add this script:

```
on (release) {
  hairColor = new Color(hair);
  hairColor.setRGB(0xCC0000);
}
```

This ActionScript tells Flash to create a new Color object named `hairColor` when this button is released and to associate that object with the **hair** movie clip instance. The second line of ActionScript uses the `setRGB()` method to change the color of this Color object (hence the **hair** movie clip instance) to `CC0000`, which is the hex value for the red in the middle of the button.

3) With the Actions panel open, select the yellow button and add this script:

```
on (release) {
  hairColor = new Color(hair);
  hairColor.setRGB(0xFFCC00);
}
```

This ActionScript is identical to the ActionScript attached to the red button except for the color value used in the `setRGB()` method, the value of which is the hex value for the yellow in the middle of the button.

4) With the Actions panel open, select the green button and add this script:

```
on (release) {
  hairColor = new Color(hair);
  hairColor.setRGB(0x009900);
}
```

The hex value for green in the middle of this button is `009900` and is used in the `setRGB()` method, just as in the two preceding scripts.

5) With the Actions panel open, select the blue button and add this script:

```
on (release) {
  hairColor = new Color(hair);
  hairColor.setRGB(0x336699);
}
```

As with the previous three buttons, this ActionScript creates a Color object that it uses to change the color of the **hair** movie clip instance.

```
on (release) {
  hairColor = new Color(hair);
  hairColor.setRGB(0xCC0000);
}
```

```
on (release) {
  hairColor = new Color(hair);
  hairColor.setRGB(0xFFCC00);
}
```

```
on (release) {
  hairColor = new Color(hair);
  hairColor.setRGB(0x009900);
}
```

```
on (release) {
  hairColor = new Color(hair);
  hairColor.setRGB(0x336699);
}
```

Now it's time to test your work!

6) Choose Control > Test Movie. Click the four buttons to view the color changes.
Every time you click one of these buttons, Flash creates a new Color object and associates it with the **hair** movie clip instance. It then uses the `setRGB()` method available to Color objects to change the color of that instance.

NOTE *Although in this exercise a Color object is created on each button, an object really only needs to be created once—after which it exists as part of the timeline. Any changes to that object can then be made simply by using methods available to that object.*

Now let's use ActionScript to change the clown's hair color to a random color.

7) Close the test movie to return to the authoring environment. With the Actions panel open, select the rainbow-colored button and add this script:

```
on (release) {
  R = random(256);
  G = random(256);
  B = random(256);
  colorHexString = R.toString(16)+G.toString(16)+B.toString(16);
  colorHex = parseInt(colorHexString,16);
  hairColor = new Color(hair);
  hairColor.setRGB(colorHex);
}
```

There are two ways to describe a color programmatically: with its RGB (red, green, blue) value or with its hex value. There are three separate RGB values, each of which can have a numeric value between 0 and 255. The RGB value of red, for instance, is R=255, G=0, B=0. The corresponding hex value (for the same color of red) is FF0000. The idea behind the first five lines of this script is to generate a random RGB value, convert it to a hex value, then use that value in the setRGB() method at the bottom of the script.

The first three lines of the above ActionScript create variables R, G, and B whose values are random numbers between 0 and 255. The next line of ActionScript uses the toString() method of the Number object to convert a base 10 number to a base 16 string value. Let's assume, for example, that when this script is executed, the following R, G, and B values will be generated:

```
R = 45
G = 202
B = 129
```

The next line of the script says to convert the value of R to a base 16 value, then convert it to a string, and then do the same thing with G and B. Using the plus (+) operator to put the converted values together, the variable coloHexString will have a string value of "2DCA81." This needs to be converted to a hex number (same value as string value, without the quotes) to use the setRGB() method. To do this, you use the parseInt() function as seen above.

The last two lines of ActionScript create a new Color object pointing to the **hair** movie clip instance and then change its color to the random value just created.

NOTE *This ActionScript can randomly generate more than 16 million possible colors.*

8) Choose Control > Test Movie, and click the rainbow-colored button several times.

As you can see, the **hair** movie clip instance changes randomly! You can even modify this technique to randomly generate colors within a certain range.

9) Close the test movie and save your work as Clown2.fla.

You should now be able to easily change the color of any movie clip instance at any time.

USING THE KEY OBJECT TO ADD INTERACTIVITY

The Key object is a useful tool for capturing key events (that is, user interaction with the keyboard) from the user. You can employ the Key object to:

- Determine whether a specific key is currently pressed

- Determine the last key pressed

- Obtain the key code value of the last key pressed

- Add a listener that watches for a key event.

- Determine whether a certain key (like Caps Lock) is toggled on or off

The Key object is a global object, which means you cannot create a new instance of it. The most common use of the Key object is to determine whether a specific key is pressed. You would use the following syntax to determine whether a key is being pressed:

```
Key.isDown(Key.TAB);
```

The above line of ActionScript—which uses the `isDown()` method of the Key object to determine whether the Space bar is currently pressed down—returns a result of either `true` or `false`. The parameter of the `isDown()` method can reference either a specific key in the Key object or the key code of a specific key. For instance, the Tab key can be referenced using `Key.TAB`, or by the number 9, which is its ASCII equivalent. Thus, the following line of script is essentially the same as the previous one:

```
Key.isDown(9);
```

In the following simple exercise, you'll move a hot-air balloon around on the screen using your keyboard and the Key object.

1) Open balloon1.fla in the Lesson04/Assets directory.

This movie contains two layers: Background and Balloon. On the Balloon layer, you'll see a movie clip instance of a hot-air balloon. In this exercise, you'll place actions on that movie clip that will be executed using clip events.

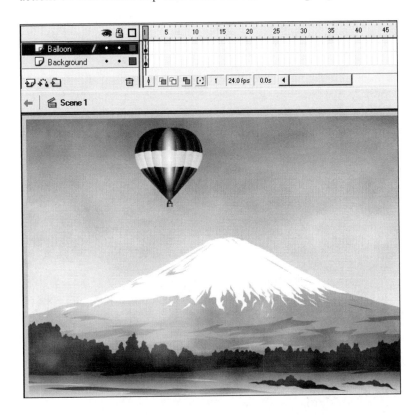

2) With the Actions panel open, select the hot-air balloon movie clip instance and add this script:

```
onClipEvent (load) {
  speed = 3;
}
```

At the end of this exercise, you should be able to move the balloon with your arrow keys. Every time you press the key, the balloon should move a certain amount. When this movie clip instance loads, the script sets the value of speed, which determines how much the balloon moves every time you press a key. When used in the following scripts, this value represents a distance of 3 pixels.

3) With the _balloon_ instance still selected, add this script at the end of the current script:

```
onClipEvent (enterFrame) {
  if (key.isDown(key.RIGHT)) {
    _x += speed;
  } else if (key.isDown(key.LEFT)) {
    _x -= speed;
  }
}
```

This script uses an `enterFrame` event to evaluate a conditional statement. `Key.RIGHT` references the right arrow key, and `Key.LEFT` references the left arrow key. Thus, each time this statement is evaluated, the movie clip instance is moved to its current x position *plus* the value of `speed` if the right arrow key is pressed (moving the instance to the right). However, if the right arrow key is not pressed, that part of the script is ignored and the next part is evaluated—which means that if the left arrow key is pressed, the movie clip instance is moved to its current x position *minus* the value of `speed` (moving the instance to the left).

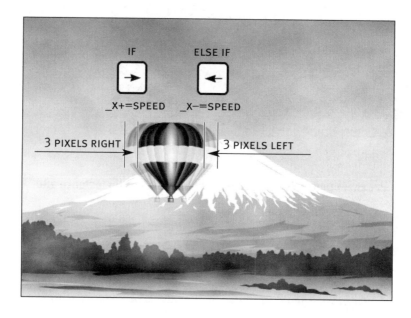

4) Add the following ActionScript to the `enterFrame` clip event:

```
if (key.isDown(key.UP)) {
  _y -= speed;
} else if (key.isDown(key.DOWN)) {
  _y += speed;
}
```

This ActionScript is similar to the ActionScript we added in the previous step. However, here the `if` statement reacts to the up and down arrow keys (rather than the right and left arrow keys). The first part of this statement says that if the up arrow key is pressed, the movie clip instance is moved to its current y position *minus* the value of `speed` (moving the instance up). If the down arrow key is pressed, the instance is moved to its current y position *plus* `speed` (moving the instance down).

5) Choose Control › Test Movie. Use the left, right, up, and down arrow keys to control the movement of the hot-air balloon.

The conditional statements you wrote are performed in each frame of the `enterFrame` clip event. If one of the keys is detected to be in the down state, the balloon will be moved accordingly.

6) Close the test movie and save your work as balloon2.fla.

You now know how to capture a key press and make something happen as a result. There are many applications for this, such as paging through a slide show or making a game.

WORKING WITH STRING AND SELECTION OBJECTS

As one of the most commonly used objects, the String object uses methods that can be very helpful for modifying and building *strings*—quote-enclosed values that contain information (like the name "Jobe") that can be easily understood by humans.

```
message = "No shoes, no service!"
```

The above ActionScript creates a variable named `message` whose value is a string. In such cases, you can think of the variable itself as an instance of the String object—which means you can use String object methods to manipulate its value.

Let's look at a few examples.

The `toUpperCase()` method of the String object forces a string to become all uppercase letters. For instance:

```
message = message.toUpperCase();
```

The above script modifies the variable `message` to contain `"NO SHOES, NO SERVICE!"` (For the opposite effect—that is, to force the entire string to become all lowercase letters—you would apply `toLowerCase()` in the same fashion.)

Note that the text value of a text field instance (the text within the field) is considered an instance of the String object. Thus, if **message** were the name of a text field instance, the previous script could be rewritten as follows:

```
message.text = message.text.toUpperCase();
```

Is there any advantage of using one over the other? Not really: Every project is different, and you may find cases where one seems to be more appropriate than the other. To review, you can create an instance of the String object by:

- Using a constructor (for example, `myNewStringObject = new String("Hello");`). The String object is identified as `myNewStringObject`

- Assigning a string value to a variable. The String object is identified as the name of the variable

- Creating a text field. The String object is identified as `nameOfTextField.text`

Since most of the projects in this book contain text fields, you'll find that the most common reference we make is `nameOfTextField.text`.

Another useful method of the String object—`indexOf()`—lets you find the first occurrence of a character or group of characters in a string. The result returned is a number corresponding to the *letter index* where the string starts. A letter index is the number of a character in relation to the whole string. The first character in a string has an index of 0; the second has an index of 1; and so on. If the `indexOf()` method finds no occurrences of the character or group of characters, it returns a value of –1. The following is an example of one use of the `indexOf()` method:

```
message.text = "No shoes no service!";
firstS = message.text.indexOf("s");
```

The variable `firstS` will be assigned a value of 3 because that's the character number of the first *s* encountered.

STRING INDEX VALUES

"No shoes no service!"
```
|   | | |   |   |   |   |
0   1 2 3   4   5   6   7
```

It can sometimes be useful to determine the number of characters in a string. This is easy to do because all instances of the string object have a length property. You can often use string length to validate user-input information in a text field. Say, for example, that you wanted a user to enter a valid U.S. Zip code; you would know that it must be five characters in length. By checking the length property of the Zip code, you could create a simple validation script like the following:

```
zipCode.text = "27609";
zipLength = zipCode.text.length
if (zipLength == 5) {
  // Correct length of zip code
} else {
  // Invalid zip code
}
```

The first line sets the text value shown in the **zipCode** text field. (We assume this is what the user has entered.) The next line creates a variable named `zipLength` and assigns it a value based on the length property of `zipCode.text`—in this case 5, because that's the number of characters the **zipCode** field contains. The last part of the script uses an `if` statement to take one set of actions if `zipLength` equals 5 and another if it doesn't.

The Selection object allows you to control various aspects of the currently focused text field, including highlighting text, getting and setting the caret's (current insertion point) position and more. A text field is considered focused if the user's cursor is placed there. Since only one text field can be focused at a time, there's never more than one Selection object.

By clicking on a text field, the user dictates which one has focus. However, you can use the `setFocus()` method to override the user's current choice—important since you can only use other Selection object methods on the text field currently in focus. (As you'll see from the following exercise, you can't always rely on the user to select—and thus bring into focus—the proper text field.)

One last method of the Selection object allows you to highlight portions of text dynamically—without the user's help. This method (`Selection.setSelection(param1, param2)`) includes two parameters: the character index of where the selection starts and the character index of where the selection should end. Say, for example, you have a text field that contains the text "Derek is the craziest person I know." To highlight the word *craziest* (assuming its text field is in focus), you would use the following:

```
Selection.setSelection(13, 20);
```

"Derek is the craziest person I know"

13   20

In this exercise, you'll create a simple word processor using many of the String and Selection object methods we've just discussed.

1) Open wordProcessor1.fla in the Lesson04/Assets folder.

There are two layers in this file, Background and Buttons. The Background layer contains the image of the word processor window as well as text fields. The Buttons layer contains the four buttons that appear at the top of the word processor window. There are three text fields on the stage. The largest one, in the center, represents the text document. It has an instance name of **inputField**. The next text field, to the right of the Find button, is appropriately called **findField**. When played, the user will be able to enter a character or string of characters into this text field to search the **inputField** text field. The search results will be displayed in the third text field, at the bottom of the window, which is called `status`. This text field is also used to display the results when counting the number of characters in the document. We will be attaching various scripts to the buttons at the top of the window to make our word processor work.

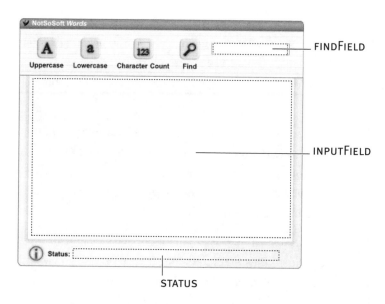

2) **With the Actions panel open, select the Uppercase button (with the capital *A*) and add the following script:**

```
on (release) {
  inputField.text = inputField.text.toUpperCase();
}
```

Flash interprets this script as saying, "On release of this button, make the letters in the **inputField** text field uppercase." When the button is pressed, the contents of the **inputField** text field are reassigned with uppercase letters.

3) **With the Actions panel open, select the Lowercase button (with the small *a*) and add the following script:**

```
on (release) {
  inputField.text = inputField.text.toLowerCase();
}
```

This script is similar to the one added in the previous step. On release of the button, the **inputField** text field is reassigned with all lowercase characters.

4) With the Actions panel open, select the Character Count button (with '123') and add the following script:

```
on (release) {
  status.text = "There are " + inputField.text.length + " characters in the
current document";
}
```

When this script is executed, a custom message will be displayed in the **status** text field. The Length property of the **inputField** text field is determined and inserted in the middle of the message. The message is built dynamically by adding, "There are " plus the value of the length property, plus the ending part of the message, " characters in the current document." If the document has 50 characters, the message will read, "There are 50 characters in the current document."

5) With the Actions panel open, select the Find button (with the magnifying glass) and add the following script:

```
on (release) {
  result = inputField.text.indexOf(findField.text);
  if (findField.text != "" && result >= 0) {
    status.text = "The first instance of these characters occurs at character
" + result;
    Selection.setFocus("_root.inputField");
    Selection.setSelection(result, result + findField.text.length);
  } else {
    status.text = "That string could not be found";
  }
}
```

The above script is the most complex one in this exercise because it does several things. The first line sets the value of the result variable using the indexOf() method of the String object. Here, we're asking the script to look in the **inputField** text field and find the index number of the first occurrence of the character or group of characters entered into the **findField** text field. In the end, result will have a value of –1 (no occurrence was found) or 0 to the string length (depending on how many characters are in the document). For example, if the first occurrence is found at index 13, result will have a value of 13. This value plays an important part in the rest of the script.

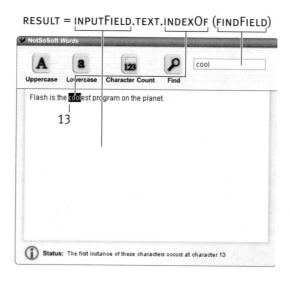

RESULT = INPUTFIELD.TEXT.INDEXOF (FINDFIELD)

The next part of the script uses an `if` statement to carry out one of two sets of actions, depending on whether a couple of conditions prove true. The first part of the statement looks at the text values of **findField** and the numeric value of `result`. It says that if **findField** is not empty (this makes sure that the **findField** text field has not been left blank) *and* the value of `result` is equal to or greater than 0 (which it will be if an occurrence of the characters entered is found), do the actions below. The `else` part of the statement deals with what happens if neither of these conditions is met. In this case, nothing will happen except the `status` text field will display the text "That string could not be found."

Assuming that both conditions are true, let's look at what the three actions under the first part of the `if` statement do. The first action will display a dynamic text message in the **status** text field. The message is built dynamically by adding "The first instance of these characters occurs at character " plus the value of `result`. If `result` has a value of 7, the message will read, "The first instance of these characters occurs at character 7." The next two actions use methods of the Selection object to highlight the character or characters in the **inputField** text field that were searched for and found. You'll remember that a text field must have focus before any of the Selection object methods can be used on it. Since we want to highlight text in the **inputField** text field, we use the following line to ensure that this field has focus before the next Selection method is used on it:

```
Selection.setFocus("_root.inputField");
```

The next line of script uses another Selection method to highlight text in the currently focused text field. This line of script reads as follows:

```
Selection.setSelection(result, result + findField.text.length);
```

We've used a couple of dynamic values with this method to determine where the selection begins and ends. Because we want the selection to begin where the first occurrence was found, we use the value of `result` as the starting point of the selection. The ending point of the selection is determined by adding the value of `result` to the value of the `length` property of the **findField** text field. How does this work? Assume you typed "I like my dog very much" in the **inputField** text field. Next, in the **findField** text field, you search for "dog." When the above script is executed, `result` will have a value of 10 (the first occurrence of "dog" is at the tenth character) and `findField.text.length` will be 3 (since the word "dog" is currently in this field, and it is three characters long). Using these values, the above line of script could be written as follows:

```
Selection.setSelection(10, 10 + 3);
```

or

```
Selection.setSelection(10, 13);
```

This will highlight Characters 10 through 13, which is where "dog" appears in the **inputField** text field.

6) Choose Control > Test Movie.

Type into the **inputField** text field and press the Uppercase and Lowercase buttons. Also press the Count Characters button to determine how many characters the document contains. Finally, try out the search function by entering one or more characters into the **findField** text field and pressing the button.

7) Close the test movie and save your work as wordProcessor2.fla.

You can see how easy it is to use the methods associated with the String and Selection objects—a good thing since you'll find yourself using the String object frequently to both validate and reformat data.

WHAT YOU HAVE LEARNED

In this lesson, you have:

- Learned what objects are and why they are useful (pages 124–127)
- Become acquainted with the various objects available in ActionScript (pages 127–134)
- Used the Color object (pages 135–140)
- Created an interactive scene using the Key object (pages 140–143)
- Created a word processor using properties and methods of the String and Selection objects (pages 143–149)

using functions

When programming, you may find yourself using the same chunks of code over and over—either by copying and pasting them or by rewriting the same lines of ActionScript. There is, however, a way to write ActionScript just once and then reuse it any time with a single action. You do this via *functions*, and the action by which you execute a function is a *call* or a *function call*. Functions are real time-savers—both during development and during code maintenance—because they reduce the amount of code you need to write or modify. Think of a function as a mini-program that serves a specific purpose within another application. You can use it to perform a set of specific actions, or you

You will create several functions that allow you to turn a Flash-TV (a simple Flash app that acts like a TV and remote control) on and off and change its channels.

can feed it information and output a result—or you can do both. Functions provide a powerful and versatile way to script your project.

In this lesson, you'll learn how to create and use functions while developing a functional remote control for a Flash-made television set.

WHAT YOU WILL LEARN
In this lesson, you will:

- Create a function
- Call a function
- Add parameters to a function
- Create a function that returns a result
- Use local variables

APPROXIMATE TIME
This lesson takes approximately 1 ½ hours to complete.

LESSON FILES
Starting File:
Lesson05/Assets/television1.fla
Lesson05/Assets/television2.fla
Lesson05/Assets/television3.fla
Completed Project:
television4.fla

CREATING FUNCTIONS

Before you use a function, you must create or define it. You can do this by using one of two possible syntaxes.

SYNTAX 1

The following code describes the first syntax:

```
function myFunction (parameter1,parameter2,etc.) {
  //actions go here;
}
```

The above code represents the most common way of creating a function as well as the syntax we'll use most frequently in this lesson. You'll see that the function declaration begins with the word *function*, followed by the name of the function (which can be anything you choose, as long as it follows typical naming conventions). Following the function name is an area enclosed by parenthesis. You can leave this area blank, or you can fill it with information (parameter data) that the function can use. By leaving the area within the parenthesis blank, you create a "generic" function—that is, one that performs the same way whenever it's called. If, however, your function contains parameters, it will perform in a unique way each time it's called based on the parameter information it receives. Giving the function information in this way is called *passing in arguments* or *passing in parameters*. You can use as many parameters as you wish; we'll tell you how to access them a bit later in this lesson.

Following the optional parameter area is an open curly brace followed by a carriage return and then some actions before the curly brace that concludes the function. In this space between the curly braces, you write the actions that you wish your function to perform. These actions may also make use of any parameter information passed to the function (as you will see soon).

TIP *You can create a function skeleton (that is, a function that does not yet contain any actions) by clicking Actions > User-Defined Functions in the Actions panel.*

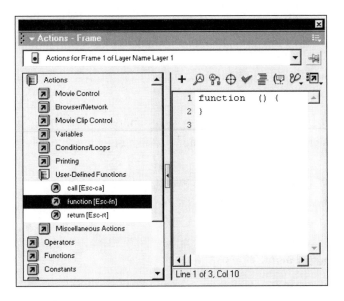

Syntax 2

The following code represents the second syntax for creating functions:

```
myFunction = function (parameter1,parameter2,etc.) {/* actions go here */ };
```

You would use the above syntax to create a function dynamically or to define your own custom *method* of an object (which we'll discuss in Lesson 6, Customizing Objects). The only difference between this syntax and Syntax 1 is in the way the function name is assigned: The function name appears first, and the function value is assigned using the "=" assignment operator. You can only use this syntax by manually typing it into the Actions list window with the Actions panel in Expert mode.

If a function contains no parameters, it can be called using the following syntax:

```
myFunction();
```

When you call a function, you're telling Flash to execute all of the actions within that function. Thus, if myFunction() contained 20 actions, all of them could be executed by using this single line of script.

If a function has been defined to accept parameter information, you can use the following syntax to call it:

```
myFunction(parameter1, parameter2);
```

The examples above assume that the function and function call reside on the same timeline. Just as each timeline contains its own variables and objects, each timeline also contains any functions you've defined there. To call a function on a specific timeline, you need to place the target path to that timeline in front of the function call, like this:

```
_root.clip1.clip2.myFunction();
```

In this exercise, you'll create a Power button on a television remote control. With this button, the Flash-television can be toggled on and off using a function.

> **TIP** *A function can be called dynamically based on a value (for instance, _root[aVariableName]();). Thus, if aVariableName had a value of "sayHello", the function call would actually look like _root.sayHello();.*

1) Open television1.fla in the Lesson05/Assets folder.

The movie's structure has already been created. The Actions layer is where you will include most of the ActionScript. Inside the TV layer is a movie clip instance named **tv**, which contains three layers on its timeline: The bottom layer (called Television) is just a graphic; the layer above that (called Screen) contains a movie clip instance called **screen**, which itself includes two layers and two frames, and contains graphical content that represents the various "programs" that will be seen when changing channels on the TV.

On the main timeline there is another layer, named Remote, that contains a movie clip instance named **remote**. Inside **remote**, you'll find a layer that contains most of the remote-control graphics, including a movie clip with an instance name of **light**, as well as another layer that contains the buttons for the remote, all of which will eventually contain scripts.

2) Select Frame 1 of the Actions layer on the main timeline. With the Actions panel open, add the following ActionScript:

```
tvPower = false;
function togglePower () {
  if (tvPower) {
    newChannel = 0;
    tvPower = false;

  } else {
    tvPower = true;
    newChannel = 1;
  }
  tv.screen.gotoAndStop(newChannel + 1);
  remote.light.play();
}
```

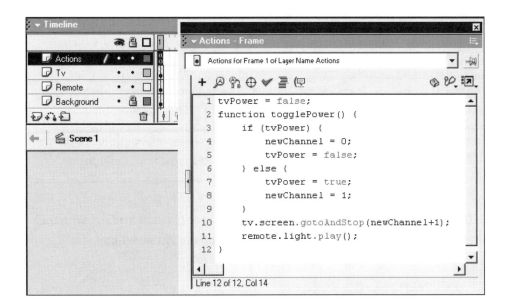

The first line of this script creates a variable named tvPower, which is used to track the current state of the TV: A value of true means the television is on; false means the television is off. The television will appear off initially, thus tvPower is set to false. The next seven lines represent a function definition for togglePower(): When called, this function will toggle the television power on and off. No parameters are passed into this function. Since this script exists on Frame 1, our togglePower() function is defined and a variable called tvPower is set to false as soon as the frame is loaded (that is, when the movie begins to play).

TIP *Because functions must be defined before they can be called, it's common practice to define all functions on Frame 1 so that they can be called at any time after that.*

The first part of the function uses an if statement to analyze the current value of tvPower. If tvPower is true (TV is on) when the function is called, the actions in the function change it to false (off) and set the value of the newChannel variable to 1; otherwise (else), tvPower is set to true and newChannel to 0. Using the if statement in this manner causes the value of tvPower to be set to its opposite each time the function is called, thus toggling the value of newChannel. By the time this statement is finished, newChannel has a value of 0 or 1.

The function then sends the **screen** movie clip instance (which is inside the **tv** movie clip instance) to a frame based on the current value of newChannel + 1. You must add 1 to the value of newChannel to prevent the timeline from being sent to Frame 0 (since newChannel will sometimes contain a value of 0, and there's no such thing as Frame 0 in a Flash movie timeline). In the end, this part of the function will send the **screen** movie clip instance to Frame 1 (showing a blank TV screen) or Frame 2 (showing Channel 1).

The function finishes by telling the light on the remote control to play (which causes it to blink, providing a visual indication that a button has been pressed).

There is now a function on Frame 1 of the main, or root, timeline. Although this function contains several actions, none of them are executed until the function is called.

3) Double-click the remote-control movie clip instance to edit it in place. With the Actions panel open, select the Power button and add this ActionScript:

```
on (release) {
  _root.togglePower();
}
```

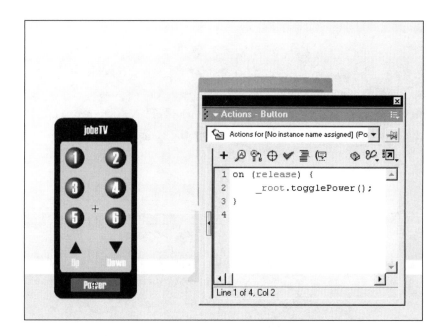

This ActionScript calls the `togglePower()` function we created in the previous step. It's important to note that since the `togglePower()` function resides on the main timeline, you must use `_root` as the target path when calling this function.

4) Choose Control > Test Movie. Then click the Power button several times to view the TV on/off functionality you've created.

Every time you press the Power button, the `togglePower()` function is called so that all of the actions within that function are performed. As mentioned, the actions within the function toggle the state of the TV.

5) Close the test movie and save your work as television2.fla.

You have now created and used a function! In the next section, we'll build on this idea to create a more powerful and versatile function.

ADDING PARAMETERS TO FUNCTIONS

In the previous exercise you learned how to create a function and call it from any timeline. In this exercise, you'll add parameters to a function and learn how to use them. The following is the syntax for creating a function that accepts parameters:

```
function convertToMoonWeight (myWeight){
  weightOnMoon = myWeight/6.04;
}
```

The sole parameter for this function is `myWeight`—which is also used *within* the function definition, just as if it were a preexisting variable.

The following is an example of the syntax used to call this function:

```
convertToMoonWeight(165);
```

When calling this function, a value is passed in (that is, placed within the parenthesis). In this case, that value is a person's weight here on Earth (165). This value (165) sets the value of the `myWeight` parameter throughout the function before it executes. Thus, in our example, sending a value of 165 to our `convertToMoonWeight()` function would set the value of `weightOnMoon` to 165/6.04, or 27.32.

```
function traceNames() {
  trace("This function was passed " + arguments.length + "arguments");
  trace("The value of the first argument is: " + arguments[0]);
  trace("The value of the second argument is: " + arguments[1]);
}
traceNames("Kelly","Hayes");
```

In this example, the following would appear in the output window:

This function was passed two arguments

The value of the first argument is: Kelly

The value of the second argument is: Hayes

Accessing the argument *array can enable you to create functions that can adapt their functionality based on how many parameters are passed to them. For more information about arrays, see Lesson 7, Using Dynamic Data.*

In this exercise, you'll add button functionality to the numeric keypad on the remote control as well as to the TV channel Up and Down buttons. The numeric buttons will work by calling a function and passing in the number of the channel to jump to. You will also modify the togglePower() function slightly.

1) Open television2.fla in the Lesson05/Assets folder.

This file is set up in similar fashion to the one we just worked on, with the exception that the **screen** movie clip instance contains frames that represent six channels rather than a single channel.

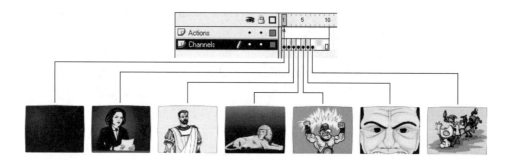

2) Select Frame 1 of the Actions layer on the main timeline and open the Actions panel. Add this ActionScript to that frame at the end of the previous function definition:

```
function changeTheChannel (newChannel) {
  if (tvPower) {
    currentChannel = newChannel;
    tv.screen.gotoAndStop(newChannel + 1);
    remote.light.play();
  }
}
```

You have just created a function that accepts a parameter. This function will change the TV channel based on the parameter (newChannel) received. All of the actions that the function will perform are enclosed in an if statement, which is used to allow channels to be changed *only* if tvPower is true. The function then proceeds to set a variable used to store the current channel of the television to the value of the parameter value sent to the function. The next two lines should be familiar from the togglePower() function we discussed in the previous exercise: They set the frame in the **screen** movie clip instance (causing the television to change channels) and instruct the light on the remote control to blink. To understand this, consider a simple example. Assume the following function call is made to this function:

```
changeTheChannel(4);
```

The function would ask whether `tvPower` is `true` (TV is on) before doing anything else. If it is, `currentChannel` is given a value of 4 (same as the parameter passed to the function). Next, the **screen** movie clip instance is moved to a frame based on the value of the parameter value passed to the function, plus one (or 4 + 1). Thus, the **screen** instance is moved to Frame 5.

Your newly created function is now ready for use. Next, we'll add function calls to the numeric buttons on our remote control.

3) Double-click the *remote* movie clip instance on the main timeline to edit it in place. With the Actions panel open, select the round button under the number 1 on the remote keypad and add this ActionScript:

```
on (release) {
  _root.changeTheChannel(1);
}
```

Repeat this step for each of the round buttons under the numbers 2 through 6. In the parameter area (in the parenthesis) of each function call, enter the channel number that the television should display for each of the buttons.

The `changeTheChannel()` function resides on the main timeline so you must call it using the path to its location: `_root`.

4) Choose Control › Test Movie. Press the Power button on the remote control to turn on the TV, then use the numeric keypad on the remote control to change the channels.

If you press the channel buttons before turning on the television, the `changeTheChannel()` function will not perform the change request. If the television is on and you press one of the channel buttons, that button number is passed into the `changeTheChannel()` function and the **screen** movie clip instance will move to the correct frame (channel).

5) Close the testing movie to return to the authoring environment. With the Actions panel open, select Frame 1 of the Actions layer.

This frame contains two function definitions, one for turning the TV on and off and another for changing channels using the numeric buttons on the remote-control keypad. However, you'll notice some redundancy between these functions: Both are set up so that when either is called, they tell the remote-control light to blink as well as send the **screen** movie clip instance to the correct frame. Since it's best to fix this type of redundancy whenever possible, let's correct this problem.

```
1  tvPower = false;
2  function togglePower() {
3      if (tvPower) {
4          changeTheChannel(0);
5          tvPower = false;
6      } else {
7          tvPower = true;
8          changeTheChannel(1);
9      }
10         tv.screen.gotoAndStop(newChannel+1);
11         remote.light.play();
12 }
13 function changeTheChannel(newChannel) {
14     if (tvPower) {
15         currentChannel = newChannel;
16         tv.screen.gotoAndStop(newChannel+1);
17         remote.light.play();
18     }
19 }
```

Line 1 of 19, Col 17

6) With the Actions panel still open, modify the `togglePower()` function to read as follows:

```
function togglePower () {
  if (tvPower) {
    changeTheChannel(0);
    tvPower = false;
  } else {
    tvPower = true;
    changeTheChannel(1);
  }
}
```

This function now makes use of the `changeTheChannel()` function to change the channel when the power is turned on or off. When the TV is turned on, the `togglePower()` function now makes a call to the `changeTheChannel()` function and passes in the number *1*. This means that every time the TV is turned on, it will start on Channel 1. When it is turned off, it goes to Channel 0 (the off state of the TV screen). This demonstrates how one function can contain a call to another.

You'll notice that in the first part of the if *statement above, the call to the* changeTheChannel() *function happens before* tvPower *is set to* false. *This is because we defined the* changeTheChannel() *function so that it only works if* tvPower *is* true *(which it is if this part of the statement is executed). If* tvPower *were set to* false *first, the function call of* changeTheChannel(0) *would do nothing. The* else *part of the statement works just the opposite: The value of* tvPower *is set to* true *first, before the function call. Once again, this is because it has to have a value of* true *before the function call will have an effect.*

Now let's create a couple of functions that will allow us to increment and decrement channels using the Up and Down arrows on the remote.

7) Select the first frame of the Actions layer on the main timeline and open the Actions panel. Insert the following line of ActionScript in this frame, just below where it says tvPower = false;**:**

```
numberOfChannels = 6;
```

This line of code creates a variable called numberOfChannels and assigns it a value of 6. This variable will be used in a function (which we'll create in a moment) that will be used to increment channels each time it's called. You'll remember that the **screen**

movie clip instance only contains graphics representing six channels; thus, this value of 6 represents the total number of channels our TV can display and will be used to prevent the incrementing of channels beyond Channel 6. Let's see how this will work.

8) Add the following ActionScript at the end of the currently selected frame:

```
function channelUp () {
  if (currentChannel + 1 <= numberOfChannels) {
    changeTheChannel(currentChannel + 1);
  }
}
```

This function—which does not accept parameters—bumps up the channel by 1 each time it's called. However, it uses a "safety mechanism" to prevent going beyond Channel 6. Recall that a variable named `currentChannel` is set every time the `changeTheChannel()` function is called (see Step 2). The value of this variable represents the channel currently displayed minus 1. Thus, if Channel 4 is currently displayed, this variable's value will be 3. Before the `channelUp()` function will execute, it uses an `if` statement to determine whether the current channel incremented up (the value of `currentChannel` + 1) will still be less than or equal to the upper channel limit (the value of `numberOfChannels`, or 6). If the condition is satisfied, the `changeTheChannel()` function is called with a parameter that has a value of the current channel plus 1. This will cause the next channel to be displayed. This `if` statement contains no accompanying `else` statement. Thus, if the condition is not satisfied, this means that Channel 6 is currently displayed and no further actions are performed.

9) Add the following ActionScript at the end of the currently selected frame:

```
function channelDown () {
  if (currentChannel - 1 >= 1) {
    changeTheChannel(currentChannel - 1);
  }
}
```

Like the `channelUp()` function, this function does not accept parameters. When called, it determines whether the value of the `currentChannel` variable *decremented* by 1 is greater than the lower bound of 1, thus preventing the user from "channeling down" beyond Channel 1. If this condition is satisfied, the `changeTheChannel()` function is called and passed the value of the `currentChannel` minus 1. This will cause the previous channel to be displayed. As with the `if` statement in the `channelUp()` function definition, this `if` statement contains no accompanying `else` statement. Thus, if the condition is not satisfied, this means that Channel 1 is currently displayed and no further actions will be performed.

Now it's time to add function calls to the Up and Down buttons on our remote control that will use the `channelUp()` and `channelDown()` functions we just created.

10) Double-click the *remote* movie clip instance on the main timeline to edit it in place. With the Actions panel open, select the Up arrow button and add this ActionScript:

```
on (release) {
  _root.channelUp();
}
```

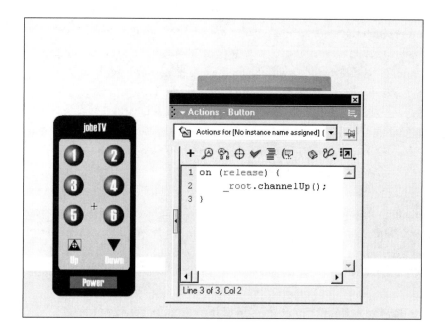

Every time this button is clicked, the `channelUp()` function in the root will be called. When the current channel reaches its upper limit (as defined by the `numberOfChannels` variable), the channels will no longer increase.

11) With the Actions panel open, select the Down arrow button and add this ActionScript:

```
on (release) {
  _root.channelDown();
}
```

Like the Up button, this action calls a function that resides in the root. Every time this button is pressed, `channelDown()` is called andthe `currentChannel` variable is decremented (as long as it's greater than the lower limit). The television is then set to the correct channel.

12) Choose Control > Test Movie, then turn the television on using the Power button and use the Up and Down buttons to change channels.

Notice that you can select any channel, and from there use the Up and Down buttons to change the channels. Using a variable that stores the current channel and functions as you have done here makes this type of functionality simple.

13) Close the test movie and save your work as television3.fla.

You have now created a functional remote control for a television. In the next exercise, you'll learn how to use functions in a new way while adding a cable box display.

USING LOCAL VARIABLES AND CREATING FUNCTIONS THAT RETURN RESULTS

The variables you've created and used thus far can be accessed at any time by any script in the Flash movie. In contrast, *local* variables are special variables that you can only create and use within the scope of a function definition. In other words, a local variable is created within the function definition, used by the function when it's called, then deleted when that function has finished executing. Local variables exist only within the function definitions where they were created.

Although local variables are not absolutely required in ActionScripting, it's good programming practice to use them. Applications that require many and frequent calculations end up creating a lot of variables—which can slow applications. By using local variables, however, you minimize memory usage. And by employing them in function definitions, you also help prevent *naming collisions*—which occur when your project gets so big that you unknowingly create and use variable names that are already in use. However, local variables in one function definition can have the same names as local variables within another function definition—even if both definitions exist on the same timeline. This is because Flash understands that a local variable only has meaning within the function definition where it was created.

There is just one way to manually create a local variable. Here's the syntax:

```
var myName = "Jobe";
```

Note the use of `var` in the above syntax: It tells Flash to consider this particular variable as a local variable. If this line of code existed within a function definition, `myName` would only have meaning to (and could only be used by) that function.

Multiple local variables can be declared on a single line using this syntax:

```
var firstName = "Jobe", lastName = "Makar", email = "jobe@electrotank.com";
```

In addition to using local variables, you can build functions to return end results—that is, returned values. Think of this as what happens when you enter numbers into a calculator: The calculator represents a function that tabulates numbers; the numbers entered represent parameter values sent to the function when it's called; and the total represents the result returned by the function once it's finished executing. Using a function return makes your code easy to read and update. The following represents the syntax for a return line:

```
return myVariable;
```

With a return, a function can perform all of its actions to determine a final result. This final result is then returned to the action line that called the function. When a `return` action is encountered in a function, execution of the actions in the function is immediately halted—a handy feature if you want to stop a function before it has finished executing. Here's an example of a function definition that uses a local variable and a return:

```
function convertToMoonWeight (myWeight) {
  var newWeight = myWeight/6.04;
  return newWeight;
}
```

This function is called in the following way:

```
myWeightOnMoon = convertToMoonWeight(165);
```

The above line of ActionScript uses a function call to determine the value of myWeightOnMoon. Since the function that's called is set up to return the value of newWeight, this will set the value of myWeightOnMoon to that value (27.32). The parameter myWeight is automatically created as a local variable and deleted when the function has executed. The local variable newWeight is also deleted when the function has finished its job. (This will make more sense in a moment.)

In this exercise, you'll add a cable-box display to our project, which displays the name of the current channel. You will create a function that builds the text to be displayed on the cable box.

TIP *You can use the* return *action to return any data types, including variable values, arrays, or any other objects.*

1) Open television3.fla in the Lesson05/Assets folder.

This file is set up in similar fashion to the one we just worked on, with the exception that it now contains a cable box below the television. This movie clip has an instance name of **cableBox**, and it contains a simple graphic and a text field with an instance name of **cableDisplay**. This text field will be filled with different channel names, depending on the channel selected.

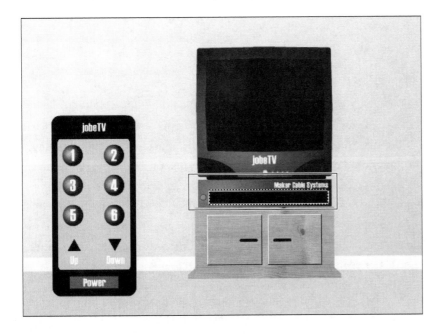

2) With the Actions panel open, select Frame 1 and enter the following ActionScript just below where it says `numberOfChannels = 6;`**:**

```
channelNames =
["","News","Classics","Family","Cartoons","Horror","Westerns"];
```

You have just created an array named `channelNames`. This array contains names that will be dynamically inserted into a string of text that will be displayed inside the cable box. There are seven string elements in this array separated by commas. Each one of these elements has what is known as an associated *index* value, beginning with 0. For example, channelNames[0] = "" (or nothing), channelNames[1] = "News," channelNames[2] = "Classics," and so on. This is important to understand as we progress.

NOTE *For more information on arrays, see Lesson 7, Using Dynamic Data.*

Next, let's create a function that uses the text elements in this array to display a message in the cable box.

3) With the frame still selected, enter the following ActionScript at the end of all scripts on Frame 1:

```
function displayCableText () {
  if (currentChannel != 0) {
    var displayText = "You are viewing " + channelNames[currentChannel] +
".";
  } else {
    var displayText = "";
  }
  return displayText;
}
```

This defines the `displayCableText()` function, which accepts no parameters. It is used to dynamically build a string of text that will eventually appear in the **cableDisplay** text field. This function then takes this string and returns it using the `return` action. The function contains a conditional statement that checks to make sure that the television channel is not the channel associated with the TV being in the off state (0). If the condition is satisfied, a local variable named `displayText` is created, and a line of text is dynamically built from the `channelNames` array as well as the current value of `currentChannel`. For example, if the value of `currentChannel` is 4 at the time this function is called and executed, this would essentially be the same as the following:

```
var displayText = "You are viewing " + channelNames[4] + ".";
```

Since "Cartoons" exists at index position 4 of the `channelNames` array, it can be further broken down:

```
var displayText = "You are viewing Cartoons";
```

If the first part of the conditional statement is not satisfied (`else`), the local variable `displayText` is created with no value (or simply ""). The function ends by returning the value of `displayText`. But where does this value actually get returned to? We'll explain that in the next step. Since `displayText` has been specified as a local variable (using `var`), it's removed from memory as soon as its value is returned,.

4) With the Actions panel still open, modify the `changeTheChannel()` function by inserting the following line of code after the fifth line of the function definition:

```
cableBox.cableDisplay.text = displayCableText();
```

```
1  tvPower=false;
2  numberOfChannels=6;
3  channelNames=["","News","Classics","Family","Cartoons","Horror","Westerns"];
4  function togglePower() {
5      if (tvPower) {
6          changeTheChannel(0);
7          tvPower=false;
8      } else {
9          tvPower=true;
10         changeTheChannel(1);
11     }
12 }
13 function changeTheChannel(newChannel) {
14     if (tvPower) {
15         currentChannel=newChannel;
16         tv.screen.gotoAndStop(newChannel+1);
17         remote.light.play();
18         cableBox.cableDisplay.text=displayCableText();
19     }
20 }
```

Line 18 of 38, Col 1

You have modified `changeTheChannel()` so that each time a channel is changed and the `changeChannel()` function is called, the **cableDisplay** text field (inside the **cableBox** movie clip instance) will be updated with the correct text. This line of ActionScript sets the value of the text field instance **cableDisplay** (which is actually the dynamic text field in our cable box) using the returned value of the `displayCableText()` function. Thus, the `displayCable()` function is called, goes to work, and comes up with a value. That value is then inserted after the equals sign. This is what's meant by a function *returning* a value. The value the function comes up with is returned to the line of script that called the function (as shown above). This is also a great example of how using functions can be a real time-saver. We've enhanced changeTheChannel() in a single location, but any script that calls the function will automatically execute this enhancement as well—very efficient!

5) Choose Control > Test Movie. Select the Power button to turn the television on. Change the channel a few times.

Every time you select a button that changes the channel, the cable box is updated with the name of the channel you're watching. You have created a simple application that uses six functions to perform several tasks.

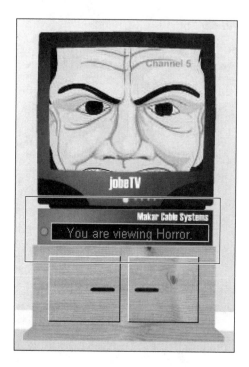

6) Close the test movie and save your work as television4.fla.

You're now finished with this file. You'll apply what you've learned here in lessons to come.

WHAT YOU HAVE LEARNED

In this lesson, you have:

- Learned how functions can make scripting a project much more efficient (pages 150–151)

- Created functions using various syntaxes (pages 152–157)

- Passed arguments into functions while calling them (pages 157–165)

- Used local variables (pages 165–170)

- Called functions from within other functions (pages 168–170)

- Returned and used the results of calling a function (pages 168–170)

customizing objects

LESSON 6

Most of us learned in shop class that you've got to use the proper tool for the job at hand—anything else can result in botched jobs or, worse, terrible injury. But what do you do if the tool for *your* task doesn't exist? When Henry Ford started producing cars on an assembly line, he didn't call the assembly-line parts store to purchase the requisite tools; he created his own—either from scratch or by enhancing existing tools.

As ActionScripters, we sometimes need to do the same: Since we're creating *new* Macromedia Flash applications, the basic scripting tools we're accustomed to using (Flash's prebuilt objects) will not always be up to the task. When this is the case, we simply roll up our sleeves and create our own—which means you need to understand something about the mechanics of the way objects work in ActionScript.

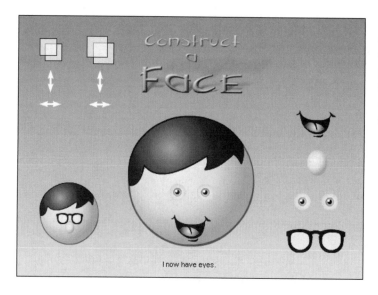

You will learn about a number of object-oriented scripting principles in the Construct a Face application you will script in this lesson

In this lesson, we'll show you the way objects work and how they're constructed so that you can create new classes of objects from the ground up as well as enhance existing ones.

WHAT YOU WILL LEARN

In this lesson, you will:

- Learn why objects are so useful
- Learn about the parent/child relationship created when an object contains another object
- Create a custom class of objects
- Work with the prototype object of a class
- Learn about object inheritance
- Create a subclass of objects
- Learn how to watch the properties of an object
- Create new object methods
- Enhance the methods of Flash's built-in objects
- Create new methods for Flash's built-in objects
- Register a movie clip to a custom object class to cause instances of that clip to inherit specific functionality

APPROXIMATE TIME

This lesson takes approximately 2½ hours to complete.

LESSON FILES

Media Files:

None

Starting Files:

Lesson06/Assets/object1.fla
Lesson06/Assets/class1.fla
Lesson06/Assets/objectProject1.fla
Lesson06/Assets/registerClass1.fla

Completed Projects:

object2.fla
class4.fla
objectProject4.fla
registerClass2.fla

UNDERSTANDING OBJECT MECHANICS

In Lesson 4, we introduced you to Flash's prebuilt objects (the objects listed in the Toolbox window of the Actions panel). In that lesson you created *instances* of prebuilt objects, changed their properties, and used various methods to make the objects perform specific tasks. In the process you got a taste of how objects facilitate interactivity. However, we couldn't explain *why* objects work the way they do until you understood functions, since these play a critical role in the creation and customization of objects. Now that you know something about functions (which we covered in Lesson 5), you're ready to get down to the real nitty-gritty of creating and customizing objects.

CREATING *INSTANCES* OF OBJECTS VS. *CLASSES* OF OBJECTS

Right about now you may be saying, "But I thought I created and customized objects in Lesson 4; how is what we're going to do here different?" Well, in Lesson 4 you created *instances* of prebuilt objects (for example, an instance of the Color object)—objects that are built into ActionScript and thus immediately available for use. We showed you the different classes of Flash's built-in objects (Array, Color, Date, String, Sound, and so on), but we didn't explain how to build your *own* class of objects (that is, your own custom tools) or how to enhance existing ones. To return to an earlier analogy, when the automobile was invented, a new class of objects was created, the Automobile class. This class of objects had doors, steering wheels, headlights, and other features. Now when an automobile rolls off the assembly line, an *instance* of the Automobile class has been created, not a new class of objects. A new class of objects would be created if someone developed an individual flying machine and named that class FlyingMachine. Instances of the FlyingMachine object would soon start rolling off the assembly line as well. Although we'll touch on this concept in more detail shortly, it's important to understand that a *class* simply describes how an object is made and works—a blueprint, if you will. Instances are what you create from that blueprint. In the end, both the blueprint and the resulting instance must be created.

NOTE *Instances are also known as* objects. *In most cases,* instances *and* objects *are one and the same.*

Since the concept of how objects work is a fairly abstract one, the exercises in the following several sections take a slightly different approach than those in the rest of the book. While most of the other exercises are graphical and tangible in nature—that is, they involve elements that you can actually see and manipulate in your project—the following deal with what's going on behind the scenes. In the following exercises, you'll use the `trace` action and the List Variables command (Debug > List Variables, in the testing environment) to view data that exists within a movie as it plays but is normally not seen. You've seen the `trace` action before, but to clarify its use, take a look at the following syntax:

```
trace(_root._totalframes);
```

If this action is placed on Frame 1 of a movie that contains 47 frames, the Output window will automatically open and display the following as soon as the movie begins playing within the testing environment:

47

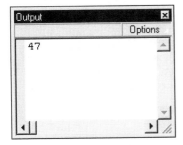

This simple action provides a great tool for learning how objects work.

Let's begin.

NOTE *If you're already familiar with how objects work, feel free to skip to the "Watching Properties" section.*

OBJECTS AS CONTAINERS

ActionScript objects are, first and foremost, containers—though special ones. As such, they not only hold stuff (for example, data and even other objects, also known as *object properties)*, they also perform specialized tasks (which are usually related to their contents). Flash's built-in String object, for instance, is used to hold a string value—for example, "Hedgehogs make great companions"—however, it also has methods that allow you to manipulate and work with that content, a principle we'll demonstrate in the following exercise.

1) Open Flash and choose File > New to start a new authoring file. With the Actions panel open, select Frame 1 and add the following script:

```
person1 = new Object();
```

This syntax creates a new instance of a generic object named `person1`.

> **NOTE** *The Object object (as used here) doesn't have a specific use—thus, it's a generic object. The above line, then, is an instance of the Object object (not a custom class), which we've created to demonstrate objects' role as containers. You will see a more extensive use of the Object object in the next lesson.*

At this point, person1 is a real nobody: We've defined no characteristics—not even a gender—for it.

2) Place the following lines of script just below the line you added in the previous step:

```
person1.gender = "male";
trace (person1.gender);
trace (person1.age);
```

The person1 object now has a property, known as gender, with a value of "male". We've added a couple of trace actions to see what values exist in our person1 object. Let's test our progress thus far.

3) Choose Control > Test Movie to test the project up to this point.

The Output window will open and display the following:

```
male
undefined
```

The first trace action returns a value of "male" because that's the value that exists at person1.gender (as set in the previous step). The second trace action returns a value of undefined for person1.age because that value has not been set anywhere yet.

Now let's add a few more property values to person1.

4) Close the test movie to return to the authoring environment. With the Actions panel open, select Frame 1. Replace the three lines of script you added in Step 2 with the following lines of script:

```
person1.age = 16;
person1.legs = 2;
person1.name = "Justin";
```

As you can see, person1 is shaping up nicely: He now has all the basic requirements to enter society.

person1

```
age = 16
legs = 2
name = "Justin"
```

At this point, a script can access any of the data associated with person1—which we'll demonstrate in the next step.

5) Add the following if statement to the end of the current script:

```
if (person1.age >= 21){
  trace("I'm going to the Disco");
}else{
  trace("I'm going to BurgerHouse");
}
```

This statement looks at the value of person1.age to determine a course of action.

6) Choose Control > Test Movie to test the project up to this point.

The Output window will open and display the following:

```
I'm going to BurgerHouse
```

Because person1.age has a value of 16, the if statement returns this result when evaluated.

Now let's make an addition to our person1 object to demonstrate how objects can contain other objects—a concept you're somewhat familiar with from using nested timelines (for example, using one MovieClip object within another MovieClip object).

7) Close the test movie to return to the authoring environment. With the Actions panel open, select Frame 1. Replace the if statement you added in the previous step with the following lines of script:

```
person1.head = new Object()
person1.head.eyes = 2;
person1.head.memories = new Array();
```

Here, we've given `person1` a `head` (finally!)—made possible by creating a new instance of the Object object and placing it inside the `person1` object. We've given `head` an `eyes` property, which has a value of 2. In addition, we've placed an Array object (named `memories`) inside of the `head` object.

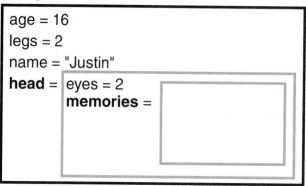

person1

```
age = 16
legs = 2
name = "Justin"
head = eyes = 2
       memories =
```

As you can see, we've placed one object (`memories`) inside of another object (`head`), which itself resides in an object (`person1`). This is opposed to placing `memories` directly in `person1`, as follows:

```
person1.memories = new Array();
```

There's a good reason for doing this, which we'll explain in a moment.

> **TIP** *If you wanted to place an existing array—named, say,* myThoughts*—into* person1.head *(as opposed to creating a new array as shown), you would use the following syntax:* person1.head.memories = myThoughts.

Now let's add some memories to the `memories` array.

8) Place the following lines of script at the end of the current script:

```
person1.head.memories[0] = "I was born into the world.";
person1.head.memories[1] = "I learned the word 'NO.' It was a very
productive day.";
person1.head.memories[2] = "I learned that if I make a bunch of noise, I get
what I want.";
```

These three lines of script will store data in the `memories` array, which is inside the `head` of the `person1` object.

9) Place the following action at the end of the current script:

```
trace(person1.head.memories[1]);
```

10) Choose Control > Test Movie to test the project up to this point.

The Output window will open and display the following text:

```
I learned the word 'NO.' It was a very productive day.
```

This is the value contained at `person1.head.memories[1]`.

11) Close the test movie and save your work as object1.fla.

We'll use what we've scripted so far in the next exercise. The thing to keep in mind for now is that objects are containers—for simple pieces of data or even for other objects. The idea behind placing a variable inside a movie clip instance, or even creating an instance of the Color, Sound, or other objects on a timeline, is a great example of this (see Lesson 4, "Using Objects"). You're placing an object (say, an instance of the Color object) on a timeline (inside an instance of the MovieClip object). When you place a variable in a timeline, you're essentially giving that instance of the MovieClip object a new property.

THE PARENT/CHILD RELATIONSHIP

When you place a timeline (that is, an instance of the MovieClip object) within another timeline (another instance), as you do with movie clips, a parent/child relationship is created (see Lesson 3, Understanding Target Paths). The same principle applies here with our objects. Continuing with our previous example, take a look at the following:

```
person1.head.memories
```

Here, `head` is a child object of `person1`; and `memories` is a child object of both `head` and `person1`. (Thus, `head` is the parent of `memories`, and `person1` is the parent of both `head` and `memories`.)

The key thing to be aware of here is that what happens to the parent happens to its children as well—which we'll demonstrate in the following exercise.

1) Open objects1.fla in the Lesson06/Assets folder. With the Actions panel open, select Frame1. Remove the `trace` action added in Step 9 of the previous exercise and attach the following script to the end:

```
delete person1.head;
trace(person1.head);
trace(person1.head.memories[1]);
trace(person1.name);
```

The first action deletes the head of person1. The trace actions that follow allow us to see how this affects our object.

2) Choose Control > Test Movie to test the project up to this point.

The Output window will open and display the following:

```
undefined
undefined
Justin
```

Here, we see that person1.head is now undefined, as is memories[1], which was inside of head. As the child of head, the memories array was deleted at the same time that head (its parent) was deleted. However, none of the other properties of the person1 object were affected—as demonstrated by the value returned by the trace action for person1.name.

person1

age = 16
legs = 2
name = "Justin"
head = eyes = 2
memories =

DELETED!

As you can see, a properly constructed object can react to circumstances in the same way as physical objects do. And when used in conjunction with actions that have a visual affect on your movie—which you'll learn about shortly—they can do even more.

180

3) Close the test movie and return to the authoring environment. With the Actions panel open, select Frame 1. Add the following lines of script at the end of the current script, right after where it says `trace(person1.name);`**:**

```
person1.head = new Object();
trace(person1.head);
trace(person1.head.memories[1]);
```

The first line adds the `head` object back to `person1`. The `trace` actions that follow will enable us to see the result. These three lines of script are placed just below the four lines you added in Step 1. Thus, when we test the project, the Output window will once again display the result of `person1.head` being deleted; however, this time that will be followed by the result of adding the `head` property back.

4) Choose Control > Test Movie to test the project up to this point.
The Output window will open and display the following:

```
undefined
undefined
Justin
[object Object]
undefined
```

The first three lines of output are the same as those explained in Step 2. The last two lines indicate what occurs when the `head` property is added back to `person1`. As a result, `person1.head` is traced as `[object Object]`, indicating that the `head` object exists again (and is an instance of the Object object) but that `person1.head.memories[1]` remains `undefined`. The reason for this is that when `person1.head.memories[1]` was removed earlier (as a result of deleting `person1.head`), it was wiped out of the computer's memory (along with the `eyes` property that was part of the `head` object). Adding the `head` property back does not bring back the `memories` array or the `eyes` property that were also deleted. In such a case, you would need to re-create the `memories` array and `eyes` property and set them with new data (as shown earlier).

5) Close the test movie and save your work as object2.fla.
This completes our use of this file. We'll build on your knowledge of objects in the next section—with a slight twist.

DEFINING A CUSTOM CLASS AND
CREATING INSTANCES OF THAT CLASS

Up to now, we've been using an instance of the generic Object object to demonstrate the way our `person1` object works. Now it's time to move to the next level of object mechanics: Creating a custom class—which in this exercise we'll define as the Person class. This class will serve as the blueprint for creating new instances of people, representing a more efficient way of creating and defining `person1`.

NOTE *We used the Object object in the above exercises primarily to illustrate the concept of objects. The Object object has many viable uses in regular projects; however, it's a general solution and one that may not be suitable for every application.*

Like the previous exercises, this one makes liberal use of the `trace` action to teach concepts.

1) Open Flash and choose File › New to start a new authoring file. With the Actions panel open, select Frame 1 and add this script:

```
Person = function(){
}
```

Although this closely resembles a function definition (it's a constructor function), it is also the beginning of a class definition.

NOTE *The terms* constructor function *and* class definition *are used interchangeably in the following discussion.*

Regular function definitions and constructor functions (class definitions) employ similar syntaxes; however, they're accessed differently. We'll explain this in greater detail in a minute, but for now take a look at the following examples. In the first, the function is executed *as a function;* in the second, the function is executed to create *an instance* of the Person class:

```
Person(); //executes as function
person1 = new Person();//creates an instance of the person class
```

NOTE *Although our class definition looks like a function, we need to approach it strictly as a class definition. It's not practical to use a single block of code both ways.*

You should think of a class definition as a blueprint, or template, for creating instances of that class. Within the curly braces of the class definition you define the characteristics that make up that class of objects. Since our Person class does not yet have any characteristics (properties), we'll update its class definition in accordance with our previous example.

2) Update the Person class definition as follows:

```
Person = function(){
  this.name = "Justin";
  this.age = 16;
  this.legs = 2;
  this.head = new Object()
  this.head.eyes = 2;
  this.head.memories = new Array();
}
```

Our class definition is now complete. In the next couple of steps, we'll discuss how to use it and explain what `this` means in the context of a class definition. We'll also show you how to create instances of our new class.

TIP *In case you hadn't noticed, we've given the Person class definition a name that starts with an uppercase letter. It's common practice to begin class names in this manner. In contrast, instances of the class are usually given names beginning in a lowercase letter. By employing this simple trick, you can make your script easier to read and understand.*

3) Add the following line of script at the end of the current script:

```
person1 = new Person();
```

This code creates an instance of the Person object named `person1`.

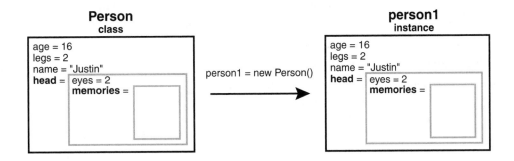

183

4) Choose Control › Test Movie to test the project up to this point. When the testing environment appears, choose Debug › List Variables.

The Output window will open up, and the following script will appear in the information it displays:

```
Variable _level0.person1 = [object #2] {
  name:"Justin",
  age:16,
  legs:2,
  head:[object #3, class 'Object'] {
  eyes:2,
  memories:[object #4, class 'Array'] []
  }
}
```

This is information about the `person1` instance that is created as a result of the action you added in the previous step. As our Person class defines, the `person1` instance has a name of "Justin", an age of 16, two legs, and so on.

It's important to understand how `person1 = new Person();` creates an instance with the properties defined by Person class. It's actually quite simple: When the line above is executed, ActionScript knows that it's time to build a new instance of the Person class. When this occurs, a temporary object (an *Activation object)* is created and sent to the Person class definition that was scripted earlier (all of which happens invisibly and automatically). The Activation object, which is pretty formless initially, is then "passed through" the class definition where various class properties (`name`, `age`, `legs`, and so on) are attached to it. During this process, the temporary Activation object is referenced by the term `this`, as shown in the class definition. Thus, when the class definition contains the following line:

```
this.age = 16;
```

It's saying that when an Activation object passes through here, its `age` property should be set to a value of 16. This process of creating an instance can be likened to moving the Activation object through an assembly line, adding parts to it as it moves along. When the activation object has completed the construction process, it is given a name (in this case `person1`) and becomes available for use.

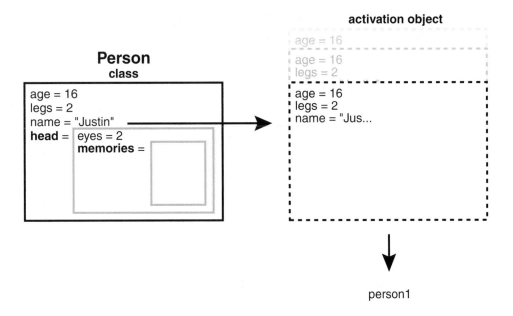

activation object

person1

Although we've defined our Person class and know how to create instances of it, each of those instances will be pretty much identical. This is because the way our Person class is currently defined, every instance created has a name of "Justin", an age of 16, and so on. Since our Person class needs to do more than create clones, let's make some changes to its class definition so that we can create instances with different property values.

5) Close the test movie to return to the authoring environment. With the Actions panel open, select Frame 1 and update the Person class definition as follows:

```
Person = function(name, age){
  this.name = name;
  this.age = age;
  this.legs = 2;
  this.head = new Object()
  this.head.eyes = 2;
  this.head.memories = new Array();
}
```

Just like a regular function definition, our Person class definition now accepts two arguments: `name` and `age`. You'll notice that those same two values are used in the first two lines of the class definition. This enables us to create instances of the Person class that have unique property values.

6) Update the line of script we added in Step 3 to read as shown below (in the first line), and then add the second line shown here below that:

```
person1 = new Person ("Justin", 16);
person2 = new Person ("Derek", 29);
```

These two actions will create two instances of the Person class. These instances have different `name` and `age` values now that the Person class definition has been updated to allow it. We can pass strings, numbers, and even object names to create and set the properties of a new instance.

Because we want to be able to create instances of the Person class easily, from any timeline (without having to enter a target path, just like Flash's built-in objects), we need to make our class definition global.

7) Update the Person class definition as follows:

```
_global.Person = function(name, age){
  this.name = name;
  this.age = age;
  this.legs = 2;
  this.head = new Object()
  this.head.eyes = 2;
  this.head.memories = new Array();
}
```

Notice the addition of `_global` to the first line of the script: This enables an instance of the Person class to be created from any timeline simply by using the following:

```
new Person();
```

If we had not added `_global` and the class definition was defined on, say, the root timeline, you would need to use the following syntax:

```
new _root.Person();
```

> **NOTE** *Even if you use _global to make a class definition accessible to all timelines without using a target path (as just described), individual instances will still exist in the timeline containing the script that created them. Thus, if you create an instance of the Person class named myBuddy and the timeline containing the script for creating that instance exists at _root.myMovieClip, the absolute target path to myBuddy will be _root.myMovieClip.myBuddy. Of course, you can make instances global, if you wish, by using the following syntax when creating them: _global.myBuddy = new Person("Dennis", 27);.*

8) Save your work as class1.fla.

We'll continue to use this file in the following exercise Although we can now create instances of our custom Person class, we still need to do one thing to fine-tune it—and that requires an understanding of the scary-sounding but powerful prototype object.

GENETICALLY PROGRAMMING AN OBJECT BY CUSTOMIZING ITS PROTOTYPE

When a baby is born, we expect to see specific characteristics: a head, two eyes, two ears, two legs, and so forth. These are characteristics we expect to see in *all* babies because they're hard-wired into our genetic code. This same type of logic applies to objects created with ActionScript. While names and ages vary, as they do when creating instances of our Person class, certain characteristics are universal to *all* instances. Let's make another change to our Person class definition in accordance with this logic.

1) Open class1.fla in the Lesson06/Assets folder. With the Actions panel open, select Frame1. Update the lines of script that make up the Person class definition with the following:

```
_global.Person = function(name, age){
  this.name = name;
  this.age = age;
}
Person.prototype.legs = 2;
Person.prototype.head = new Object();
Person.prototype.head.eyes = 2;
Person.prototype.head.memories = new Array();
```

Here, you can see we've moved some of the properties that were formally part of the class definition and attached them to the Person class' prototype object—a special object associated with a class. This object—which is automatically created in the background whenever a new class is defined—contains properties and values that are universal to the class. You can think of this object as sitting right next to the class definition, as a kind of special attachment.

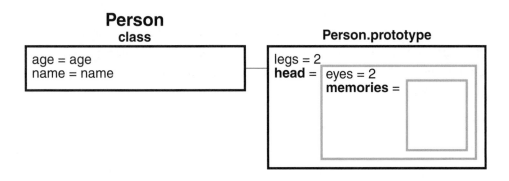

187

All classes of objects, including those built into ActionScript, have an associated prototype object. We will be tinkering with the prototype objects of these classes later in the lesson.

Nothing of value exists in a custom class' prototype object until we script it—which is why we've added three properties to this object (and assigned their values) immediately after the class definition (as shown above). These prototype object properties are automatically *inherited* by all instances of that class, and their values are accessible in the same manner as described earlier. It's important to understand how this prototype object works, so let's look briefly at that.

When a new instance of the Person class is created, the class definition will add two properties to that instance, representing `name` and `age`. The following shows what happens when the value of one of those properties is accessed:

```
myVariable = person1.age;
```

First, ActionScript looks at `person1` and determines whether an `age` property is attached directly to that instance. When it sees that there is (the property was attached when the instance was passed through the class definition), it assigns the value of that property to `myVariable`. Now, let's say that line of script looks like this instead:

```
myVariable = person1.legs;
```

You'll remember that the Person class definition doesn't include a `legs` property; however, `myVariable` will still be given a value of 2. The reason for this is that in this scenario, ActionScript still looks at the instance *first* to determine whether the `legs` property is attached. If not, ActionScript says, "Well, `person1` is an instance of the Person class. Since I can't find the `legs` property on the instance, I'll look at the `Person.prototype` object to see if it exists there." At this point, ActionScript will see that `Person.prototype.legs` has been given a value of 2, and that `person1.legs` thus has a value of 2 as well. ActionScript will subsequently assign that value to `myVariable`.

ActionScript will always look for the property at the instance level first (we'll discuss the term *instance level* in a moment). If it finds one, it quits looking; if it doesn't, it looks at the prototype object of the instance's class. Think of a class' prototype object as a mirror. Any properties attached to it will be reflected in each instance of that class. Even though the instance doesn't actually contain the property, it appears that it does to ActionScript.

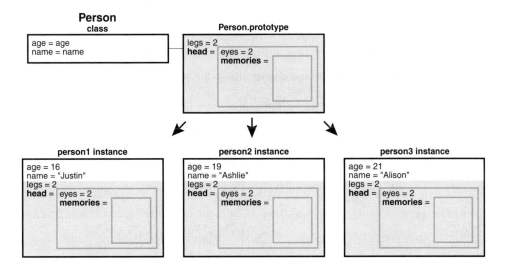

You may be may be thinking that these properties worked just fine as part of the class definition (as in the previous exercise): Why would we want to move them to this prototype object? The reason to do so is that the prototype object enables *class-wide* enhancements—that is, changes to all instances of a particular class. If you change a property value on a class' prototype object, all newly created or existing instances of that class automatically inherit that new value (with one exception, which we'll discuss in a moment). To help you understand this concept a bit better, let's do some testing.

2) Add the following lines of script at the end of the current script:

```
person1 = new Person ("Justin", 16);
person2 = new Person ("Derek", 29);
trace (person1.legs);
trace (person2.legs);
```

The first two lines create two instances of the Person object. The `trace` actions will display the `legs` property value of each instance in the Output window.

3) Choose Control > Test Movie to test the project up to this point:
The Output window will open and display the following:

```
2
2
```

You can see that both `person1` and `person2` share the same value for their `legs` property. However, we can make a class-wide change (that is, change the value for all instances) by adjusting the value of the `legs` property on the `Person.prototype` object. Let's do that.

4) Close the test movie to return to the authoring environment. With the Actions panel open, select Frame 1 and update the value of `Person.prototype.legs` from 2 to 5. Then choose Control › Test movie to test the results again.

The Output window will open and display the following:

```
5
5
```

You can see that by simply changing a single value on the `Person.prototype` object, both `person1` and `person2` both get new values for their `legs` property. If you had 100 instances, each would reflect this new value. Adding, deleting, or updating properties on a class' prototype object causes those changes to be immediately reflected in all instances of that class (with an exception, which we'll discuss in the next section).

So why do we need to be able to set property values in both the class definition and the prototype object? The reason for this is that most object instances have both unique properties and universal properties (ones that they share with instances of the same class). For example, we all have different names and ages (properties you would likely set in the class definition), but we also have certain shared characteristics, such as two legs, a head, and memories (properties you would likely set using the prototype object).

5) Close the test movie to return to the authoring environment. With the Actions panel open, select Frame 1 and change the value of `Person.prototype.legs` back to 2. Save your work as class2.fla.

We'll continue to use this file in the following exercise.

INSTANCE-LEVEL PROPERTIES

As mentioned in in the previous section, when attempting to access a property value—as when assigning `myVariable` the value of `person1.legs` (`myVariable = person1.legs;`)—ActionScript will always look for the specified property at an instance level first. Only after it's looked there will ActionScript check the instance's prototype object. An instance-level property is a property that's set in the class definition when an instance is created, or it's a value set by directly addressing the instance. The `person1` instance we created in the previous exercise has the following properties:

```
name  = "Justin" // instance level
age = 16 // instance level
legs = 2 // prototype level
head = new Object() // prototype level
head.eyes = 2 // prototype level
head.memories = new Array() // prototype level
```

Why is it important to distinguish between instance- and prototype-level properties? When an instance-level property and a prototype level property share the same name, the instance-level property value overrides the prototype property value (though only as it relates to that instance).

For example, the `person1` instance currently gets its `legs` property from the `Person.prototype` object because it wasn't assigned that property at its creation. However, by setting the property value by addressing the instance itself—for example, `person1.legs = 1;`—we create an instance-level `leg` property for `person1`, whose value overrides the prototype value used up to this point. All other instances will still have two legs—except for `person1`, which now only has one. The prototype value still exists for this instance, it's just hidden by the instance-level property with the same name. This could be likened to placing your left hand in front of your right hand. Your left hand (instance level) is all you can see; however, your right hand (prototype level) is still there—it's just hidden from your view.

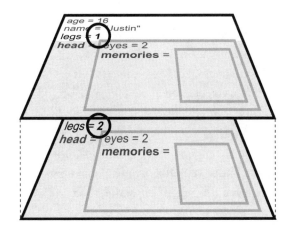

person1 instance

Person.prototype

We can delete the instance-level `leg` property by using the following:

```
delete person1.leg;
```

As a result, `person1` will once again start reflecting the `leg` property (and its value) as set by the Person class prototype object.

Another important aspect of instance-level properties is that they allow instances to have properties in addition to those set in the class definition or inherited by the Prototype. To add such properties, you simply address the instance itself. For example:

```
person2.favoriteFood = "Pizza";
```

At this point, `person2` is the only instance that has a `favoriteFood` property. We could easily add this property to other instances (either by assigning it directly or adding it to the prototype object), but until we do so, `person2` is the only instance that includes the `favoriteFood` property.

NOTE *If we added the property to the class definition, only new instances created from that point forward would be given the property, not existing instances. The reason for this is that the constructor function (class definition) only attaches properties to instances during their creation.*

Instance-level properties allow you to individualize instances without sacrificing the benefits of object classes.

CREATING SUBCLASSES

Our Person class has become quite functional: We can create instances and give them names and ages, and they all inherit properties from the prototype object. But just as in real life, there can be classes of people *within* our Person class: doctors, lawyers, Flash developers, and so on—each a *sub*class of people. These subclasses share the characteristics of the Person class (names, ages, legs, a head), but each has unique characteristics as well. If, for example, you created a Doctor class, it could have unique characteristics such as specialty, the "Dr." title, and so on *as well as* all of the characteristics of the Person class.

1) Open class2.fla in the Lesson06/Assets folder. With the Actions panel open, select Frame1. Remove the two `trace` actions at the end of the script, then add the following:

```
_global.Doctor = function(almaMater){
  this.almaMater = almaMater;
}
Doctor.prototype.title = "Dr.";
```

Here, we've created a constructor function that defines a new class of objects, the Doctor class. Each new instance of this object class is given an `almaMater` property, whose value is sent to the constructor function when an instance is created. We've also given the Doctor class a prototype property named `title`, with a value of "Dr.". Because all doctors share this title (that is, it doesn't change from one doctor to the next), placing it on the prototype object of the Doctor class is appropriate.

192

Doctor
class

almaMater = almaMater

Doctor.prototype

title = "Dr."

Let's create an instance of our new class.

2) Place the following actions at the end of the current script:

```
frankenstein = new Doctor("Transylvania");
trace(frankenstein.almaMater);
trace(frankenstein.title);
trace(frankenstein.legs);
```

The first action creates a new instance of the Doctor class named `frankenstein`. The `trace` actions that follow will output the result.

3) Choose Control > Test Movie to test the project up to this point:

The Output window will opens and display the following:

```
Transylvania
Dr.
undefined
```

You can see that the `almaMater` property is set (that is, an instance-level property was added at the instance's creation) and that the `title` property is set (via the `Doctor.prototype` object); however, the `legs` property does not exist.

Our goal is to make the Doctor class a subclass of the Person class, so that all instances of the Doctor class inherit properties such as `legs`, `head,` and so forth. This does not happen automatically: Somewhere in our script, we must tell ActionScript that the Doctor class is a subclass of the Person class.

4) Close the test movie to return to the authoring environment. With the Actions panel open, select Frame 1 and place the following line of script just above `Doctor.prototype.title = "Dr.":`

```
Doctor.prototype = new Person();
```

This line of script creates a connection between the Doctor and Person classes. It's telling the Doctor prototype object to inherit from the Person prototype object.

As a result, all instances of the Doctor class will reflect the properties not only of `Doctor.prototype`, but `Person.prototype` as well. The converse is not true; Instances of the Person class will only reflect the properties of `Person.prototype`. Doctor is now a subclass of Person, and the Person itself is the *superclass* of the Doctor class.

There's a reason we've placed the above line of script *above* the line assigning the `title` property on the `Doctor.prototype` object. When the above line is executed initially, it in essence wipes the `Doctor.prototype` object clean, replacing all existing properties with those in the `Person.prototype` object. If the `title` property were attached to the `Doctor.prototype` object prior to this happening, it would have been lost. Instead, as our script shows, we add the `title` property to the `Doctor.prototype` object on the very next line, which solves the problem.

At the bottom of the script, you should still see the following `trace` actions, which previously returned (shown in Step 3) the results shown:

```
trace(frankenstein.almaMater);// returned "Transylvania"
trace(frankenstein.title);// returned "Dr."
trace(frankenstein.legs);// returned undefined
```

Let's test the results now.

5) Choose Control › Test Movie to test the project up to this point:

The Output window will open and display the following:

```
Transylvania
Dr.
2
```

You'll see that `frankenstein` now has two legs (whereas before this property was undefined). This is the result of Doctor instances inheriting properties from both the `Doctor.prototype` and the `Person.prototype` objects, as discussed in the previous step. For this reason, `frankenstein` also has a `head`, `memories` in his head, and so on. If you change a `Person.prototype` property now, those changes will be reflected not only in instances of the Person class but in instances of the Doctor class as well (since it's a subclass of the Person object). In essence, when Flash looks for the `legs` property on the `frankenstein` instance (as an instance level property), it doesn't find it. The next place it looks is the `Doctor.prototype` object (because `frankenstein` is an instance of the Doctor class). The property can't be found there either. Finally, Flash looks on the `Person.prototype` object (because Doctor is a subclass of the Person class)—and this is where the `legs` property is found.

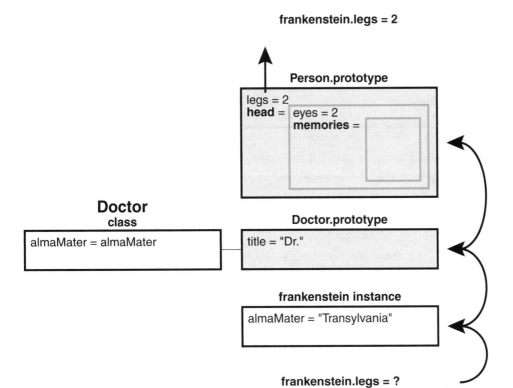

frankenstein.legs = 2

Person.prototype

legs = 2
head = eyes = 2
memories =

Doctor
class

almaMater = almaMater

Doctor.prototype

title = "Dr."

frankenstein instance

almaMater = "Transylvania"

frankenstein.legs = ?

Now you may be wondering about the `name` and `age` properties of the Person class. Since these properties are not part of the `Person.prototype` object, do instances of the Doctor class inherit those? Currently, no. To fix this, we need to update the Doctor class definition.

6) Close the test movie to return to the authoring environment. With the Actions panel open, select Frame 1 and update the Doctor class definition as follows:

```
_global.Doctor = function(name, age, almaMater){
  this.base = new Person(name, age);
  this.name = this.base.name;
  this.age = this.base.age;
  delete this.base;
  this.almaMater = almaMater;
}
```

The first thing you'll notice about the updated Doctor class definition is that it now accepts two *new* values (in addition to `almaMater`, which it had before): `name` and `age`. All three values are used in the lines that follow to create an instance of the Doctor class.

The first line uses the `name` and `age` values passed to this constructor function to create a new instance of the Person class. Yes, the Doctor constructor function is creating an instance of the Person class. As you can see, this instance is given a name/path of `this.base`. As soon as ActionScript sees this line, it will create that instance. As a result, `this.base` is assigned a `name` and `age` property (as all instances of the Person class are). The next two lines in the constructor function set the `name` and `age` property values of the Doctor instance being created (`this.name` and `this.age`) based on the property values that belong to `this.base` (the instance of the Person class created in Line 1.) The fourth line in the constructor function deletes the `this.base` instance, showing that its use was temporary. The fifth line sets the `almaMater` property for the instance being created (as discussed in Step 1).

> **NOTE** *This demonstrates how dynamic constructor functions can be when the need arises: The function can create temporary objects (as shown), do math calculations, perform actions, and more.*

Right about now you may be thinking, Couldn't we have just set up the class definition to read as follows?

```
_global.Doctor = function(name, age, almaMater){
  this.name = name;
  this.age = age;
  this.almaMater = almaMater;
}
```

Although the above would suffice under most circumstances, what would happen if our Person class definition was set up to do something dynamic with the `name` and `age` values passed to it (such as reversing the value of `age` or capitalizing all the characters in the `name` sent to it)? With this latter approach, instances of the Doctor class would not see these affects—a limitation not shared by our initial approach.

7) Update the line that currently reads: `frankenstein = new Doctor("Transylvania");` **to read as follows:**

```
frankenstein = new Doctor("Frankenstein", 85, "Transylvania");
```

This change is necessitated by the addition of the `age` and `name` parameters to the Doctor constructor function (as discussed in Step 6). As a result, when the `frankenstein` instance is created, it is given a `name` value of "Frankenstein", an `age` value of 85, and an `almaMater` value of "Transylvania".

8) Place the following actions at the end of the current script:

```
trace(frankenstein.name);
trace(frankenstein.age);
```

These trace actions will allow us to see the results of our updates. In addition to these, there should be a total of five trace actions at the end of this script (three of which were added in Step 2).

9) Choose Control > Test Movie to test the project up to this point:

The Output window will open and display the following:

```
Transylvania
Dr.
2
Frankenstein
85
```

The `frankenstein` instance is now complete.

Now would be a good time to introduce and examine the `__proto__` property. Every prototype object of a class and every instance of a class has a `__proto__` property value. This value indicates where an instance or class should look when a property cannot be found within itself. Yes, we already know that the `frankenstein` instance will look to the `Doctor.prototype` object in such a case. Thus, `frankenstein.__proto__` is `Doctor.prototype` (instance inherits from a prototype object). Since the Doctor *class* inherits from the Person *class*, `Doctor.prototype.__proto__` is `Person.prototype` (one class' prototype inherits from another class' prototype object). This `__proto__` property is set automatically when an instance or a subclass is created (as we've described thus far), and it can be changed whenever the need arises. For example, if you had created a Lawyer class and wanted to associate `frankenstein` with that class (rather than the Doctor class), you would simply use the following line of script:

```
frankenstein.__proto__ = Lawyer.prototype;
```

Now `frankenstein` can now be considered an instance of the Lawyer class, inheriting the prototype characteristics of that class. In the meantime, his Doctor-specific characteristics (those that he inherited from the `Doctor.prototype` object) have been wiped clean!

Lastly, let's take a look at two important aspects of Object classes: composition and inheritance. Understanding these will help you better conceptualize properties and inheritance. These two concepts can be summed up in two words: *has* and *is*. When you look at the two classes of objects we've created thus far (Person and Doctor), you'll notice the following:

- Person instance *has* a name: This is composition.
- Person instance *has* a head: This is composition.
- Person instance *has* a leg (property): This is composition.
- Doctor instance *is* a Person: This is inheritance.
- Doctor instance *has* a title: This is composition.

These concepts have real-world representations as well. For example:

- A cheeseburger *is* a sandwich *is a* food: This is inheritance.
- A car *has* a body *has* a door *has* a window: This is composition.

Knowing how to look at objects in this manner can go a long way in helping you develop custom classes of objects in the most efficient manner: *Is* relationships are good candidates for subclassed objects, while *has* relationships can cue you to *properties* that a certain class of objects should have.

There are several additional aspects of inheritance, but those are beyond the scope of the book. Now that you understand how custom classes of objects are created (and how they resemble real-world objects), the application development process should be a bit easier to conceptualize. At the end of the next section, we'll bring everything together, explaining the significance of what you've learned and demonstrating how you can put it to use in your projects.

10) Close the test movie to return to the authoring environment. Save your work as class3.fla.
We'll continue to use this file in the following exercise

CREATING CUSTOM METHODS FOR CUSTOM CLASSES

While the objects we've created thus far contain property values that can be evaluated and used in various ways, they cannot perform tasks. To understand what this means, let's take a look at some of the things that Flash's built-in objects can do:

- Movie clip instances can `play()`, `stop()`, `loadMovie()`, `getURL()`, and so forth.
- Sound object instances can `loadSound()`, `setVolume()`, `setPan()`, and so forth.

In contrast, our custom Person and Doctor classes don't do anything besides just sit there. We'll change that in this section by creating methods for our custom classes—enabling instances of those classes to perform useful tasks.

The first thing you need to be aware of is that a method is nothing more than a function that has been assigned to a class by placing it on that class' prototype object. To see how this works, let's begin an exercise.

1) Open class3.fla in the Lesson06/Assets folder. With the Actions panel open, select Frame1. Remove the five `trace` actions at the end of the script, then add the following:

```
Person.prototype.talk = function(){
  trace("Hello, my name is " + this.name + ". I am " + this.age + " years
old.");
}
```

NOTE *Alternate syntax for creating this method would be:*

```
//Define a function first
function soonToBeMethod(){
    trace("Hello, my name is " + this.name + ". I am " + this.age + " years
old.");
}
//Set the function as the talk method of the Person class
Person.prototype.talk = soonToBeMethod;
```

This creates a new method for the Person class of objects. We've made the function a method of the Person class by placing it on the Person class' prototype object.

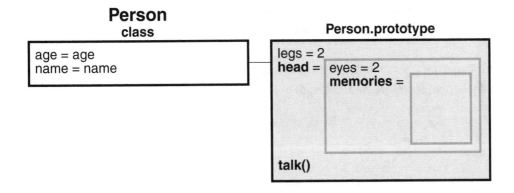

This custom method, named `talk()`, can be used by any instance of that class. In our case, this would be `person1` or `person2`. Thus, either one of these instances can use this method in the following manner:

```
person2.talk();
```

This method does just one thing: It outputs a message to the Output window when the movie is tested. You can see that the `trace` action in the method definition uses the terms `this.name` and `this.age`. When a function is a method, `this` is a reference to the instance that calls the method. Thus, if `person2` calls this method, these could be replaced to read `person2.name` and `person2.age`.

NOTE *When the term `this` is used in a regular function, it refers to the timeline that contains the function definition.*

2) Place the following line of script at the end of the current script:

```
person2.talk();
```

This will cause `person2` to invoke the `talk()` method.

3) Choose Control > Test Movie to test the project up to this point.
The Output window will open and display the following:

```
Hello, my name is Derek. I am 29 years old.
```

While the `talk()` method has enabled instances of our Person class to actually do something, we can customize it a bit further.

4) Close the test movie to return to the authoring environment. With the Actions panel open, select Frame 1 and update the `talk()` method as follows:

```
Person.prototype.talk = function(tone){
  var message = "Hello, my name is " + this.name + ". I am " + this.age + "
years old.";
  if (tone == "scream"){
    trace(message.toUpperCase());
  }else{
    trace(message);
  }
}
```

You'll notice that the method now accepts a parameter named `tone`. The method will operate in one of two ways based on the value of this passed parameter. Let's look at the method's updated definition.

First, a local variable named `message` is created and given an expression as its value. This expression is the same one that was used inside the `trace` actions before.

> **NOTE** *As mentioned in the previous lesson on functions, a local variable is a variable that only has meaning within the function definition where it exists. If we hadn't made `message` a local variable, its value would be accessible by scripts anywhere. As a local variable, it will get deleted as soon as the method finishes executing.*

After you've set the `message` variable's value, you'll notice an `if` statement. This statement says that if the value of `tone` equals "scream", convert the value of `message` to all uppercase characters and then display it in the Output window. If `tone` has any other value, `message` will be output normally. The use of the String object method `toUppercase()` demonstrates how a method from a different class can be used to define the functionality of other methods. Custom methods can contain actions, methods, and so on—practically anything ActionScript offers to facilitate interactivity.

5) Add the following line of script to the end of the current script:

```
person2.talk("scream");
```

This will cause `person2` to invoke the `talk()` method, while passing it a value of "scream". Since the last two lines of script both invoke the `talk()` method (in different ways; one passes it the value "scream"), the Output window will display the results of both.

6) Choose Control > Test Movie to test the project up to this point.

The Output window will open and display the following:

```
Hello, my name is Derek. I am 29 years old.
HELLO, MY NAME IS DEREK. I AM 29 YEARS OLD.
```

Let's look at one more interesting aspect of our `talk()` method.

7) Close the test movie to return to the authoring environment. With the Actions panel open, select Frame 1 and update the `talk()` method calls (last two lines currently on Frame 1) as follows:

```
frankenstein.talk();
frankenstein.talk("scream");
```

```
3      this.age = age;
4  }
5  Person.prototype.legs = 2;
6  Person.prototype.head = new Object();
7  Person.prototype.head.eyes = 2;
8  Person.prototype.head.memories = new Array();
9  person1 = new Person ("Justin", 16);
10 person2 = new Person ("Derek", 29);
11 _global.Doctor = function(name, age, almaMater){
12     this.base = new Person(name, age);
13     this.name = this.base.name;
14     this.age = this.base.age;
15     delete this.base;
16     this.almaMater = almaMater;
17 }
18 Doctor.prototype = new Person();
19 Doctor.prototype.title = "Dr.";
20 frankenstein = new Doctor("Frankenstein", 85, "Transylvania");
21 Person.prototype.talk = function(tone){
22     var message = "Hello, my name is " + this.name + ". I am "
23     if (tone == "scream"){
24         trace(message.toUpperCase());
25     }else{
26         trace(message);
27     }
28 }
29 frankenstein.talk();
30 frankenstein.talk("scream");
```

Line 30 of 30, Col 29

The `talk()` method is actually a method of the Person class, but since the Doctor class is a subclass of the Person class, Doctor class instances can access this method as well—which is why the `frankenstein` instance can use it as shown.

The Doctor class can also have methods unique to it: You would simply place functions on the `Doctor.prototype` object, as demonstrated with the `Person.prototype` object in Step 1.

202

8) Choose Control › Test Movie to test the project up to this point.

The Output window will open and display the following:

```
Hello, my name is Frankenstein. I am 85 years old.
HELLO, MY NAME IS FRANKENSTEIN. I AM 85 YEARS OLD.
```

While our `talk()` method performs a simple task, custom methods can get quite complex.

9) Close the test movie to return to the authoring environment. Save your work as class4.fla.

The knowledge you've gained about object mechanics will prove useful in the sections to follow, as you learn how to extend Flash's prebuilt objects. Although you've seen how objects can be used to organize and work with data, Flash is primarily a visual medium—which means you're probably wondering how objects can help in that realm. You're now ready to make that journey.

WATCHING PROPERTIES

By now you know that you can give objects (including movie clips) properties (also known as variables). In a typical Flash application, the value of these properties can change at any time. And just as with real-world objects, a property change can have a couple of results: Not only is the object with the changed property affected, but a number of other objects can be affected as well, in a chain reaction of changes. For example, assume weather is an object and that the condition of the weather (a property of weather, as in `weather.condition`) went from sunny to rainy (`weather.condition = "rainy";`). As a result, the sky gets dark, car lights come on, and windshield wipers start working. ActionScript employs the `watch()` method to watch various properties (variables, such as `condition` in our example) of objects, so that if a change occurs in the property value, a function can be called so that your project can react to the change. If you were to use this method, it would look something like this:

```
nameOfObject.watch("propertyToWatch", nameOfFunction);
```

If **weather** were the name of a movie clip instance on the main timeline, `condition` were the name of a variable in that movie clip instance, and `watchCondition()` were the name of the function we wanted to invoke when the value of `condition` were changed, the syntax would look like this:

```
_root.weather.watch("condition", watchCondition);
```

NOTE *An object can initiate a watch within itself using* `this.watch("propertyToWatch", nameOfFunction);`.

The `watchCondition()` function that is called would be set up as follows:

```
function watchCondition(id, oldval, newval){
  message.text = id + " used to be " + oldval " but now it's " + newval";
  if (newval == "rainy"){
    sky.gotoAndStop("dark");
    lights.gotoAndStop("on");
    wipers.gotoAndPlay("on");
  }else if (newval == "sunny"){
    sky.gotoAndStop("bright");
    lights.gotoAndStop("off");
    wipers.gotoAndStop("off");
  }
}
```

Notice the `id`, `oldval`, and `newval` parameters, which are passed to the function. These parameters are automatically sent to the function when it is called as a result of the `watch()` method firing. The `id` parameter represents the name (as a string value) of the property being watched; `oldval` represents its old value (before the change), and `newval` represents the new value that caused the `watch()` method to fire. You can see in the above example how these parameter values can be used in the function.

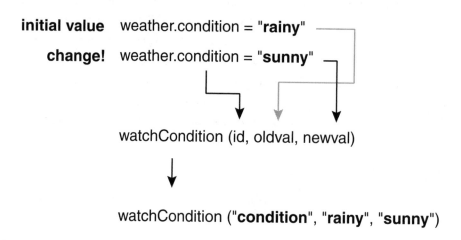

initial value   weather.condition = "**rainy**"

change!   weather.condition = "**sunny**"

watchCondition (id, oldval, newval)

watchCondition ("**condition**", "**rainy**", "**sunny**")

NOTE *Although our example doesn't show it, a reference to* `this` *in the function would be considered a reference to the object whose property is being watched.*

NOTE *You must always define the function that will be called by the watch before you initiate the* `watch()` *method if everything is to function properly. This is because in the parameters of the* `watch()` *method, you identify a function to call when the property changes. You can't specify a function to call if it doesn't exist yet.*

If you no longer want a property to be watched, you can invoke the `unwatch()` method as follows:

```
weather.unwatch("condition");
```

This line of script prevents changes to `condition` from causing the `watchCondition()` function to be called.

The following are some important points to remember about using the `watch()` method:

- The `watch()` method works for most objects in ActionScript that have properties (variables), including custom object instances (as discussed in the previous exercises in this lesson). However, you cannot watch ActionScript's predefined properties, such as `_x`, `_y`, `_alpha`, and so on.

- You can only set one watch for any property. Setting a new watch on the same property will cancel the previous one.

- If you attempt to 'domino' watches—where a watched property is changed, executing a function that changes another watched property, which as a result executes another function that changes another watched property, and so on—you will get unexpected results.

In the exercise that follows, we'll create a scene in which changes to watched properties will affect different elements.

1) Open objectProject1.fla in the Lesson06/Assets folder.

We've already set up most of the elements in this scene so that you can focus on the ActionScript. This scene contains four layers: The Background layer contains the gradient background and the project logo. The Head layer contains two instances of the Head movie clip symbol. The smaller instance is named **smallHead**, and the larger instance is named **bigHead**. (We'll take a closer look at this movie clip in a moment.) The Head layer also contains a text field at the bottom of the stage named **message**. The Buttons layer contains all of the buttons our project will use. There are four buttons to the right of the **bigHead** instance, which we'll use in this exercise: Their instance names are **mouthButton**, **noseButton**, **eyesButton**, and **glassesButton**.

(The remaining buttons, at the top left of the stage, will be used in the exercises that follow.) The Actions layer will contain scripts (which we'll add in the following exercises as well).

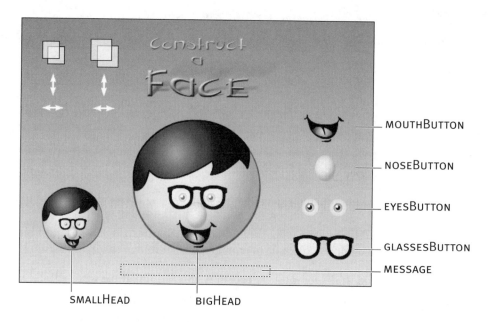

2) Double-click the *bigHead* instance to edit it in place.

The main things to be aware on this clip's simple timeline are four movie clip instances: **glassesClip**, **eyesClip**, **noseClip**, and **mouthClip**. These instances, which are graphical representations of what their names imply, will be made visible and invisible as watched property values are changed. Our project contains two instances of this clip, which we will set up to react in opposite ways. For example, if the **noseClip** instance in the **bigHead** instance is made visible, the **noseClip** instance in the **smallHead** instance will be made invisible.

3) Return to the main timeline. With the Actions panel open, select the *bigHead* instance and add the following script:

```
onClipEvent(load){
  glassesClip._visible = false;
  eyesClip._visible = false;
  noseClip._visible = false;
  mouthClip._visible = false;
  glasses = false;
  eyes = false;
  nose = false;
  mouth = false;
}
```

206

This script uses a `load` event to execute this script as soon as the **bigHead** instance appears in the scene—which it does when the movie begins to play. We will be adding the majority of script for this exercise within this `load` event. For now, let's take a look at the first several lines of our script.

These first four lines will make the instances discussed in the previous step invisible. Thus, **bigHead** will appear faceless upon loading, and the **smallHead** instance will be unaffected (that is, it will have a face) because these actions target the instances in **bigHead** only.

The next four lines create and set variable values. The variable names and values coincide with the current state of the aforementioned movie clip instances. It is these four variables (properties) that will be watched for changes. These are their initial values.

Let's next define the functions that will be called when one of these property values changes.

4) Add the following function definition at the bottom of (but within) the `load` event:

```
function watchGlasses(id, oldval, newval){
 _root.message.text = "I now have " + id + ".";
  glassesClip._visible = newval;
   _root.smallHead.glassesClip._visible = oldval;
    _root.glassesButton.enabled = false;
}
```

We will eventually set up a watch that will execute this function when the value of glasses changes. Notice the three parameters sent to the function of id, oldval, newval: All three of these parameter values are used in the function. The first line in the function will display a message in the **message** text field that makes use of the value of id. Because this function will be set up to watch the value of glasses, id will therefore have a string value of "glasses" when this function is called. The resulting message will read, "I now have glasses." The next line of script makes use of the newval parameter value. In the previous step, we gave glasses an initial value of false; thus, when that value is changed to true (causing this function to execute), newval will have a value of true, which is the new value that the property/variable is being set to. Thus, on the second line, glassesClip._visible is set to true, which will make the **glassesClip** inside of **bigHead** appear. The next line makes use of the oldval parameter to set the visibility of the **glassesClip** in the **smallHead** instance. Since oldval has a value of false (the value of glasses prior to the change), the **glassesClip** will be made invisible in **smallHead**. The last action will disable the **glassesButton** button. While we haven't given this button any functionality yet, it will be used to change the value of glasses, thus executing this function. After it has been used to change the value of glasses, it gets disabled (thus, it can only be used once).

5) Add the following additional function definitions at the bottom of (but within) the load event:

```
function watchEyes(id, oldval, newval){
  _root.message.text = "I now have " + id + ".";
  eyesClip._visible = newval;
  _root.smallHead.eyesClip._visible = oldval;
  _root.eyesButton.enabled = false;
}
function watchNose(id, oldval, newval){
  _root.message.text = "I now have a " + id + ".";
  noseClip._visible = newval;
  _root.smallHead.noseClip._visible = oldval;
  _root.noseButton.enabled = false;
}
function watchMouth(id, oldval, newval){
  _root.message.text = "I now have a " + id + ".";
  mouthClip._visible = newval;
  _root.smallHead.mouthClip._visible = oldval;
  _root.mouthButton.enabled = false;
}
```

These three functions will handle what happens when the value of `eyes`, `nose` and `mouth` change, respectively. As set up in Step 2, these properties all have initial values of `false`; thus, the appropriate function will execute when that value changes to `true`. These functions work in similar fashion to the one discussed in the previous step. The only changes are in the names of the function, the instance they make visible (in **bigHead**) and invisible (in **smallHead**), and which button they disable.

Now that we've created our functions, let's set our watches.

N O T E *Remember that functions used by the `watch()` methods must be defined first—prior to setting a watch, as shown here.*

6) Add the following lines of script at the bottom of (but within) the `load` event:

```
this.watch("glasses", watchGlasses);
this.watch("eyes", watchEyes);
this.watch("nose", watchNose);
this.watch("mouth", watchMouth);
```

These four lines will tell Flash to watch for changes in value to the properties shown, and then which function to execute when it does. The first line sets a watch on the `glasses` property/variable. When the value of this property changes, the `watchGlasses()` function is executed (as discussed in Step 4). Notice the use of `this` in setting the watch. This first line says, in essence, "Watch for changes in the `glasses` property value in 'this' object." If `glasses` were a variable in a different instance, we would simply use the target path to that instance (and/or function) to set the watch as follows:

```
_root.myMovieClip.watch("glasses", _root.myFunction);
```

The remaining three lines of the above script watch the `eyes`, `nose`, and `mouth` properties, and execute the specified function when their values change.

The last thing we need to do is set up our four buttons to change the values of the properties we've been discussing.

7) Select the *mouthButton* button, to the right of the *bigHead* instance, and attach this script:

```
on(release){
  _root.bigHead.mouth = true;
}
```

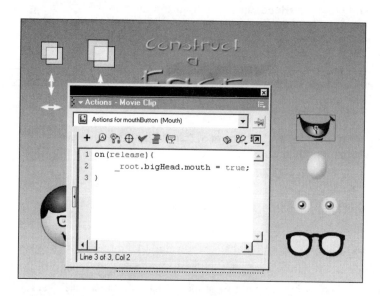

When released, this button will change the value of the mouth property in the **bigHead** instance from false to true, triggering the watch set up in the previous step.

8) Add the following scripts to the remaining buttons:

Attach to the **noseButton** button:

```
on(release){
  _root.bigHead.nose = true;
}
```

Attach to the **eyesButton** button:

```
on(release){
  _root.bigHead.eyes = true;
}
```

Attach to the **glassesButton** button:

```
on(release){
  _root.bigHead.glasses = true;
}
```

These scripts will cause each button to work in similar fashion to the button scripted in the previous step. The only difference is the property value that each button changes.

9) Choose Control > Test Movie to test the project up to this point.

Initially, **bigHead** will appear faceless. Pressing and releasing a button on the right will update the value of `mouth`, `nose`, `eyes`, or `glasses` (depending on which button is clicked), which in turn will cause one of the functions we defined to execute. Several changes will occur in the scene, as scripted within the function.

10) Close the test movie and save your work as objectProject2.fla.

This completes the exercise. You've seen how by using watched properties, a single change in value can trigger a function to execute. Although we could have placed function calls on our buttons to accomplish the same thing, sometimes watching properties, as shown here, can work better—especially if a change in an object's property can have a significant bearing on your project's functionality. It's easy to simply watch that property and change its value as needed rather than worry about function calls. In addition, working with properties is a bit easier to conceptualize.

ENHANCING EXISTING OBJECT METHODS

Flash's built-in object classes (MovieClip, TextField, XML, and so on) come with a number of predefined methods that are useful in most situations. You may at times, however, need more functionality than they can provide. Using what you've learned thus far in this lesson, you can easily extend and enhance these methods to do just about anything imaginable.

You can enhance existing methods in two ways, depending on the type of object you're working with. There are some objects you cannot create instances of: These are singular and universal to your project, and include the Mouse, Key, Selection, and Math objects. You cannot, for example, create an instance of the Mouse object—it's universal, meaning you use the methods of the Mouse object to control the singular mouse that appears on screen. This is in contrast to object classes, for which you can create instances (MovieClip, TextField, and so on). When you cannot create an instance of an object, you can enhance a method of that object, using syntax that resembles the following:

```
MathPlus = new Object();
MathPlus.__proto__ = Math;
MathPlus.oldMax = Math.max;
MathPlus.max = function(x, y, z){
  firstComparison = MathPlus.oldMax(x, y)
  secondComparison = MathPlus.oldMax(firstComparison, z);
  return secondComparison;
}
Object.prototype.Math = MathPlus
trace(Math.max(23, 56, 4));
```

This script will enhance the `max()` method of the Math object, which is normally used to find the higher of two numbers. For example, the following will set `myVariable` to a value of 456, the higher of the two numbers.

```
myVariable = Math.max(456, 23);
```

The above script enhances this method to find the highest of *three* numbers. Here's how: The first line creates a generic object named `MathPlus`. The next line uses the `__proto__` property to make this object instance inherit the functionality of the Math object.

NOTE *We do not use `MathPlus = new Math();` to establish inheritance in this scenario (as shown earlier when setting up inheritance between the Doctor and Person classes) because you cannot create instances of the Math object (thus, `new Math()` has no meaning). If we want the `MathPlus` object to inherit the functionality of the Math object, we must use the `__proto__` property as shown—which does basically the same thing but in a different way. (We discussed this property in Step 9 of the section "Creating a Subclass" earlier in this lesson.)*

At this point, `MathPlus` can do everything the Math object does. Thus, `Math.round(34.7);` and `MathPlus.round(34.7);` will do the same thing. The reason for doing it this way is that we can't directly manipulate the methods of the Math object (or any other object for which you can't create instances). Thus, to get around this, we create a proxy object that inherits the Math object's functionality (`MathPlus`), change the functionality of the proxy object, and then (in a strange twist) tell ActionScript to think of the proxy object (`MathPlus`) object as the new Math object.

On the next two lines of script, two new methods are defined for the `MathPlus` object: `oldMax`, which is given the functionality of the original `Math.max()` method, and `max`, which is set up as the new and improved `max()` method. We needed to create `oldMax` because the new `max()` method still needs the original `max()` method's functionality. However, we needed to give it a new name because our improved method is now named `max`. The function that defines the new `max()` method is set up to accept three values (x, y, z). The new method definition uses these parameter values in various ways to find the highest of the three numbers. In the line after the function definition that sets the new `max()` method's functionality, the new `MathPlus` object is assigned to the Math method of the Object class' prototype (meaning that the `MathPlus` object becomes the new Math object).

212

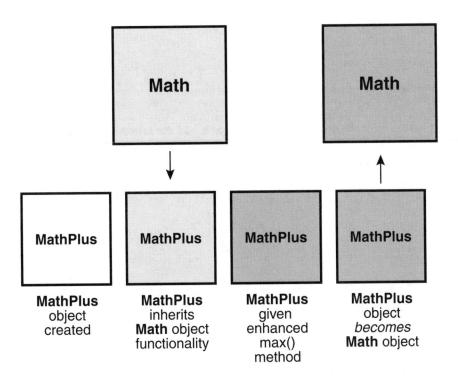

You can also enhance the Math object by extending the `random()` method to generate a random number *between a range*. To do that, you would use the following additional syntax (assuming `MathPlus` has been created and inheritance set as shown on Lines 1 and 2 of the previous example):

```
MathPlus.oldRand = Math.random;
MathPlus.random = function(min, max){
  return MathPlus.floor(MathPlus.oldRand() * ((max - min) + 1)) + min;
}
```

You can see that this syntax is structured similarly to the previous example. Similar syntax is also used to extend methods of the Mouse, Key, and Selection Objects.

Enhancing the methods of classes of objects, where instances can be created (for example, with MovieClip, TextField, and so on) is a bit different—but not by much. In this exercise, we'll extend the `duplicateMovieClip()` method. Using this method, you can already specify which movie clip you want to duplicate, what the duplicate's name will be, and the depth at which the duplicate should be placed (for more information about this action, see Lesson 14, Controlling Movie Clips Dynamically). Now, we'll enhance it so that you can also move the original movie clip (the one that is duplicated) to specified x and y coordinates after the duplication process.

1) Open objectProject2.fla in the Lesson06/Assets folder.

Since we worked on this project in the previous exercise, you should be familiar with the elements it contains. In this exercise, we'll place scripts on Frame 1 as well as on the double-square buttons on the top-left part of the screen.

2) With the Actions panel open, select Frame 1 and add the following script:

```
MovieClip.prototype.oldDuplicateMovieClip =
MovieClip.prototype.duplicateMovieClip;
MovieClip.prototype.duplicateMovieClip = function(name, depth, moveX,
moveY){
  this.oldDuplicateMovieClip(name, depth);
  this._x = moveX;
  this._y = moveY;
}
```

We've placed this script on Frame 1 so that it will execute as soon as the movie begins to play and the `duplicateMovieClip()` method will be enhanced and available for use by movie clip instances from that point forward.

While we couldn't directly manipulate the methods of the Math object (which require a proxy object, as discussed), we can directly manipulate the methods of the MovieClip class because these methods exist on the `MovieClip.prototype` object, which is easy to change.

The first line of the script places all of the functionality of the original `duplicateMovieClip()` method into `oldDuplicateMovieClip`. We did this because we need to retain its functionality when defining how the enhanced version of the method should work. The next line begins the function that defines the new and improved `duplicateMovieClip()` method. This method is set up to accept two additional parameters: `moveX` and `moveY` (which we'll explain how to use in a moment). The first line of the function uses the `oldDuplicateMovieClip()` method to perform the task of the original `duplicateMovieclip()` method—that is, duplicate a movie clip, give it a name, and assign it a depth. The use of `this` in the function definition references the original movie clip instance (the one being duplicated). The next two lines use the `moveX` and `moveY` parameter values to move the original instance the specified amounts. Our new `duplicateMovieClip()` method is ready for use by all movie clip instances!

3) With the Actions panel open, select the smaller of the double-square buttons and attach this script:

```
on(release){
  smallHead.duplicateMovieClip("myHead1", 10, 200, 150);
}
```

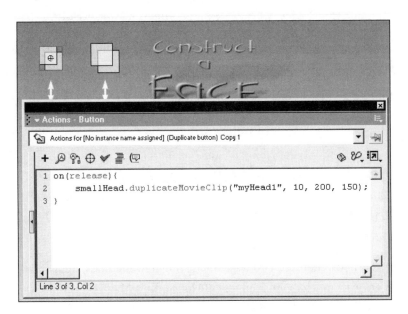

When the button is released the **smallHead** instance is duplicated. The duplicate is given a name of **myHead** and a depth of 10. The last two values represent the values for moveX and moveY, respectively, which are used to move the original instance after the duplication process. Thus, **smallHead** is moved to an x coordinate of 200 and a y coordinate of 150.

4) With the Actions panel still open, select the larger of the double-square buttons and attach this script:

```
on(release){
  bigHead.duplicateMovieClip("myHead2", 20, 100, 200);
}
```

This will duplicate the **bigHead** instance in the same way as described in the previous step.

5) Choose Control > Test Movie to test the project up to this point.

Pressing either of the buttons we just scripted will duplicate the specified instance, then move the instance to the specified x and y coordinates.

This is a simple example of how you can enhance an existing method; however, you can extend them in complex ways as well—and in the process make use of any number of other ActionScript actions. You can extend methods for other classes (for example, TextField, Sound, Color, XML, and so on) in the same way as shown in Step 2 (that is, by changing the functions on their prototype objects).

6) Close the test movie and save your work as objectProject3.fla.

This completes this exercise. We'll continue to build on this project in the following exercise.

DEFINING CUSTOM METHODS FOR PREBUILT OBJECTS

In the previous exercise you learned how to *enhance* an existing method of the MovieClip object class. But what do you do if you need a method that hasn't been invented? You create your own!

As with enhancing methods, there are two ways of creating new methods, depending on whether you're creating one for a built-in *object* (Mouse, Key, Math, Selection) or a *class of objects* (MovieClip, TextField, and so on).

To create a new method for a built-in object (we'll use the Math object again), you would use the following syntax:

```
Math.totalWithTax = function(total, taxPercent){
  convertedPercent = taxPercent / 100;
  totalTax = total * convertedPercent;
  return total + totalTax;
}
trace(Math.totalWithTax(24.00, 6)); // Outputs 25.44
```

Here you can see that to add a method (like the `totalWithTax()` method) to the Math object, you simply attach a function to it as shown. This method is now available for use anywhere in your movie. You would use this same approach to attach new methods to other built-in objects.

In the following exercise, we'll show you how to add a new method to a *class* of built-in objects (primarily the MovieClip object, though you can use the same approach to create new methods for any built-in object class). The method that we create will allow a movie clip instance to be flipped horizontally or vertically—functionality ActionScript doesn't currently provide through a built-in method.

1) Open objectProject3.fla in the Lesson06/Assets folder.

Since we worked on this project in the previous exercise, you should be familiar with its elements. In this exercise, we'll place scripts on Frame 1 as well as on the double-headed arrow buttons on the top-left part of the screen.

2) With the Actions panel open, select Frame 1 and add the following script at the end of the current script:

```
MovieClip.prototype.flip = function(mode){
  if (mode.toLowerCase() == "h"){
    this._xscale = -this._xscale;
  }else if (mode.toLowerCase() == "v"){
    this._yscale = -this._yscale;
  }
}
```

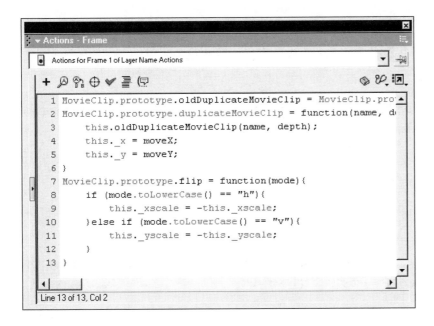

We've placed this script on Frame 1 so that it will execute as soon as the movie begins to play and the `flip()` method will be added to the `MovieClip.prototype` object and available for use by movie clip instances from that point forward. As you can see, this new method is nothing more than a function that accepts a single parameter named `mode`. This will be a value of either "h" or "v", indicating whether flipping should occur horizontally or vertically.

The function uses an `if` statement to determine the value of `mode`, so that it knows how to react. The `if` part of the statement first converts the value of `mode` to a lowercase character then compares that value to "h". If that value is "h", the function knows to do a horizontal flip (which is what the line of script that follows does). It does this by reversing the current `xscale` value of the currently referenced movie clip instance (`this`). Thus, if that value is currently 75, it will be set to -75; if it's –34, it will be set to 34. The function reverses these values by using the minus operator (-). When used as shown, that operator turns a negative value into a positive and vise-versa. Scaling a movie clip instance in this fashion gives the effect of flipping.

The `else` part of the statement deals with what happens if `mode` has a value of "v", indicating a vertical flip. In this case, the `yscale` property of the currently referenced instance is reversed, which gives the effect of flipping it vertically.

NOTE *We converted the value of* `mode` *to a lowercase character to deal with a situation in which we might accidentally use "H" or "V" instead of "h" or "v". "H" does not equal "h"; thus, the conversion helps minimize errors that might occur when attempting to use the new method.*

3) With the Actions panel open, select the up-down arrow button under the smaller of the double-square buttons and attach this script:

```
on(release){
  smallHead.flip("v");
}
```

When the button is released, the **smallHead** instance is flipped vertically.

4) With the Actions panel still open, select the left-right arrow under the button you just added a script to and attach this script:

```
on(release){
  smallHead.flip("h");
}
```

This will flip the **smallHead** instance horizontally.

5) Attach the same actions discussed in the previous two steps to the up-down, and left-right buttons under the larger of the double-square buttons, replacing the `smallHead` reference in the script with `bighead`.

6) Choose Control › Test Movie to test the project up to this point.

Pressing any of these buttons will cause the appropriate movie clip instance to flip.

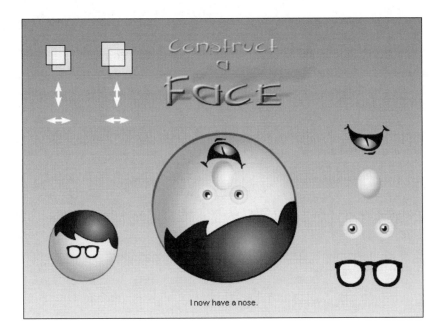

This is just a simple example of how you can add a custom method to a class of objects. You can create methods for other classes (for example, TextField, Sound, Color, XML, and so on) in similar fashion to that shown in Step 2.

7) Close the test movie and save your work as objectProject4.fla.

This completes this exercise. We will build on a slightly modified version of this project in the following exercise.

> **TIP** *For a great resource for custom and enhanced ActionScript methods, visit http://www.layer51.com/proto/.*

> **TIP** *You can create a library of custom methods (or classes of objects for that matter) by writing the necessary code in a standard text editor then saving the file as something like customScript.as (an .as file is understood by Flash to contain Actionscript code). Then, if you needed to use any of these classes or custom methods, you would simply place an* `#include` *action on Frame 1 of your movie, indicating the file name of the .as file containing the script you would like to include (something like* `#include "customScript.as"`*). This action automatically imports and inserts the code in the .as file at the same point as the* `#include` *action (a transparent process). You can create as many different .as files as you want to organize your reusable custom code.*

REGISTERING CLASSES

One of the most exciting enhancements to ActionScript in Flash MX is the ability to easily create subclasses of movie clips. You can now create a custom class (as described earlier in this lesson); use movie clip event handlers, custom methods and more to add functionality to that class; and then associate one or more movie clip symbols in the library with that class so that every instance of that symbol automatically inherits the functionality of the custom class. Although this may seem like a complex concept (since it's so powerful), it's actually quite simple. Let's take a look at an example. To begin with, assume there are a couple of symbols in the library with Linkage identifier names of clipOne and clipTwo.

NOTE *It's important to note that in the following text, when we refer to a* movie clip *or* clip, *we're talking about the master clip in the library.* Movie clip instance *or simply* instance *refer to, well, instances of the clip.*

Next, we'll create a custom class:

```
_global.CustomClass = function(){
}
```

This creates a new class named CustomClass. Next, let's set this class to inherit the functionality of the MovieClip class by placing the following line of script just below the last.

```
CustomClass.prototype = new MovieClip();
```

Next we'll add additional functionality to the class by adding to its prototype object:

```
CustomClass.prototype.onRollOver = function(){
  this._alpha = 50;
}
CustomClass.prototype.onRollOut = function(){
  this._alpha = 100;
}
CustomClass.prototype.onEnterFrame = function(){
  this._rotation += 10;
}
```

Our custom class is now set up to handle interactivity in three ways using event handler methods. Now we want instances of the clipOne movie clip (as mentioned earlier) to inherit this functionality. To do this, we'll use the `Object.registerClass()` method as follows:

```
Object.registerClass("clipOne", CustomClass);
```

Instances of the clipOne movie clip will now react to `rollOver`, `rollOut`, and `enterFrame` events as defined by CustomClass. The reason for this is that they're no long technically considered instances of the MovieClip class of object but rather instances of the CustomClass class of objects.

> **NOTE** *The use of `this` when scripting the functionality of the event handler methods as shown refers to the individual instance that inherits the functionality.*

If you no longer wish instances of the clipOne movie clip to inherit the functionality of CustomClass, you would use the following syntax:

```
Object.registerClass("clipOne", null);
```

The effect of registering and unregistering a movie clip with a custom class is not applied to existing instances of the specified movie clip; it's only applied to *new* instances placed in your movie (either directly on the timeline during development, or dynamically using `duplicateMovieClip()` or `attachMovie()`). Existing instances retain their current functionality. To better understand this, let's take a look at our current example. Say you define CustomClass on Frame 1 of your movie. On this same frame you've placed an instance of the clipOne movie clip and named it **myInstance**. On Frame 2, you place the action that registers clipOne with CustomClass:

```
Object.registerClass("clipOne", CustomClass);
```

At this point, even though we've registered clipOne with CustomClass, the instance of clipOne named **myInstance** (which we placed on Frame 1) does not inherit the functionality of CustomClass because it was created within the movie (on Frame 1) *before* the `registerClass()` method was invoked (on Frame 2). Only instances of clipOne placed manually in the movie on Frame 3 and beyond, or dynamically from that point forward, will inherit the functionality of CustomClass.

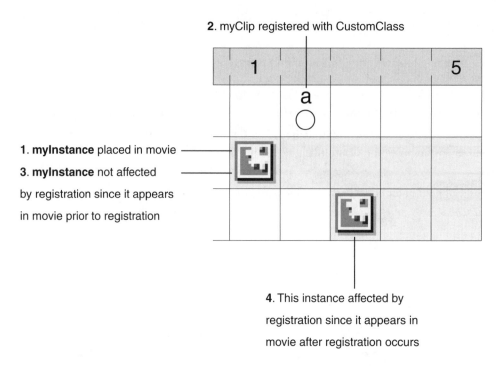

2. myClip registered with CustomClass

1. **myInstance** placed in movie

3. **myInstance** not affected by registration since it appears in movie prior to registration

4. This instance affected by registration since it appears in movie after registration occurs

But what do you do if you want to place instances of clipOne on Frame 1 and have them inherit the functionality of CustomClass on that same frame? We'll address that issue in the exercise for this section. Just be aware of how this works; otherwise, it may lead to hours of frustration.

A movie clip, such as clipOne, can only be registered with one class at a time. If a clip is registered with a class and you then register it with a different class, the latter registration will replace the former.

However, this *does not* mean that you can't register multiple clips with CustomClass— you can! To register additional movie clips with a class, simply invoke additional `registerClass()` methods:

```
Object.registerClass("clipTwo", CustomClass);
Object.registerClass("myClip", CustomClass);
Object.registerClass("anotherClip", CustomClass);
```

These actions cause instances of clipTwo, myClip, and anotherClip inherit the functionality of CustomClass.

222

If you only want to associate individual instances of a clip to a custom class, just set the instance's `__proto__` *property to the prototype object of the custom class, as follows:*

```
myMovieClip.__proto__ = CustomClass.prototype;
```

In this case only the **myMovieClip** *instance will inherit the functionality of CustomClass. When changing the* `__proto__` *property in this manner, the change is immediately reflected in the instance.*

In the following exercise we'll create a custom class, set up the class' functionality, and then assign a movie clip symbol in the library to that custom class using the `registerClass()` method.

1) Open registerClass1.fla in the Lesson06/Assets folder.

Since we worked on this project in the previous exercise, you should be familiar with its elements: however, we've altered its structure slightly from the way we left it in the previous exercise. The project now contains two scenes that are identical but for one thing: Scene1 has a button to navigate the project to Scene 2, and Scene 2 includes a button to navigate to Scene 1. In addition, a `stop()` action has been added to Frame 1 of Scene 1 so that the user can navigate between scenes by using the buttons.

The buttons to the right of the **bigHead** instance have been replaced with four instances of a movie clip symbol named Icons. In the authoring environment, these instances appear the same (as a graphic of a mouth); however, the Icons movie clip actually contains all of the graphics that were previously used for our buttons (eyes, nose, and glasses). By the time we've finished scripting and playing this project, these four instances will appear as the buttons did in the previous exercises.

The reason we've replaced the buttons is because in this exercise we'll be setting up the Icons movie clip—and thus these four instances—to inherit its functionality from a custom class we will create. As a result, the four instances will act like enhanced versions of the buttons we previously used.

These four instances have been given instance names (from top to bottom) of **mouth**, **nose**, **eyes**, and **glasses**. Remember these instance names: They will play an important role later in this project. Most of the scripting we'll add in this exercise will be placed within the Icons movie clip's timeline. Before we do that, however, let's examine this clip in the library.

2) Choose Window > Library to open the Library panel. Locate the movie clip named Icons. Right-click (or Control-click on a Mac) on the clip and choose Linkage from the menu that appears.

This opens the Linkage Properties dialog box. Here you can see that we've given the Icons movie clip an Identifier name of "icons" (to identify it in the library). You'll also note that the option for "Export in first frame" has been selected: This will cause the clip (and in some cases a script it contains) to load before anything else in the movie, including the first frame—functionality that will be important to remember later in the exercise.

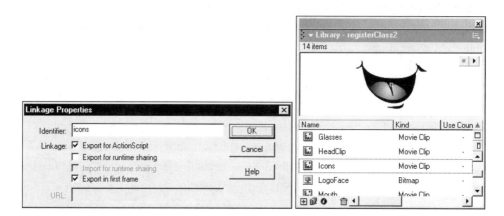

NOTE *For more information about linkage properties settings, see Lesson 14, Controlling Movie Clips Dynamically.*

3) Click Cancel to close the Linkage Properties dialog box. Close the Library panel. On the stage, double-click one of the instances of the Icons movie clip to edit it in place.

This clip's timeline contains four layers, each of which stretches across 40 frames. There are four keyframes (on the Labels layer) labeled **mouth, nose, eyes**, and **glasses**. At each of these frame labels, the graphic on the stage (on the Graphics layer) changes to reflect the name of the label. The Hit State layer has a small transparent square that exists behind the graphic on the Graphics layer. This square serves a very useful purpose, which we will explain shortly. Frame 1 of the Actions layer will contain all of the script we will be adding in this exercise.

4) With the Actions panel open, select Frame 1 and add the following script:

```
_global.Custom1 = function(){
}
Custom1.prototype = new MovieClip()
```

The first two lines create a new class named `Custom1`. As you can see, this class definition is very simple. The next line creates inheritance, where the Custom1 class inherits all of the functionality of the MovieClip class. Next, we'll defining new functionality specific to the Custom1 class.

5) Add this script at the end of the current script:

```
Custom1.prototype.scale = function(amount){
  this._xscale = amount;
  this._yscale = amount;
}
```

This block of code defines a new method for the Custom1 class, called `scale()`, which is set to scale an instance by the value specified by `amount` when the method is invoked. You'll see it used in a moment.

> **NOTE** *The use of* `this` *in the script (and the additions that follow) refer to any instance that inherits this class' functionality. Thus, if there is an instance named* **myClip** *that has the functionality of Custom1,* `myClip.scale(50);` *would scale that instance 50 percent.*

6) Add the following script to the end of the current script:

```
Custom1.prototype.onLoad = function(){
  this.gotoAndStop(this._name);
}
```

This part of the script uses an `onLoad` event handler method to set what instances of this class should do upon loading. A `gotoAndStop()` action will move each instance to a frame label based on its name. The four instances of the Icons movie clip will inherit this class' functionality. These instances—**mouth**, **nose**, **eyes**, and **glasses**—have the same names as the four labels on this movie's timeline. Thus, when an instance loads (`onLoad`), it will look at its name (`this.name`) and go to the frame label that matches its name. As a result, the four instances will appear as the buttons appeared in the previous exercises.

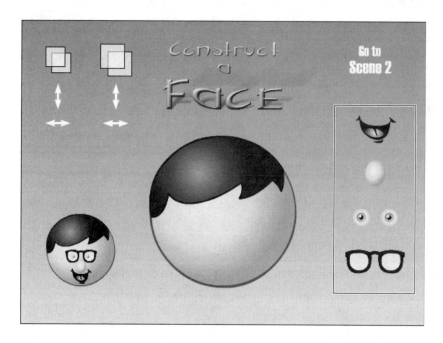

6) **Add this script to the end of the current script:**

```
Custom1.prototype.onPress = function(){
  thisX = this._x;
  thisY = this._y;
  startDrag(this, true);
  this.scale(70);
}
```

This part of the script uses an onPress event handler method to set what instances of this class should do when they are pressed. The first two lines capture the current x and y positions of the instance and store those values in variables named thisX and thisY. (We'll use these in a moment). The next action causes the instance to become draggable. The last action makes use of the scale() method we created for this class in Step 5, so that when the instance is pressed, it becomes 70 percent of its actual size.

7) Add this script to the end of the current script:

```
Custom1.prototype.onRelease = function(){
  stopDrag();
  if (this.hitTest("_root.bigHead")){
    this._x = thisX;
    this._y = thisY;
    _root.bighead[this._name] = true;
    this.scale(100);
    this.enabled = false;
  }else{
    this._x = thisX;
    this._y = thisY;
    this.scale(100);
  }
}
```

This part of the script uses an `onRelease` event handler method to set what instances of this class should do when they are pressed and released. The first thing that occurs when the instance is released is that it ceases to be draggable. Next, an `if` statement is used to take one of two sets of actions, depending on the location of the instance when it's released. The first part of the statement uses the `hitTest()` method to determine if the instance is hitting the **bigHead** instance on the main timeline at the time it's released. If it is, then five actions are executed. The first two will set the x and y position of the instance to the values of `thisX` and `thisY`, respectively, moving the instance back to its position when originally pressed. The next action uses the instance name to set a property value in the **bigHead** instance to `true`. Thus, if the just-released instance has an instance name of **nose**, this line of script would be evaluated to read as follows:

```
_root.bigHead.nose = true;
```

This changes the value of the `nose` property in the **bigHead** instance, which you'll remember is a watched property. This will cause the face to gain a nose as scripted in an earlier exercise.

The following action scales the instance back to its original size. And the last action disables the instance so that the `onPress` event handler method (as it relates to this instance) can't be triggered again.

227

If the `else` part of the statement executes, this means that the instance was not hitting the **bigHead** instance when it was released. In this case, only three actions execute. They simply snap the instance back to its original position and scale it back to its original size. When this occurs, the instance can be pressed and dragged again. When released, the aforementioned `if` statement will execute again and take the appropriate action.

The functionality of the class is now complete. We simply need to associate the Icons movie clip with this class so that instances of that movie clip inherit this class' functionality.

8) Place the following line of script at the end of the current script:

```
Object.registerClass("icons", Custom1);
```

This will register instances of the Icons movie clip (with a Linkage identifier name of "icons") to inherit the functionality of the Custom1 class we just set up.

9) Choose Control › Test Movie to test the project to this point.

As soon as it begins playing, you'll notice a problem with the way our project is functioning. The four instances of the Icons movie clip haven't seemed to inherit the functionality of Custom1, as we set up. If you press the Go to Scene 2 button, you'll notice that the four instances in that scene *have* inherited the functionality of the Custom1 class. If you press the Go to Scene 1 button, the instances that weren't functioning properly before are now. If you go back to Scene 2, then back to Scene 1, you'll see that all of the instances are still working. The `registerClass()` method is not taking effect in Scene 1 when the movie initially plays, but it does in all subsequent scene changes. Let's fix the problem and then discuss why it's occurring.

10) Close the test movie to return to the authoring environment. You should return to the Icons movie clip timeline. With the Actions panel open, select Frame 1 and move all of the code you added in the previous steps below the `#initclip` action but before the `#endinitclip` action, as shown:

```
#initclip
//code added in previous steps
#endinitclip
```

These actions are used to enclose what is known as an *initialization code block*. Before we explain what this is, let's look at how the movie now functions.

```
1  #initclip
2  _global.Custom1 = function(){
3  }
4  Custom1.prototype = new MovieClip()
5  Custom1.prototype.scale = function(amount){
6      this._xscale = amount;
7      this._yscale = amount;
8  }
9  Custom1.prototype.onLoad = function(){
10     this.gotoAndStop(this._name);
11 }
12 Custom1.prototype.onPress = function(){
13     thisX = this._x;
14     thisY = this._y;
15     startDrag(this, true);
16     this.scale(70);
17 }
18 Custom1.prototype.onRelease = function(){
19     stopDrag();
20     if (this.hitTest("_root.bigHead")){
21         this._x = thisX;
22         this._y = thisY;
23         _root.bighead[this._name] = true;
24         this.scale(100);
25         this.enabled = false;
26     }else{
27         this._x = thisX;
28         this._y = thisY;
29         this.scale(100);
30     }
31 }
32 Object.registerClass("icons", Custom1);
33 #endinitclip
```

11) Choose Control > Test Movie to test the project to this point.

As soon as the project begins playing, you'll see that the four instances on the right are now functioning properly: You can press and drop them as scripted. They have all the functionality of the Custom1 class. If you navigate to Scene 2 you can see that the instances on that scene work properly as well. So what happened?

In the first test of our movie, the effect of registering the Icons movie clip symbol with the Custom1 class obviously didn't happen with the four instances that were initially loaded when the movie first played. To understand why, you need to look at the flow of how things are occurring when the movie first plays. The following is a breakdown of that flow:

1) Movie (SWF) loads and initializes.

2) Frame 1 loads.

3) Instances on Frame 1 are created (including four instances of Icons clip).

4) Actions on Frame 1 of the main timeline execute.

5) Frame 1 actions on *instances* execute. (This is where the actions that define Custom1 exist. This is also where the `registerClass()` method is invoked.)

6) New instances of the Icons movie clip from this point forward have the functionality of the Custom1 class.

By examining this flow, we can see that the initial four instances were not functioning properly because they were appearing on the stage (third step in the flow) *prior* to being registered to Custom1 (fifth step in flow). You'll remember that we mentioned earlier that the effect of registering and unregistering a movie clip with a custom class is not applied to existing instances of the specified movie clip, only *new* instances placed in your movie. Existing instances retain their current functionality. Because the initial four instances in our movie are created in the third step of the flow, they are considered existing instances by the time the registration process occurs in the fifth step of the flow—and thus they didn't work as expected. But what about the instances in Scene 2 of our initial test? They worked as expected because navigating to that scene could be thought of as the seventh step in the flow. Registration had occurred, so the instances in that scene would be affected by it. Navigating back to Scene 1 as we did could be thought of as the eighth step in the flow. Even though we returned to the scene where the initial instances didn't work properly, at the point we returned to the scene, registration had occurred—and thus the instances now functioned properly. This explains why our initial test worked the way it did. But how did the actions we added in the previous step solve the problem?

In order for the initial four instances to inherit the functionality of Custom1, we needed a mechanism to execute the registration process prior to Frame 1 loading and the instances being created (second and third steps in flow). The `#initclip` and `#endinitclip` actions provide us with the means to do this. These are special movie clip-only actions (that is, they can only be used on Frame 1 of a movie clip) that allow you to control the way your movie initializes—and thus the order in which actions are executed. Here's how they work.

You'll remember that the Icons movie clip in the library was set to "Export in first frame" in the Linkage Properties dialog box (see Step 2 of the exercise). This setting means that the clip will load into memory even before Frame 1. By using `#initclip` and `#endinitclip` on Frame 1 of the Icons clip as we have, we're telling Flash to do something extra at that time. We're telling it to execute any script between these two actions. Thus, the script gets executed *prior* to Frame 1 of the main timeline loading. This changes the flow we discussed earlier to look like this:

1) Movie loads and initializes.

2) Actions between `#initclip` and `#endinitclip` are executed. (This is where the actions that define Custom1 exist. This is also where the `registerClass()` method is invoked, registering instances of the Icons clip to the Custom1 class.)

3) New instances of the Icons movie clip from this point forward have the functionality of the Custom1 class.

4) Frame 1 loads.

5) Instances on frame 1 are created (including four instances of Icons clip)

6) Actions on Frame 1 of the main timeline execute.

7) Frame 1 actions on instances execute (any actions outside of the `#initclip` and `#endinitclip` actions).

As a result, the registration process now occurs prior (second step in flow) to the instances on Frame 1 being created (fifth step in flow). The registration process is now successful on those initial four instances on Frame 1, as our tests indicated.

You don't need to script the creation of a custom class and the registration of a movie clip to that class in the way that we've demonstrated in this exercise—it's usually just the most efficient way of doing so. As long as you understand how the way your movie executes scripts affects the registration process, you're free to do as you wish.

NOTE *All of the components included with Flash use the initialization scheme demonstrated here (using `#initclip` and `#endinitclip`) to achieve their functionality. You would do well to follow this scheme when creating custom components of your own.*

If you deselect the "Export in first frame" option on the Linkage Properties dialog box for a clip that contains actions between #initclip and #endinitclip, instead of being executed before Frame 1 of the movie, that code will instead be executed before the frame that contains the first instance of the clip. For example, if the first instance doesn't appear until Frame 47, the code is executed before Frame 47 loads. As a result, the instance(s) on Frame 47 will be properly registered (as just demonstrated).

To help you understand how this all works, let's add a couple of final scripts to our project.

12) Close the Test movie to return to the authoring environment. Navigate to Scene 1. Choose Window > Library to open the Library panel, and find the HeadClip movie clip symbol in the library. Right-click (or Control-click on a Mac) that symbol and choose Linkage from the menu that appears. When the Linkage Properties dialog box appears, check the Export for ActionScript option and give this clip an identifier name of headClip.

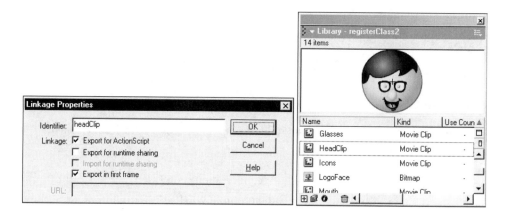

This clip is the clip of the head in the scene. We needed to give it an identifier name so that we could register instances of it to inherit functionality from another simple class we will define next.

13) **With the Actions panel open, select the Go to Scene 2 button and add the following script within the** `on(release)` **event handler just above where it says** `nextScene();:`

```
_global.Custom2 = function(){
}
Custom2.prototype = new MovieClip();
Custom2.prototype.onEnterFrame = function(){
  this._rotation += 5;
}
Object.registerClass("Icons", Custom2);
Object.registerClass("HeadClip", Custom2);
```

The first six lines create a new class named Custom2 and set it up so that instances of it will spin 5 degrees with each `enterFrame` event that occurs. The last two lines register the Icons and HeadClip movie clips with the Custom2 class so that instances of those clips created after the button-press will inherit the functionality of the Custom2 class. Notice we've placed these actions *before* the `nextScene()` action: This is to register the clips *before* moving to the next scene, where instances of these clips (which exist in that scene) are created. If we placed the script after the `nextScene()` action, its flow would change so that the movie would move to the next scene first, the instances would be created, then the clips would get registered. This means that the instances in that scene would be created prior to registration—and thus the registration would have no effect on them initially. By setting it up so that registration occurs before moving to the next scene, registration occurs before the instances in that scene are created—and thus they're registered as intended.

When the button is pressed and this script is executed, the registration of the Icons clip to the Custom2 class (as shown in Line 7 above) will wipe out its initial association with the Custom1 class (as set up and discussed in the previous exercises). Thus, instances on the Icons clip in Scene 1 will initially have the functionality of the Custom1 class, but once this button is pressed, subsequent instances will have the functionality of Custom2 (in addition to instances of the HeadClip movie clip).

This script demonstrates how a custom class can be defined, and that registration can happen anywhere in your movie. As long as you're aware of the flow of how registration occurs, you're free to implement its use just about any way you choose.

14) Choose Control > Test Move to test the project up to this point.

When the movie plays, the instances to the right of **bigHead** have the functionality of the Custom1 class. Press the button to navigate to Scene 2, and those instances, as well as the instances of the HeadClip movie clip, now have the functionality of the Custom2 class. You can no longer drag and drop them; they simply spin around, as defined by the Custom2 class.

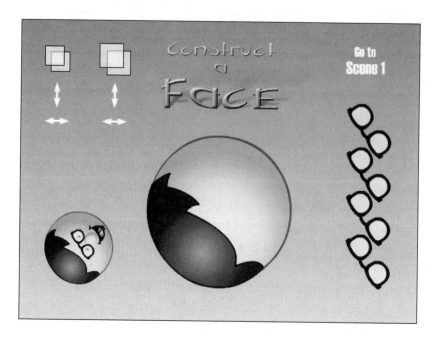

15) Close the test movie and save your work as registerClass2.fla.

Believe it or not, this completes this lesson. It's been a long lesson, but you now have a very thorough knowledge of objects, inheritance, classes, subclasses, methods and more. You're well equipped to tackle the development of more complex projects. This understanding will also help you in the remaining lessons in this book.

WHAT YOU HAVE LEARNED

In this lesson, you have:

- Learned why objects are useful (pages 172–181)

- Created a custom class of objects (pages 182–186)

- Worked with the prototype object of a class in order to extend instances of that class (pages 187–192)

- Created a subclass of objects (pages 192–198)

- Learned about object inheritance (pages 197–198)

- Created new object methods for custom objects as well as Flash's built-in objects (pages 198–203)

- Learned how to watch the properties of an object in order to easily make changes in a scene when an object's property value changes (pages 203–210)

- Enhanced the existing methods of Flash's built-in objects (page 211)

- Registered movie clips to a class to make them inherit specific functionality (pages 220–234)

using
dynamic data

When using Flash to create an application, you can easily enter information directly onto the stage using the Text tool. Text that you enter in this way is said to be *hard coded* because it's permanent once the SWF file is published. If you want to alter data that's hard coded into your Flash application, you must edit the Flash source file—a cumbersome and unnecessary process since Flash lets you define areas where text can be displayed *dynamically*. Instead of being set when the SWF is published, dynamic data is processed and stored *while* the SWF file is running, which means you can change it as often as you want. Dynamic data can be user-supplied information, data loaded from another file, or even information you can't control, such as the current time. You can use this type of data to display information, make decisions, manipulate the position of movie clips, and much more.

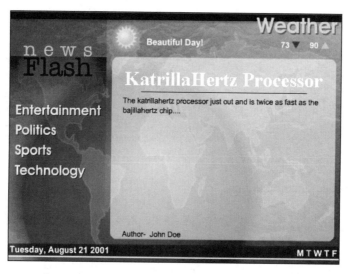

The weather and news stories of our project will be generated using structured, dynamic data.

In this lesson, you'll build a simple news Web site to learn how to use dynamic data. You'll start by creating the objects and variables that store information for this site. Then you'll create the arrays to store groups of related information. Once the information structure is complete, you'll create text fields on the stage to display this information.

WHAT YOU WILL LEARN

In this lesson, you will:

- Learn the power of dynamic data

- Create text fields

- Create variables

- Create arrays

- Store information in objects

- Retrieve information from storage dynamically

APPROXIMATE TIME

This lesson takes approximately 1 hour to complete.

LESSON FILES

Media Files:

None

Starting File:

Lesson07/Assets/newsFlash1.fla

Completed Project:

newsFlash5.fla

CREATING VARIABLES

Each timeline in your project can contain its own set of variables—containers, so to speak, for storing information (data). When you create variables, you must give them names—monikers you cannot change, though you can alter their contents. The following is the syntax for creating a variable:

```
myFullName = "Jobe Makar";
```

The ActionScript to the left of the equals sign represents the variable name; the portion to the right represents its *value*.

NOTE *You can name a variable anything you choose, as long as you follow these simple rules: It must begin with a character, and it cannot contain spaces, special characters (@, #, $, %, and so on), or punctuation marks.*

TIP *Name your variables according to the data they contain—for example,* numberOfDays, *favoriteDogsName,* totalTax, *and so on—so you can remember and use them easily throughout your project.*

Once you've created a variable and assigned it a value, you can use that value in any script simply by referencing its name. Take a look at the following:

```
favoriteNumber = 66;
```

This creates a variable named favoriteNumber and assigns it a value of 66. To use that value in a script, you would use syntax similar to the following:

```
on (release) {
  gotoAndPlay (favoriteNumber); // Moves the timeline to frame 66
    cat._xscale = favoriteNumber; // Scale cat movie clip instance  66%
vertically
  }
```

As you can see, variables derive their power from universally available data—that is, information that can be used in any script. If the value of your variable changes, the scripts that use it will execute differently, since some of the actions are based on the current value of that variable.

Data Storage	Scripts

myFavoriteNumber = 66	gotoAndStop (myFavoriteNumber);
	
	cat._xscale = myFavoriteNumber;
	
	if (userInput > myFavoriteNumber);
	   message = "Lower it, buddy!';
	} else {
	   message = "That's fine!";
	}

There are three main types of variable values:

- String
- Boolean
- Number

A *string* is a text value. For instance, `myFullName = "Jobe Makar"` has the string value "Jobe Makar." Strings are most often used to store text, such as `latestNews = "We just got a new dog!"` String values are defined using quotation marks (""). Thus, the syntax `myFavoriteNumber = "27"` assigns a *text* value of "27" to `myFavoriteNumber`, not a number value of 27.

A *Boolean* value is a `true` or `false` value such as the following:

```
playMusic = true;
```

TIP *In ActionScript, `true` has a numerical value of 1 and `false` has a numerical value of 0. Choosing to use true/false or 0/1 when assigning Boolean values is a matter of preference.*

In programming, Boolean values are often used to indicate whether something is on or off: A script can look at the Boolean's current state (on or off, true or false) and act accordingly. For example, if you were to create a music toggle button for a Flash movie, you might want to set a Boolean variable to store the music's state—on or off (`musicPlaying = true` or `musicPlaying = false`). You could attach a script to the button so that when pressed, it would check to see if the music was on or off (`true` or `false`). If the music were currently on (`musicPlaying = true`), the idea would be to turn the music off and then switch the value of the variable to `false`. If the music were off (`musicPlaying = false`), the music would need to be turned on and the value of the variable set to `true`. Since the value of `musicPlaying` is being switched between `true` and `false` with each successive button click, the script on the button would evaluate its current value and turn the music on or off.

> **NOTE** *In Lesson 9, Conditional Logic, we'll cover Boolean values (and their uses) in more depth.*

A *number* value is just what it sounds like, a number. Numbers are used to store numeric values—often for mathematical use. You can use numeric values for people's ages, for scores in a game, and to track the number of times someone has clicked a button—to name just a few uses. The following demonstrates how you would create a variable and assign a number value to it:

```
radius = 32;
```

Instead of assigning direct values (or *literals*)—for example, 32, "dog," or something else—to variables, you can use an expression to set a variable's value. An *expression* is a phrase—or a collection a variables, numbers, text, and operators—that evaluates to a string, number, or Boolean value. For example:

```
bottlesOfBeerOnTheWall = 99;
oneFellDown = 1;
bottlesLeft = bottlesOfBeerOnTheWall - oneFellDown;
```

The third line in this script uses an expression to set the value of `bottlesLeft`. The expression substitutes the values of the variables (99 and 1) and then performs a subtraction. The end result is that the variable `bottlesLeft` is assigned a value of 98. It's important to note that depending on how the expression is structured, it will result in a string, Boolean, or number value.

When using expressions to set variable values, the expression doesn't have to be lengthy. Take a look at the following example:

```
someone = "Jobe Makar";
coffeeBoy = someone;
```

In this example, a variable called `someone` is created in the first line of ActionScript. In the second line, the value of the `coffeeBoy` variable is set to the string "Jobe Makar" by referencing the value of `someone`. If the value of `someone` changes at a later time, `coffeeBoy` will not reflect the change.

> **NOTE** *A variable can also gain its value as the result of a function. For more on this, see Lesson 5, Using Functions.*

A Flash project can contain many timelines, each with its own set of dynamic data (variables, arrays, and so on). The timeline where dynamic data resides depends on which timeline it was placed when it was created. The following ActionScript creates a variable named myVariable in the current movie:

```
myVariable = 100;
```

The following creates a variable named myVariable and places it on the root, or main, timeline:

```
_root.myVariable = 100;
```

Notice the use of a target path in this variable's creation. By using target paths in this manner, you can create or access data on a specific timeline.

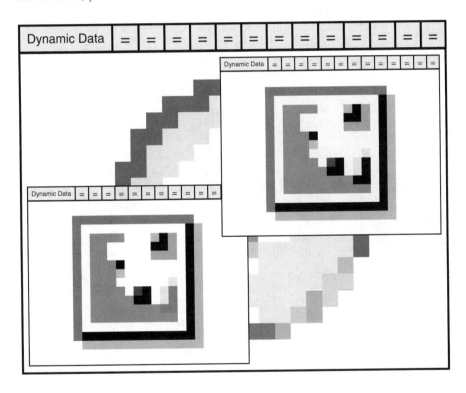

TIP *If a project is not working as it should, check for errors in target paths to pieces of data. A single line of script that tries to access a piece of data on an incorrect timeline can cause major problems in your applications.*

Since dynamic text fields can be used to display the value contained in a particular piece of data, in this exercise you'll set and use variables that will ultimately control what's displayed on the screen for the news site project.

1) Open newsFlash1.fla in the Lesson07/Assets folder.

This file currently contains no actions, but the frame and movie clip structure have already been created.

There are three frame labels on the main timeline: initialize, refresh, and sit. The first label, initialize, is where you'll create the data for this site. The next label, refresh, will contain actions used to pull out the data to be displayed in various places on screen. And the final frame, sit, is just a place where the playhead can rest until we need the screen to change its display again.

Move to the refresh frame label, and you'll see that graphics have already been created and inserted. The screen doesn't yet contain any text fields to display data.

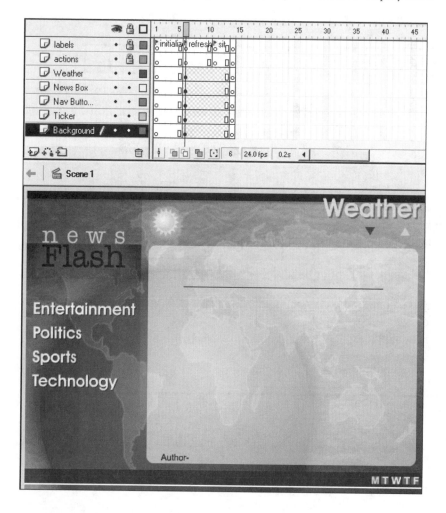

2) Select Frame 1 of the Actions layer on the main timeline. Open the Actions panel and enter the following ActionScript:

```
// ----Monday--------
monday = new Object();
monday.date = "Monday, August 20 2001";
// ----Tuesday--------
tuesday = new Object();
tuesday.date = "Tuesday, August 21 2001";
```

To structure the data for this application, you'll use objects—each of which will be named for a different day of the week and will store all of the news for that day accordingly. Note that we only discuss the ActionScript for Monday and Tuesday because the ActionScript for the rest of the week works in the same way.

By entering the above ActionScript on Frame 1 of the timeline, you create two objects, `monday` and `tuesday`. You also add a date variable (or *object property)* on each object to store each day's date.

3) Save your work as newsFlash2.fla.

You've created the variables needed thus far. You'll create more variables in a later exercise.

CREATING ARRAYS

Suppose you have a guest list for a party: You can store that information in ActionScript with variables like the following:

```
name1 = "John Smith";
name2 = "Kelly McAvoy";
name3 = "Chris Taylor";
name4 = "Tripp Carter";
```

If Kelly tells you she can't make it to your party, besides being upset that only three people will be attending, you'll have to rename the variables beneath her name and shift them up your list. You can simplify this tedious task—as well as many other similar data storage and manipulation chores—by using *arrays*.

Think of arrays as supervariables: While a regular variable can only contain a single value, an array can contain multiple values—which means you could store that entire guest list in a single array.

However, you must create an array in order to use it. Since arrays are objects, you use the Array object constructor method to create them. The syntax to create an array is as follows:

```
myArray = new Array();
```

You can populate an array with values (separated by commas) when you create it, as in the following:

```
guestList = new Array("John Smith","Kelly McAvoy","Chris Taylor","Tripp Carter");
```

Or you can use an alternative syntax:

```
guestList = ["John Smith","Kelly McAvoy","Chris Taylor","Tripp Carter"];
```

Each value in an array is identified by an index number—0, 1, 2, and so on—that denotes its position in the array. In the array we just created, "John Smith" has an index number of 0, "Kelly McAvoy" has an index number of 1, and so on. To access a value in an array, you would use the following syntax:

```
myFavoriteGuest = guestList[1];
```

Here, the variable myFavoriteGuest is assigned a value of "Kelly McAvoy" because this is the value that exists at index position 1 in our guestList array.

The guestList array was created with four elements. You can add or modify elements at any time by referencing the specific element in the array. For instance, the following will update the value at index 2 from "Chris Taylor" to "Kris Tailor":

```
guestList[2]="Kris Tailor";
```

An array element can contain any data type, including strings, numbers, and Boolean values, as well as entire objects. An array element can even contain another array. You'll learn more about arrays and methods of the Array object in later lessons. The following exercise—in which you'll use arrays to store groups of related information for each day of the week—represents just the beginning.

1) With newsFlash2.fla still open, select Frame 1 of the Actions layer. Add the following ActionScript just below the `monday.date="Monday, August 20 2001` **variable set:**

```
monday.weather = new Array();
monday.weather[0] = "rainy";
monday.weather[1] = "Very wet";
monday.weather[2] = 85;
monday.weather[3] = 62;
```

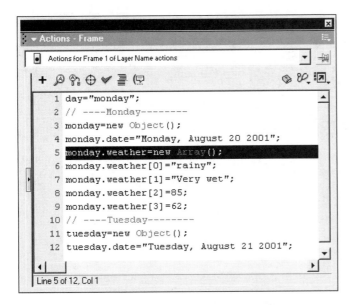

You have created an array called `weather` that's used to store weather data. The array is on the object `monday`. Remember: You'll store all information pertaining to Monday on the `monday` object.

On the frames that contain graphics, you'll see a small weather icon (which currently displays the sun). This icon is a movie clip instance whose timeline contains three frame labels that hold weather icons that correspond to three different weather conditions. The frame labels are **sunny, rainy**, and **stormy**. The value of the first element (the 0th index) of the `weather` array will later be used to send this movie clip instance to the correct frame. Here it's set to "rainy" because Monday is supposed to be rainy. The second element of the `weather` array contains a blurb about Monday's weather, which will later be displayed on the screen.

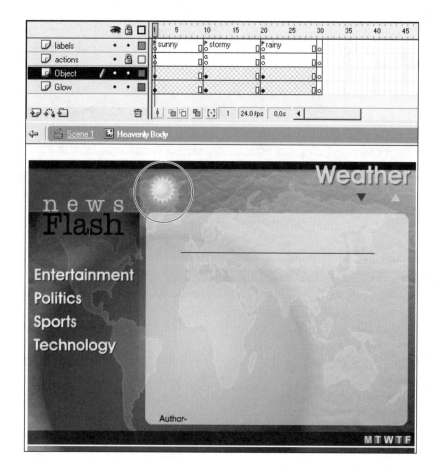

The high and low temperatures for Monday are stored in the third and fourth elements of the `weather` array, respectively. These values will be accessed later so that they can be displayed on the news page.

You have just created an array that stores four pieces of related information in an easily accessible way.

2) With Frame 1 still selected, insert the following ActionScript after `tuesday.date="Tuesday, August 21 2001",:`

```
tuesday.weather = new Array();
tuesday.weather[0] = "sunny";
tuesday.weather[1] = "Beautiful Day!";
tuesday.weather[2] = 90;
tuesday.weather[3] = 73;
```

Here we have created another array named weather, only this array is on the tuesday object. It contains weather information pertaining to Tuesday. The first element of this array now contains the value "sunny" so that the weather icon movie clip instance will display a sun. The value of each array element here is different from that of the weather array for Monday, but the index numbers of corresponding values are the same: Although the high temperatures for Monday and Tuesday differ, they're both stored at the Number 2 index position in each array.

Now that you've created and structured your weather data, it's time to create and structure some news stories.

3) Create arrays to contain news articles for individual categories by entering the following ActionScript just below monday.weather[3]=62**:**

```
monday.entertainment = new Array();
monday.entertainment[0] = "MTV is 20!";
monday.entertainment[1] = "The popular TV network MTV has now been on the
air for 20 years…";
monday.entertainment[2] = "Jobe Makar";
monday.politics = new Array();
monday.politics[0] = "Jesse Ventura Wins";
monday.politics[1] = "Former WWF wrestler Jesse Ventura is elected governor
of Minnesota…";
monday.politics[2] = "Happy Camper";
monday.sports = new Array();
monday.sports[0] = "Head Tennis";
monday.sports[1] = "The Head Atlantis tennis racquet is one of the most
popular racquets in history…";
monday.sports[2] = "Jane Doe";
monday.technology = new Array();
monday.technology[0] = "BajillaHertz Processors!";
monday.technology[1] = "The bajillaHertz processor has just hit the shelves
and is faster than light…";
monday.technology[2] = "John Doe";
```

This news site can display four sections of stories: Entertainment, Politics, Sports, and Technology (as denoted by the navigation buttons on the left of the screen). For each of these sections, we've created an array and stored information about one article for that Monday. In the first section of this step, we created an array called entertainment. The first element of the entertainment array stores the news story's headline; the second element contains the actual news article; and the third element stores the name of the author. The politics, sports, and technology arrays contain the same type of information (headline, story, and author) at the same index positions.

Although this information will be accessed on a later frame, by building a logical object-oriented storage structure for it now, you ensure that it will be easy to access when needed.

4) Add this news article ActionScript just after `tuesday.weather[3]=73`**:**

```
tuesday.entertainment = new Array();
tuesday.entertainment[0] = "Amazing Sci-Fi";
tuesday.entertainment[1] = "Sentrillion Blazers is the must see sci-fi movie
of the year!...";
tuesday.entertainment[2] = "Jobe Makar";
tuesday.politics = new Array();
tuesday.politics[0] = "Tax Refund";
tuesday.politics[1] = "Bush issues large tax refund...";
tuesday.politics[2] = "John Doe";
tuesday.sports = new Array();
tuesday.sports[0] = "Ryder Cup Begins";
tuesday.sports[1] = "The European golf tournament you have been waiting for
has just begun...";
tuesday.sports[2] = "Jane Doe";
tuesday.technology = new Array();
tuesday.technology[0] = "KatrillaHertz Processor";
tuesday.technology[1] = "The katrillahertz processor just out and is twice
as fast as the bajillahertz chip...";
tuesday.technology[2] = "John Doe";
```

This ActionScript stores the headlines, stories, and authors for the four news sections on Tuesday. The array names are the same as they were for Monday; the only difference is the information stored. Tuesday's information structure is exactly the same as that for Monday.

5) Save your work as newsFlash3.fla.

You have now created the information storage structure for your news site. Because all of the script we've discussed thus far is placed on Frame 1, this data is created as soon as the movie begins to play. Next, you must add the capability to retrieve the information and display it on screen.

CREATING DYNAMIC TEXT FIELDS AND RETRIEVING INFORMATION

In Flash there are three types of text:

• Static text

• Input text

• Dynamic text

You compose *static* text on the stage using the Text tool. However, since you can't change the font, font size, or content of any static text area once a SWF file has been created, you'll generally use static text for text that changes infrequently. Web site navigation buttons, for example, are good candidates for static text.

Input text defines a text area that can be edited by users at run time. In other words, this is where users enter text. Input text fields are generally employed to gather textual information from the user—which your movie then either uses or sends to a server for processing. This type of text field is commonly found in Flash forms.

A *dynamic* text field is a text area on the stage that can be *populated*, or filled with text, as a movie plays—which means the text can change as the movie plays. A dynamic text field can also be set to display simple HTML-formatted text. A news section of a Flash Web site is a good example of where dynamic text would be useful. When using a dynamic text field to display HTML-formatted text, you can set attributes like color, font, and hyperlinks dynamically.

NOTE *All input and dynamic text fields placed in a project are instances of the Text Field object. As such, you can control and change them using properties and methods of that object class.*

The Property inspector is where you configure text fields. If you select the text tool from the Tools panel and then open the Property inspector from Windows > Properties, you'll see that it includes a drop-down menu (at the top) where you can select one of the three text types (static, dynamic, or input). Depending on which text type you select, different text options are available.

If you select Static Text from the drop-down list in the Property inspector, you can choose from the following options:

- **Use Device Fonts**. If you select this option, Flash will use fonts installed on the user's computer rather than any special fonts you've included.
- **Selectable**. If you select this option, the mouse cursor will change to an I-bar so that on mouse-over the text can be highlighted and copied.
- **Bold**. If selected, text is bolded.
- **Italics**. If selected, text is italicized.
- **Alignment**. You can change the alignment of the text to be left justified, right justified, or centered using the appropriate paragraph icon.
- **Text Orientation**. This allows you to choose whether text in a static text field appears horizontally or vertically.
- **Format**. Pressing this button brings up the Format Option dialog box where you can adjust indentation, line spacing, and margins.
- **Character display attributes**. You can choose the font, point size, and kerning for the text using this option.

- **Position attributes**. At the bottom left of the Property inspector is information about the screen position and the height and width of the text field. This can be modified here.

- **URL Link**.Enter a URL here to make the text field respond as regular hyperlinked text.

If you choose Input Text from the drop-down list, you have the following options:

- **Single Line, Multiline, Multiline no wrap, Password**. If you select Single Line, only one line of text can be entered into this text field. (The following options impose restrictions on the length of that line.) If you select Multiline, multiple lines of text can be entered and lines that exceed the width of the text field will automatically wrap to the next line. "Multiline no wrap" prevents text from wrapping. Thus, text that extends beyond the boundaries of the text field is simply not shown. With Password selected, stars serve as visual replacements for anything you type (and the machine remembers the correct content).

- **Instance Name**. If you assign instance names to input text and dynamic text fields, you can use ActionScript to control or access information from a text field. If you gave a text field an instance name of, say, **box**, you could access its text using the reference `box.text`.

- **Var**. You can also give text fields variable names. When you assign a variable name directly to a text field, its contents always reflect the value of that variable. Likewise, if the text field is modified, the value of the variable changes to match the modified field.

- **HTML**. Although input text fields are normally employed to accept user input, you can also use them to display dynamically generated text. If you select this option, the text field will be able to interpret any HTML 1.0 code (tags for bold, underline, and so on) that's included in the dynamic text that populates the field.

- **Border/Bg**. If selected, this option will add a white background and black border to the text box—a useful way to automatically show where the text field is located on the screen. If you leave this option unselected your user might not be able to see where the input field is located on the stage.

- **Maximum Characters**. This allows you to limit the number of characters that can be entered into the text field. (If this option is set to 0, users can enter an unlimited number of characters.)

- **Character**. When you press this button, you're presented with the Character Options dialog box, which enables you to configure several display options pertaining to the currently selected text field. One of these options is to embed this text field's fonts into the SWF at the time it's published—allowing Flash to display very smooth edges on your text. If, on the other hand, you select the No Characters radio button (the default behavior), the font won't be embedded. If you select the All Characters radio button, all characters of the current font will be embedded into the movie—usually adding 20K to 30Kto its file size. If you know you're only going to display numbers, uppercase letters, lowercase letters, or punctuation, there are individual radio buttons and checkboxes for embedding only those characters—one way to keep your file size smaller. The text-entry area on the bottom of this Character Options dialog box lets you enter specific characters that you want embedded—useful, for example, if you were creating a percent preloader for your movie (in which case you could select the "Numerals (0-9)" button and type *loaded* into the text-entry area).

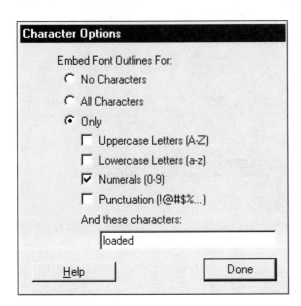

All of the options for Input Text are also available for Dynamic Text, which also includes this additional option,

- **Selectable**. This is the same as the Selectable option for Static Text.

In the following exercise you'll create all of the needed text fields for the News Flash Web site. All of the text fields used here are dynamic text fields.

1) With newsFlash3.fla still open, move the playhead to the frame labeled refresh.
On this frame, you can see the News Flash site graphics. On the left side of the stage there are four buttons that correspond to news sections. On the top middle of the stage there's a movie clip instance that contains several weather icons; the name of this movie clip instance is **icon**. The top right of the screen contains two arrows, one that points up and one that points down. This is where the high and low weather temperatures will be displayed. On the bottom right, you'll see a movie clip that contains the letters *M T W T F* referring to the five business days in a week.

2) Select the News Box layer. Select the Text tool from the toolbar and open the Property inspector. Select "Dynamic Text" from the drop-down list.
In the next several steps, you'll be creating dynamic text fields in various areas of the stage. Once you've created a text field, you can edit the instance name from the Property inspector.

3) Create a text field to the right of the weather icon by clicking on the stage. Embed the font by clicking the Character button on the Property inspector and then choosing the All Characters radio button. Adjust the width of this text field to approximately 150 pixels, and change the font of the text to _sans and the font size to 14.

This text field will display info about the days' weather. The text that will be dynamically placed in this field should be white; to make sure this is the case, choose white from the Property inspector while the text field is selected. All of the text fields created for this project will be either white or black. Make sure that Single Line (not Multilines) is displayed on the Property inspector. The Embed Fonts (All Characters) option should be set (by pressing the Character button on the Property inspector) when creating any of the text fields in this project.

4) With the text field still selected, edit its instance name from the Property inspector to read *weatherBlurb*.

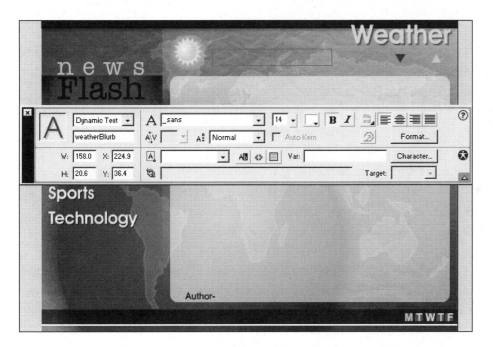

This text field is now complete. Whenever the value for `weatherBlurb.text` is set in the main timeline, the information displayed in this text field will be updated.

5) With the Text tool still selected, click and drag to create another text field the width of the light-blue area just above the black line on stage. Change the current font to _typewriter and the font size to 20, and select the bold option. Using the Property inspector, choose the center option for the text. Give the text field the instance name *headline*.

This text field will display the headline of an article with the Courier font.

6) Click and drag to create another text field under the *headline* text field approximately the size of the unoccupied light-blue area. Change the current font to _sans, the font size to 12, and the current color to black. Select Multiline from the drop-down list, and then select Word wrap. Assign the instance name *article* to this text field.

This text field is where the actual article will be displayed. When the value for `article.text` is set in the main timeline, the information displayed in this text field will be updated.

7) Click and drag to create another text field about 130 pixels wide just to the right of the word *Author* on the bottom of the light-blue area. Change the Property inspector so that Single Line is selected. Assign this text field the instance name *author*.

Like the other text fields, the information displayed in this text field will be updated whenever the value for `author.text` is changed.

8) Click and drag to create another text field in the bottom left of the screen positioned on the dark-gray bar. Change the current font to _sans, white, bolded, with a font size of 14. Assign this text field the instance name *date*.

This text field will display the date of the day that you select to view the news.

9) Click and drag to create two text fields, one just to the left of the blue arrow and another just to the right of the blue arrow in the Weather section of the site. Change the font size to 13. Assign the instance name *low* to the left text field and *high* to the other one.

These two text fields will display the low and high temperatures for the selected day.

10) Save your work as newsFlash4.fla.

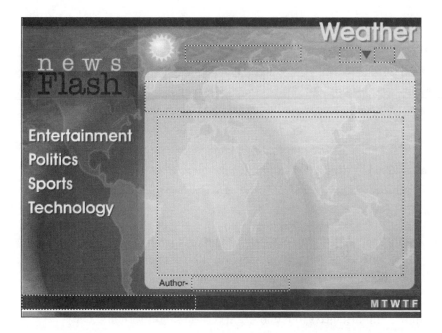

You have now created all of the visual areas on the stage that will contain dynamic data. However, you still need to retrieve the stored information and use it to populate the text fields.

RETRIEVING THE DATA

Now that you've created a data-storage architecture, you need to develop a way to retrieve the information from storage—and that involves some new syntax that provides a means of writing a dot syntax path dynamically. Square brackets are used to evaluate an expression. Here's how it works:

Assume we have three variables that contain animal sounds:

```
dog = "bark";
cat = "meow";
duck = "quack";
```

We'll create a variable and assign it a text value of "dog," "cat," or "duck" (note that these text values have the same names as our variables). We'll start with "dog":

```
currentAnimal = "dog";
```

255

Using the following syntax, we can access the value of the variable named dog:

```
animalSound = this[currentAnimal];
```

Here, animalSound is assigned a value of "bark." The expression to the right of the equals sign looks at currentAnimal and sees that it currently contains a text value of "dog." The brackets surrounding currentAnimal tell ActionScript to treat its value as a variable name. Thus, this line of script is seen by Flash as the following:

```
animalSound = this.dog;
```

Since dog has a value of "bark," that's the value assigned to animalSound. If we were to change the value of currentAnimal to "cat," animalSound would be assigned a value of "meow."

Note that you must use this in the expression to include the target path of the variable used to set the dynamic variable name (in this case currentAnimal) as it relates to the variable to the left of the equals sign (in our case animalSound). Using this denotes that these two variables are on the same timeline. If animalSound existed in a movie clip instance's timeline while currentAnimal was on the root, or main timeline, the syntax would look like this:

```
animalSound = _root[currentAnimal];
```

A couple of other examples include the following:

```
animalSound = _parent[currentAnimal];
animalSound = myMovieClip[currentAnimal];
```

This syntax is critical to the way you'll be retrieving information from the objects in this exercise. You'll remember that all of the objects are built with the same array names and structure; they just have different parent object names (monday and tuesday). We can use the aforementioned syntax to access the data in these objects dynamically based on the current value of a variable.

1) With newsFlash4.fla still open, select Frame 1 of the Actions layer. Open the Actions panel and enter the following two variables:

```
day = "monday";
section = "entertainment";
```

256

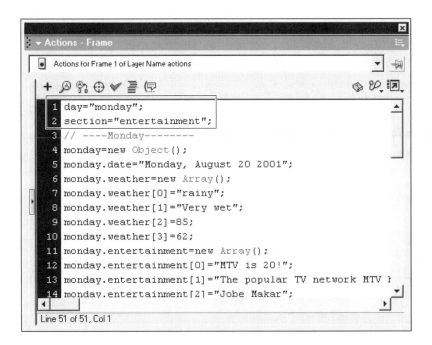

When our application plays for the first time, we want Monday to appear initially and Entertainment news to be displayed. These two variables allow us to accomplish this—you'll see how in the next few steps!

NOTE *The above two variables are known as* initializing *variables. Since the information our application displays will depend on which buttons the user clicks, these variables provide some starting settings (prior to user input).*

2) Select the frame labeled refresh in the Actions layer. Enter this ActionScript onto that frame:

```
date.text = this[day].date;
```

This uses the syntax we introduced at the beginning of this exercise. The value of the variable `date.text` is set by dynamically referencing another variable. Since `day` initially has a value of "monday" (as set in the last step), ActionScript sees the above code as the following:

```
date.text = monday.date;
```

You'll remember that `monday.date` contains the text value of "Monday, August 20 2001" and **date** is the name of the text field in the bottom-left portion of the screen. Thus, as a result of this action, "Monday, August 20 2001" will be displayed in the **date** text field.

You can begin to see how dynamically named variables can be useful. If the variable day had a value of "Tuesday," this line of code would reference the date variable in the object called tuesday.

In a moment, we'll explain why we placed this action on the frame labeled refresh.

3) With the current frame still selected, add the following ActionScript to the bottom of the current script:

```
days.gotoAndStop(day);
icon.gotoAndStop(this[day].weather[0]);
weatherBlurb.text = this[day].weather[1];
```

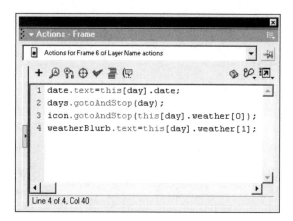

These three actions depend on the current value of day (which we set to an initial value of "monday" in Step 1) when they are executed. Here's how.

The movie clip instance named **days** in the bottom right portion of the stage contains five buttons (M, T, W, T, F) that will enable the user to select the day's news that he or she wishes to see. This movie clip also contains five frame labels ("Monday," "Tuesday," and so on), one for each day of the business week. Each of the frame labels displays a different day in yellow. The first line of ActionScript above tells the **days** movie clip instance to go to the appropriate frame, based on the current value of day. This cues the user to what day's news he or she is viewing. Since day has an initial value of "monday," that day will appear in yellow.

The weather icon (instance name **icon**) contains three frame labels, one for each weather type ("Sunny," "Stormy," "Rainy"). You'll remember that the zero element of the weather array in the monday and tuesday objects contains one of these three

258

values. The second line of ActionScript above dynamically pulls that value from the `weather` array using the correct object and sends the **icon** movie clip instance to the correct frame. Flash sees the following:

```
icon.gotoAndStop(this[day].weather[0]);
```

as

```
icon.gotoAndStop(this.monday.weather[0]);
```

Or, taking it one step further, since `monday.weather[0]` has a value of "rainy":

```
icon.gotoAndStop("rainy");
```

In the same way, the last action will populate the **weatherBlurb** text field with the value of `monday.weather[1]`, which is "Very Wet."

Keep in mind that if `day` had a value of "Tuesday," these actions would be executed based on the respective values in the `tuesday` object.

4) Add the following ActionScript to the selected frame:

```
high.text = this[day].weather[2];
low.text = this[day].weather[3];
```

Using the same syntax as in the previous step, the **high** and **low** text fields are populated by referencing the second and third elements of the `weather` array dynamically.

5) Add these final actions to the currently selected frame:

```
headline.text = this[day][section][0];
article.text = this[day][section][1];
author.text = this[day][section][2];
```

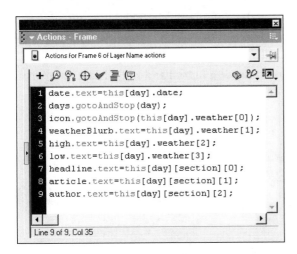

The dynamic referencing performed in this step is one level deeper into the storage objects than referenced in the previous step. We're trying to *dynamically* pull information about a news article from an object and an array because the day can be either Monday or Tuesday and the section can be Entertainment, Politics, Sports, or Technology. The initialization variables you set in Step 2 of this exercise set `section = "entertainment."` Using the values of our initialization variables, Flash will read the above three lines of ActionScript as follows when the movie first plays:

```
headline.text = this.monday.entertainment[0];
article.text = this.monday.entertainment[1];
author.text = this.monday.entertainment[2];
```

The only text field instances affected by the current `section` variable are **headline**, **article**, and **author**.

The ActionScript added in Steps 2 through 5 exists at the refresh label on the timeline. It's important to note that our application will be sent back to this frame label whenever the value of `day` or `section` is changed so that the information on the screen can be updated.

6) Move to the frame labeled sit and select it in the Actions layer. With the Actions panel open, enter a `stop();` action.

When you test the movie, you don't want the entire movie to loop repeatedly. Instead, the movie will initialize the storage variables on Frame 1 and then move to the refresh label and populate the text fields on the screen. Once this has been done, the movie will halt on the sit frame.

7) Choose Control > Test Movie.

Your on-screen text fields should be populated with information pertaining to Monday entertainment. The weather icon movie clip should display the correct icon, and the **days** movie clip instance (on the bottom right) should have the M (for Monday) highlighted.

8) Close the test movie. Select the Entertainment button and add this ActionScript:

```
on (release) {
  section = "entertainment";
  this.gotoAndPlay("refresh");
}
```

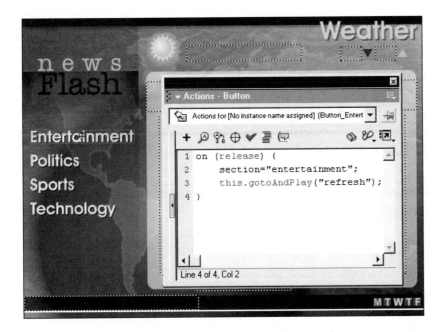

When that button is released, the `section` variable is set to `"entertainment"` and the screen is refreshed. This changes the display to an entertainment-related article (if one isn't already showing).

9) Select the Politics button and add this ActionScript:

```
on (release) {
  section = "politics";
  this.gotoAndPlay("refresh");
}
```

This ActionScript does the same thing as the ActionScript attached to the Entertainment button—the only difference is that `section` is set to `"politics."`

10) Select the Sports button and add this ActionScript:

```
on (release) {
  section = "sports";
  this.gotoAndPlay("refresh");
}
```

The ActionScript added to this button is identical to that on the other two buttons; however, this time `section` is set to `"sports."`

11) Select the Technology button and add this ActionScript:

```
on (release) {
  section = "technology";
  this.gotoAndPlay("refresh");
}
```

The `section` variable is set to `"technology,"` and the screen is then refreshed to show the updated information—the same as in the previous three buttons.

12) Choose Control > Test Movie. Click the four category buttons to see the headlines, articles, and authors change.

The information should change very easily now. If you wanted to add more sections of news stories, it would be easy to do so using this object-oriented coding technique.

13) Close the test movie and double-click the *days* movie clip instance on the bottom right of the screen. On the Buttons layer, select each button individually and add the following using the appropriate day:

```
on (release) {
  _parent.day = "monday";
  _parent.gotoAndPlay("refresh");
}
```

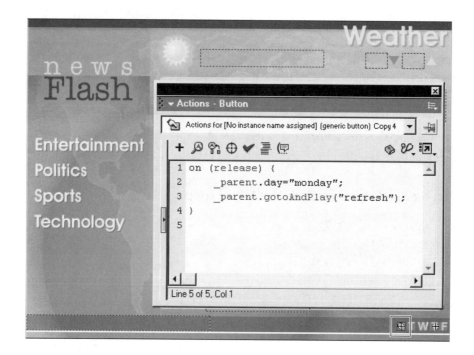

For the button that overlaps *T* (for Tuesday), change the ActionScript to `_parent.day = "tuesday."` This ActionScript is similar to that used to update sections: It changes the `day` variable and then refreshes the screen.

In this project, all of the buttons are used to set the values of either the `day` or `section` variables. The playhead is then sent back to the frame labeled refresh. Since the refresh frame contains all of the ActionScript used to populate our text fields, each time the timeline is sent back to this frame, it will refresh the content on the screen based on the current values of `day` and `section`.

14) Choose Control > Test Movie. Click the M and T on the bottom right of the screen to change the display. Notice that the weather and date change.

The way we've coded this makes it easy to add day objects without changing the information retrieval code.

15) Close the test movie and save your work as newsFlash5.fla

You have now completed a project in which displayed information is retrieved dynamically from a logical storage structure. The next logical step in a project like this would be to put all of our project's data into a database or text file. The information would then be grabbed and routed into the storage structure that you created. We'll cover loading information in and out of Flash in Lesson 11, Getting Data In and Out of Flash, and Lesson 12, Using XML with Flash.

WHAT YOU HAVE LEARNED

In this lesson, you have:

- Created variables (pages 238–243)
- Created arrays and accessed them dynamically (pages 243–248)
- Created text fields and learned the common uses of each type (pages 248–254)
- Stored information in objects and retrieved this information dynamically (pages 255–263)

manipulating data

Every day you're presented with various types of information—the weather, a special on a lunch menu, the past-due amount on your credit card. Some of this information you take as is, and some you manipulate (to make it more understandable or to answer questions). For instance, if you were to receive a past-due notice on your credit card, you might want to use that card's finance rate to determine how much more money you'll owe. Taking a piece of data and using it to arrive at another piece of data is known as *data manipulation*, and it can be as simple as converting a person's weight from kilograms to pounds or as complicated as translating text from English to

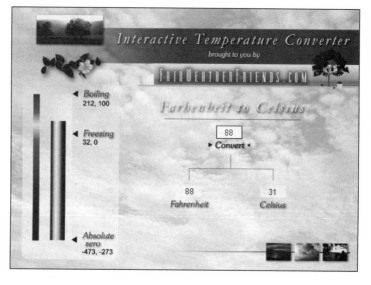

Manipulating data by converting it from one scale of measurement to another is what this temperature converter does, converting Fahrenheit values to Celsius.

Mandarin. Regardless of its complexity, data manipulation is essential to building applications and presenting information in a useful way.

In this lesson, you will manipulate both string and numerical data using expressions.

WHAT YOU WILL LEARN

In this lesson, you will:

- Build expressions
- Learn about precedence
- Manipulate numbers with the Math object
- Gain experience with the methods of the String object

APPROXIMATE TIME

This lesson takes approximately 30 minutes to complete.

LESSON FILES

Media Files:

None

Starting Files:

Lesson08/Assets/tempConverter1.fla

Lesson08/Assets/madlibs1.fla

Completed Projects:

tempConverter2.fla

madlibs2.fla

DATA TYPES

If you've made it through the preceding lessons, you've already been introduced to all of the data types. However, since you've never looked at all of them together, here's a quick review:

- **String**. This data type represents a text value (such as a name or title) or a value placed within quotation marks (such as `"hello"` or `"dog"`).

- **Number**. Numbers represent any numerical value that does not appear within quotes. For example, *6* represents the numeric value as shown, while "6" (with quotes) represents a string value. Understanding the difference between the two is crucial when it comes to manipulating data, especially when using the addition operator (+, which you'll learn about in the section, "Operators"). For example, "6" + "2" equals a string value of "62," but 6 + 2 (no quotes) equals a value of 8.

- **Boolean**. A Boolean value can have one of two states: usually `true` or `false` or 1 or 0.

- **Object**. Objects serve as storage devices for any data type, including other objects. They also can contain properties and methods that allow you to control and use them for various tasks. To review the types of objects available and how to use them, see Lesson 4, Understanding and Using Objects.

In this lesson, we'll focus on data manipulation using strings and numbers.

BUILDING EXPRESSIONS

An expression is a phrase—or a collection of variables, numbers, text, and operators—that evaluates to a value. To understand this, take a look at the following example:

```
oneDozen = 6 * 2;
```

To the right of the equals sign, you see `6 * 2`: This is an expression. When this line of ActionScript is executed, the expression `6 * 2` is replaced by the result of 6 multiplied by 2, or 12. Thus, `oneDozen` equals 12. In addition to the already-mentioned scripting elements, an expression can contain variables, arrays, even function calls—anything that when evaluated returns a value. For example:

```
total = subTotal + tax;
```

Here, the value of `total` is based on the result of adding the variable `subTotal` to the variable `tax`; `subTotal + tax` is the expression.

```
discount = totalPrice * employeeDiscount[2];
```

Here, the value of `discount` is based on the result of multiplying the variable `totalPrice` by the value of the third element in the `employeeDiscount` array; `totalPrice * employeeDiscount[2]` is the expression.

```
usDollars = 10;
japaneseYen = convertToYen(usDollars);
```

Here, the value of `japaneseYen` is based on the value returned by a call to the `convertToYen()` function—making the function call itself the expression.

NOTE *For more information about functions, see Lesson 5, Using Functions.*

Expressions are used to:

- Set variable values
- Set array-element values
- Determine whether conditions are being met (using the comparison operators)
- Dynamically name movie clips, variables, and objects
- Call functions dynamically
- More

By using expressions, you can avoid hard-coding values that will remain the same no matter what. And by assigning and manipulating values via expressions, you can make the data used by your scripts dynamic—resulting in more interactive projects. You'll find that many of the scripts in this book rely on expressions—that's because without them, your project plays back in exactly the same way each time it's viewed.

OPERATORS

Operators are the "marks" within an expression that control the way in which the expression's values are evaluated. There are various types of operators; the ones you use will depend on the ways in which you need to manipulate values.

NOTE *In this section, we'll review both arithmetic and string operators. For information about logical and comparison operators, see Lesson 9, Using Conditional Logic.*

ARITHMETIC OPERATORS

Even if you're not very familiar with ActionScript, you will be familiar with most of the arithmetic operators. These operators are used in expressions to manipulate numeric values.

- **Addition operator (+)**. Adds two numeric values together. **Example:** `totalCost = productPrice + tax;` This adds the two variables to arrive at a final result.

- **Increment operator (++)**. A shorthand method for adding 1 to a value. **Example:** `++myAge;` This increases the value of the `myAge` variable by 1—the equivalent of `myAge = myAge + 1;`

- **Subtraction operator (-)**. This operator subtracts two values and can be used in the same way as the addition operator. **Example:** `moneyInWallet = paycheck – moneySpent;` This subtracts one value from another to return a new number.

- **Decrement operator (--)**. This operator reduces the value of a variable by 1. **Example:** `--bottlesOfBeerOnTheWall;` There is now 1 less bottle of beer on the wall.

- **Multiplication operator (*)**. This operator multiplies one numeric value by another. Example: `hoursPerWeek = 24 * 7;` The number of hours per week is the product of these two numbers being multiplied together.

- **Division operator (/)**. Divides one numeric value by another. **Example:** `hourlyRate = payCheck / hoursBilled;` This divides the value of `hoursBilled` into the value of `payCheck`.

- **Modulo operator (%)**. Divides the value on the left by the value on the right and returns the value of the remainder. **Example:** `4 % 2;` The result of this would be 0 because 4 can be evenly divided by 2, hence there is no remainder. **Example:** `7 % 3;` The result of this is 1 because 3 divides into 7 twice with a remainder of 1.

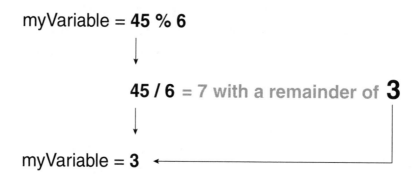

STRING OPERATORS

Unlike numbers, which can be manipulated using several different operators, strings can be manipulated by only one operator—the Concatenation operator (though they can also be manipulated using various methods of the String object). Although other operators work with strings (namely assignment operators and comparison operators), they cannot be used to *directly* manipulate a string. (For more on comparison operators, see Lesson 9, Using Conditional Logic.)

- **Concatenation operator (+).** *Concatenation* means to link or join two or more things—exactly what this operator does with strings of text in ActionScript. The concatenation operator—which uses the same symbol as the addition operator (see above)—joins two text strings to create a single string. **Example:** `birthDayMessage = "You are " + age + " years old.";` If `age` has a value of 26, then the '+' symbol joins the three parts of the message together to form, "You are 26 years old."

TIP *Unlike some other programming languages, ActionScript does not require you to declare that a variable will hold a string or a number value when you create it. You can sometimes treat a string as a number, and vice versa. With this benefit comes an occasional problem, however: Because the plus (+) symbol is used as both a concatenation operator and an addition operator, Flash must determine whether you're treating a value as a string or a number. This can create some odd issues when loading information from external sources. For example, Flash may see two numbers as strings.* `PayCheck1` + `PayCheck2` *may get concatenated instead of added (45 + 65 may end up being "4565" rather then 110). When getting data from an external source or a user-input field, it's sometimes prudent to use the* `Number()` *function—for example,* `Number(PayCheck1)` + `Number(PayCheck2)`—*to ensure that your values are treated as a numeric value (if that's their function).*

PRECEDENCE

Expressions can often include several operators. When this is the case, it's important to understand the order in which parts of the expression are evaluated, or the *order of precedence*. A value can't be involved in two mathematical operations simultaneously—that is, you can't subtract from a value at the same time you're using that value to multiply another number (like the 5 in the expression `myNumber = 20 * 5 – 3`; one of these evaluations must be completed before the other can begin). Based on the rules of precedence, expressions are evaluated in the following order:

1) Data in parentheses is evaluated before data outside parentheses. For precise control over how an expression is evaluated, you can nest parentheses.

2) Multiplication and division are evaluated before addition or subtraction. Because multiplication and division have equal precedence, evaluation occurs from left to right when both are used (in the absence of parenthesis).

3) Addition and subtraction are evaluated last. Because these operations have equal precedence, evaluation occurs from left to right when both are used (in the absence of parenthesis).

Let's take a look at a few examples:

```
myVariable = 5 + 7 - 3;
```

Because addition and subtraction have the same precedence, this expression is simply evaluated from left to right, with `myVariable` being assigned a value of 9.

```
myVariable = 5 + 7 * 3;
```

Because multiplication takes precedence over addition, 7 is multiplied by 3, then 5 is added to that result. In the end, `myVariable` is assigned a value of 26.

```
myVariable = (5 + 7) * 3;
```

Because data in parentheses takes precedence, 5 is added to 7, then that result is multiplied by 3. In the end, `myVariable` is assigned a value of 36.

```
myVariable = ((2 + 8) * (4 - 2)) / 5
```

Even though multiplication and division usually take precedence over addition and subtraction, nested parenthesis are used to add 2 to 8, then to subtract 2 from 4. These two results are multiplied, then divided by 5. The result is that `myVariable` is assigned a value of 4.

$$myVariable = ((2 + 8) * (4 - 2)) / 5$$

$$\downarrow \quad \downarrow$$

$$myVariable = (10 * 2) / 5$$

$$\downarrow$$

$$myVariable = 20 / 5$$

$$\downarrow$$

$$myVariable = 4$$

MANIPULATING NUMERICAL DATA USING MATH

Earlier in this lesson, we introduced you to the numeric operators, which allow you to perform simple arithmetic in your expressions. Flash's Math object allows you to access a variety of useful methods that allow you to further manipulate numbers. We'll introduce you to a few of the most commonly used methods of the Math object here; you'll use many of the other methods in other lessons in this book.

Common methods of the Math object include the following:

- `Math.abs()` The absolute-value method is used to return the scalar (positive) value of a number. **Example:** `distance = Math.abs(here – there);` If subtracting the value of `there` from `here` results in a negative value (for example, –375), the `Math.abs` method will convert it to a positive value (for example, 375), ensuring a positive result.

- `Math.round()` The round method accepts a number as a parameter and returns an integer. If the digit in the tenth placeholder of the number is 5 or greater, the number is rounded to the next highest integer; if it's less than 5, it's rounded to the next lowest integer. **Example:** `cupsOfCoffee = Math.round(3.7);` Since 7 is greater than or equal to 5, this number is rounded up to the next highest integer, or 4.

- `Math.floor()` This method works like `Math.round()` except that it always rounds down to the next lowest integer.

- `Math.ceil()` This method works like `Math.round()` except that it always rounds up to the next highest integer.

- `Math.sqrt()` The square-root method accepts a positive number as an argument and returns the square root of that number. **Example:** `answer = Math.sqrt(9);` `answer` is assigned a value of 3.

In this exercise, using operators, expressions and Math object methods, you will write a simple algorithm that will convert Fahrenheit temperatures to Celsius. You will also program a thermometer to display the correct mercury level.

1) Open tempConverter1.fla in the Lesson08/Assets folder.

All of the symbols and text fields have been created and are on the stage so that we can focus on ActionScript. The main timeline contains four layers: Actions, Thermometer, Temperature Input, and Background.

The Background layer contains the main graphics. The Temperature Input layer contains an input-text field with an instance name of **temperature**. This is where the temperature to be converted will be input. This layer contains also two additional text fields—**fahrenheit** and **celsius**—which will be used to display those values.

Also on this layer is a button containing the text "Convert." The Thermometer layer contains a movie clip instance named **mercury** that will be scaled vertically to indicate the proper temperature. We'll use the Actions layer in a moment.

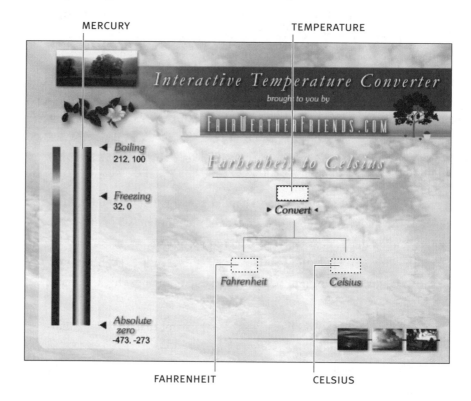

2) With the Actions panel open, select Frame 1 of the Actions layer and add the following script:

```
function changeTemp () {
}
```

The above script represents the beginning of a function definition. Ultimately, this function will be executed when the Convert button is pressed, and it will do the following:

1. Convert a Fahrenheit value to Celsius.

2. Make sure that the Fahrenheit value entered to convert is within the range on the thermometer.

3. Scale the mercury on the thermometer to the correct height.

3) At the beginning of the function definition you started in the preceding step, create the following variables:

```
boilingPoint = 212;
absoluteZero = -460;
```

Our thermometer covers a large temperature range—from absolute zero (approximately -460 degrees Fahrenheit) to the boiling point of water (212 degrees Fahrenheit), temperatures that will be treated as the highest and lowest acceptable input temperatures.

4) To ensure that the input temperature is within acceptable limits, add the following script just below `absoluteZero = -460`:

```
if (temperature.text > boilingPoint) {
  temperature.text = boilingPoint;
} else if (temperature.text < absoluteZero) {
  temperature.text = absoluteZero;
}
fahrenheit.text=temperature.text;
```

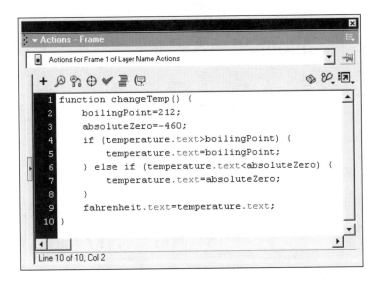

This part of the function is an `if`/`else if` statement that acts as a data filter. It says that if the value the user inputs (`temperature.text`) is greater than the value of `boilingPoint` (which is 212), the user-input value will be automatically set *to* the value of `boilingPoint`. Otherwise, if the user inputs a value less than `absoluteZero` (-460), that value will be automatically set to the value of `absoluteZero`. After the filter, the value of `temperature.text` is set to display in the **fahrenheit** text field instance.

273

Filter statements such as the above are used frequently in programming since it's rare for a function to accept all possible input extremes.

5) Just below the statement we added above, add the following expression, which is used to convert Fahrenheit to Celsius:

```
celsius.text = Math.round((5 / 9) * fahrenheit.text - 17.777);
```

The expression to the right of the equals sign converts a Fahrenheit value to Celsius. This expression sets the value of `celsius.text`, which is the name of the corresponding text field on the stage. Thus, this line is used to display the converted value in that text field.

Notice the use of parentheses in the expression. As Flash executes this line of code, it will evaluate the first part of the expression that it can find that is fully enclosed in parentheses (in this case, `5 / 9`). Flash then performs the multiplication, then the subtraction. The `Math.round()` method is not invoked until its entire argument is evaluated and replaced with a numeric result. This method will then round the value to the next integer up or down depending on the value in the tenth place of the argument.

$$\text{fahrenheit.text} = 56$$

$$\downarrow$$

$$\text{celsius.text} = \text{Math.round}(\mathbf{(5 / 9)} * 56 - 17.777)$$

$$\downarrow$$

$$\text{celsius.text} = \text{Math.round}(\mathbf{.5555 * 56} - 17.777)$$

$$\downarrow$$

$$\text{celsius.text} = \text{Math.round}(\mathbf{31.108 - 17.777})$$

$$\downarrow$$

$$\text{celsius.text} = \mathbf{Math.round(13.331)}$$

$$\downarrow$$

$$\text{celsius.text} = \mathbf{13}$$

274

6) Add the following lines to the end of the current script:

```
scalePercent = (Math.abs(absoluteZero – Fahrenheit.text) /
Math.abs(absoluteZero – boilingPoint)) * 100;
mercury._yScale=scalePercent;
```

These two lines of code first create a variable to store the percent used to scale the **mercury** movie clip instance, then use that value to scale it.

The expression used to set the value of `scalePercent` is based on the ratio of the difference between absolute zero and the temperature submitted when compared against the full temperature range. To help you understand this, let's assume that the user has entered a value of 56 in the **fahrenheit** text field. We know that `absoluteZero` equals -460 and that `boilingPoint` equals 212. Thus, the expression is evaluated as follows:

```
(Math.abs(-460 – 56) / (Math.abs(-460 – 212)) * 100;
```

or

```
(Math.abs(-516) / (Math.abs(-672)) * 100;
```

or

```
((516) / (672)) * 100;
```

or

```
(.767) * 100
```

or

```
76.7
```

The absolute-value method of the Math object is used here to ensure that the expression evaluates to a positive percentage value. (A negative percentage value wouldn't make sense in the context of this script.)

The second line of the above script scales the **mercury** movie clip instance vertically using the value of `scalePercent`. Thus, the instance is scaled to 76.7 percent of its original value, which works well because the **mercury** movie clip was built in Flash to be the maximum height when at normal size (100 percent).

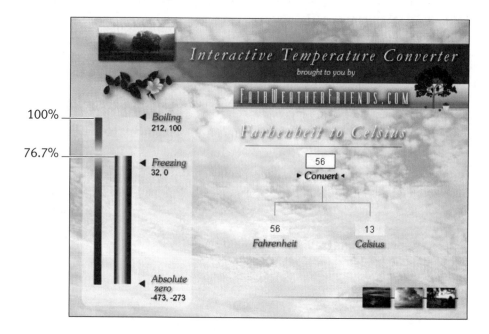

7) **With the Actions panel open, select the Convert button and add the following script:**

```
on (release, keyPress "<Enter>") {
  changeTemp();
}
```

When the button is released or the Enter key pressed, the `changeTemp()` function you just built will be called.

8) **Choose Control › Test Movie. Enter a temperature value and press the button.**
When the button is pressed, you'll see the **mercury** movie clip scale appropriately. The **celsius** and **fahrenheit** fields on the screen will also get populated with data. Try entering a temperature that falls outside the acceptable range, and you'll see that the filter `if/else if` statement catches and replaces it with either the upper or lower boundary.

9) **Close the test movie and save your work as tempConverter2.fla.**
You have now used the Math object in an expression. With it, you converted Fahrenheit to Celsius and scaled a movie clip based on a percent calculated.

MANIPULATING STRINGS

Thus far in this lesson, we've dealt mostly with numbers. Now it's time to learn about the powerful methods of the String object, which you were introduced to in Lesson 4. Using String object methods, you can find specific characters in a string, change the case of the string, reverse the characters in the string, and more.

The following are some of the most commonly used String object methods:

- `length` This String object property returns the number of characters in a string. **Example:** `numCharacters = userName.length;` Here the value of `numCharacters` based on the number of characters in the `userName` variable. If `userName` is `"Jobe"` the result is 4.

- `substr(start, length)` The substring method, which returns part of a string, accepts two parameters: starting index and the length (or number) of characters to count (including starting character). If the length parameter is omitted, this method will by default count until the end of the string. **Example:** `name.substr(1, 2);` If the value of `name` is `"Kelly"` the result would be "el". The letter *e* has an index of 1, and the number *2* tells the substring to include two letters.

- `toLowerCase()` This method forces all of the letters in a string to be lowercase. **Example:** `message.toLowerCase();` If the value of `message` is `"Hello"` the result is "hello".

- `toUpperCase()` This method forces all of the letters in a string to be uppercase. **Example:** `message.toUpperCase();` If the value of `message` is `"Hello"` the result is "HELLO".

> **NOTE** *As mentioned in Lesson 4, the* `text` *property of a text field instance can also be considered an instance of the String object—and thus can be manipulated as such. For example,* `myTextField.text.toUpperCase();` *will cause all the text in the* **myTextField** *text field to appear in uppercase letters.*

In this exercise, you will create a simple silly word-game application. With it, you can enter words in a basic form and a paragraph will be generated.

1) Open madlibs1.fla in the Lesson08/Assets folder.

This file includes three layers: Background, Text Fields, and Actions. The Background layer contains the main site graphics. The Text Fields layer contains five input-text fields, a dynamic-display text field, and a Submit button. (We'll use the Actions layer in a moment.)

The five input-text fields are (from the top down) **verb1**, **properNoun**, **verb2**, **adjective**, and **noun**. These will allow the user to enter words that will be used to generate the paragraph. The bigger text field, at the bottom-right of the stage, is named **paragraph** and will be used to display the paragraph.

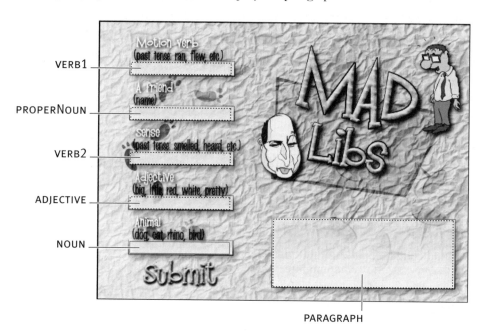

PARAGRAPH

2) With the Actions panel open, select Frame 1 of the Actions layer and add the following script:

```
function generate () {
}
```

This is the beginning of a function definition. This function will be called when the Submit button is pressed. The final function will take all of the user-input words and modify them when needed. A sentence of text will then be generated that includes these words.

3) With Frame 1 still selected, add the following four lines of script to the generate() **function definition:**

```
verb1.text = verb1.text.toLowerCase();
verb2.text = verb2.text.toLowerCase();
adjective.text = adjective.text.toLowerCase();
noun.text = noun.text.toLowerCase();
```

```
1  function generate() {
2      verb1.text=verb1.text.toLowerCase();
3      verb2.text=verb2.text.toLowerCase();
4      adjective.text=adjective.text.toLowerCase();
5      noun.text=noun.text.toLowerCase();
6  }
7
```

These four actions force the text entered into the corresponding text fields to be lowercase—primarily for grammatical reasons (none of these fields will include proper nouns or represent the first word in the sentence).

4) Add the following script to the end of the current generate() **function, just below** noun.text = noun.text.toLowerCase():

```
properNoun.text = properNoun.text.substr(0,1).toUpperCase() +
properNoun.text.substr(1).toLowerCase();
```

In the above script, properNoun.text makes reference to the **properNoun** text field on the stage, which is used to enter a person's name. For grammatical reasons, the leading character in a person's name (that is, the character at index 0) should be capitalized and the rest of the letters lowercased. To ensure that this is the case, we use the substr() method in our expression. As you can see from the above, you can use two methods concurrently and in a contiguous fashion. First, properNoun.text.substr(0, 1) returns the first letter of the value of properNoun.text, which it is then forced to uppercase using the toUpperCase() method. The string concatenation operator (+) is then used to concatenate the first half of the expression with the second. The second half also uses the substr() method. The difference here is that it begins counting with the character at index 1 (the second letter). Because the length value (the second parameter of the substr() method) is not specified, it finds the rest of the characters in the string and uses the toLowerCase() method to make those letters lowercase.

Thus, "kelly" would be changed to "Kelly" or "kEILy" to "Kelly."

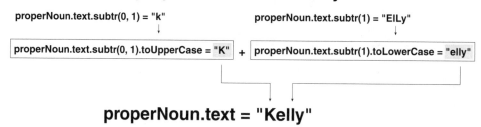

5) **Add the following final line of script to this** `generate()` **function:**

```
paragraph.text = "You " + verb1.text + " into love with " + properNoun.text
+ " when you " + verb2.text + " " + properNoun.text + " eating a " +
adjective.text + " " + noun.text + ".";
```

This line of script uses the concatenation operator several times to insert various variable values in hard-coded text strings to build a complete sentence.

TIP *Be careful when concatenating several strings that each string section has opening and closing quotes; if any are missing, an error will result. The Actions panel cues you to errors in code by providing red highlighting above the Parameters setting area of the panel to indicate an error in that line's syntax.*

6) **With the Actions panel open, select the Submit button and add the following script:**

```
on (release, keyPress "<Enter>") {
  generate();
}
```

When the button is released or the Enter key pressed, the `generate()` function you just created will be called.

7) **Choose Control > Test Movie.**

Enter text into each of the input-text boxes, then press the Submit button and read the sentence you created. Try it again, this time entering text with varying case. You can see how easy it is to manipulate strings with ActionScript.

8) Close the test movie and save your work as madlibs2.fla.

Now you know something about using methods of the String object—an important aspect of learning ActionScript since text plays an important role of many projects and you need to know how to manipulate it. The exercise in this section introduced you to the basics; as you progress through the book, you'll find additional examples of ways to control text to suit your project's needs.

WHAT YOU HAVE LEARNED

In this lesson, you have:

- Been formally introduced to expressions (pages 264–269)
- Learned about precedence in ActionScript (pages 269–270)
- Used the Math object to modify data (pages 271–276)
- Use the String object to modify strings and build a sentence (pages 277–281)

using conditional logic

Every day we're confronted with all kinds of situations—large and small—that require us to make decisions about what actions we'll take. Although we may not be doing it consciously, we're constantly saying to ourselves, "If this is the case, I need to do this": If it's hot, wear shorts; if it's rainy, wear pants; and so on. This process of taking different actions based on current circumstances, or *conditions*, is known as *conditional logic*—and it's something we all apply naturally.

Conditional logic is a critical component of interactivity. It allows you to program your project to react intelligently—to the movement or position of the mouse, to the current day of the week, and to many other dynamic conditions that exist as

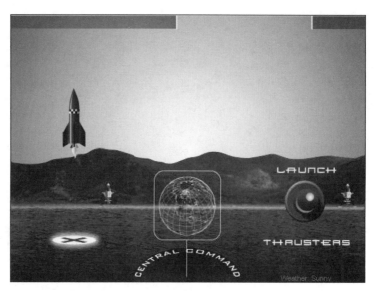

A successful rocket launch demands perfect conditions. This lesson's project will emulate a launch to demonstrate some of the principles and techniques used in conditional logic.

your movie plays. By employing conditional logic, you can transform simple linear presentations and animations into dynamic projects that offer a unique experience each time they're viewed.

In this lesson, we'll introduce you to some of the ways you can use conditional logic to bring about graphical changes in your movies based on varying conditions.

WHAT YOU WILL LEARN

In this lesson, you will:

- Learn how to control your script's flow using `if`, `if/else`, and `if/else if` statements

- Become familiar with the various operators used in conditional logic and their functions

- Learn about the conditions that can exist in your movie

- Script a project to react to various conditions

- Create a scripted boundary to restrict an object's movement

- Turn a script on and off using conditional logic

- Program a project to react to user interaction

- Learn how to detect and react to object collisions

APPROXIMATE TIME

This lesson takes approximately 1 hour to complete.

LESSON FILES

Media Files:
None

Starting File:
Lesson09/Assets/rocketLaunch1.fla

Completed Project:
rocketLaunch6.fla

CONTROLLING A SCRIPT'S FLOW

Typically, actions in your scripts execute consecutively, from beginning to end—a sequence that represents your script's flow. Using conditional logic, you can control this flow by scripting specific actions to execute *only* when a specific condition (or condition) is met or exists in your movie. By implementing conditional logic in your scripts, you give your movie the ability to make decisions and take action based on various conditions you've set it up to analyze—an ability that allows your movies to take on a life of their own. The following *conditional statements*, or phrases, are used to implement conditional logic in your scripts.

IF/THEN STATEMENT

At the heart of conditional logic is the simple If/Then statement. Take a look at the following example:

```
if (moneySaved > 500) {
buyStuff();
}
// next line of actions...
```

In the above script, the `buyStuff()` function is called only if the variable `moneySaved` has a value greater than 500. If `moneySaved` is equal to or less than 500, the `buyStuff()` function call is ignored and actions immediately below the `if` statement are executed.

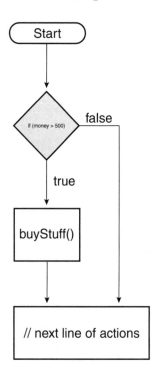

At its core, a conditional statement looks at a circumstance (whatever is placed within parentheses) and determines whether that circumstance is `true` or `false`. If it is `true`, actions within the statement are executed; if `false`, they're ignored. Thus, when creating an `if` statement, you're essentially stating the following:

```
if (…what is shown here is true) {
  Do this;
}
```

The data you place within parenthesis represents the condition to be analyzed; the data within the curly braces ({}) represents the actions to be taken if the condition exists.

As in real life, sometimes your `if` statement needs to analyze multiple conditions before taking a single action or set of actions. Take a look at the following example:

```
if (moneySaved > 500 && billsPaid == true) {
  buyStuff()
}
```

In this script the AND operator (`&&`) has been added to the statement so that now the `buyStuff()` function is called only if `moneySaved` is more than 500 *and* `billsPaid` is `true`. If either condition is `false`, `buyStuff()` will not be called. Using the OR operator (`||`) allows you to take a slightly different approach. Take a look at the following example:

```
if (moneySaved > 500 || wonLottery == true) {
  buyStuff()
}
```

In this script, the `buyStuff()` function is called if *either* `moneySaved` has a value greater than 500 *or* `wonLottery` has a value of `true`. Both conditions do not need to be `true` as is the case when using the AND operator.

You can mix these operators together to create sophisticated conditional statements like the following:

```
if (moneySaved > 500 && billsPaid == true || wonLottery == true) {
  buyStuff()
}
```

In this script the `buyStuff()` function is called only if `moneySaved` is more than 500 *and* `billsPaid` is `true` *or* if `wonLottery` has a value of `true`.

Following is a list of the common operators (known as *comparison operators* because they're used to compare values) used in conditional logic, as well as a brief description and example of how they are used:

OPERATOR	DESCRIPTION	EXAMPLE
==	Checks for equality	if (name == "Derek"). This says, "If name has an exact value of Derek, do the following…"
!=	Checks for inequality	if (name != "Derek"). This says, "If name has a value other than Derek, do the following…"
<	Less than	if (age < 30). This says, "If age has a value less than 30, do the following…"
>	Greater than	if (age > 30). This says, "If age has a value greater than 30, do the following…"
<=	Less than or equal to	if (age <= 30). This says, "If age has a value less than or equal to 30, do the following…"
>=	Greater than or equal to	if (age >= 30). This says, "If age has a value greater than or equal to 30, do the following…"
&&	Logical AND	if (day == "Friday" && pmTime > 5). This says, "If day has a value of Friday and pmTime has a value greater than five, do the following…"
||	Logical OR	if (day == "Saturday" || day == "Sunday"). This says, "If day has a value of Saturday or Sunday, do the following…"

TIP *A common mistake when checking equality is to insert a single equals sign (=) where a double equals sign (==) belongs. Use a single equals sign to assign a value (for example,* money = 300*); use a double equals sign to check for equality. Thus,* money == 300 *does not assign a value of 300 to money. Rather, it asks whether money has a value of 300.*

TIP *Although comparing numbers is straightforward—after all, most of us understand that 50 is less than 100—comparing text values may be less obvious. "Derek" doesn't equal "derek" even though the same letters are used. With string values, A has a lower value than Z, and lowercase letters have greater values than uppercase letters. Thus, if A has a value of 1, z has a value of 52 (ABCBEFGHIJKLMNOPQRSTUVWXYZabcdefghijklmnopqrstuvwxyz).*

IF/ELSE IF STATEMENT

An `if/else if` statement is similar to the basic `if` statement we just discussed; however, it enables your script to react to multiple conditions. Take a look at the following example:

```
if (money > 500) {
  buyTV("35 inch");
} else if (money > 300) {
  buyTV("27 inch");
}
```

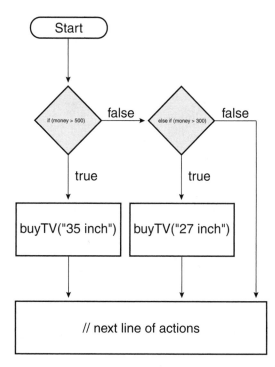

This script executes varying actions depending on the value of money. It says, "If money has a value greater than 500, buy the 35-inch TV." If money has a value less than 500, this part of the script is ignored and the next condition is examined. The next condition says that if money has a value greater than 300, buy the 27-inch TV. Thus, if money has a value of 450 when this script is executed, the first part of the statement is ignored (because 450 is not greater than 500), but the second part of the statement is executed (because a value of 450 *is* greater than 300). If money had a value of less than 300, both parts of this statement would be ignored.

You can create several lines of `if/else if` statements that can react to dozens of conditions.

287

IF/ELSE STATEMENT

An `if/else` statement allows your script to take action if none of the conditions in the statement prove true. Consider this the fail-safe part of the statement.

```
if (money > 500) {
  buyTV("35 inch");
} else if (money > 300) {
  buyTV("27 inch");
} else {
  workOvertime ();
}
```

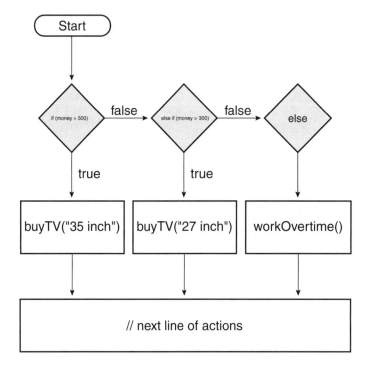

In this script, if `money` does not have a value of at least 300, neither of the conditions analyzed will be `true`, and thus neither of the actions under them will be executed. Instead, the actions under the `else` part of the statement are executed—a bit like saying the following:

```
if (…this is true) {
  // Do this
} otherwise if (…this is true) {
  // Do this
} otherwise, if none of the above conditions are true {
  // Do this
}
```

CONDITIONAL STATEMENT VARIATIONS

The statements we've discussed up to this point (and the syntax used) form the basis of most conditional logic you'll use in your projects. However, as with most things in ActionScript, there's more than one way to script a conditional statement. Let's take a look at a couple of these variations and how you might use them to shorten your code and make it easier to read. The following variations have no real advantage over the ones we've already discussed; it really comes down to personal preference.

A `switch` statement—which is a variation on the `if/else` statement—can be extremely useful when you want a script to take a specific set of actions when an exact value exists. Take a look at how the following statement works:

```
switch (favoriteBand) {
case "Beatles":
  gotoAndPlay("Beatles");
  break;
case "U2":
  gotoAndPlay("U2");
  break;
default:
  gotoAndPlay("Slim Whitman");
}
```

First, in parentheses, there is a single expression (most often a variable), which is evaluated once. The value of the expression is then compared with the values for each `case` in the structure. If there's a match, the block of code associated with that `case` is executed. If no match is found, the default statement (at the end) is executed. `break` is used in each `case` in order to prevent the code from running into the next case automatically if a match has already been found. What can be checked in each `case` includes string values (shown), numeric values, and Boolean values of `true` and `false` (though for Boolean values, the variation we describe next represents an easier and more appropriate choice).

The *ternary operator* (?:)lets us write a simple `if/else` statement in one line. Take, for example, the following:

```
myMood = (money > 1000000) ? "Happy" : "Sad";
```

If the condition within the parenthesis evaluates to true, the first expression, "Happy," is set as the value of myMood. If the condition is false, the second expression, "Sad," is used. This single line of ActionScript accomplishes the same thing as the following lines of code:

```
if (money > 1000000) {
  myMood = "Happy";
} else {
  myMood = "Sad";
}
```

Here's an example of an extended way to use the ternary operator:

```
myMood = "I'm " + (money > 1000000) ? "happy" : "sad";
```

In this example, myMood will have a value of either "I'm happy" or "I'm sad," depending on whether the value of money is greater than or less than 1000000.

The ternary operator is commonly used to toggle variable states. Take, for example, the following:

```
playSound = (playSound) ? false : true;
```

Every time the above line of ActionScript is executed, the variable playSound is changed from true to false or from false to true.

DETERMINING CONDITIONS

Your project may well contain numerous conditions you can take advantage of in your scripting to control the way it works or interacts with the user. Although a condition can take many forms, at its core, it represents a circumstance that is either true or false. The following are some of the common conditions that conditional statements look for:

- If one object comes in contact with another object
- If something is on or off
- If a movie clip's position, size, or any other property is greater than, less than, or equal to another value.
- If the user has a specific interaction with the mouse or keyboard
- If text or numeric values are greater than, less than, or equal to another value
- Any combination of the above

REACTING TO MULTIPLE CONDITIONS

For a successful rocket launch to occur, a number of conditions must be met. One of the most important variables affecting a rocket launch is weather, which helps determine not only how the rocket is propelled but how it's controlled as well. In this exercise, we'll begin scripting our project so that the rocket will react differently based on randomly generated weather conditions.

1) Open rocketLaunch1.fla in the Lesson09/Assets folder.
This file contains a single scene made up of seven layers, named according to their content. Let's take a quick look at the various elements in the scene.

The Weather layer contains a movie clip instance the size of the movie itself. This movie clip represents the background sky in the scene. Its timeline contains three frame labels: Sunny, Rainy, and Night. At each of these frame labels, the sky graphic changes to match the name of the label. At Sunny, the sky appears sunny; at Rainy, it appears overcast, and at Night, it looks dark.

The Ground/Central Graphics layer contains the mountains, ground, and main Central Command graphics. There is also a small movie clip instance of a red dot, which blinks to indicate the launch location on the globe.

The Rocket layer obviously contains our rocket—that is, a movie clip instance named **rocket**. Its timeline contains two frame labels: off and on. At the off label, the rocket doesn't show a flame; at the on label, it does. This provides a visual indicator of when the rocket is in motion.

The Control Panel layer contains several elements, the most conspicuous of which is the red Launch button. This will be used not only to launch the rocket but also to reset the scene after a launch has been attempted. Below this button is a movie clip instance named **thrustBoost** that includes the text "Thrusters." This clip also contains two frame labels: on and off. At the on label, the text appears big and red to provide a visual indication that thrust is being applied to the rocket. This layer's last element is a text field in the lower-right portion of the stage with an instance name of **weatherText**. It will provide a textual indication of current weather conditions.

The Status layer contains a movie clip instance named **status** that appears as a small circle in the middle of the sky. It appears this way because the first frame of its timeline contains no graphical content. There are three frame labels on this movie clip's timeline: off, abort, and success. At the off frame label, the clip appears as it does now. At the abort label, a text message appears that reads, "Launch Aborted." At the success label, a text message appears that reads, "Launch Successful." This clip will provide a text message about the launch's success or failure.

The Guides layer contains a movie clip instance of two red bars. The space between the red bars represents the launch window—the area the rocket must pass through to have a successful launch.

The Sound Clips layer contains a movie clip instance named **sounds** that also appears as a small circle just above the stage, on the left side. Its timeline contains frame labels named intro, launch, abort, and success. At each of these labels is a sound clip that's representative of the frame label where it exists (for example, at the launch label is a launch sound, at the abort label is an abort sound, and so on). Various scripts will send this clip to these frame labels to provide audio effects for our project.

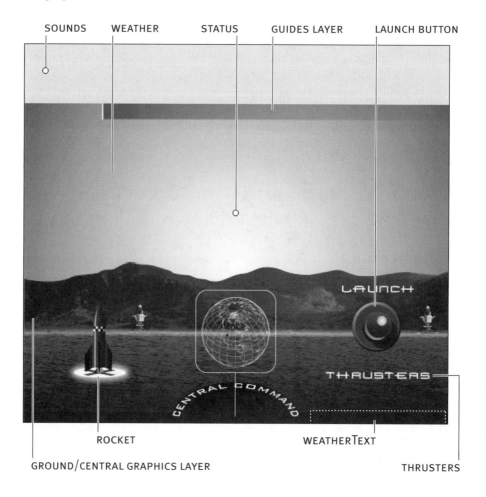

Let's begin scripting the project.

2) With the Actions panel open, select the *weather* movie clip instance and add the following script:

```
onClipEvent (load) {
  randomWeather = random (3);
  if (randomWeather == 0) {
    conditions = "Sunny";
    _root.rocket.noThrust = 3;
    _root.rocket.thrust = 6;
  } else if (randomWeather == 1) {
    conditions = "Rainy";
    _root.rocket.noThrust = 2;
    _root.rocket.thrust = 4;
  } else {
    conditions = "Night";
    _root.rocket.noThrust = 1;
    _root.rocket.thrust = 2;
  }
}
```

This script is executed as soon as this movie clip instance loads. Its first action sets the value of the `randomWeather` variable, based on a randomly generated number (three possibilities of 0, 1 or 2). Next, an `if` statement is used to analyze the value of `randomWeather` so that the values of three other variables can be set. If `randomWeather` has a value of 0, the variable named `conditions` is created on this timeline and assigned a string value of "Sunny." In addition, two variables are created on the **rocket** movie clip instance's timeline: one named `noThrust` and the other `thrust`, with values of 3 and 6, respectively. If `randomWeather` does not have a value of 0, then that part of the statement is ignored, at which point an `else if` statement checks to see if `randomWeather` has a value of 1. If it does, the same variables we just discussed are instead assigned values of "Rainy," 2, and 4, respectively. If `randomWeather` doesn't have a value of 1 either, that part of the statement is ignored as well, at which point the actions under the `else` statement are executed. Remember that an `Else` statement enables you to define what happens if none of the previous conditions in the statement have proven true but you still want *something* to happen. In this case, if the previous conditions proved `false`, the actions under the `else` statement are executed, setting the value of the variables we've been discussing to "Night," 1, and 2, respectively.

The value of the `conditions` variable will be used in a moment to set how the weather will appear graphically in the scene. The other two variables will soon be used to establish how fast the **rocket** instance will move based on the weather condition generated.

3) With the Actions panel open, add the following script inside the `load` event, just below the last part of the `if` statement:

```
gotoAndStop (conditions);
_root.weatherText.text = "Weather: " + conditions;
```

These two actions occur as soon as the `if` statement is analyzed, and both use the value of `conditions` to react in unique ways. The first action will move this movie clip instance to a frame label based on the value of `conditions`. If `conditions` has a value of "Rainy", this movie clip instance will move to that frame label, where the weather will appear rainy. The next action determines what will be displayed in the **weatherText** text field in the bottom-right portion of the stage. Once again, if `conditions` has a value of "Rainy", this text field will display "Weather: Rainy".

IF (RANDOMWEATHER == 0)   IF (RANDOMWEATHER == 1)   ELSE

 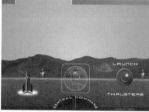 

_ROOT.ROCKET.NOTHRUST = 3   _ROOT.ROCKET.NOTHRUST = 2   _ROOT.ROCKET.NOTHRUST = 3
_ROOT.ROCKET.THRUST = 6   _ROOT.ROCKET.THRUST = 4   _ROOT.ROCKET.THRUST = 6

4) Choose Control > Test Movie to test the functionality of our project up to this point.
As soon as the movie plays, the **weather** movie clip is loaded and the script we just added is executed. Depending on the random number generated in the script, the graphical representation of the weather is affected as well as the text displayed in the bottom-right portion of the screen.

NOTE *Closing the test movie and then choosing Control > Test Movie again should give you different results because a different random number will be generated, causing the scene to react and appear accordingly.*

5) While still in the testing environment, choose Debug > List Variables.
This opens the Output window, allowing you to see the value of variables on different timelines. A quick glance will reveal the values of the `thrust` and `noThrust` variables in the **rocket** timeline. We will use these values shortly.

```
Output                                                            ×
Generator Installed                                          Options
Level #0:
  Variable _level0.$version = "WIN 5,0,30,0"
  Variable _level0.weatherText = "Weather: Rainy"
Movie Clip:  Target="_level0.instance1"
Variable _level0.instance1.randomWeather = 1
Variable _level0.instance1.conditions = "Rainy"
Movie Clip:  Target="_level0.rocket"
Variable _level0.rocket.noThrust = 2
Variable _level0.rocket.thrust = 4
```

6) Close the test environment to return to the authoring environment and save your work as rocketLaunch2.fla.

We will build on this file in the next exercise.

DEFINING A BOUNDARY

Boundaries are something we contend with on a daily basis. Although boundaries can take many forms—physical, financial, mental—in the end they're nothing more than an indicator of something's limit. To make a boundary work, you must simply define its limits, then take appropriate action when (or just before) those limits are exceeded. Think of driving a car: Lines on the road define the boundaries our cars are supposed to remain within. If we're approaching the line on the left (the left boundary), we move our steering wheel to adjust; if we're approaching the line on the right, we once again make the requisite adjustment—conditional logic in action! Written in ActionScript, those actions might look like the following:

```
if (car._x > leftOfRoad) {
  turnWheel ("right");
} else if (car._x > rightOfRoad) {
  turnWheel ("left");
}
```

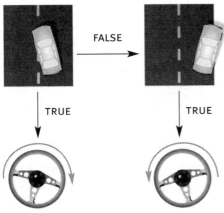

To make a boundary work in Flash, you must define its limits, then use an `if` statement to check the affected element each time an event occurs that might cause it to exceed its defined boundaries. This will become clearer as we progress through this exercise.

In Flash, boundaries are used for the following:

- To prevent movie clip instance properties (including x, y, alpha, xscale, yscale, and so on) from being changed beyond specified amounts

- To invoke an action (property change or method) when something is within or exceeds a specified boundary

- To prevent data values from exceeding defined limits (useful when validating data)

In this exercise, we'll dynamically animate the red bars at the top of our project, which represent a moving "launch window" that our rocket must pass through to complete a successful launch.

1) Open rocketLaunch2.fla in the Lesson09/Assets folder.

This file continues on the one we worked with in the last exercise.

2) With the Actions panel open, select one of the two red bars at the top of the stage and add this script:

```
onClipEvent (enterFrame) {
  if (_x < 0) {
    direction = "right";
  } else if (_x > 550) {
    direction = "left";
  }
  if (direction == "right") {
    _x = _x + 3;
  } else {
    _x = _x - 3;
  }
}
```

Obviously, the two red bars at the top of the stage are part of the composite movie clip instance to which this script is attached. This script uses two `if` statements to move this movie clip instance back and forth, from left to right. Using the `enterframe` event causes these statements to be evaluated 24 times a second (the frame rate of the movie).

The first statement is used to analyze the position of this clip as it moves within a specified boundary. It says that if the horizontal position of this instance is less than 0 (that is, its center point exceeds the left side of the stage), set the value of `direction` to "right." Otherwise, if its horizontal position is greater than 550 (that is, its center point exceeds the right side of the stage), set the value of **direction** to "left." The way this is scripted, the value of **direction** changes *only* if one of the limits of the boundary is exceeded. This will occur as a result of the movie clip being put into motion, which is what the next **if** statement does. It says that if **direction** has a value of "right," move the instance to its current horizontal position *plus* 3. This moves the instance to the right. Otherwise (**else**; if **direction** has a value of "left"), move the instance to its current horizontal position *minus* 3. This moves the instance to the left. With these two statements being analyzed as well as these actions executing 24 times a second, the red bars are set in motion, but their movement is restricted to a specified area.

NOTE *When creating boundaries in your scripts, it's important to note which event handler might cause an element to exceed a boundary so that you can use that event to analyze the boundary conditional statement. For example, if you wanted to take a specific action when a movie clip instance's vertical position exceeded an established boundary while being dragged around the stage, the* **mouseMove** *event handler would be ideal since it could easily cause a dragged movie clip instance to exceed its boundary.*

These two statements work in harmony: The direction of the red bars' movement is determined by which boundary it last exceeded (which sets the value of **direction** to either "left" or "right")—that is, they will move in the opposite direction of the boundary exceeded. Eventually, a boundary will be exceeded again, and the process will be repeated in the opposite direction. In other words, if **direction** has a value of "right," the instance will move right, eventually exceeding the right part of the boundary—at which point the value of **direction** is set to "left" and the process is reversed.

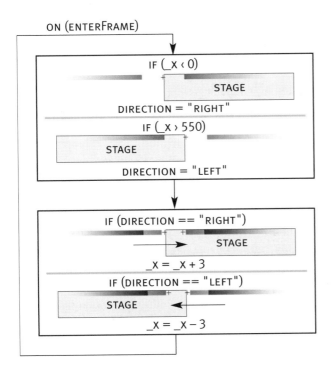

3) Choose Control › Test Movie to test the project's functionality thus far.

When the movie begins playing, the red bars are set in motion. When either of the boundaries we defined in the last step is exceeded, the bar is set in motion in the opposite direction.

4) Close the test environment to return to the authoring environment and save your work as rocketLaunch3.fla.

We will build on this file in the next exercise.

TURNING POWER ON/OFF

Sometimes certain actions should be executed *only* if something is turned on. A real-world example of this would be a car: Try driving one without starting it, and chances are, you won't get far. That car is designed so that it will only run after you've given it power by turning the ignition. In similar fashion, something can happen in your movie to trigger your script's functionality (turn it on).

Think of it this way: Events power scripts by triggering actions. The scripts themselves represent the mechanism, or "machine," for accomplishing various tasks. Conditional logic can be used as an On/Off switch in your scripts, allowing actions to execute, as the result of an event, only under certain circumstances.

Take, for example, the following script:

```
onClipEvent (enterFrame) {
  clock._rotation = clock._rotation + 1;
}
```

With this script, a movie clip instance named **clock** is rotated by 1 degree with each enterFrame event—regardless of what else is happening in your movie. If you wanted to "unplug" your clock—so that it would only rotate if it had "power"—you could revise the preceding script to read as follows:

```
onClipEvent (enterFrame) {
  if (power == true) {
clock._rotation = clock._rotation + 1;
  }
}
```

With this script, the clock only rotates if the variable `power` has a value of `true`. You can set the value of this variable to `false` or back to `true` again by using a script attached to a button, frame, or other movie clip instance—in essence, creating an On/Off switch for the script.

Many desktop software applications make use of this scripting functionality to allow users to turn on and off program capabilities through preference settings dialog boxes. Because Flash projects are usually steeped in multimedia and animation—which are often triggered by an executing script—you can use this capability to restrict a script's power until you need it, essentially turning off timelines, animations and more.

In the following exercise, we'll use the above scripting concepts to put our rocket in motion only after the Launch button has been pressed and released.

1) Open rocketLaunch3.fla in the Lesson09/Assets folder.

This file continues on the one we worked with in the last exercise.

2) With the Actions panel open, select the *rocket* movie clip instance and add the following script:

```
onClipEvent (load) {
  speed = noThrust;
}
```

This script is executed as soon as the movie clip loads. Its only purpose is to set the value of a variable named `speed` to the value of `noThrust`. You'll remember the script on the **weather** movie clip instance that sets the values of `thrust` and `noThrust` based on the value of `randomWeather` (this was the first exercise in this lesson, in case you need to review). Thus, when this script is executed, `noThrust` will have a value of 1, 2, or 3, which is the value that `speed` is set to. The value of the `speed` variable will be used in a moment to set the speed at which the rocket will move initially.

3) Add the following script below the script you just added:

```
onClipEvent (enterFrame) {
  if (launch) {
    _y = _y - speed;
    if (_y < _root._y) {
      launch = false;
      gotoAndStop ("off");
      _root.status.gotoAndStop ("success");
      _root.sounds.gotoAndPlay ("success");
    }
  }
}
```

```
1  onClipEvent (load) {
2      speed = noThrust;
3  }
4  onClipEvent (enterFrame) {
5      if (launch) {
6          _y = _y - speed;
7          if (_y < _root._y) {
8              launch = false;
9              gotoAndStop ("off");
10             _root.status.gotoAndStop ("success");
11             _root.sounds.gotoAndPlay ("success");
12         }
13     }
14 }
```

This script is executed (24 times a second) using the `enterFrame` event (24 times a second). The first part of it says that if `launch` is `true`, move the rocket to its current position minus the value of `speed`. This causes the instance to move upward only if `launch` is `true`. If `launch` is `false`, nothing happens. We will shortly script the Launch button to set the value of `launch` to `true` when it is released, thus setting this instance (**rocket**) in motion. As mentioned in the last step, the value of `speed` dictates the rate at which the rocket moves upward.

TIP *In the above statement, using* `if (launch)` *is the same as using* `if (launch == true)`. *The former is simply a shortcut. Likewise, if we wanted to check whether* `launch` *had a value of* `false`, *we could simply use* `if (!launch)`.

Just below the line of script that moves the instance upward, you'll see another `if` statement—notable for its right indentation: This indicates that it, too, is *only* analyzed when `launch` is `true`, just like the line of script above it. This second `if` statement is said to be *nested* inside the first. The reason for this is that it checks to see if this instance's vertical position exceeds the top of the stage—which is guaranteed to happen eventually because the instance is in upward vertical motion when `launch` is `true`. However, because the condition will *only* exist if `launch` has been set to `true` and the instance has been set in motion, it's only necessary to check for it under those circumstances—which is why that `if` statement is nested. If the statement weren't nested, it would be constantly analyzed—whether or not the rocket were in motion (`launch` were `true` or `false`)—which would be a waste of processor power.

Using this nested statement, once the boundary (the top of the stage) has been exceeded, four actions are executed: The first sets the value of `launch` to `false`—in essence, turning off this script. (In other words, the action gives the script the ability to turn itself off.) The next action sends this instance to the frame labeled off—the point on this movie clip's timeline where the flame does not appear under the rocket. The next action sends the **status** movie clip instance to the frame labeled success, causing the message "Launch Successful" to appear in the middle of the screen. The last action sends the **sounds** movie clip instance to a frame labeled success. At this label, a short audio clip plays, indicating that the launch was successful.

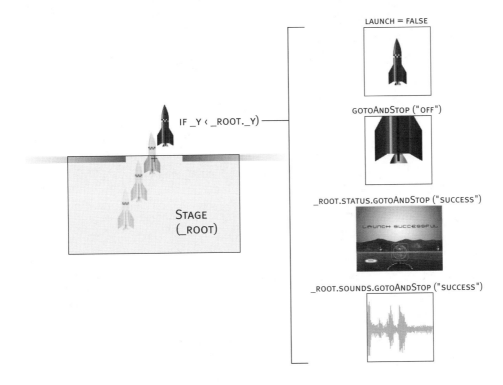

LAUNCH = FALSE

GOTOANDSTOP ("OFF")

IF _Y < _ROOT._Y)

_ROOT.STATUS.GOTOANDSTOP ("SUCCESS")

_ROOT.SOUNDS.GOTOANDSTOP ("SUCCESS")

STAGE
(_ROOT)

As already mentioned, this script depends on the value of launch being true to do anything. We'll next script the Launch button that sets this value.

4) With the Actions panel open, select the Launch button and add this script:

```
on (release) {
  rocket.launch = true;
  rocket.gotoAndStop ("on");
  sounds.gotoAndPlay ("launch");
}
```

Using this script, when this button is released, three actions are executed: The first action sets the value of the launch variable on the **rocket** movie clip instance's timeline to true (which in turn sets the rocket in motion, as discussed in the previous step). The next action sends the **rocket** instance to the frame labeled on, causing the flame to appear at the bottom of the rocket. The last action sends the **sounds** instance to the frame labeled launch, where an audio clip of a rocket blasting off begins to play.

5) Add this script to the end of the last script:

```
on (press) {
  rocket.launch = false;
  rocket.gotoAndStop ("off");
  status.gotoAndStop ("off");
  sounds.gotoAndPlay ("intro");
  rocket._x = 98;
  rocket._y = 352;
}
```

We want this button to take several actions when pressed—all of which deal with resetting elements and variables in the scene so that a rocket launch can be attempted more than once. The first action sets the value of launch on the **rocket** instance's timeline to false to halt the rocket's upward motion. The next three actions move the **rocket**, **status**, and **sounds** movie clip instances to frame labels that return them to their initial states. The last two actions place the **rocket** instance back on the launch pad.

6) Choose Control › Test Movie to test the functionality of the project up to this point.

Press and release the Launch button. As soon as the button is released, the value of launch is set to true. This "turns on" the script on the **rocket** instance, causing it to move upwards. Once it goes beyond the top of the stage, the script is turned off and several other actions occur, indicating a successful launch. Pressing and holding the Launch button at this point will reset the scene. Releasing it again restarts the process.

7) Close the test environment to return to the authoring environment and save your work as rocketLaunch4.fla.

We will build on this file in the next exercise.

REACTING TO USER INTERACTION

Users will interact with your movie in two primary ways—via mouse or keyboard, either of which can be used any number of ways. Users can interact with your movie by moving the mouse around the screen, pressing and releasing buttons, and so forth. Using conditional logic, you can script your movie to react in various ways based on the user's interaction with it.

In the following exercise, we'll add functionality to our project that allows the user to press the Space bar on the keyboard to apply "thrusters" to move the rocket upward at a quicker-than-normal pace.

1) Open rocketLaunch4.fla in the Lesson09/Assets folder.

This file continues on the one we worked with in the previous exercise.

There are a couple of important things to keep in mind as you begin working on this exercise: The first thing to remember is that when the **weather** movie clip instance is loaded, a script is executed that does several things based on the value of a variable named randomWeather. Not only does it display a random weather graphic, it also sets the values of the variables thrust and noThrust. The variable thrust is given a value double that of noThrust at the time they are set. Thus, if noThrust has a value of 2, thrust has a value of 4. The second thing to remember is that when the **rocket** instance loads, the speed variable on its timeline is set to the value of noThrust; thus, if noThrust has a value of 2, that's what speed is set to. You'll remember that the value of speed is used to determine how fast the rocket moves upward. In this exercise, we'll set the value of speed to either thrust or noThrust, depending on whether the

Space bar is pressed down. Because thrust has a value twice that of noThrust, this will propel the rocket upward twice as fast when the Space bar is pressed.

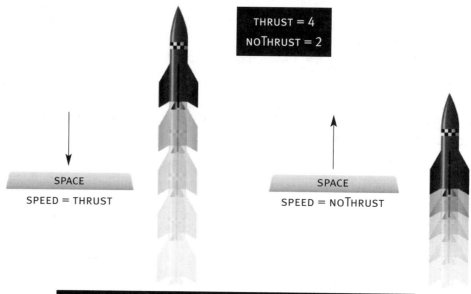

THRUST = 4
NOTHRUST = 2

SPACE
SPEED = THRUST

SPACE
SPEED = NOTHRUST

DISTANCE ROCKET IS MOVED IS BASED ON THE VALUE OF SPEED

2) With the Actions panel open, select the *rocket* **movie clip instance and add the following script just below the last script that appears:**

```
onClipEvent (keyDown) {
  if (launch && key.isDown(key.SPACE)) {
  speed = thrust;
  _root.thrustBoost.gotoAndStop ("on");
  }
}
```

This script is executed whenever a key is pressed—at which point a conditional statement looks for two conditions. If launch has a value of true *and* if the Space bar is pressed down, two actions are executed. The first action sets the value of speed to the value of thrust to move the rocket upward at twice its current rate. The next action tells the **thrustBoost** movie clip instance (just below the Launch button in the scene) to go to the frame labeled on where big, red text that reads 'Thrusters' is displayed.

Obviously, we want a mechanism that allows the rocket to return to its initial speed; that's what the next script does.

3) Add the following script just below the script we added in the last step:

```
onClipEvent (keyUp) {
  if (!key.isDown(key.SPACE)) {
  speed = noThrust;
  _root.thrustBoost.gotoAndStop ("off");
  }
}
```

```
1 onClipEvent (load) {
2     speed = noThrust;
3 }
4 onClipEvent (enterFrame) {
5     if (launch) {
6         _y = _y - speed;
7         if (_y < _root._y) {
8             launch = false;
9             gotoAndStop ("off");
10            _root.status.gotoAndStop ("success");
11            _root.sounds.gotoAndPlay ("success");
12        }
13    }
14 }
15 onClipEvent (keyDown) {
16     if (launch && key.isDown(key.SPACE)) {
17         speed = thrust;
18         _root.thrustBoost.gotoAndStop ("on");
19     }
20 }
21 onClipEvent (keyUp) {
22     if (!key.isDown(key.SPACE)) {
23         speed = noThrust;
24         _root.thrustBoost.gotoAndStop ("off");
25     }
26 }
```

This script is similar in syntax to the last one we added; however, it works in just the opposite way. For starters, it's executed whenever a key is *released* on the keyboard. A conditional statement then checks to see if the space bar *is not* pressed down. If it's not, two actions are executed. The first sets the value of speed back to the value of noThrust (its initial value). The next tells the **thrustBoost** movie clip instance to go to the frame labeled off where the "Thrusters" text appears as it did initially.

4) Choose Control › Test Movie to test the functionality of your project up to this point.
Press and release the Launch button. As soon as the button is released, the rocket is set in motion. Pressing the space bar should cause the rocket to move upward at twice its current speed. Releasing the space bar should return the rocket's speed to its initial value.

5) Close the test environment to return to the authoring environment and save your work as rocketLaunch5.fla.
We'll build on this file in the next exercise.

DETECTING COLLISIONS

Many Flash applications, especially games, are able to detect object collisions—one of the most easily understood applications of conditional logic.

To detect collisions between two objects (movie clip instances), ActionScript provides the `hitTest()` method of the Movie Clip object. Using this method in conjunction with a conditional statement allows you to take action when two movie clips collide. You simply define in the script the various actions you want to take, depending on which object is hit. Take a look at the following script:

```
onClipEvent (enterFrame) {
  if (hitTest ("wallOfCotton")) {
    pain = 0;
  } else if (hitTest ("wallOfCardboard")) {
    pain = 5;
  } else if (hitTest ("wallOfBricks")) {
    pain = 10;
  }
}
```

If the movie clip instance to which this script is attached collides with the movie clip instance named **wallOfCotton**, `pain` is set to 0. If it collides with **wallOfCardboard**, `pain` is set to 5. And finally, if it collides with **wallOfBricks**, `pain` is set to 10. As you can see, the `hitTest()` method is very straightforward.

In this exercise, we'll use the `hitTest()` method in conjunction with a conditional statement to take specific action if the **rocket** movie clip instance collides with either of the two red bars (our launch window) that are in motion. If the instance hits either one of them, the launch will abort; if it passes through the space between them, the launch will be successful.

1) Open rocketLaunch5.fla in the Lesson9/Assets folder.

This file continues on the one we were working with in the last exercise.

2) Double-click one of the two red bars at the top of the stage to edit this clip in place.

Obviously, both red bars are part of this movie clip instance. However, each of the red bars is also a movie clip instance itself, with one flipped horizontally in the opposite direction of the other. Because each of these bars is a movie clip instance, you can use them to react to a collision with the **rocket** movie clip instance.

3) With the Actions panel open, select one of the red-bar instances and add the following script:

```
onClipEvent (enterFrame) {
  if (hitTest("_root.rocket")) {
    _root.rocket._x = 98;
    _root.rocket._y = 352;
    _root.rocket.launch = false;
    _root.rocket.gotoAndStop ("off");
    _root.status.gotoAndStop ("abort");
    _root.sounds.gotoAndPlay ("abort");
  }
}
```

This script is executed using the `enterFrame` event, which means this conditional statement is analyzed 24 times a second. The condition that is being looked for is whether the **rocket** movie clip instance (`root.rocket`) has collided with this instance. Whenever it does, the actions in the statement are executed. The first two reset the rocket to its original position on the stage. The next action sets the value of `launch` on the **rocket** instance's timeline to `false`, causing it to cease moving upward. The next action also moves that instance's timeline to the frame labeled off. At this label the flame does not appear under the rocket. Next the **status** movie clip instance is moved to the frame labeled abort. This will display a message in the middle of the screen stating that the mission has been aborted. Lastly, the **sounds** movie clip instance is moved to the frame labeled abort, where a short audio clip will play, indicating that the launch has been aborted.

4) With the Actions panel open, select the other red bar and place the above script on it as well.

If the **rocket** instance collides with this instance, the actions described in the previous step will occur.

```
onClipEvent (enterFrame) {
    if (hitTest("_root.rocket")) {
        _root.rocket._x = 98;
        _root.rocket._y = 352;
        _root.rocket.launch = false;
        _root.rocket.gotoAndStop ("off");
        _root.status.gotoAndStop ("Abort");
        _root.sounds.gotoAndPlay ("abort");
    }
}
```

```
onClipEvent (enterFrame) {
    if (hitTest("_root.rocket")) {
        _root.rocket._x = 98;
        _root.rocket._y = 352;
        _root.rocket.launch = false;
        _root.rocket.gotoAndStop ("off");
        _root.status.gotoAndStop ("Abort");
        _root.sounds.gotoAndPlay ("abort");
    }
}
```

5) Choose Control › Test Movie to test your project up to this point.

Your project is now fully functional! Press and hold the Launch button to experience what happens at prelaunch. Release it to launch the rocket. Apply thrusters with the idea of getting the rocket between the space in between the red bars. If you do, the launch will be successful; if you don't, it will abort.

6) Close the test environment to return to the authoring environment and save your work as rocketLaunch6.fla.

This completes the lesson.

By now, you have seen that by creating scripts that use conditional logic, the dynamism of your project can increase several-fold, providing a unique experience to every person that views and interacts with it.

WHAT YOU HAVE LEARNED

In this lesson, you have:

- Learned how to control the flow of a script using `if`, `if/else` and `if/else if` statement (pages 284–290)

- Learned about the various operators used in conditional logic (page 286)

- Scripted a project to react to various conditions (pages 290–295)

- Created a scripted boundary to restrict an object's movement (pages 295–298)

- Turned a script on and off using conditional logic (pages 298–302)

- Programmed a project to react to user interaction (pages 303–306)

- Learned how to detect and react to object collisions (pages 306–308)

automating scripts with loops

We've all had to perform repetitive tasks—whether complicated or simple, they require us to perform at least one step in a process repeatedly. For example, if you were sending out 100 wedding invitations, repetitive steps could include folding papers, stuffing envelopes, closing envelopes, and affixing stamps—each of which you must do 100 times! In ActionScript, performing a set of repeated steps, or *actions*, multiple times is called *looping*. ActionScript lets you loop through a set of actions as many times as needed—which means that instead of writing an action (or set of actions) several times, you can write it once and then loop through it any number of times. In this lesson, you'll learn how to use the three loop types offered by ActionScript.

The drop-down list as well as the 2-by-2 grid of pictures in this application will be created dynamically using loops.

WHAT YOU WILL LEARN

In this lesson, you will:

- Learn about the usefulness of loops

- Learn about the types of loops

- Set loop conditions

- Create a nested loop

- Use loop exceptions

APPROXIMATE TIME

This lesson takes approximately 45 minutes to complete.

LESSON FILES

Media Files:

None

Starting Files:

Lesson10/Assets/pictureShow1.fla

Lesson10/Assets/phoneNumberSearch1.fla

Completed Project:

pictureShow3.fla

phoneNumberSearch2.fla

WHY LOOPS ARE USED

Loops enable Flash to perform an action (or set of actions) repeatedly—which means that with just a few lines of ActionScript, you can force an action to be executed several thousand times! In ActionScript, you can use loops for any of the following—many of which would be difficult or impossible to perform without them:

- To create dynamically generated drop-down lists
- To validate data
- To search text
- To dynamically duplicate movie clips
- To copy the contents of one array to a new array
- To detect collisions in games between projectiles and objects

You can use loops to automate any number of tasks. Take, for example, dynamically creating movie clip instances: If your project called for 100 instances of the same movie clip (spaced evenly), you could drag one instance from the library and create a four- or five-line looping statement to automatically duplicate the instance 100 times and position those duplicates on the stage—a great improvement over dragging 100 instances from the library and then aligning each and every one. What's more, you can modify your looping statement to use it various ways in your project.

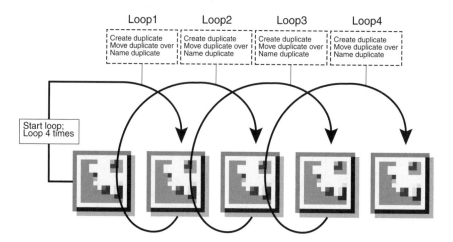

Loops are also dynamic. Suppose you scripted a loop to dynamically create a menu of 15 choices (buttons). By altering the loop slightly, you could easily add and remove choices dynamically. In contrast, adding or removing a button from a *manually* created menu involves adding or removing the choice, then moving all of the other choices up or down one—perhaps even rescripting here and there.

As you move through this lesson (and the rest of the book), you'll begin to see the value of using loops in your scripts.

TYPES OF LOOPS

ActionScript can take advantage of three loop types—all of which perform an action (or set of actions) while a specific condition is `true`.

WHILE LOOP

The syntax for creating this most common type of loop is as follows:

```
while (someNumber < 10) {
  // perform these actions
}
```

The expression `someNumber < 10` is the condition that determines how many iterations the loop will perform. With each iteration (pass through the statement), the actions inside the loop are executed. The logic that determines how the condition is evaluated (and thus how the loop is exited) is discussed in the next section, "Writing and Understanding Loop Conditions." Here is an example of the `while` loop:

```
i=0;
while (++i <= 10) {
  myClip.duplicateMovieClip("myClip" + i, i);
}
```

The script above duplicates **myClip** 10 times.

FOR LOOP

The `for` loop is a compact, all-in-one looping solution for loops that rely on incrementing or decrementing a variable. This is because it lets you initialize a loop variable, set the loop condition, and increment or decrement that variable all in one line of ActionScript. Although the `for` loop employs a different syntax than the `while` loop, everything you can accomplish with the `while` loop can also be done with the `for` loop. Personal preference will dictate which one you use. The syntax of the `for` loop is as follows:

```
for (someNumber = 0; someNumber < 10; ++someNumber) {
  // perform these actions
}
```

The three elements within parentheses separated by semicolons are used to specify the number of iterations the loop will perform. In this example, the variable `someNumber` is created and assigned an initial value of 0. The script then goes on to state that as long as `someNumber` is less than 10, the loop will execute the actions contained therein. The last element specifies that `someNumber` will be incremented by 1 with each loop iteration, eventually causing `someNumber` to have a value of 10 (which means the loop will cease after nine iterations).

The `for` loop's structure means that it's used primarily to loop through a set of actions a specific number of times. Here is the same example given for the `while` loop using the `for` loop syntax:

```
for (i=0; i<=10 ; ++i) {
  myClip.duplicateMovieClip("myClip" + i, i);
}
```

The `for` loop above duplicates **myClip** 10 times.

FOR .. IN LOOP

This loop—which employs the following syntax—is used to loop through all of an object's properties:

```
for (i in _object) {
  // perform these actions
}
```

The `i` in the above loop is a variable that (with each loop iteration) temporarily stores the name of the property it references. The value of `i` can then be used in the actions within the loop. For a practical application of this, take a look at the following script:

```
car = new Object();
car.color = "red";
car.make = "BMW";
car.doors = 2;
for (i in car) {
  result = result + i + ": " + car[i] + newline;
}
```

The first thing that happens in this script is that a generic object is created and given a name of `car`. The next three lines assign properties (which you can think of as simply variables within the `car` object) and corresponding values to the `car` object. Next, a `for . . in` loop is set up to loop through all of that `car` object's properties, using `i` as a the variable that temporarily stores the name of each property. The value of `i` is then used in the action within the loop. When the loop is finished, `result` will contain a string of text that contains the name of each property as well as its value.

On the first iteration of the loop, `i` will have a string value of "doors" (since that was the name of the last property defined, as shown). Thus, during the first loop, the expression that sets the value of `result` would look like this:

```
result = result + "doors" + ": " + 2 + newline;
```

Thus, after the first loop, `results` will have a string value of:

```
"doors: 2"
```

In the expression that sets the value of result, the variable i (without brackets) refers to the property *name* (such as "doors", "make", or "color"). Using car[i] (that is, placing i between brackets) is the same as writing car.doors—and thus is a reference to that property's *value*.

CAR OBJECT

PROPERTIES

Loop3	COLOR = "RED"	I="COLOR" CAR[I] = "RED"
Loop2	MAKE = "BMW"	I="MAKE" CAR[I] = "BMW"
Loop1	DOORS = 2	I="DOORS" CAR[I] = 2

When complete, result will have a string value of:

```
"doors: 2
make: BMW
color: red"
```

Because the car object has three properties, the for . . in loop in this script will only perform three iterations automatically.

You can use this type of loop for any of the following:

- To find the name and value of every variable in a timeline or object
- To find the name of every object in a timeline or object
- To find the name and value of every attribute in an XML document

TIP *When you create a variable on an object, it's stored in what's known as an associative array. As you know, in a regular array, elements are referenced by number (starting with 0). In an associative array, in contrast, elements are referenced by name. The loop above loops through the associative array that contains all of these references in a specific timeline or object.*

315

WRITING AND UNDERSTANDING LOOP CONDITIONS

For the rest of this lesson, we'll use the while loop exclusively. The actions within this type of loop are performed continuously—as long as the condition evaluates to true. Take, for example, the following:

```
i = 0;
while (i < 10) {
  // perform these actions
}
```

The condition in the above loop is i < 10. This means that as long as the value of i is less than 10, this statement is true and the actions within the loop are repeated. However, the above looping statement is missing a key ingredient—a means for the condition to eventually become false. Without this functionality, the loop could continue forever—which in the real world will cause applications to freeze because Flash can't do anything else until the looping statement completes its job. To prevent this from happening in the example above, the value of i must be incremented so that its value eventually equals 10—at which point the condition will prove false, and the loop will stop. The great thing about loops is that you can build this functionality in by using the increment operator (++). Take a look at the following example:

```
i = 0;
while (i < 10) {
  perform these actions
  ++i
}
```

Incrementing the value of i causes the loop to perform 10 iterations. The value of i is initially set to 0; however, with each loop that value increases by one. On the tenth loop, i = 10, which means i < 10 is no longer true and thus the loop halts. The following is a shortcut method of writing the same thing:

```
i = 0;
while (++i < 10) {
  // perform these actions
}
```

This loop will perform nine iterations. The value of i is initially set to 0; however, with each iteration (including the first), that value is incremented by one within the conditional statement of the loop itself. On the tenth loop, i = 10, which means i < 10 is no longer true and thus the loop halts.

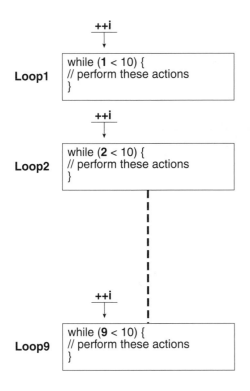

You can also use the decrement operator, which might look something like this:

```
i = 10;
while (--i > 0) {
  // perform these actions}
}
```

The condition in a loop does not have to depend on an incremented value; it can be any sort of condition. It can also be the result of a function call that returns a value of `true` or `false`, as in the following:

```
while (someFunction()) {
  // perform these actions
}
```

In this exercise you'll create a drop-down list using a `while` loop.

1) Open pictureShow1.fla in the Lesson10/Assets folder.

The main timeline includes two layers: Background and Dynamic Elements. Not surprisingly, the Background layer contains the project's background graphic. The Dynamic Elements layer includes four movie clip instances: three above the stage that contain pictures and an instance on the stage (named **dropDownList**) that contains a button labeled Menu and another movie clip instance named **item**. The

item instance—which is *inside*, or part of, the **dropDownList** instance—is made up of two elements, a dynamic text field with an instance name of **itemName** and a button that appears as a partially transparent white box. This instance plays an important part in this exercise because it will be duplicated in a process to dynamically generate clickable menu choices.

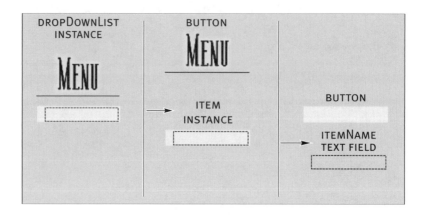

Most of the scripts in this exercise will be attached to movie clip instances—that is, they'll be triggered by clip events.

2) With the Actions panel open, select the *dropDownList* movie clip instance and add the following script:

```
onClipEvent (load) {
  buttonNames = ["Paris","New York","London"];
  item._visible = false;
}
```

In the above script, you're using the `load` clip event on the **dropDownList** movie clip instance to initialize a couple of things: The first action creates an array named `buttonNames`, which contains names that will appear in the drop-down list.

The second action makes the **item** movie clip instance invisible. (Since you'll only be using it as a template for creating duplicates, the instance itself does not need to be visible.)

3) Just below the last line of ActionScript on the `load` clip event enter this function:

```
function populateList () {
  spacing = item._height + 2;
  numberOfButtons = buttonNames.length;
}
```

This function will duplicate the **item** movie clip instance, align the duplicates under the Menu button, and change the text displayed in the duplicated instances.

Because this function dynamically generates the list of choices, we need to consider vertical spacing between the list-choice buttons in our script. In its first action, this function creates a variable named `spacing`. This variable's value is determined by retrieving the height of the **item** movie clip instance and adding two to that value. Our loop will use this value to set the spacing between the top of one duplicated movie clip instance and the top of the movie clip instance underneath it.

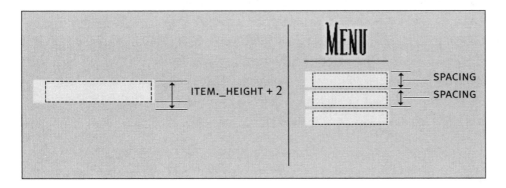

The `numberOfButtons` variable gets its value from the length of the `buttonNames` array (that is, how many elements it contains). The `while` loop used to build the drop-down list will then use that value to determine how many iterations to perform. Because the length of `buttonNames` is currently 3 (because the array contains three city names), the loop we are about to set up will loop three times, creating a list button with each loop. If we placed another city's name in the array, its length property would be 4, which means the loop would automatically adjust accordingly and create four list buttons.

4) Add the following ActionScript to the `populateList()` function just below its last line of code:

```
var i = -1;
while (++i < numberOfButtons) {
  name = "item" + i;
  item.duplicateMovieClip(name, i);
  this[name].itemName.text = buttonNames[i];
  this[name]._x=0;
  this[name]._y = i * spacing;
  this[name].pictureID = i + 1;
}
```

You've just scripted a `while` loop that duplicates the **item** movie clip instances needed for the drop-down list, positions them, and gives them a name to display.

Before the loop is defined, the script creates a local variable named `i` and assigns it a value of `-1`.

The letter `i` is commonly used as the name of an incremental variable in loops.

The next line of ActionScript starts the `while` loop and defines the condition that makes the loop continue working. It basically states that while the incremented value of `i` is less than the value of `numberOfButtons`, keep looping. When the loop begins, `i` will have a value of `0`. This is because although `i` is initially assigned a value of `–1`, the increment operator (`++`) increments its value by one prior to each loop—including the first. Because `numberofButtons` will have a value of `3` (as discussed in the previous step) and `i` is incremented by one with each iteration, the condition this loop analyzes will prove `false` after three iterations.

The first action in the script creates a variable called `name`, which is assigned a dynamic value based on the current value of `i`. Since that value is incremented with each iteration of the loop, in the first iteration of the loop, `name` is assigned a value of `"item0"` and in the second iteration it is assigned a value of `"item1"` and so on. The next line uses the `duplicateMovieClip()` method to create a new instance of the **item** movie clip. There are two parameters to this method, separated by a comma: The first assigns an instance name to the duplicate that is created, and the other parameter assigns the duplicate a depth (think of this as the stacking order). As defined in the method's parentheses, we'll use the current value of the `name` variable (dynamically set with the last action) as the instance name of the duplicate, and we'll use the current value of `i` to set the depth.

With the next four actions in the loop, `this[name]` references the name of the duplicate just created. You'll remember from Lesson 7 that this special syntax provides a dynamic way of referencing a variable name in ActionScript. As discussed in the preceding paragraph, in the loop's first iteration, `name` is assigned a value of `"item0"`. Hence, with the first iteration of the loop, these lines of script could be rewritten as follows:

```
item0.itemName.text = buttonNames[i];
item0._x= 0;
item0._y = i * spacing;
item0.pictureID = i + 1;
```

Because in each loop iteration, the value of `name` is updated as well as used to name the duplicate created, these actions reference the duplicated instance.

320

Each duplicate contains the two elements included in the original **item** movie clip instance: the white button and the dynamic text field named **itemName**. Thus, the third line in the looping statement—`this[name].itemName.text = buttonNames[i];`—sets the value of `itemName.text` (and thus the text that will be displayed over the button) in the duplicated instance. That value is set by using the current value of `i` to reference a string in the `buttonNames` array created in Step 2. In the loop's first iteration, the value of `i` is `0`, which means that the value of `itemName.text` would be `buttonNames[0]`, or the first element in that array, which you'll remember is Paris.

The next two lines of script position the duplicated instance on the stage. As shown in the script, each of the duplicates will have the same x position, 0. The y position of the duplicate is dynamic, and is determined by multiplying the variable `i` by `spacing`. This has the effect of spacing the duplicates evenly, an equal distance apart, vertically.

Finally, the last action in the loop creates a variable named `pictureID` inside the duplicated instance. The value that the variable is assigned is based on the current value of `i` plus 1. This variable will not be used until the next exercise, where it will be employed to determine which set of pictures to display.

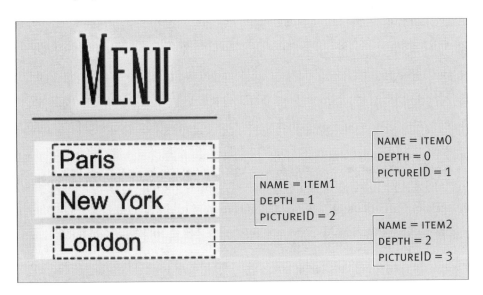

5) **Double-click the *dropDownList* movie clip instance to edit it in place. Select the Menu button, and with the Actions panel open, add the following script:**

```
on (release) {
  populateList();
}
```

AUTOMATING SCRIPTS WITH LOOPS

When this button is released, the `populateList()` function we just defined is called and a set of list buttons (dynamically created by the function) appears.

6) Choose Control > Test Movie. Click the Menu button to test your script.

When you click the Menu button, the `populateList()` function is called, and several duplicates of the **item** movie clip instance are created, positioned, and populated with text—all almost instantaneously.

7) Close the test movie and save your work as pictureShow2.fla.

You have now created a drop-down list using a `while` loop. In the next exercise you'll put this list to work by making something happen when you click on a list item.

NESTED LOOPS

As you've seen up to this point, loops provide a great way of automating a set of scripting tasks. However, loops can accomplish more than a straight, linear, repetitive execution of a set of actions. A *nested loop*, or a loop placed inside another loop, can be useful for creating a looping sequence that executes a set of actions, changes a bit, executes those same actions again, changes a bit, and so on. The following is an example of a nested loop:

```
var i = 0;
while (++i <= 10) {
  var j = 0;
  while (++j <= 10) {
    // perform these actions
  }
}
```

The actions in the above loops will be executed 100 times. Here's the underlying logic: The outer loop (which uses `i`) is set to loop 10 times. With each iteration of this outer loop, two things occur: The variable `j` is reset to 0, which then enables the inner loop (which uses `j`) to loop 10 times itself. In other words, on the first iteration of the outer loop, the inner loop will loop 10 times; on the second iteration, the inner loop will again loop 10 times; and so on.

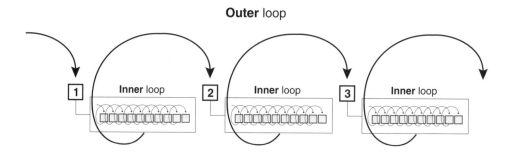

Outer loop

Nested loops are great for breaking up repetitive tasks into a hierarchical process. To help conceptualize this, think about writing a letter. A letter represents a nested-looping process in which you start on Line 1 and write 100 characters, then drop to Line to 2 and write 100 characters, and so on. If you were to write a 25-line letter, an imaginary script to do the work might look like the following:

```
var i = 0;
while (++i <= 25) {
  var j = 0;
  while (++j <= 100) {
    // type a character
  }
  // drop down to the next line
}
```

Keep in mind, too, that you aren't restricted to nesting just one loop inside of another: You can use as many loops within loops as your project requires.

In this exercise, you'll use nested loops to create a grid of images that appear when an item in the drop-down list is selected.

1) Open pictureShow2.fla in the Lesson 10/Assets folder.

On the top of the stage, you'll see three movie clip instances: **pictures1**, **pictures2**, and **pictures3**. In this exercise, you'll duplicate one of these three movie clips (depending on which item in the drop-down list is selected) to form a grid of images on the screen.

2) With the Actions panel open, select the *dropDownList* movie clip instance and add the following function to the load event:

```
function itemClicked (pictureID) {
  picToDuplicate = "pictures" + pictureID;
  xSpacing = 160;
  ySpacing = 120;
  xStart = 190;
  yStart = 30;
}
```

In a moment, we'll set up the list buttons that were duplicated in the previous exercise to call this function and pass it a parameter value—pictureID—when clicked. When finished, this function will copy one of the three picture movie clip instances at the top of the stage four times to form a two-by-two grid and to send each duplicated instance to a unique frame to display an image.

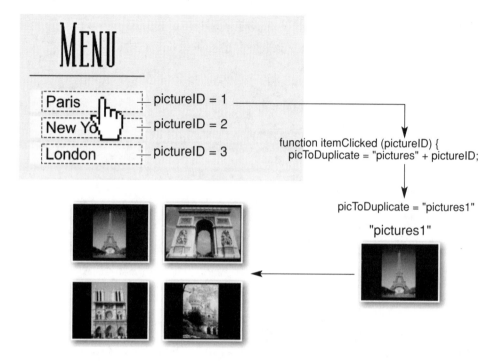

The first line in this function creates a variable called `picToDuplicate`. This variable's value—which is based on the `pictureID` value (of 1, 2, or 3) passed to the function when it was called—will be set to **picture1**, **picture2**, or **picture3**, which happen to be the names of the instances on stage containing pictures. We'll use this value in a moment to identify which of these instances to duplicate.

The `xSpacing` variable represents the amount of space you want to allot between the left sides of the two movie clip instances found on the same horizontal row. The `ySpacing` variable indicates how much space you want between two movie clips in the same column. The values of these spacing variables are fairly arbitrary and will depend largely on how much space you like to see between movie clips.

The next two variables, `xStart` and `yStart`, represent the starting position of the first duplicated movie clip in relation to the stage. Any subsequent movie clip duplicates will be positioned relative to this point.

324

3) Add the following script to the bottom of the `itemClicked()` **function (that is, add it to the function definition):**

```
v = 0;
i = -1;
while (++i < 2) {
  j = -1;
  while (++j < 2) {
    ++v;
    name = "picture" + v;
    _root[picToDuplicate].duplicateMovieClip(name, v);
    _root[name]._x = xStart + i * xSpacing;
    _root[name]._y = yStart + j * ySpacing;
    _root[name].gotoAndStop(v);
  }
}
```

Here you see a loop with a nested loop—the portion of the function that actually creates the two-by-two grid of movie clip instances. A single loop would create just a single column of movie clip instances. A nested loop, in contrast, creates two instances in a column, alters the script slightly to "move" the column coordinates, then creates another two instances in a column (which we'll explain in a moment). The following describes the logic that allows it to work.

The outer loop (beginning at Line 3) in the above script increments i by one (++i), thus setting a value of 0. The condition of this outer loop says that as long as i is less than 2, execute the actions below. Thus, because 0 is less than 2, the actions within the loop are executed. The first action sets the value of j to -1. Immediately following that, a nested (inner) loop appears, which uses the value of j. First, j is incremented by one (++j) and the condition is set that says as long as j is less than 2, continue to loop through the actions that follow. The script will continue to do nothing else but execute the actions in this inner loop until that condition becomes `false`. During the first iteration of this inner loop the value of v is incremented by one (++v), giving it a value of 1. This variable's value is used several times in the lines of script that follow. Using by-now-familiar ActionScript, the appropriate picture movie clip instance is duplicated and positioned. During the second iteration of this inner loop, the value of j is incremented by one (as shown in the loop's conditional statement), giving it a value of 1, which is still less than 2—thus, the actions within that loop are executed once again. This inner loop cannot perform a third iteration because j would be incremented again (++j), making it equal to 2 (a condition that exits the inner loop). As a result, the script revisits the outer loop. At that point, i (used by the outer loop) is incremented by one (++i), giving it a value of 1, which is still less than 2, so the actions in the outer loop are executed again. As a result, the value of j is reset to -1, and the actions in the inner loop are executed two more times (as previously described). This can be a tricky concept to grasp, so review the logic until you understand it.

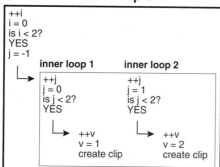

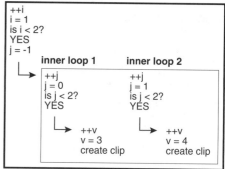

To achieve the effect of creating a two-by-two grid of movie clips (the proper spacing), take a look at the following lines of script:

```
_root[name]._x = xStart + i * xSpacing;
_root[name]._y = yStart + j * ySpacing;
```

The first line uses the current value of i to set the horizontal spacing; the second line uses the current value of j to set the vertical spacing when a movie clip is duplicated. You've already learned that with each outer loop iteration, the inner loop performs two iterations. Thus, while i has a value of 0, the value of j is both 0 and 1, then i is incremented to a value of 1, and once again, the value of j is set to both 0 and 1. Knowing the values of xStart, xSpacing, yStart, and ySpacing, as well as how the values of i and j are incremented in the looping process, we can determine the spacing for each clip as follows:

First instance duplicated

```
_x = 190 + 0 * 160;// x set to 190
_y = 30 + 0 * 120;// y set to 30
```

NOTE *Remember that in an expression, multiplication always occurs before addition (as shown).*

Second instance duplicated

```
_x = 190 + 0 * 160;// x set to 190
_y = 30 + 1 * 120;// y set to 150
```

Third instance duplicated

```
_x = 190 + 1 * 160;// x set to 350
_y = 30 + 0 * 120;// y set to 30
```

Fourth instance duplicated

```
_x = 190 + 1 * 160;// x set to 350
_y = 30 + 1 * 120;// y set to 150
```

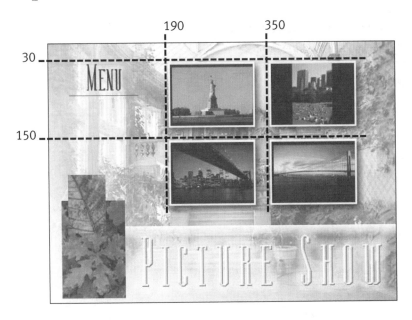

4) Add this final action as the last line in the `itemClicked()` function definition:

```
removeButtons();
```

```
  ▼ Actions - Movie Clip                                                    ▣
  [▣] Actions for dropDownList (Menu)                                    ▼  ⇥
  + ♫ ⊕ ✔ ≣ ⊡                                              ⊗ ⊗ ⊡
  24    function itemClicked(pictureID) {                              ▲
  25        picToDuplicate="pictures"+pictureID;
  26        xSpacing=160;
  27        ySpacing=120;
  28        xStart=190;
  29        yStart=30;
  30        v=0;
  31        i=-1;
  32        while (++i<2) {
  33            j=-1;
  34            while (++j<2) {
  35                ++v;
  36                name="picture"+v;
  37                _root[picToDuplicate].duplicateMovieClip(name,v);
  38                _root[name]._x=xStart+i*xSpacing;
  39                _root[name]._y=yStart+j*ySpacing;
  40                _root[name].gotoAndStop(v);
  41            }
  42        }
  43        removeButtons();
  44    }
  45  }                                                                 ▼
  ◀                                                               ▶
  Line 46 of 46, Col 1
```

This action calls a function you're about to create named `removeButtons()`, which will remove the drop-down-list buttons after one has been clicked and the picture grid created.

5) Create the `removeButtons()` function at the end of the `load` event of the currently selected movie clip instance:

```
function removeButtons() {
  var i = -1;
  while (++i < numberOfButtons) {
    name = "item" + i;
    this[name].removeMovieClip();
  }
}
```

This function uses a simple `while` loop to loop through and remove all of the buttons (which are actually the duplicate movie clip instances **item0**, **item1**, and **item2**) that make up the drop down-list choices under the Menu button. This loop works in similar fashion to the loop we used to *create* the duplicates that make up the list. Let's analyze this loop's syntax.

You'll remember that the variable `numberOfButtons` (used in the third line of the script) was originally created and assigned a value in the `populateList()` function discussed in the previous exercise. Its value is based on the `length` property of the `info` array. Because that array has three elements, the above loop will perform three iterations. On each loop the variable `name` is set based on the current value of i. The `removeMovieClip()` method is then used to remove the duplicate movie clip instances referenced by the current value of `name`—removing the list of choices beneath the Menu button.

6) Double-click the *dropDownList* movie clip instance to edit it in place. Double-click the *item* movie clip instance to edit it in place. Select the white button, open the Actions panel, and add the following script:

```
on (release) {
  _parent.itemClicked(pictureID);
}
```

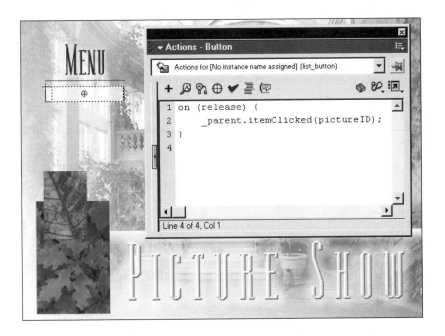

When you click the Menu button, a drop-down list is created by duplicating the **item** movie clip instance. Because the above script is attached to a button *inside* the **item** movie clip instance, the buttons in the duplicates will include this same script. However, during the duplication process (accomplished via the `populateList()` function we created in the previous exercise), a variable called `pictureID` is created inside each duplicate instance—and in each instance, the variable has a different value. That value is 1, 2, or 3, depending on the value of `i` when the duplicate is created (review the structure of the `populateList()` function if this is unclear). When this button is clicked in any of the duplicated movie clip instances, the above script passes the value of the `pictureID` variable in that instance to the `itemClicked()` function that was defined on the **dropDownList** movie clip instance. The result is that a grid of images is formed on the stage. To make better sense of this, review the image in Step 2 of this exercise.

7) Choose Control > Test Movie to test your work.

Click the Menu button to display the list of choices. As you click any of the list buttons, you'll see that the grid of images is being created based on the value of `pictureID` that is being passed to the `itemClicked()` function. You'll also notice that the list choices are removed via the `removeButtons()` function.

8) Close the test movie and save your work as pictureShow3.fla.

In this exercise, you used nested loops to create a grid of images on the screen. While we could have manually dragged and placed four movie clip instances on the stage to accomplish the same thing, by using a nested loop, we've automated the entire process in such a way that with a couple of minor adjustments, our script can create anything from a two-by-two grid to a 100-by-100 grid. Using loops, and especially nested loops, in this fashion not only helps automate processes you might perform manually in the authoring environment, it also enables your projects to scale up or down dynamically based on conditions that exist while it plays.

LOOP EXCEPTIONS

In general, a loop continues to perform iterations until its condition is no longer `true`. There are two actions you can use to change this behavior: `continue` and `break`.

With the `continue` action, you can stop the current iteration (that is, no actions in that iteration will be executed) and jump straight to the next iteration in a loop. Take, for example, the following:

```
total = 0;
i = 0;
while (++i <= 20) {
  if (i == 10) {
    continue;
  }
  total += i;
}
```

The `while` statement in this script loops from 1 to 20, and with each iteration, adds the current value of `i` to a variable named `total`—except when `i` equals 10. When `i` equals 10, the `continue` action is invoked, which means no more actions are executed on that iteration, and the loop skips to the eleventh iteration. This would create a set of numbers that read "1 2 3 4 5 6 7 8 9 11 12 13 14 15 16 17 18 19 20." Note that there's no number *10*, indicating that no action occurred on the tenth loop.

The `break` action is used to exit a loop—even if the condition that keeps the loop working remains `true`. Take, for example, the following:

```
total = 0;
i = 0;
while (++i <= 20) {
  total += i;
  if (total >= 10) {
    break;
  }
}
```

This script increases the value of a variable named `total` by 1 with each iteration. When the value of total is 10 or greater (as checked by an `if` statement, as shown), a `break` action occurs and the `while` statement halts, even though it's set to loop 20 times.

In this exercise, you'll use `continue` and `break` in a simple search routine.

1) Open phoneNumberSearch1.fla in the Lesson10/Assets folder.

This file contains two layers: Actions and Search Assets. The Actions layer will contain the search routine for this project. The Search Assets layer contains the text fields, button, and graphics for this exercise.

In this exercise, you'll produce a simple application that lets you enter a name in a search field to return the phone number for that individual. There are two text fields on screen, one with an instance name of **name** that will be used to enter the name to search, and the other with an instance name of **result** that will be used to display the search result. There is an invisible button over the Search button graphic that will be used to call a search function.

2) With the Actions panel open, select the first frame in the Actions layer and add the following script:

```
info = [["John","919-555-5698"],["Kelly","232-555-3333"],["Ross","434-555-
5655"]];
```

This creates a two-dimensional array called `info`, which contains three elements, each of which is its own array, or *sub-array*. The first element of each sub-array is a name, and the second element of each sub-array is a phone number.

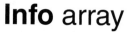

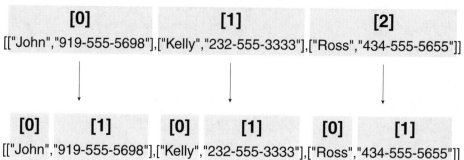

To access the first name in this array, you would use `info[0][0]`; the first phone number would be accessed using `info[0][1]`. This represents John's name and number. This syntax will play an important role in the search function we're about to script.

3) Add the following function definition just under the `info` array:

```
function search () {
  matchFound = false;
  i = -1;
  while (++i < info.length) {
  }
}
```

You've begun to define the function that will search the `info` array for a specific phone number. The first action in this function creates a variable called `matchFound` and assigns it an initial value of `false`. (We'll show you how this variable will be used in a moment.)

We've set up the `while` statement to loop once for every element in the `info` array.

4) Add the following actions to the `while` loop in the `search()` function:

```
if (info[i][0].toLowerCase() != name.text.toLowerCase()) {
  continue;
  }
  result.text = info[i][1];
  matchFound = true;
  break;
}
```

With each iteration of the loop, the above `if` statement uses the current value of `i` to determine whether there are any mismatches between names in the `info` array (made all lowercase) and the user-entered name in the **name** text field (forced to lowercase).

When a mismatch is encountered, the `continue` action within the `if` statement is evoked and you skip to the next loop. By using `toLowerCase()` to convert any names to lowercase, the search becomes case-insensitive.

If a name in the `info` array and the **name** text field match, `continue` is not invoked and the actions *after* the `if` statement are executed: Using the value of `i` at the time a match was found, the first action sets the value of the variable `result.text` to the matching phone number; `matchFound` is set to `true`; and the `break` action is executed to halt the loop.

To demonstrate how this works, imagine that someone has entered *Kelly* into the **name** text field. The location of "Kelly" in the `info` array is as follows:

```
info[1][0]
```

On the first iteration of the loop, the value of `i` is `0`, which means the `if` statement in the loop would look like the following:

```
if (info[0][0].toLowerCase() != name.text.toLowerCase()) {
  continue;
}
```

Here the statement asks if "john" (the name at `info[0][0]`, made lowercase) is not equal to "kelly'" (entered into the **name** text field, made lowercase). Since "john" does not equal "kelly," the `continue` action is invoked and the next loop begins. Because `i` is incremented by one with each loop, on the next iteration, the `if` statement will look like the following:

```
if (info[1][0].toLowerCase() != name.text.toLowerCase()) {
  continue;
}
```

Here the statement is asking if "kelly" (the name at `info[1][0]`, made lowercase) is not equal to "kelly" (entered into the **name** text field, made lowercase). Since "kelly" does equal "kelly," the `continue` action is skipped and the next three actions are executed. The first action sets the value of `result.text` to `info[i][1]`. Because `i` has a value of `1` when this is executed, `result.text` is set to `info[1][1]`—Kelly's phone number, which is now displayed. Next, `matchFound` is set to `true` and the `break` action exits the loop.

Although the break *action is not a necessity, it helps shorten search times. Think of how much time you could save by using a* break *action to avoid unnecessary loops in a 10,000-name array!*

5) Add this final if **statement as the last action in the** search() **function:**

```
if (!matchFound) {
  result.text = "No Match";
}
```

This statement, which is not part of the loop, checks to see whether matchFound still has a value of false (as it was set initially) once the loop is complete. If it does, the action in this if statement sets the value of result.text to "No Match." The syntax !matchFound is a shorthand way of writing matchFound == false.

6) With the Actions panel open, select the invisible button over "search" and add the following script:

```
on (release, keyPress "<Enter>") {
  search();
}
```

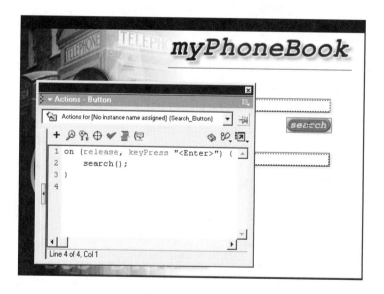

If the mouse is released or the Enter key pressed, the search() function will be called.

7) Chose Control > Test Movie. Enter *John*, *Kelly*, or *Ross* into the search field and press the Search button. Enter any other name and then press the Search button.

A phone number should appear when a name is valid, and "No Match" should appear when a name is not contained within the `info` array.

8) Close the test movie and save your work as phoneNumberSearch2.fla.

In this exercise, you used the loop exceptions `continue` and `break` to create a search routine. You'll soon find out that in practice, the `break` command is more common than the `continue` command: This is because programmers often use `if` statements rather than `continue` to bypass actions in a loop.

WHAT YOU HAVE LEARNED

In this lesson, you have:

- Learned about the usefulness of loops (pages 310–312)
- Been introduced to the three loop types available in ActionScript (pages 313–315)
- Applied `while` loops in several ways (pages 316–322)
- Created and used a nested loop (pages 322–330)
- Used the `continue` and `break` loop exceptions (pages 330–335)

getting data in and out of Flash

LESSON 11

One of Flash's most useful features is its ability to communicate with external sources. Being able to send and receive data to and from other locations makes Flash a real application development tool: It enables you to do things like load news dynamically, facilitate user log in and registration, and build Flash chat applications.

In this lesson, we'll show you the various ways Flash is able to send and receive data. You'll then use this knowledge to build a simple Flash polling application that lets you vote for a movie and then displays the poll results, as well as a journal that saves entries to your hard drive.

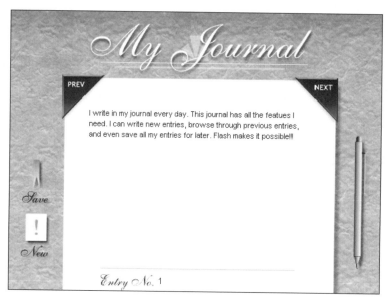

This journal application (which you'll create in this lesson) will allow you to add new entries, browse all previous entries, and save entries for later.

WHAT YOU WILL LEARN

In this lesson, you will:

- Learn about the types of data format that Flash can load

- Learn about the objects designed for data transfer

- Send and receive data from a server

- Save data to your hard drive using shared objects

APPROXIMATE TIME

This lesson takes approximately
1 hour to complete.

LESSON FILES

Media Files:

Lesson11/Assets/poll.asp

Lesson11/Assets/poll.mdb

Starting Files:

Lesson11/Assets/poll1.fla

Lesson11/Assets/journal1.fla

Completed Projects:

poll2.fla

journal2.fla

Bonus File:

Lesson11/Bonus/highscoreList.fla

UNDERSTANDING DATA SOURCES AND DATA FORMATS

A *data source* is a place from which Flash can load external data (that is, data not directly programmed into the movie). For example, Flash can load data from a simple text file—and that text file is considered a data source. *Data transfer* is the act of retrieving data from a source or sending data from Flash to another application. In this section, you'll learn about the different types of data sources, as well as the Flash objects and methods used to communicate with these sources in the data transfer process.

Any data that you plan to load into Flash from an external source must be structured (formatted) in a certain way. Flash supports the following formats:

- **URL string.** In this type of name-value pair formatting, variables and their values are defined as a string of text. For example, the text string `name=Jobe&website=http://www.electrotank.com&hairColor=brown` defines three variables (`name`, `website`, `hairColor`) and their respective values (`Jobe`, `http://www.electrotank.com`, `brown`). Once this text string has been loaded, Flash will automatically break it into its respective variable name-values, making them available for use as any other variables. As you can see, an equals sign is used to associate a variable name with its value, while an ampersand (&) marks the end of one variable and the beginning of another. The format supports an unlimited number of variables. Keep in mind, however, that only simple variables can be stored in this format; data contained in objects, arrays, or any other data type *cannot*. You will use this format in an exercise later in this lesson.

- **XML.** This popular formatting standard allows data to be stored in a logical structure. For example,

```
<States>
  <State>
    <Name>North Carolina</Name>
    <Capital>Raleigh</Capital>
  </State>
  <State>
    <Name>Virginia</Name>
    <Capital>Richmond</Capital>
  </State>
</States>
```

Once an XML document is loaded into Flash, a script (which you must write) is used to extract information from it.

338

NOTE *See Lesson 12, Using XML with Flash, for more information on the XML format.*

- **Shared objects.** We'll describe these in detail later in this lesson; for now, just understand that shared objects are like Flash cookies: They allow you to store objects (data) locally, on the user's hard drive. This means that once a user views and exits a Flash movie (as a projector or online), the data created while the movie was playing (user's name, last section visited, and so on) is saved. This in turn means that this data can be retrieved the next time the user plays the movie on the same computer. By using shared objects, you can store not only variables and their values but *any* kind of data object—arrays, XML objects, even custom objects. You can make this process of saving data transparent to users, or you can provide buttons for them to initiate the action. And you can have multiple shared-object data files on a single computer because each movie usually (though not always) creates its own data file.

Now that you're familiar with the various data formats Flash supports, let's review the sources from which Flash can load data:

- **Text files.** Flash can load text files (*.txt) containing data formatted using the URL string format mentioned above. Text files can be loaded using `loadVariables()` or the `load()` method of the `LoadVars` object, both of which we'll discuss later in this lesson. You can easily create these types of data sources using Windows Notepad or Apple SimpleText.

- **Server-side scripts.** These are scripts placed on ASP, CFM, CGI, or JSP pages and executed by a server. Although invisible to the user, the scripted page actually generates formatted data (HTML, XML, and so on) that's sent back to the requesting source. Imagine, for example, visiting a page called news.asp that contains a server-side script, and probably no real content: The script—which is executed when a user visits the page—is used to dynamically generate and send to the user's browser an HTML-formatted page containing the latest news (probably extracted from a database). Server-side scripts can return data in both the XML format and the URL string format—which means that by communicating with a page that contains a server-side script, Flash can load dynamic data created on the fly.

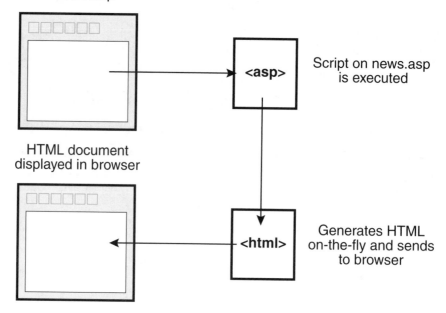

Browser requests page
at news.asp

`<asp>`

Script on news.asp
is executed

HTML document
displayed in browser

`<html>`

Generates HTML
on-the-fly and sends
to browser

- **XML files.** An XML file is simply a text file that contains XML-formatted data; such files usually include an xml extension.

- **XML socket.** Socket servers are applications that run on a server and connect several simultaneous users to one another. Flash can send or receive information via the socket using the XML format. (You'll learn more about socket servers—including how to build a chat application with them—in Lesson 12.)

- **Shared objects.** As mentioned above, shared objects are used to create data files that store information on a user's hard drive—which you can then retrieve and build back into a movie (as you will see in the last exercise in this lesson).

> **TIP** *Flash has a security feature that prevents you from loading data across domains. For example, if you were to upload a movie to www.site1.com and attempt to load data from www.site2.com, your load would fail.*

GET VS. POST

When working with server-side scripts (as mentioned above), there are two ways to transfer data between the server and Flash: via GET or POST. These two ways of sending variables and their associated values are used in regular HTML pages and in Flash whenever data entered into a form is sent to a server to be processed. (We'll discuss the specific methods Flash uses to send data in the following exercises.)

When you send variables using GET, you're simply concatenating variable name/value pairs onto the URL itself. For example, if you wanted to use GET to send my name and e-mail address to a script located on the register.asp page, you'd specify the URL as: `http://www.somedomain.com/register.asp?name=jobe&email=jobe@electrotank.com`. The question mark preceding the variables tells the script and server that everything that follows comprise variables. Although GET is easier to use than POST, it won't work for every situation because it has a 1,024-character limit.

Now let's take a look at how POST is used. When variable data is sent using POST, that data is contained within the header of the HTTP request—which means you cannot see it being transferred. Because POST doesn't have a character limit, it provides a slightly more versatile way of sending variable data.

Using GET

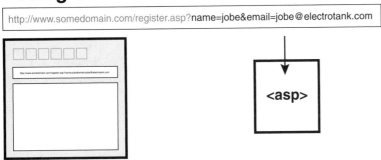

Using POST

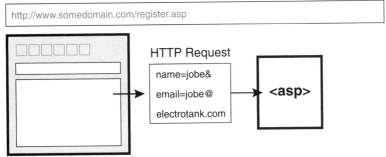

We'll return to the topic of GET and POST in the exercise that accompanies the next section, "Using the LoadVars Object."

TIP *Since GET and POST are not always easily interchangeable, most scripts are programmed to accept variables either via GET or POST but usually not via both.*

USING THE LOADVARS OBJECT

You will use the `LoadVars` object when working with data in the URL string format. This object enables you to *load* variable data from a text file or *send and load* variable data to and from a server-side script.

> **NOTE** *While variable data contained in a text file can be loaded into Flash, Flash cannot save data to a text file directly; you must use a server-side script to do that.*

Creating a `LoadVars` object in Flash is simple. Take a look at the following example:

```
container = new LoadVars();
```

This creates a new LoadVars object named `container`. To load variables from a URL into a `LoadVars` object, use the `load()` method:

```
container.load("http://www.myDomain.com/myFile.txt");
```

> **TIP** *At any time you can get the total number of bytes loaded so far or the total bytes that will be loaded using the `getBytesLoaded()` and `getBytesTotal()` methods of the LoadVars object.*

When data has been loaded into a LoadVars object, you can access it by referencing the name of the particular LoadVars object that contains the data you want, followed by the variable name of that piece of data. For example, if you were to load the following string into a LoadVars object named `myData`:

name=Jobe&age=25&wife=Kelly

These variable values could be referenced as follows:

```
myData.name
myData.age
myData.wife
```

For example:

```
usersAge = myData.age;
```

Here, `usersAge` would have a value of 25. In the same manner, a variable value in a LoadVars object (`myData`) can be set from within a script in Flash in the following manner:

```
myData.age = 45;
```

This means that variable values inside a LoadVars object can be set not only by loading external data into the object but also by setting its value internally (using a script inside the movie);

TIP *When loading variables into a LoadVars object, Flash will overwrite variable values where they may already exist in the object and append new variable values that don't already exist.*

If you wish to send the variables in a LoadVars object to a server-side script for processing, you would use the `send()` method. That syntax is as follows:

```
myLoadVarsObject.send("http://www.mydomain.com/process.cfm");
```

A response is not sent back to Flash when you use this method—which means you would only use it to send variable data to the server for processing.

The `sendAndLoad()` method allows you to specify a LoadVars object whose contents you want to send and the LoadVars object in which you want the response to load:

```
myLoadVarsObject.sendAndLoad("http://mydomain.com/process.asp",
receivingLoadVarsObject);
```

In this case, the variables in `myLoadVarsObject` are sent to the URL shown for processing. The server will send data back to Flash, and that data will be loaded into `receivingLoadVarsObject`. At that point, you can work with the `receivingLoadVars` object to extract the data the server sent back. If you want to send variables in a LoadVars object and have that same object receive the data the server sends back, simply use the `load()` method (which we'll describe in the following exercise).

Using the `toString()` method of the `LoadVars` object, you can create a URL-formatted string that represents the variables/values contained in the object.

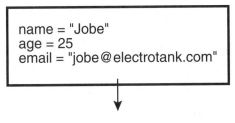

myLoadVarsObject

```
name = "Jobe"
age = 25
email = "jobe@electrotank.com"
```

myLoadVarsObject.toString()

name=Jobe&age=25&email=jobe@electrotank.com

The LoadVars object has two properties: `contentType` and `loaded`. The `contentType` property (which you can change before sending out variables) simply gives you the mime type specified in the HTTP header of the loaded document. The `loaded` property simply returns `true` if data has finished loading into the object, `false` if it has not, and `undefined` if a `load()` method has not yet been invoked.

There is only one event available to the `LoadVars` object: `onLoad`. You would use this event to call a function when data has finished loading into the object. Each time data is loaded into the object, this event is fired again.

To load variables from a specified URL into a `LoadVars` object and then have it call a function when loading is complete, you must:

1. Define a function

2. Create a new `LoadVars` object using the new `LoadVars` constructor

3. Specify the function to be called when the loading has completed

4. Invoke the `load()` method of the `LoadVars` object

For example:

```
function myFunction(){
  trace("Data is loaded");
}
container = new LoadVars();
container.onLoad = myFunction;
container.load("http://www.somedomain.com/myFile.asp");
```

In this example, `myFunction()` is called when a string of data from the specified URL has been completely loaded into the `container` LoadVars object.

NOTE *If you're familiar with Flash 5's use of the `loadVariables()` method, you should know that while it still works in Flash MX, it's preferable to use LoadVars objects.*

In the following exercise, you'll create a simple polling system using a LoadVars object. This object will send and load data to and from an ASP page in the URL string format. This page contains a server-side script that enables it to read and write to a Microsoft Access database. When variable data is *sent* to the ASP page, it interprets it and updates the values in the database accordingly. When a LoadVars object requests that data be *loaded* into it from the ASP page, the page is set up so that it gets the data from the various fields in the database, encodes that data into the URL string format, and then sends that data to the LoadVars object.

You will find this scripted page (poll.asp) and the accompanying database (poll.mdb) in the Lesson11 folder on your CD-ROM. To complete this lesson successfully, you will need access to a Windows server so that the server-side script on the ASP page can be executed. Before you begin this exercise, you will need to upload poll.asp and poll.mdb to a Windows server and make a note of their location (URL).

1) Open poll1.fla in the Lesson 11/Assets folder.

We've already created the layers, frames, frame labels, and movie clips you'll need so that you can focus on the ActionScript.

With the timeline at Frame 1, you'll notice the following text: "What was the best movie of 2001?" Below this text is some space, then a Submit button. You will place four Radio Button components in the empty space between these two elements. These radio buttons will represent the selection method for your choice of the best movie of 2001. When a user presses the Submit button, the movie will execute a script, sending data to the server (based on which radio button is selected) and at the same time moving the playhead to Frame 3, labeled **waiting**, where it will wait for a response from the server. When a response is received (data is loaded into a LoadVars object), the movie will move to the frame labeled **display**. This frame will contain a script used to interpret the response from the server (data will be extracted from the LoadVars object). This data will then be used to determine the percent of the total number of votes that each of the four movies listed has received. Each movie's overall percentage value will then be displayed in a text field as well as graphically, using simple bar graphs.

345

2) Move the playhead to Frame 1 and select the frame in the layer called Text and Buttons.

You will add four instances of the Radio Button component to this layer (beneath the question but above the Submit button).

3) Open the Components panel. Locate the Radio Button component and drag four instances of it onto the stage. Align these four components in a vertical column under the question on the screen.

You have just added four Radio Button components to the stage. If you select one of them and look at the Property inspector, you'll see a list of that component's properties, all of which are editable. The first property, Label, is the name that will be displayed next to the button. The next property, Initial State, is a Boolean value that determines whether this radio button should be selected or unselected initially. The Group Name property is a name that binds groups of radio buttons together. The four radio buttons we have added will be part of the same group; thus, each of their Group Name property values will be the same (we'll use the default value of radioGroup for all four buttons). Only a single radio button from the group can be selected at a time. In addition, each radio button in the group is assigned an associated value (its Data property). When one of the radio buttons is selected, *its* Data property value becomes the overall group's data value. Thus, if a radio button is selected and its Data property value is 47, the group's data value is updated to 47 as well (a fact that will be important to remember for this project). Below the Data property in the Property inspector, you'll see the Label Placement property. This property is used to determine whether the radio button's label should be left- or right-justified. Finally, the Change Handler property lets you define a function that you want to call when the button is pressed; you can leave this blank.

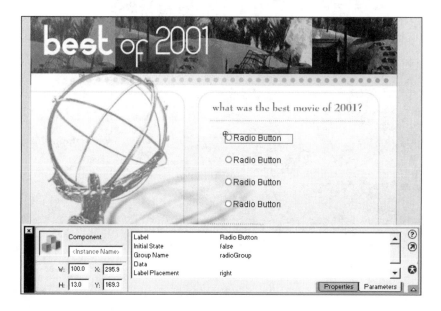

4) Select the top radio button and change its Label property to "A Beautiful Mind." Change the Label properties of the next three radio buttons to "Lord of the Rings", "Harry Potter", and "American Pie II" respectively.

As you change the label names of the radio buttons (from top to bottom on the screen), you should be able to see that the text is updated in the component itself.

NOTE *If this doesn't happen, choose Control > Enable Live Preview.*

5) Change the Data property of the four Radio Button components to 1, 2, 3, and 4, from top to bottom.

When the movie is published and a radio button is selected, its Data property value is set as the data value of the radioGroup. You retrieve this data value for use at any time by invoking the `getData()` method of the Radio Button component object. For example, if a radio button with a Data property value of 3 was selected, and this radio button was part of a group of radio buttons with a group name of radioGroup, the following syntax:

```
selectedValue = radioGroup.getData();
```

would assign a value of 3 to `selectedValue`.

6) With the Actions panel open, select Frame 1 in the Actions layer and add `stop()`;

This `stop()` action prevents the movie from playing past Frame 1 until we instruct it to do so.

7) With Frame 1 still selected, add the following line of script:

```
pollURL = "http://www.myDomain.com/poll.asp";
```

This creates a variable name `pollURL` and assigns it a value that represents the location (URL) of the poll.asp page you uploaded to your server at the beginning of this exercise. (The URL shown should be replaced with the actual location of poll.asp, as it resides on your server.)

8) Next, add this line of ActionScript:

```
poll = new LoadVars();
```

This creates a new LoadVars object. With this object, we can load data from a remote location and make use of the convenient methods and properties described earlier in this lesson.

9) Define the `pollLoaded()` **function by adding the following ActionScript at the end of the current script:**

```
function pollLoaded() {
  _root.gotoAndStop("display");
}
```

This function is used to move the playhead to the frame labeled **display**. (The next step explains when this function gets called.)

10) To associate the function we just defined with the onLoad **event of the** poll **LoadVars object, add the following line of ActionScript:**

```
poll.onLoad = pollLoaded;
```

This script says that when the last byte of data is completely loaded into the poll LoadVars object, the pollLoaded() function will be called. Thus, when the data has finished loading, the timeline will move to the frame labeled display (since that function is set up to move the timeline to that label). In a moment, we'll add a script at the display frame that will use the loaded data to display the results in several bar graphs.

11) Next, add this function definition just below the last line of script:

```
function submitChoice() {
  var choice = radioGroup.getData();
  poll.load(pollURL + "?choice=" + choice);
  _root.gotoAndStop("waiting");
}
```

```
Actions - Frame

Actions for Frame 1 of Layer Name Actions

 1  stop();
 2  pollURL = "http://63.151.44.251/projects/tfts/poll.asp";
 3  poll = new LoadVars();
 4  function pollLoaded() {
 5      _root.gotoAndStop("display");
 6  }
 7  poll.onLoad = pollLoaded;
 8  function submitChoice() {
 9      var choice = radioGroup.getData();
10      poll.load(pollURL+"?choice="+choice);
11      _root.gotoAndStop("waiting");
12  }

Line 1 of 16, Col 1
```

This function—which is used to submit the user's choice for best movie of 2001—is called when the Submit button is clicked.

The first line of the function definition creates a local variable named `choice`. This variable is assigned the current data value of the radioGroup group of radio buttons. Thus, if the user selected the second radio button, `choice` would have a value of 2.

The next line of ActionScript invokes the `load()` method of the `poll` LoadVars object. Using an expression, the URL of the poll.asp page is specified (`pollURL`), and the variable `choice` is added to the end of the string in order to send this to the server using the GET method of transferring variable data. If the user pressed Radio Button 3, this argument would look something like the following: `"http://www.mydomain.com/poll.asp?choice=3"`. Remember, everything after the question mark in the above argument is a variable. In this case, we're sending a vote (`choice=3`) to the poll.asp page. That page will then update the values in the database based on this vote and load the results into the `poll` LoadVars object. Those results are then used in the actions described in Step 14.

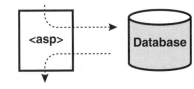

poll LoadVars Object

```
totalVotes = 65
item1total = 27
item2total = 15
item3total = 9
item4total = 14
```

The final line of script in this function tells Flash to go to the frame labeled waiting. The movie will stay on this frame until the data is loaded back into Flash from the server. At that point, the `pollLoaded()` function will be called (as described in the previous step), moving the timeline to the frame labeled display.

12) With the Actions panel open, select the Submit button and add the following script:

```
on (release) {
  submitChoice();
}
```

The submitChoice() function we defined in the previous step is executed when the button is clicked.

13) Move the playhead to the frame labeled *display*.

On this frame you'll see four movie clip instances with horizontal bars in them, one bar graph for each movie on which the user is voting. All of these are instances of the same movie clip: Their instance names are **barGraph1**, **barGraph2**, **barGraph3**, and **barGraph4**. Note that all of these instance names end with numbers: These are used to display the results of the poll. Each of these instances includes two text fields—**topPercent** and **bottomPercent**—that are used to display a textual representation of the percent. Both of these text fields display the same text; **bottomPercent** is simply there to provide a slight shadow effect behind **topPercent**. This movie clip also contains a horizontal bar with an instance name of **bar**. It will be horizontally scaled based on the value of the percent.

14) Select the frame in the Actions layer and add this loop:

```
for (i=1; i<=4; ++i) {
  var graphName = "barGraph" + i;
  var votes = poll["item" + i + "total"];
  var totalVotes = poll.totalVotes;
  var percent = Math.round((votes / totalVotes) * 100);
  _root[graphName].bar._xscale = percent;
}
```

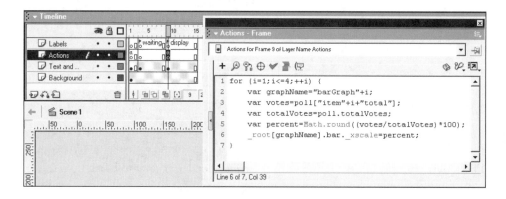

When the playhead has made it to this frame label (display), it means the user has submitted his or her choice and the server has accepted it, added it to the current results, and loaded the resulting data into the poll LoadVars object. You'll remember that in Steps 9 and 10, we scripted our movie so that it would move to this frame label only after the resulting data from the server had been loaded completely into the poll LoadVars object. The script on this frame will now use that data. The variables loaded from the remote script into the LoadVars object are named `totalVotes`, `item1total`, `item2total`, `item3total`, and `item4total`. Obviously, `totalVotes` has a numeric value representing the total number of all votes submitted (which will be used in a moment to figure percentage values). The other variables hold the number of individual votes that each of the movies received. Since these variables have been loaded into the `poll` LoadVars object, you can access their values using the following syntax:

```
poll.totalVotes
poll.item1total
poll.item2total
poll.item3total
poll.item4total
```

The loop in the above script calculates the percentage of votes received by each movie and scales the bar in the appropriate movie clip instance based on that number. The first line of script in the loop defines the variable called `graphName`. Since the value of this variable is based on the concatenation of the string "barGraph" with the current value of `i`, it is actually a reference to the name of the movie clip instance that will be worked with during the current loop (**barGraph1**, **barGraph2**, and so on). Once again, using the value of `i`, the next action in the loop sets a variable called `votes` equal to the total number of votes for the current item (`poll.item1total`, `poll.item2total`, and so on). Then, a variable called `totalVotes` is assigned a value that represents the total number of votes cast for all of the movies. Next, the `percent` variable is calculated by dividing the current item's number of votes by the total votes and multiplying by 100. This is then rounded using the `Math.round()` method of the Math object. Finally, the **bar** clip in the current movie clip (as referenced by the current value of `graphName`) is scaled to match the `percent` value. This loop will repeat these actions four times, scaling each of the bar graphs in the process.

Script as seen during loop number 2

```
var graphName = "barGraph2";
var votes = poll.item2total;
var totalVotes = poll.totalVotes;
var percent = 23
_root.barGraph2.bar._xscale = 23;
```

barGraph1

barGraph2

barGraph3

barGraph4

poll LoadVars Object

```
totalVotes = 65
item1total = 27
item2total = 15
item3total = 9
item4total = 14
```

NOTE *For more information about loops, see Lesson 10, Automating Scripts Using Loops.*

15) Add these two lines of ActionScript to the end of but within the loop:

```
_root[graphname].topPercent.text = percent + "%";
_root[graphname].bottomPercent.text = percent + "%";
```

The text to be displayed in the **topPercent** and **bottomPercent** text fields, above the scaled **bar** movie clip instance, is set using the value of the percent variable and concatenating "%" to the end of it.

16) Choose Control > Test Movie to test your work. Select a movie radio button and press the Submit button.

When you press the Submit button, your choice is sent to the poll.asp page, which then updates the database and returns the results of the poll to the poll LoadVars object. Your movie then moves to the frame labeled display and shows you the results!

17) Close the test movie and save your work as poll2.fla.

You have just completed a basic application that uses the LoadVars object to talk to external scripts. You can now use this knowledge to build more complex and useful applications.

USING SHARED OBJECTS

A SWF file can save data (variables as well as array, XML, and other data objects) to a user's hard drive using shared objects—similar to but more powerful than the cookies used by Web browsers: You can use them to store information generated by the user while viewing your movie (name, last frame visited, music preference, and more). Shared objects can be used by movies played in a Web browser, as well as those turned into stand-alone projectors.

NOTE *You can also use shared objects with Flash Application Services provided by Macromedia (visit macromedia.com for details on Flash Application Services).*

Here's an example of a script you might use to create a shared object:

```
myObject = SharedObject.getLocal("stuff_I_saved");
```

If the shared object "stuff_I_saved" already exists on the user's hard drive, its data is loaded instantly into myObject. If "stuff_I_saved" does not yet exist, it is created—and still referenced by myObject. In the latter case, myObject would be empty—that is, it would contain no data.

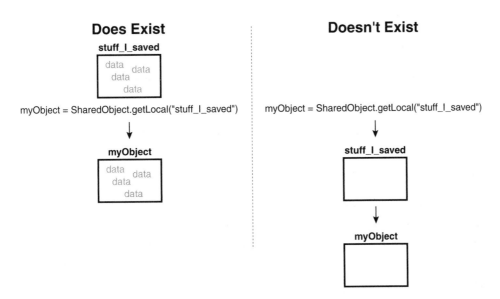

As you can see from the above syntax, the shared object's name is actually "stuff_I_saved". However, in ActionScript you can't reference the shared object directly using that name; thus, a reference to the shared object is created using `myObject`. This means that whenever you reference `myObject` in a script, you're actually referencing the shared object named "stuff_I_saved"—a tricky concept but essential to understanding how ActionScript deals with shared objects.

Data is saved to a shared object using the `data` property. Take a look at the following example:

```
myObject.data.userName = userName.text;
```

This would save the `userName` variable (and its value, the text in the **userName** text field) in the shared object. You can save entire objects as well. For example, if you wanted to save an array contained by your project, you would use the following syntax:

```
myObject.data.savedArray = nameOfArray;
```

A single shared object can contain multiple bits of data simultaneously:

```
myObject.data.savedArray = nameOfArrayObject;
myObject.data.savedXML  = nameOfXMLObject;
myObject.data.userName  = userName.text;
```

A particular piece of data can be erased from a shared object using `null`, as in the following example:

```
myObject.data.userName = null;
```

If `userName` were a piece of data in the shared object, the above script would delete it.

Extracting data from a shared object is similar to creating data in one:

```
userName.text = myObject.data.userName;
```

The above script will display, in the `userName` text field, the value of `userName` in the shared object. If this variable doesn't exist in the shared object, the value displayed in the text field will be "undefined."

When the SWF session ends (that is, the movie is closed or exited), all the information under the `data` property of your shared object is *automatically* written to the shared object file, ready to be retrieved using the `getLocal()` method described earlier. You can *force* a shared object to be written and saved at any time by using the `flush()` method. For example:

```
myObject.flush();
```

The above line of ActionScript forces your shared object and all the data it contains to be saved. Since `myObject` references the shared object named "stuff_I_saved", this is the object that will actually be saved.

Flash stores all shared objects in a central location on the user's hard drive—the *exact* location will depend on where the movie that created them resides (more on this in a moment).

On Windows, all shared objects are stored in the following general directory:

Windows\Application Data\Macromedia\Flash Player\

On a Mac, the location is:

System Folder\Preferences\Macromedia\Flash Player\

These are both general paths—that is, when a movie creates a shared object, a new subdirectory is created at one of the above locations. For example, if you were to view a movie at the following URL:

http://www.electrotank.com/fun/games/MiniGolf.swf

Any shared object created by this movie would, by default, be saved at the following path on a Windows machine:

Windows\Application Data\Macromedia\Flash Player\electrotank.com\fun\games\MiniGolf

Notice how this subdirectory's path structure matches that of the URL.

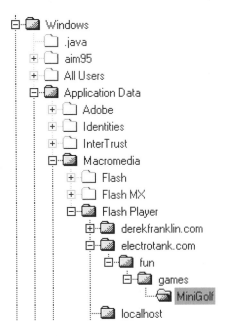

Because movies played locally (such as projectors) don't exist at a URL, Flash will save shared objects that they create to a localhost directory:

Windows\Application Data\Macromedia\Flash Player\localhost

All these directory paths are *default* paths where shared object data is stored. You actually have a lot of latitude as to where a shared object is stored or retrieved from within the general directory. Using the previous example, imagine playing a movie at the following URL:

http://www.electrotank.com/fun/games/MiniGolf.swf

This movie has the following shared object:

```
myScores = SharedObject.getLocal("scoreData");
```

When this shared object is saved, it is saved at the following path in Windows:

Windows\Application Data\Macromedia\Flash Player\electrotank.com\fun\games\MiniGolf\scoreData.sol

Flash will look for this same location again when the movie is played from that URL. However, the getLocal() method lets you add an optional directory path where the shared object should be saved and looked for. Assuming the movie at the aforementioned URL has a shared object declaration of the following:

```
myScores = SharedObject.getLocal("scoreData", "/fun");
```

The shared object would be saved to (and looked for) at the following path:

Windows\Application Data\Macromedia\Flash
Player\electrotank.com\fun\scoreData.sol

Armed with this knowledge, you can create movies at different locations that use the same shared object—useful if you want all of the movies on your site to reference a "master" shared object containing information about the user. Simply save a shared object in the main directory ("/").

NOTE *Be careful when using a single shared object across movies: Any one of the shared objects has the potential of overwriting the data it contains with new data.*

A single movie can create, save, and load multiple shared objects simultaneously.

TIP *You can configure the amount of data that a given URL can store by using the Flash player. If you right-click on the window of an open SWF and select Settings, you will see the Local Storage controls. You can block any site from storing information on your machine.*

NOTE *A bonus file called highscorelist.fla has been included on the CD-ROM in the folder for this lesson. It offers a complex but useful way to store game scores locally—and by so doing enables multiple users of the same computer to have their scores saved and then returned in order. You can use the custom-created highScoreList object defined in this file to control the list. Among other things, you can sort the list by ascending or descending scores, delete the list, edit a score, start a new list, or add a score to the list.*

In this exercise, you'll create a journal that saves text entries in an array as a shared object.

1) Open journal1.fla in the Lesson11/Assets folder on your CD-ROM.

You will notice one frame with four layers, which are named according to their contents. The stage contains two text fields that will be used to display information. The large one in the center, **journalBody**, will be used for journal entries. The smaller text field at the bottom of the screen, **entryNumber**, will be used to display the current journal entry number. The Buttons layer contains Prev, Next, New, and Save buttons.

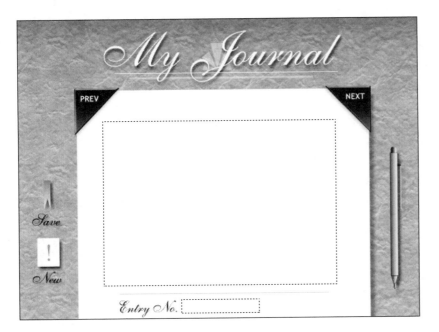

This application will allow you to start a new journal entry, save it, and browse through the entries you've created.

2) With the Actions panel open, select Frame 1 in the Actions layer and add this script:

```
myJournal = SharedObject.getLocal("JournalObject");
```

This line of ActionScript creates a reference to the shared object `JournalObject`. This object can be read and modified using the `myJournal` reference set up here. Thus, in the following scripts, when using `myJournal`, we're actually working with the shared object named `JournalObject`.

3) Add this conditional statement just below the line of script you added in the previous step:

```
if (myJournal.data.journal == undefined) {
  myJournal.data.journal = [];
}
```

This statement looks in the shared object for an array named `journal`. If it doesn't find one (`undefined`), the action within the statement creates it.

NOTE *If an array is created, it automatically becomes part of the shared object when the movie is exited or the shared object is saved.*

The `journal` array will only appear `undefined` the first time the movie is played. Each subsequent time the movie is played, the array will exist and thus this action will be ignored.

TIP *It's a good idea to check for `undefined` data values in a shared object, as shown above. This allows you to assign default values the first time a movie is played by the user.*

4) Add this function definition at the end of the current script:

```
function displayEntry(num) {
  _root.entryNumber.text = num;
  _root.journalBody.text = myJournal.data.journal[num - 1];
}
```

This function does two things: It sets the value of two text fields on the stage—**entryNumber** and **journalBody**—based on the value of `num`. For example, if `num` had a value of 1 when the function was called, "1" would appear as the current entry number in the **entryNumber** text field. The second line in the function uses the value of `num` to determine which entry in the `journal` array (of the shared object) to display in the **journalBody** text field. Still assuming that `num` has a value of 1, this line of script could be broken down to read as follows:

```
_root.journalBody.text = myJournal.data.journal[1 - 1];
```

or

```
_root.journalBody.text = myJournal.data.journal[0];
```

The reason for subtracting 1 from the value of num in this expression is because what is shown as entry "1" in the **entryNumber** text field is actually the 0th element in the journal array. Thus, the conversion is necessary to keep the two elements in sync. We could have just made the first entry "0", but that doesn't make sense. With this in mind, it's important to understand that other entry numbers and array elements follow the same sequence (entry "3" is array element 2, and so on). Several of the scripts that follow employ similar logic.

5) Add this function call to the end of the current script:

```
displayEntry(myJournal.data.journal.length);
```

Since this function call exists on Frame 1, it's executed as soon as the movie plays. The displayEntry() function (which we defined in the previous step) is called and passed a value based on the length value of the journal array in the shared object. This will display the final entry the user made before exiting the movie. For example, if the journal array has three entries, the displayEntry() function is passed a value of 3 and the third journal entry is displayed. If the journal array has just been created (as described in Step 3), it will contain a single, empty element—thus, a length of 1 gets sent to the function.

6) Next, add the following function definition to handle saving data:

```
function save() {
  var num = Number(_root.entryNumber.text) - 1;
  myJournal.data.journal[num] = _root.journalBody.text;
  myJournal.data.flush();
}
```

As mentioned earlier, data is automatically saved to a shared object when a movie is exited. By using the flush() method, as shown here, you can save data at any time while the movie is playing. This function will be called when the Save button is pressed (see Step 11). Let's take a look at how this function works.

The first line in the function creates a variable named num. The value of this variable is set to the current value displayed in the **entryNumber** text field, minus one. The Number() function is used to make sure num contains a numerical value. The num value will be used in the next line of the function to reference the appropriate array index of the current journal entry as it relates to the current entry number. As mentioned in Step 4, the number displayed in the **entryNumber** text field is actually one more than the associated array index it references—which is why one is subtracted from the current entry value in the first line of script. (Keep reading: This will make more sense in a moment!)

The next line in this function definition uses the value of num to update the journal array with the text displayed in the **entryNumber** text field. As always, the best way to understand this is by using a sample scenario. Imagine that the current entry number displayed in the **entryNumber** text field is 9. When this function is called, num would be set to a value of 8 (nine minus one). The second line in the function would be evaluated as follows:

```
myJournal.data.journal[8] = _root.journalBody.text;
```

This will place the text in the **journalBody** text field into Index 8 of the journal array. Note once again that the current *entry number* is 9, but the currently referenced index number of the array is 8 (see Step 4 for more on this). This line of script can affect the data in the array in two ways: If Index 8 was previously empty (undefined), it will now contain text; if it previously included text, that text will be overwritten.

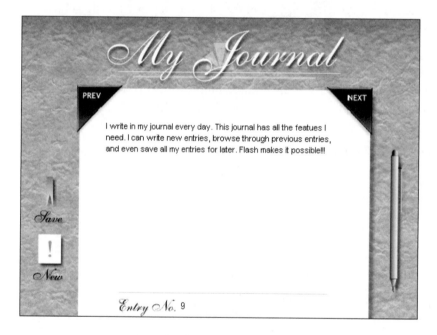

The last action in the function uses the flush() method to force the data and shared object to be saved to the user's hard drive—for our project, that will include all of the entries that exist in the journal array.

360

7) Now add this function definition to create a new journal entry:

```
function newEntry() {
  _root.entryNumber.text = myJournal.data.journal.length + 1;
  _root.journalBody.text = undefined;
  Selection.setFocus("_root.journalBody");
}
```

The first action in this function sets the current journal entry number (**entryNumber** text field) to the length of the journal array, plus one. Thus, if the journal array has two entries, it has a length of 2. Adding one will cause "3" to appear in the **entryNumber** text field. This action causes all new entries to be inserted at the *end* of the array. The last two actions in this definition are used to empty the **journalBody** text field, and then to give it focus, so that the user can immediately begin typing his or her entry. To better understand this, let's take a look at how this function works in harmony with the save() function discussed in the previous step.

Assume there are two entries in the journal array. This means that the array has entries at index positions 0 and 1 (important to remember), and that it has a length of 2. When the above function is executed, the **entryNumber** text field will display "3" (the length of the journal array plus one) and the **journalBody** text field will be emptied. The user now types text into this text field and presses the Save button, which will call the save() function defined in the previous step. At that point, the save() function will subtract one from whatever is displayed in the **entryNumber** text field, which will in turn save the current text in the **journalBody** text field to index position 2 of the journal array. The journal array would now contain *three* entries at index positions 0, 1, and 2, and its length would be 3. If the above function were called again, the process would begin again.

8) Next, add the following function definition, which will be used to display the next entry in the journal:

```
function nextEntry () {
  var num = Number(_root.entryNumber.text) + 1;
  if (num > myJournal.data.journal.length) {
    num = myJournal.data.journal.length;
  }
  displayEntry(num);
}
```

When executed, this function displays the next journal entry in the array. It does this by first assigning a value to num, based on the current numerical value displayed in the **entryNumber** text field, plus one. This value represents the next journal entry to be displayed. To prevent our application from displaying an entry that does not exist, the value of num is compared against the total number of entries in the journal array (the length property of journal). If the value of num is greater (as the if statement asks), you're attempting to display a nonexistent entry. In that case, the action within the if statement will reset the value of num to the length property value of the journal array—in effect causing the last entry in the array to be displayed instead. The final action in this function calls the displayEntry() function and passes it the value of num, enabling it to display the appropriate journal entry.

9) Create the following function, which will be used to display previous journal entries:

```
function previousEntry() {
  var num = Number(_root.entryNumber.text) - 1;
  if (num < 1) {
    num = 1;
  }
  displayEntry(num);
}
```

This function works similarly to the function described in the last step. First, num is given a value representing the current entry number minus one. The if statement is used to prevent our application from displaying anything beyond journal entry 1. Here's how it works.

Suppose the user is currently viewing entry number 6. When this function is called, num would be assigned a value of 5 (six minus one) and that value would be checked to make sure it's not less than 1. Since it's not, the action within the if statement is ignored and the displayEntry() function is called and passed a value of 5, displaying journal entry 5.

If the user were viewing entry 1 when this function was called, num would initially be assigned a value of 0. The if statement would determine that this value is indeed less than 1 and thus *change* its value to 1. The displayEntry() function would then be passed a value of 1. Since entry 1 is already being displayed, it will appear as if nothing has changed on screen. As mentioned, this mechanism prevents browsing past entry 1, since no entries exist at *entry number* 0 or less.

10) With the Actions panel open, select the New button and add this function call:

```
on (release) {
  newEntry();
}
```

When the user presses this button, the `newEntry()` function is called, advancing the current entry number by one and clearing the **journalBody** field so that new text can be entered.

11) With the Actions panel open, select the Save button and add this ActionScript to it:

```
on (release) {
  save();
}
```

When the user clicks this button, the `save()` function will be executed—at which point the current text in the **journalBody** field either replaces an existing entry or is added as a new entry in the `journal` array (as described in Step 6).

12) With the Actions panel open, select the Prev button and add this ActionScript:

```
on (release) {
  previousEntry();
}
```

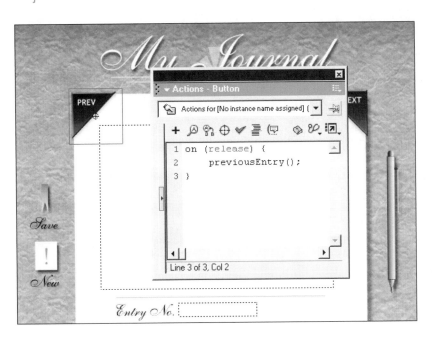

363

The call to the previousEntry() function changes the display to show the journal entry created before the current one displayed.

13) Finally, select the Next button and add this script:

```
on (release) {
  nextEntry();
}
```

This ActionScript simply calls the nextEntry() function when the button is clicked. The screen is then updated to display the next entry in the list of journal entries.

14) Choose Control > Test Movie to test your work. Enter some text as a journal entry. Press the Save button to save the entry, then the New button to create a new journal entry. Press the Save button and then restart the movie.

When you restart your movie, the shared object will be loaded (as described in Steps 2 and 3) and any data previously saved can be browsed using the Prev and Next buttons.

15) Close the test movie and save your work as journal2.fla.

In this lesson you have learned the basics of creating, retrieving, and saving shared objects.

You can also use shared objects to save any of the following:

- User's name
- Last frame visited
- User's music preference
- Date of user's last visit
- User's ordering preferences
- Scores (for games)
- Appointments, addresses, lists
- Property values (x, y, alpha, rotation) of elements
- More…

WHAT YOU HAVE LEARNED

In this lesson, you have:

- Learned about the data formats that Flash can accept (pages 338–340)

- Discovered how GET and POST are used to transfer data (pages 340–341)

- Gained experience using the LoadVars object (pages 342–352)

- Created an application that communicates with a server (pages 345–352)

- Saved and retrieved data locally using shared objects (pages 352–364)

using XML with Flash

Imagine what it would be like if every electrical appliance in your home had a different type of plug—chances are, you'd end up putting most of those gizmos back in the cupboard and doing the task manually. Or what if none of the screwdrivers or wrenches in your tool shed even came close to fitting the screws, nuts, and bolts that hold stuff together? Fortunately, neither scenario is likely because people figured out long ago that by creating products according to guidelines, or *rules of standardization*, they could have far more productive societies.

This simple chat application— which you will script in this lesson—uses an XML socket connection.

In essence, standards facilitate linkages between disparate items—battery and flashlight, Macromedia Flash and multiuser game server, and so on. And on the Web, where tons of data is transferred every second, having a standardized way of moving data between systems is essential. The powerful and easy-to-use XML is quickly becoming that standard.

In this lesson, we'll introduce you to the XML format, as well as show you how to use the XML object and the XMLSocket object in Flash. By lesson's end, you will have made Flash talk to ASP pages for user log-in and registration, and you will have created a very simple real-time chat using a socket server.

WHAT YOU WILL LEARN

In this lesson, you will:

- Learn about the XML format
- Send and load XML from the server
- Create new XML objects
- Learn to parse an XML document
- Use methods, properties, and events of the XML object
- Connect to a simple socket server using Flash

APPROXIMATE TIME

This lesson takes approximately 1 ½ hours to complete.

LESSON FILES

Media Files:

None

Starting Files:

Lesson12/Assets/LoginRegister1.fla

Lesson12/Assets/Chat1.fla

Completed Projects:

LoginRegister2.fla

Chat2.fla

LEARNING XML BASICS

Although the name *XML*, or *eXtensible Markup Language*, sounds a bit cryptic, don't worry: The language itself is actually quite easy to understand. In a nutshell, XML provides a way of formatting and structuring information so that receiving applications can easily interpret and use that data when it's moved from place to place. Although you may not realize it, you already have plenty of experience structuring and organizing information. Consider, for example, the following.

If you wanted to write a letter to a friend, you would structure your thoughts (information) in a format you know your friend will recognize. Thus, you would begin by writing words on a piece of paper, starting in the upper left corner, breaking your thoughts into paragraphs, sentences, and words. You could, of course, use images to convey your thoughts, or write your words in circular fashion, but that would most likely just confuse your friend. By writing your letter in a format your friend is accustomed to, you can be confident your message will be conveyed—that is, you will have transferred your thoughts (data/information) to the letter's recipient.

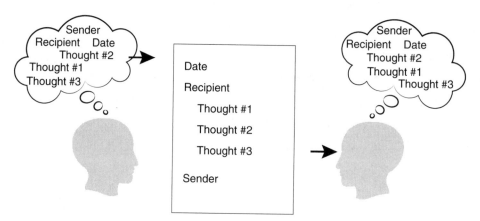

You can use XML in much the same way—as a format for conveying information. If, for instance, you wanted to send data out of Flash for processing by a Web server, you would first format that data in XML. The server would then interpret the XML-formatted data and use it in the manner intended. Without XML, you could send chunks of data to a server, but the server probably wouldn't know what to do with the first chunk, or the second, or even how the first chunk related to the second. XML gives meaning to these disparate bits of data, so that the server can work with them in an organized and intelligent manner.

XML's simple syntax resembles HTML in that it employs tags, attributes, and values—but the similarity ends there. While HTML uses predefined tags (for example, *body*, *head*, and *html*), in XML you create your own (that is, you don't pull them from an existing library of tag names). Before going any further take a look at this simple XML document:

```
<MyFriends>
  <Name Gender="female">Kelly Makar</Name>
  <Name Gender="male">Mike Grundvig</Name>
  <Name Gender="male">Free Makar</Name>
</MyFriends>
```

Each tag in XML is called a *node*, and any XML-formatted data is called an *XML document*. The above document has a *root node* called `MyFriends` and three *child nodes*. Each XML document can contain only one root node. The first child node has a *node name* of `Name` and a *node value* of `Kelly Makar`. The word `Gender` in each child node is an *attribute*. Attributes are optional, and each node can have an unlimited number of attributes. You will typically use attributes to store small bits of information that are not necessarily displayed on the screen (for example, a user identification number).

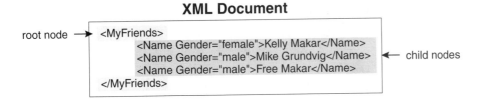

As you can see in this example, the tags (which we made up and defined) give meaning to the bits of information shown (`Kelly Makar`, `Mike Grundvig`, and `Free Makar`). This is why XML is so useful.

This next XML document shows a more extended use of XML;

```
<AddressBook>
  <Person>
    <Name>Kelly Makar</Name>
    <Street>121 Baker Street</Street>
    <City>Some City</City>
    <State>North Carolina</State>
  </Person>
  <Person>
    <Name>Tripp Carter</Name>
    <Street>777 Another Street</Street>
    <City>Elizabeth City</City>
    <State>North Carolina</State>
  </Person>
</AddressBook>
```

This example shows how the data in an address book would be formatted in XML. If there were 600 people in the address book, the Person node would appear 600 times with the same structure.

So how do you actually create your own nodes and structure? How does the destination (ASP page, socket, and so on) know how the document is formatted? And how does it know what to do with each piece of information? The simple answer is that this intelligence has to be built into your destination. Thus, if we were to build an address book in Flash and wanted the information it contained to be saved in a database, we would send an XML-formatted version of that data to an ASP (or another scripted page of choice), which would then *parse* that information and insert it into the appropriate fields in a database. The important thing to remember is that the ASP page must be designed to deal with data in this way. Since XML is typically used to transfer rather than store information, the address book data would be stored as disparate information in database fields rather than as XML. When needed again, that information can be extracted from the database, formatted to XML by a scripted page, and sent along to Flash or any other application that requested it.

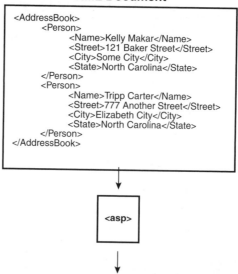

XML Document

```
<AddressBook>
    <Person>
        <Name>Kelly Makar</Name>
        <Street>121 Baker Street</Street>
        <City>Some City</City>
        <State>North Carolina</State>
    </Person>
    <Person>
        <Name>Tripp Carter</Name>
        <Street>777 Another Street</Street>
        <City>Elizabeth City</City>
        <State>North Carolina</State>
    </Person>
</AddressBook>
```

`<asp>`

ID	Name	Street	City	State
1	Kelly Makar	121 Baker street	Some City	North Carolina
2	Tripp Carter	777 Another Street	Elizabeth City	North Carolina

That said, you may sometimes use text files that contain XML-formatted information—for example a static XML file for storing information about which ASP pages to call or what port and IP to connect to when attempting to connect with a socket server.

Now that you know the basics of the XML structure, here are some rules you need to follow when you begin using it:

- You cannot begin node names with the letters *XML;* many XML parsers will break when they see this.

- You must properly terminate every node—for example, you would terminate `<Name>` with `</Name>`.

- You must URL-encode all odd characters (which you can do by using the `escape()` function in Flash). Many parsers will interpret certain unencoded characters as the start of a new node that is then not terminated properly (since it wasn't a node in the first place.) An XML document with non-terminated nodes will not pass through an XML parser completely. Attributes are less forgiving than text nodes because they can fail to pass through the parser on more characters, such as a carriage return or an ampersand. If you URL-encode the text then you will not experience any trouble with this.

- Most XML parsers are case-sensitive—which means all tags of the same type must have the same case. If you start a node with `<Name>` and terminate it with `</name>`, you're asking for trouble.

- You can only have one root node.

One more thing to note before you begin working with XML is that the clean XML structure shown in the examples here is not necessary. The carriage returns and tabs are there to make it easier for *us* to read. These tabs and carriage returns are called *white space*, and you can add or delete them without affecting the overall structure.

USING THE XML OBJECT

It's time to start using some XML! Nearly everything you do with XML in Flash involves the XML object and falls into one of the following categories: formatting XML, parsing XML (extracting the information), loading XML, or sending XML. With the XML object you will be able to load XML from an external source such as a static file or a server side script. Once this XML document is loaded you can access its information using the methods and properties of the XML object. Also using the methods and properties of the XML object you can create your own XML document. Once this document is created you can use it in your Flash movie or send it out to a server side script. All the ActionScript needed to do these things is covered in this section.

FORMATTING XML

The XML object in Flash has several methods, all of which you can use to create and format XML documents. Truth is, though, you're unlikely to employ them because they're difficult to use—and there's a better way! We'll show you how to

371

create a string and then convert it into an XML object—a much easier (and more common) way of formatting XML objects.

To create an XML object in Flash, you must use its constructor. Here is how you would create an empty XML object:

```
myXML = new XML();
```

To populate the object with XML-formatted data when it is created, you can pass (inside the parentheses of the constructor) the name of a variable that holds an XML-formatted string or another XML object.

If, in Flash, we wanted to create the following XML document:

```
<MyFriends>
  <Name Gender="female">Kelly Makar</Name>
  <Name Gender="male">Free Makar</Name>
</MyFriends>
```

We would do two things:

1. Create the document as a string.

2. Convert the string to an XML object using the XML object constructor, new XML().

Here is an example:

```
myString = "<MyFriends><Name Gender=\"female\">Kelly Makar</Name><Name
Gender=\"male\">Free Makar</Name></MyFriends>";
myXML = new XML(myString);
```

The above ActionScript creates the XML document as a string and then converts it to an actual XML object called myXML. This object can then be sent to the server using the send-related methods described later in this section of the lesson.

PARSING XML

The word *parse* simply means to analyze something or break it down into its parts. Thus, when someone speaks of writing a script to parse an XML document, they're talking about writing a script that extracts information from that XML document. The XML object has many properties to help you do this. We'll use the XML object you created in the previous subsection, myXML, to illustrate the use of a few of the most common properties.

`firstChild`: This property points to the first node in the tree structure. For example: `myXML.firstChild.firstChild` returns `<Name Gender="female">Kelly Makar</Name>`. The first child node of the XML document is the root node (`MyFriends`) and the root node's first child is `Name`, as shown.

`childNodes`: This property returns an array of the child nodes at any given point in the tree structure. For instance: `myArray = myXML.firstChild.childNodes`. Here, `myArray` contains two elements whose values are the same as those of the two `Name` nodes.

`nextSibling`: This property points to the next node in the same level of the tree structure. Thus, `myXML.firstChild.firstChild.nextSibling` returns `<Name Gender="male">Free Makar</Name>`.

`attributes`: This property returns an associative array of attribute names. For instance: `myXML.firstChild.firstChild.nextSibling.attributes.Gender` returns `"male"`.

myXML.firstChild.firstChild.nextSibling.attributes.Gender

```
<MyFriends>
        <Name Gender="female">Kelly Makar</Name>
        <Name Gender= "male" >Free Makar</Name>
</MyFriends>
```

The above represent the most commonly used properties of the XML object; others work in the same way, referencing different parts of the tree structure.

Loading XML

Typically, you'll only work with XML in Flash when you're loading it or sending it out. To load XML from a remote source, you would do the following:

1. Create an XML object.

2. Use the `load()` method of the XML object to load XML-formatted data from an external source.

For example:

```
myXML = new XML();
myXML.load("http://somedomain.com/info.xml");
```

Although in this example, the document being loaded is a static XML file, it doesn't have to be. It can point to an ASP page (or another scripted page) whose result is an XML document.

It's easy to determine when the XML has finished loading into an object by using the `onLoad` event available to the XML object. You can define this event to call a function when the document is finished loading. Take a look at the following example:

```
function init () {
  //parse script here
}
myXML = new XML();
myXML.onLoad = init;
myXML.load("http://somedomain.com/info.xml");
```

As the second line from the bottom shows, when the XML document is finished loading, the `init` function will be called.

Sending XML

The XML object allows you to send XML to a URL. It also lets you send XML *and* load the resulting document simultaneously.

To send XML to a URL, use the `send()` method and specify a destination URL. For instance:

```
myXML = new XML("<Message><Text>Hi!</Text></Message>");
myXML.send("http://somedomain.com/somedestination.asp");
```

To send XML and receive a response, all in one shot, use the `sendAndLoad()` method of the XML object. With this method, you must specify an XML object whose contents you wish to send, a URL in which to send the XML document, and an XML object in which to receive the response. As shown with the `load()` example in the previous subsection, you must define an `onLoad` event to handle the loaded XML. Here is an example:

```
URL = "http://www.electrotank.com/projects/tfts/using_xml/UserLogin.asp";
function init () {
  trace(objToReceive);
}
xmlToSend =
"<Login><UserName>Jobem</UserName><Password>hayes</Password></Login>";
objToSend = new XML(xmlToSend);
objToReceive = new XML();
objToReceive.onLoad = init;
objToSend.sendAndLoad(URL, objToReceive);
```

The above ActionScript creates an XML object (`objToSend`) containing log-in information, and then sends that information to a URL where it waits for a response from the destination. When the response is fully loaded into the receiving XML object (`objToReceive`), the `init` function is called.

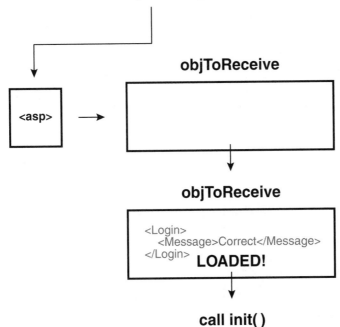

Now that you know a little bit about the XML format and XML objects (as well as their objects and properties), it's time to put that knowledge to use! In this section, you'll format a few simple XML documents, perform some easy parsing, and use sendAndLoad() to create a simple Flash application that acts as a registration/log-in screen.

The Flash file used in this section communicates with ASP pages. To fully build and test this file, you'll need access to a server where you can run ASP scripts (which usually means a Windows server). To test the files in this exercise, you'll need to upload two ASP files (AddUser.asp and UserLogin.asp) and one MS Access database file (XMLExample.mdb) to the same directory on a Windows server. (These files can be found in the Lesson12/Assets folder.)

The AddUser.asp page accepts an XML document structured as follows:

```
<Register>
  <UserName>jobem</UserName>
  <Email>jobe@electrotank.com</Email>
  <Password>secret</Password>
</Register>
```

If the user was registered properly, this page (AddUser.asp) will return the following result:

```
<Register>
  <Message>User Inserted</Message>
</Register>
```

If a user of the same name already exists, it will return this result instead:

```
<Register>
  <Message>User Exists</Message>
</Register>
```

The UserLogin.asp page accepts an XML document structured as follows:

```
<Login>
  <UserName>jobem</UserName>
  <Password>secretword</Password>
</Login>
```

If the information provided was correct, this page returns the following result:

```
<Login>
  <Message>Login Correct</Message>
</Login>
```

If the information provided was incorrect, the page returns this result instead:

```
<Login>
  <Message>Login Incorrect</Message>
</Login>
```

1) Open LoginRegister1.fla from the Lesson12/Assets directory.

We've already created all of the frames, text fields, and buttons in this file. The file contains four layers: The Actions layer is where we'll write all of the ActionScript; the Labels layer contains the frame labels we need; the Assets layer contains text fields and buttons; and the Background layer contains the interface graphics.

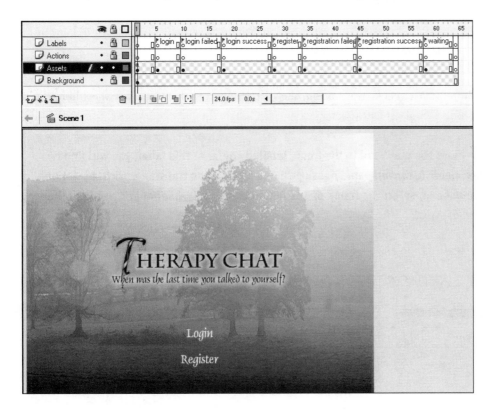

2) With the Actions panel open, select Frame 1 and add a stop() action.

By placing the Stop action here, we prevent the movie from automatically playing.

3) With the Actions panel open and the timeline at Frame 1, select the Login button and add this script:

```
on (release) {
  _root.gotoAndStop("login");
}
```

When the user clicks this button, he or she will be taken to the log-in frame (where he or she can log in).

4) With the Actions panel open and the timeline at Frame 1, select the Register button and add this script:

```
on (release) {
  _root.gotoAndStop("register");
}
```

When the user clicks this button, she will be taken to the register frame where she'll be able to register a new account.

5) Move the playhead to the frame labeled Login. At this label, you will find two text fields (*userName* and *password*) and a button on the stage. With the Actions panel open, select the frame on the Actions layer at that label and add the following line of script:

```
loginURL = "http://yourdomain.com/projects/tfts/using_xml/UserLogin.asp";
```

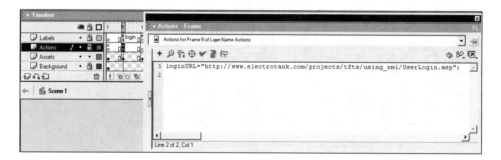

This is the ASP page that accepts the log-in XML document. It will parse the document that you send and return an answer to let you know whether the user provided the correct information. Make sure you enter the correct path to the file that you uploaded.

6) With the same frame still selected, add this function definition:

```
function loginSubmit () {
  xmlToSend =
"<Login><UserName>"+userName.text+"</UserName><Password>"+password.text+"</P
assword></Login>";
  objToSend = new XML(xmlToSend);
  objToReceive = new XML();
  objToReceive.onLoad = loginResponse;
  objToSend.sendAndLoad(loginURL, objToReceive);
  _root.gotoAndStop("waiting");
}
```

Although it hasn't been scripted to do so yet, this function will be called when the Submit button (currently on the stage) is pressed. The first line of the function uses the values entered in the **userName** and **password** text fields to format the XML that we're sending to the ASP page and then places that formatted data into a string variable named xmlToSend. Next, we create a new XML object named objToSend and pass into it the XML-formatted string we just created. The reason for doing this is that the sendAndLoad() method only works with XML objects—we can't apply it to a string. Next, we create a new object named objToReceive. This is the XML object that the ASP page's response is loaded into. Next, using the onLoad event, we tell the objToReceive object to call the loginResponse() function once the XML data has been loaded into it. (We'll create the loginResponse() function in the next step.

The next action in the function invokes the sendAndLoad() method by specifying the object to send, the destination URL, and the object in which to load the response. Finally, the last action will send the timeline to a frame named waiting, which informs the user that the information was sent but a response has not yet been returned.

7) Add this function definition just below the one you added in the previous step:

```
function loginResponse () {
  var response = objToReceive.firstChild.firstChild.firstChild.nodeValue;
  if (response == "Login Correct") {
    _root.gotoAndStop("login success");
  } else if (response == "Login Incorrect") {
    _root.gotoAndStop("login failed")
  }
}
```

This function is called as soon as the last byte of XML is loaded into the XML object called `objToReceive`, as shown in the previous step. It's used to parse the XML response from the server.

The first line in this function creates a variable named `response` and sets its value based on the data extracted from the returned XML document. Remember that the response of the UserLogin.asp page is in this format:

```
<Login>
  <Message>Login Correct|Login Incorrect</Message>
</Login>
```

As a result, `response` will have a value of either "Login Correct" or "Login Incorrect", depending on what's extracted from this XML document. An `if` statement then uses this value to send the timeline to the frame labeled either login success or login failed. This will move it from the waiting frame, which you'll remember is used as an interim location while waiting for a response from the server.

8) Select the Submit button and add this function call:

```
on (release, keyPress "<Enter>") {
  loginSubmit();
}
```

When this button is clicked the `loginSubmit()` function will be called and executed. This will activate the log-in process, as described in the previous few steps.

In summary, when the `loginSubmit()` function is called, XML data is sent to the server and the timeline is moved to the waiting frame. When a response is sent back from the server, the `loginResponse()` function is automatically called and the timeline is sent to either the frame labeled login success or that labeled login failed.

Let's next script our project to handle the registration process.

9) Move the playhead to the frame labeled register. At this label, you will find three text fields (*userName*, *email*, and *password*) and a button on the stage. With the Actions panel open, select the frame on the Actions layer at that label and add the following line of script:

```
registrationURL = "http://yourdomain.com/using_xml/AddUser.asp";
```

This is the ASP page that accepts the registration XML-formatted document. It will process the information and return a result. Make sure you enter the correct path to the file that you uploaded.

10) With the same frame still selected add this function definition:

```
function registrationSubmit () {
xmlToSend="<Register><UserName>"+userName.text+"</UserName><Email>"+email.te
xt+"</Email><Password>"+password.text+"</Password></Register>";
  objToSend = new XML(xmlToSend);
  objToReceive = new XML();
  objToReceive.onLoad = registrationResponse;
  objToSend.sendAndLoad(registrationURL, objToReceive);
  _root.gotoAndStop("waiting");
}
```

The above ActionScript is similar to that used in the `loginSubmit()` function defined in Step 6—the only differences are in the format of the XML and some reference names. Notice that the XML document here contains three pieces of user information: `userName.text`, `email.text`, and `password.text`. This is the information entered into the text fields by the user. The destination script will parse this document and extract that information.

11) Add this function definition just below the one you added in the previous step:

```
function registrationResponse () {
  var response = objToReceive.firstChild.firstChild.firstChild.nodeValue;
  if (response == "User Inserted") {
    _root.gotoAndStop("registration success");
  } else if (response == "User Exists") {
    _root.gotoAndStop("registration failed")
  }
}
```

This function is called when the last byte of information is loaded into `objToReceive`. This function is very similar to the `loginResponse()` function defined in Step 7. Remember that the AddUser.asp page returns a document of this format:

```
<Register>
  <Message>User Inserted|User Exists</Message>
</Register>
```

As a result, `response` will have a value of either "User Inserted" or "User Exists" depending on what is extracted from this XML document. An `if` statement then uses this value to send the timeline to either the frame labeled registration success, or the frame labeled registration failed.

12) Add this function call to the Submit button:

```
on (release, keyPress "<Enter>") {
  registrationSubmit();
}
```

When the user clicks this button or presses the Enter key, the `registrationSubmit()` function is called. This activates the registration process we described in the previous few steps. In summary, when the `registrationSubmit()` function is called, XML data is sent to the server and the timeline is moved to the waiting frame. When a response is sent back from the server, the `registrationResponse()` function is automatically called and the timeline is sent to either the frame labeled registration success or the one labeled registration failed.

13) Choose Control > Test Movie to test your work. Press the Register button and then submit some information. Reopen the movie and then try to log in.
You have just created a simple application that illustrates some uses of the XML object. Test it a few times to make sure you're comfortable with the ActionScript.

14) Close the test movie and save your work as loginRegister2.fla
Now you're ready to start creating some pretty advanced data-driven applications!

INTRODUCING SOCKET SERVERS

A socket server is an application that can accept "socket" connections. Socket connections are persistent—which means they let you remain connected to a server, rather than making a connection just long enough to download information and then disconnecting. Unlike a scripted page, a socket server is an application that's always running. It can accept numerous simultaneous connections and exchange information between them. Thus, while you're connected to a socket server, you can send or receive information any time. Using socket connections to continually transfer data to and from the server is how most chats and multiplayer games are created in Flash.

A key thing to understand about using socket connections with Flash is that you don't have to request information to get it—for example, in a chat application a message can be *pushed* into Flash at any time without Flash having to ask for it.

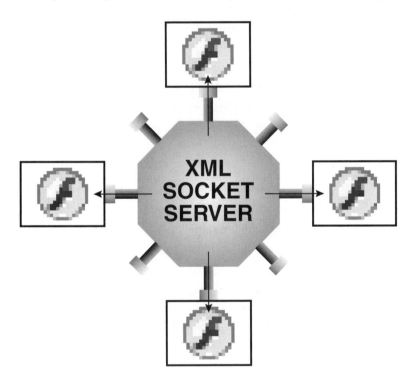

You cannot, however, just drop a socket server into the CGI-bin of your Web site or place it in a normal Web-accessible directory. Usually written in Java, C, C++, or Visual Basic, socket servers require root-level access to the Web server—which usually means you need to be running your own dedicated server to install and use a socket server. You can, however, set up a socket server on your own personal computer so that you can develop with it.

For the next exercise, we'll show you how to get a server up and running on your local machine so that you can go on to build a simple chat application that connects to a socket server. To test it, you'll need to use Windows 98, Windows 2000, Windows XP, or Mac OS X.

The accompanying CD-ROM contains a simple Java-based socket server, called AquaServer. (It was written by Branden Hall of Figleaf Software.) You need to have Java 2 Runtime Environment (JRE) version 1.3.1 or higher installed on your machine to run our socket server, as well as to test the chat program you build in the next section. (Mac OS X comes with the correct version of JRE installed.)

1) Download and install the JRE (for Windows users), by going to http://www.sun.com. Click on Downloads > Java Technology > Java 2 Runtime Environment v 1.3.1 (or higher). Download the installer and follow the instructions to install it.

In the next section, we'll tell you to start the server on a specific port. This is what you must do to start the server on a specific port on Windows:

2) Copy all of the files for this lesson from the CD-ROM into a directory on your hard drive. Open the MS-DOS prompt or Command Prompt (depending on your Windows version) by selecting Start > All Programs (or Program Files) > Accessories > Command Prompt (or MS-DOS).

3) Navigate to the directory that contains the files for this lesson by typing cd and the full path to that directory (for example, cd C:\Documents and Settings\Jobe Makar\Desktop\FlashFiles). Then press the Enter key.

The letters cd stand for change directory.

4) In the console window, type java AquaServer 9999 and press the Enter key.

This statement is case-sensitive, so make sure you type it exactly as written above. The console window should display information telling you that the server has started running and is listening on port 9999.

If you installed the JRE properly, this should work without a hitch, though you must leave the console window open for as long as you wish the server to run. When you close the window, the socket server will stop running.

AquaServer is one of a few free socket servers designed expressly for work with Flash. Although you cannot currently use any free socket server for commercial purposes, there are some extremely fast and stable commercial sockets servers developed specifically for Flash, including the following

• ElectroServer: www.electrotank.com/ElectroServer

• Unity: www.moock.org/unity/

USING THE XMLSOCKET OBJECT

Before you can connect Flash to a socket server, you must create a new XMLSocket object. You can then use the methods of that object to connect to a server and exchange information. In this section, we'll show you how to create and use an XMLSocket object while also using the XML object methods and properties introduced earlier in this lesson.

To create a new XMLSocket object, you must use the constructor for XMLSocket. Here's an example:

```
server = new XMLSocket();
```

The above line of ActionScript creates a new XMLSocket object named `server`. To connect the XMLSocket to a server, you simply employ the `connect()` method of the XMLSocket object using the following syntax:

```
server.connect(hostName,port)
```

The `hostName` parameter is the IP address on which the socket server resides—usually a numeric sequence (for example, 65.134.12.2). Since you'll be connecting to your own machine in this exercise, you can use either the sequence "127.0.0.1" or "localhost". Both 127.0.0.1 and localhost are valid references to your own computer. If you were to type http://localhost into your Web browser's address bar, it would try to connect to your computer as if it were a Web site. The `port` parameter refers to the port on which the server is listening. Flash can only connect to ports higher than 1024. For example:

```
server = new XMLSocket();
server.connect("localhost", 9999)
```

You can close a connection with a socket by using the `close()` method—which would look like the following:

```
server.close();
```

To send information via the socket connection, simply use the `send()` method and pass in the object you wish to send. For instance:

```
server.send("<Text>Hi</Text>");
```

The XMLSocket can respond to the following types of events:

- `onConnect`—This event fires when the connection is accepted or when it fails.

- `onXML`—This event fires when information arrives via the socket connection. This lets you know that new information has arrived so that you can use it.

- `onClose`—This event fires when the connection with the socket is lost.

As we did with the onLoad event in the XML object, we have to define these event handlers with the XMLSocket that we create.

For example:

```
function serverConnected (success) {
  trace(success);
}
server.onConnect = serverConnected;
```

Here you see that the serverConnected() function is called when the onConnect event is fired. The success parameter, shown in the function definition, has a value of true if the connection was successful and false if the connection was not successful.

The onXML event is used as follows:

```
function xmlReceived (data) {
  trace(data);
}
server.onXML = xmlReceived;
```

The xmlReceived() function is called each time information arrives via the socket. The data parameter contains the XML document pushed into Flash.

The onClose event handle can be defined and used as follows:

```
function socketClosed () {
    //notify the user
}
server.onClose = socketClosed;
```

You would typically use this type of event to let the user know that a connection has been lost.

In this exercise, you'll build a simple chat application that connects to AquaServer (the free server provided on the CD-ROM). When this server receives a message, it automatically broadcasts that message to all connected users. It's not suitable as a long-term chat solution but a perfect tool for learning purposes. More advanced servers let you connect to or create a "room"—from there, you can then do fancier things (for example, sending a message to a specific user, to the entire room, or to everyone in the chat).

1) Open chat1.fla in the Lesson12/Assets folder.

The file contains four layers: The Actions layer where we'll keep the ActionScript; the Labels layer which contains all of the labels for the movie; the Assets layer containing the text fields and buttons; and the Background layer which contains the interface graphics.

We'll begin by scripting the underlying functionality of our chat application. Later, we'll add appropriate actions to the various buttons it contains.

2) With the Actions panel open, select Frame 1 and add this script:

```
stop();
function setChatText (msg) {
  chatText += msg;
  chatBox.htmlText = chatText;
  scrollBar.setScrollPosition(chatBox.maxscroll);
}
```

The first line contains a `stop()` action to prevent the movie from playing past this frame until we instruct it to. The next line starts a function definition. This function is used to update the text displayed in the chat window (an HTML-enabled text field named **chatBox**). The chat window exists at the frame labeled chat. When called, this function receives a single parameter named `msg`, which is an HTML-formatted text string with appropriate break tags (<BR>) and other formatting. The first line of

387

the function concatenates this string of text with the value of the variable `chatText`, which is used to store the entire chat transcript. (Think of this variable as containing a raw-HTML representation of the chat session.) The next line in the function definition uses the value of `chatText` to set what is displayed in the chat window (**chatBox**). Because the chat window is an HTML-enabled text field, it will interpret the raw HTML in `chatText` and display it properly.

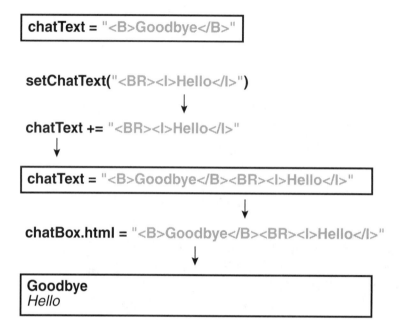

If you look on the frame labeled chat, you'll see that there is a Flash scroll-bar component attached to the **chatBox** text field. A method of this component—`setScrollPosition()`—is used to set the scrolling amount of the text field to which it's attached. Thus, the last line of script sets the scroll position of the **chatBox** to be as large as possible.

Our application—especially the `onXML` event (as you'll see in Step 4 below)—makes extensive use of this function.

3) Add this function definition to the same frame, just below the function defined in the previous step:

```
function initializeChat (itWorked) {
  if(itWorked) {
    _root.gotoAndStop("login");
  } else {
    _root.gotoAndStop("failed");
  }
}
```

This function will be called using the `onConnect` event (as shown in Step 8). This event handler will automatically send a value of `true` or `false` to this function (the `itWorked` parameter), depending on whether a successful connection is made. An `if` statement is used to analyze this value and then to act accordingly. If the connection was successful (that is, `itWorked` has a value of `true`), the timeline will be moved to the login frame label. If the connection is not successful, the timeline will be moved to the failed label. This function prevents the user from proceeding to the log-in screen unless he or she is connected to the server.

4) Next, add the following function definition to the same frame, just below the function you defined in the previous step:

```
function received (info) {
  var from = info.firstChild.firstChild.attributes.from;
  var message = info.firstChild.firstChild.firstChild.nodeValue;
  setChatText("<BR><B><FONT FACE=\"arial\" SIZE=\"15\"
COLOR=\"#333333\">"+from +"</B></FONT>: <FONT FACE=\"arial\" SIZE=\"15\"
COLOR=\"#999999\">"+message+"</FONT>");
}
```

This function will be assigned as the `onXML` event handler (as shown in Step 8), which means it will be called whenever information has arrived from the server. The `info` parameter represents the actual XML data received. The data received (chat messages) is identical to the data that's *sent* to the server. It's formatted as follows:

```
<doc>
  <message from="jobe">Hello world</message>
</doc>
```

The first two lines use properties of the XML object to set the values of two local variables, `from` and `message`. Based on the format of our XML document's structure (as shown above), the `from` variable will contain the user name of the person who sent the message, and the `message` variable will contain the actual message sent. Lastly, the `from` and `message` variables are used to format a line of HTML code, which is added to the chat window using the `setChatText()` function (defined in Step 2).

NOTE *For information on how to use HTML-formatted text in Flash, see Lesson 13, Validating and Formatting Data.*

5) To let a user know when the connection has closed, add this function definition to the frame:

```
function connectionClosed () {
  setChatText("<BR><B><FONT FACE=\"arial\" SIZE=\"15\" COLOR=\"#666666\">The
connection has been terminated.</B></FONT>");
}
```

In a moment, we'll assign this function as the onClose event handler (shown in Step 8). When the socket connection is closed or lost, this function is called. It then makes a function call itself, to the setChatText() function, which you'll remember is used to update what's displayed in the chat window. Thus, when the connection is lost, the following message will appear in the chat window: "The connection has been terminated."

6) To manually close the connection, add this function definition:

```
function closeConnection () {
  server.close();
}
```

By calling this function, you can force the socket connection to be closed. As soon as it is closed the onClose event will fire. In a moment we will set up a button to call to this function.

7) Add this function definition to the same frame:

```
function send (messageToSend) {
  server.send("<doc><message
from=\""+screenName+"\">"+messageToSend+"</message></doc>");
}
```

This function actually sends a message to the server using the send() method—you simply pass in the message to send (massageToSend) to the function, the value of which will be any text the user has entered to send. This text is then formatted into an XML document that looks like the following:

```
<doc>
  <message from="jobe">Hello</message>
</doc>
```

That document is then sent to the server, and all open chat windows (other users) will receive this data, which calls the received() function defined in Step 4.

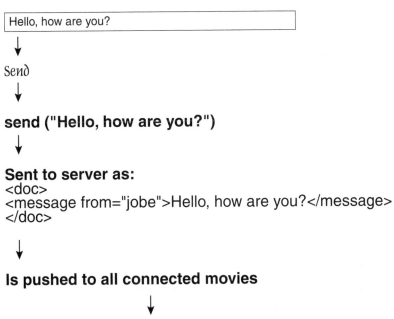

Hello, how are you?

↓

Send

↓

send ("Hello, how are you?")

↓

Sent to server as:
<doc>
<message from="jobe">Hello, how are you?</message>
</doc>

↓

Is pushed to all connected movies

↓

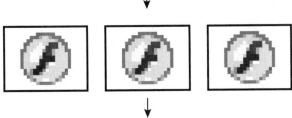

↓

**received() function is called in each movie
in order to update what is displayed in
the chat window**

8) Add the following lines of script, just below the script you added in the previous step:

```
XML.prototype.ignorewhite = true;
server = new XMLSocket();
server.onConnect = initializeChat;
server.onXML = received;
server.onClose = connectionClosed;
server.connect("localhost", 9999);
```

The first line above sets the ignoreWhite property of all XML objects to true. When true, all white space (for example, tabs and carriage returns between nodes) are ignored—a good practice, which also makes your parsing code shorter. Remember, Flash sees tabs and carriage returns as nodes, so if you don't set ignoreWhite to true, you will end up with extraneous nodes. Regular spaces and carriage returns contained within the nodes are untouched. Using ignoreWhite only affects what is between nodes.

391

The rest of the ActionScript entered above creates a new XML socket object named server and then assigns functions to be called on each of the possible events. The last line of this code opens a connection with the server. Remember: Everything we've coded thus far is on Frame 1, which means that it will be executed (or defined, whichever the case may be) as soon as the movie begins to play.

9) Move the playhead to the frame labeled failed. With the Actions panel open, select the Try Again button and attach this script:

```
on (release) {
  _root.gotoAndStop(1);
}
```

If the connection attempt fails, then the playhead is moved to the frame labeled failed. By adding this button, you allow the user to try to reconnect by sending the timeline back to Frame 1, which contains the code that initiates connection with the server (the last line in the previous step).

10) Move the playhead to the frame labeled login, where you'll find a text field (named *nameField*) and a button on the stage. With the Actions panel open, select the frame on the Actions layer at that label and add the following line of script:

```
selection.setFocus("nameField");
```

When the movie is moved to this frame label so that the user may log in, this line of code sets the cursor into the **nameField** text field. This makes it possible for the user to *immediately* begin typing his or her screen name—rather than have to click the text field first. It's a simple script we've added for the sake of convenience.

11) With the playhead still at the login frame and the Actions panel open, select the Submit button and add this ActionScript:

```
on (release, keyPress "<Enter>") {
  if (nameField.text != "") {
    screenName = nameField.text;
    _root.gotoAndStop("chat");
  }
}
```

This script is used to set the user's screen name, which is used whenever messages are sent (as in Step 7). When the user presses the Submit button, an if statement is used to make sure that he or she has entered something in the **nameField** text field. The text entered is then used to set the value of screenName—which is obviously the user's screen name. The last action is used to send the timeline to the frame labeled chat, where the user can begin to send and receive messages.

12) Move the playhead to the frame labeled chat, where you will find two text fields (*chatBox* and *chatMessage*) and two buttons on the stage. With the Actions panel open, select the frame on the Actions layer at that label and add the following line of script:

```
setChatText("<FONT FACE=\"arial\" SIZE=\"20\" COLOR=\"#666666\"><b>You have
just joined the chat!</b></FACE>");
selection.setFocus("chatMessage");
```

Since these actions are placed on a frame, they're executed as soon as the timeline is moved to the frame labeled chat. The first line of ActionScript here calls the `setChatText()` function (defined in Step 2), which is used to display a simple message in the chat window indicating to the user that he or she has joined the chat.

CHATBOX

CHATMESSAGE

The next line places the cursor into the **chatMessage** text field, which is where the user types the message he or she wishes to send. As with the script discussed in Step 10, this script is added for convenience.

393

13) With the Actions panel open, select the Send button and add this script:

```
on (release,keyPress "<enter>") {
  if (chatMessage.text != "") {
    send(chatMessage.text);
    chatMessage.text = "";
  }
}
```

This script is used to send a message from the user when the button is pressed and released. An `if` statement is used to determine whether the user has entered something into the **chatMessage** text field. If text has been entered, it's used in a function call to the `send()` function defined in Step 7.

The last action in the script will empty the **chatMessage** text field so that the user can begin typing a fresh message into it.

14) With the Actions panel open, select the Close Connection button on the stage and add this script:

```
on (release) {
  closeConnection();
}
```

This action calls the `closeConnection()` function defined in Step 6. When the user clicks the button, the socket connection will be forced to end.

15) Start AquaServer on port 9999.

Refer to the previous section for instructions on how to do this.

16) Choose Control > Test Movie to test what you have created: Log in and send some chat messages.

The HTML-formatted messages should pop into your window. You can open up several instances of this SWF file and try chatting between them. If you click the Close Connection button, you should notice that you can no longer chat.

17) Save your work as chat2.fla

You're finally finished! As you can see, there are many steps involved in creating even the most basic chat application. However, now that you're comfortable with XML, you'll soon be building bigger, more complex applications.

WHAT YOU HAVE LEARNED

In this lesson, you have:

- Learned the basics of XML format (pages 368–371)

- Learned and used several of the XML object methods and properties (pages 371–375)

- Created a simple Flash registration and log-in application (pages 376–382)

- Been introduced to socket servers (pages 383–384)

- Built a real-time Flash chat application from scratch (pages 385–394)

validating and formatting data

LESSON 13

Many applications collect information from users—phone numbers, email addresses, and so on—for later use, or to send to a database where it can be stored and retrieved as needed. However, if these applications trusted users to enter properly formatted, error-free information, they probably wouldn't function properly—that, or your database would quickly fill with useless data. The fact is, users often enter data incorrectly—which is why it's a good idea to validate data before it's used or processed. Validating data usually entails writing a script to check the way data was entered against a set of guidelines or rules. If data-entry errors are found, the user can be prompted to reenter the data, or (in some cases) the script can make the needed adjustments without further input from the user.

Our fictional product contains a product registration form that allows us to collect data from the user, validate it, and display any errors found.

In this lesson, we'll create an application that includes a form requiring user-input data that needs to be validated. After our application validates this information, it will display a custom confirmation page—a common way of thanking the user for providing the requested information.

WHAT YOU WILL LEARN

In this lesson, you will:

- Learn why validation is important

- Define validation requirements

- Set up a method to handle errors found in the validation process

- Create functions for validating strings, numbers, and sequences

- Format dynamic data using HTML

- Create text fields dynamically

- Format text using TextFormat objects

APPROXIMATE TIME

This lesson takes approximately 2 hours to complete.

LESSON FILES

Media Files:

None

Starting File:

Lesson13/Assets/validate1.fla

Lesson13/Assets/flashWriter1.fla

Completed Project:

validate7.fla

flashWriter3.fla

THE LOGIC BEHIND VALIDATING DATA

Every day we validate things—from words in a sentence (to make sure they make sense) to change received from purchases. Thus, the concept is a natural and easy one for us to understand. Take the following phone number: 555-34567

Chances are, you quickly recognized the above phone number to be invalid. How? Your brain analyzed the phone number and noted that it contained eight numbers. After comparing this fact to the rule that defines valid local phone numbers as those that include seven numbers, your brain made a determination of true (the number was valid) or false (it was invalid). If you determine that the above number is valid, you can place the phone call. If, however, the number is invalid, your brain will log an error message—something like "That number is wrong. I need to get the correct number and then try to call."

```
Submitted phone #:   555-34567
    Valid phone #:   555-3456
          Errors:                    X
```

If we were to break down the validation process, it would look like the following:

- Define criteria for valid data.

- Analyze submitted data.

- Compare this data against defined criteria.

- Continue if data is valid; determine and note error if data is invalid, resolve, then try again.

In ActionScript, this process of analyzing information, comparing it to a set of rules, and then determining the data's validity is known as a *validation routine*. Just as your brain analyzes data instantaneously, an ActionScript validation routine takes just a split second to complete.

You usually need to validate data within a Flash application whenever you require the user to enter information into an input-text field—for example, on forms (name, address, phone number, and so on), in passwords, on quizzes (to verify answers), and in e-commerce shopping carts (quantities, sizes, colors, and so on).

USING VALIDATION ROUTINES

You can think of a validation routine as a mini-scripting machine within your project that validates the data it receives and then acts accordingly (based on whether that data is valid or invalid). As such, most validation routines comprise functions composed primarily of conditional (if) statements.

It's typical to split validation routines into separate functions, one for each type of data to be validated (for example, one function for validating strings, another for numbers, and so on). This allows you to script a function once and then use it anywhere in your project, as opposed to writing the validation routine repeatedly whenever a certain type of data needs to be validated.

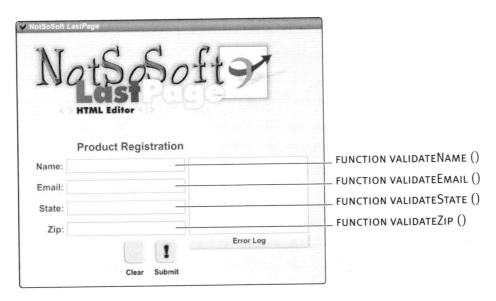

You can create two main types of validation routines (functions that validate data):

- Those that do not receive parameters but work in a specific way
- Those that receive parameters to provide additional functionality to your application

Let's take a look at each.

With a validation routine that is not sent parameters, you define the function to work in a specific way—usually to validate a specific piece of data. Say you wanted to create a routine to validate a seven-digit telephone number (which includes nine characters in all: seven digits and two hash [-] marks) that the user enters into a text field named **telephone**. The structure of that function would look like the following:

```
function validateTelephone () {
  if (telephone.length == 9) {
    // number is valid, so do these specific actions
  } else {
    // number is invalid, so do these specific actions
  }
}
```

This routine can only validate the data in the **telephone** text field because that's the field that's been defined in the script. Let's now look at how versatile we can make this function by allowing it to accept a couple of parameters:

```
function validateTelephone (lookForAreaCode, pNumber)
if (lookForAreaCode == true && pNumber.length == 12) {
  message.text = "That is a valid 10-digit telephone number";
} else if (lookForAreaCode == false && pNumber.length == 9){
  message.text = "That is a valid 7-digit telephone number";
  } else {
  message = "That is not a valid telephone number";
  }
}
```

When called, this validation function receives two parameters: `lookForAreaCode`, a `true` or `false` value that indicates whether or not to look for an area code in the number to be validated, and `pNumber`, which represents the number to be validated. If `lookForAreaCode` is `true` when called, the number (`pNumber`) sent to the function is valid *only* if it contains 10 numbers. If `lookForAreaCode` is `false`, the number sent to the function is valid only if it contains 7 numbers.

A call to this validation routine would look like the following:

```
validateTelephone(true, 812-555-1234);
```

After processing this call, the function would display the following in the **message** text field: "That is a valid 10-digit telephone number."

TIP *You'll remember from previous lessons that the values sent to a function can actually be variables. Thus, you could use the above function to validate the text in any text field by referencing that field's name and text property (`textField.text`) in the second parameter of the function call.*

By creating a validation routine that accepts parameters and validates data accordingly, you increase the routine's usefulness because you can employ it to validate *similar* data in various ways.

Conditional statements play an important role in validating data since that process really entails nothing more than evaluating various conditions to determine whether user-input data is valid. The rules that define valid data are considered *validation points*. To define validation points, you must consider the following:

- **Length.** Does the data contain the correct number of characters? A typical U.S. Zip code, for example, contains five digits. Thus, if a user-entered Zip code includes less than five characters, this is an error. Or take a name: Because most names include more than one character, you would have an error if the length of the data entered were one. (A length of zero means nothing has been entered. If you require *something* to be entered, this would be an error.)

- **Value.** Is the value of the data entered more, less, or equal to that which is considered valid? If you were asking for someone's age (which you should never do), you might define a lower limit of 18 and an upper limit as 100. If the value entered were more or less than either of these, this would be an error.

- **Type.** Is the data entered a number when it should be a string, or vice-versa? When asking for someone's weight (which, again, you should never do), *pizza* would be an error because a number is required.

- **Sequence.** Is the data properly formatted? Some data needs to contain numbers, letters, and other characters, all placed in a specific sequence—for example, phone numbers (123-4567), dates (01/23/45), account numbers (1-2345-67-890), and so on. Missing or misplaced dashes, slashes, or other characters represent errors.

Validation Points

Length	Value	Type	Sequence
Must contain 5 characters	Must equal "Macromedia"	Must be a number	Must be a in this format xx/xx/xx
Fred ⊘	Micromidia ⊘	Three ⊘	12/30/56 ✓
7271966 ⊘	Macromedia ✓	3 ✓	072/7/66 ⊘
Hello ✓	Puppy ⊘	Thirty7 ⊘	10-03-83 ⊘

Most validation routines contain conditional statements that are used to validate data based on *multiple* validation points. We will be using and discussing each of these validation points in more detail in the exercises that follow.

HANDLING ERRORS

Different projects require varying solutions for handling the errors that the validation process brings to light. In some cases, you may wish to provide a graphical indicator (for example, a red *X* next to the field containing the error), while in others a text message may suffice.

The conditional statement itself (within the validation routine) usually determines how to handle any error that it detects. Take, for example, the following:

```
if (dataValid) {
  // perform these actions
} else {
  // Execute action to denote an error
```

Because error handling plays a major role in the validation process, you should think about how you want errors to be handled in a particular project or situation before you script anything else.

In this exercise, we'll lay the foundation for the error handling process in our project.

1) Open validate1.fla in the Lesson13/Assets folder.

This project contains two scenes: Registration and Confirm. We'll work on the Confirm scene in a later exercise; for now, we'll concentrate on the Registration scene, which includes a form that the user must fill out, and thus data that needs to be validated. This scene contains four layers named according to their content: The Background layer contains the scene's graphical content—with the exception of the buttons, which reside on the Buttons layer. The Text Fields layer contains five text fields. Four of the text fields are placed above background graphics that represent the form's input areas. From the top down, these fields are named **name**, **email**, **state**, and **zip**. Because the user will be required to enter data into these fields, they are input-text fields. To the right of these text fields is a larger text field named **errorLog**. This multiline dynamic text field will be used to display errors found in the form's validation process. If the Property inspector is open, you will note that the HTML option has been selected for this field. By selecting this option, you instruct Flash to enable this text field to *interpret* the HTML sent to it rather than display the actual code.

2) With the Actions panel open, select Frame 1 on the Actions layer and add this script:

```
stop ();
errors = new Array();
```

The first action prevents the timeline from moving beyond Frame 1 of this scene until we instruct it to do so.

The second action creates an array named errors that will hold error messages that need to be displayed as the result of the validation process. (We'll explain this in more detail as we move forward.)

3) Add this function definition to the end of the current script:

```
function clearForm () {
  name.text = "";
  email.text = "";
  state.text = "";
  zip.text = "";
  errorLog.text = "";
  errors.length = 0;
}
```

When called, this function resets the value of scene elements—including the input-text fields and the **errorLog** text field—to their initial values. It also removes any error messages within the error array.

4) With the Actions panel still open, select the Clear button at the bottom of the screen and add this script:

```
on (release) {
  clearForm();
}
```

This script calls the clearForm() function that we just defined, causing the actions within that function to be executed when the button is released.

5) Save this file as validate2.fla.

We'll build on this file throughout this lesson. The most important aspect of this exercise was the creation of the errors array, which will play a major role in the way our application handles any errors it detects in the validation process.

VALIDATING STRINGS

As mentioned earlier, when validating different types of data (names, phone numbers, email addresses, and so on) it's best to break the process into specialized functions, or validation routines. We will begin that process in this exercise.

The first type of data our form asks for is the user's name. For our form, the data entered must meet two requirements:

- **Length.** The name must be at least two characters long.

- **Type.** Text must be used; a number cannot be accepted as a valid name.

In this exercise, we'll create a function for validating the name entered into our project's registration form.

1) Open validate2.fla in the Lesson13/Assets folder.

We'll build on the project from the last exercise.

2) With the Actions panel open, select Frame 1 on the Actions layer and add this function definition at the end of the current script:

```
function validateName () {
  if (name.text.length < 2 || isNaN(name.text) == false) {
    errors.push("Please enter a valid name.");
  }
}
```

```
 1 stop();
 2 errors = new Array();
 3 function clearForm() {
 4     name.text = "";
 5     email.text = "";
 6     state.text = "";
 7     zip.text = "";
 8     errorLog.text = "";
 9     errors.length = 0;
10 }
11 function validateName() {
12     if (name.text.length < 2 || isNaN(name.text) == false) {
13         errors.push("Please enter a valid name.");
14     }
15 }
```

Line 15 of 15, Col 2

When called, this function checks the data entered in the **name** text field for two conditions, its length and type (the validation points we defined at the beginning of this exercise). The conditional statement here says that if the **name** text field contains less than two characters or is a number, the string "Please enter a valid name" should be pushed into the `errors` array. Although we've used the `length` property in other scripts, some of this syntax is new and thus requires explanation.

One of the validation points we've defined for the **name** text field is that a number entered into it would need to be considered an error. To validate whether data is a number or text string, we would use the `isNaN()` function. This built-in function verifies that the argument passed to it (within the parentheses) is *not* a number (hence the name `isNaN`, or *is Not a Number*). Take a look at the following examples:

`isNaN("Box")` returns a value of `true` because the value of "Box" is a string—which means it's true that it's not a number.

`isNaN(465)` returns a value of `false` because 465 is a number—that is, it's false to state that 465 is not a number.

Thus, `isNaN(name.text) == false` is the same thing as saying, "If **name** is a number."

If *either* of the conditions in the statement exist, data has been improperly input. As a result, the action within the `if` statement is executed. This action uses the `push()` method of the array object to add an element to the end of the `errors` array. (This element is what's enclosed in the parentheses.) If you think of the `errors` array as a book, using the `push()` method is like adding a page to the end of the book, with the string within the parentheses representing the text on that page. The page number of this page would be its index position within the array.

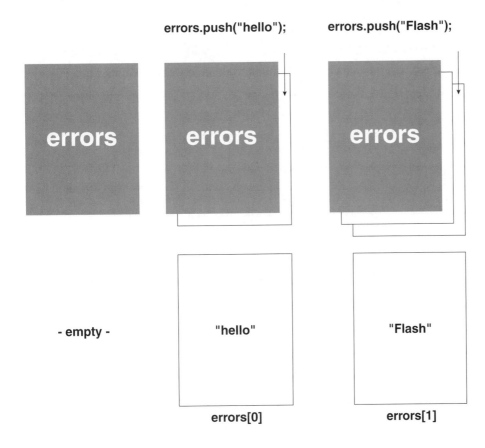

errors.push("hello");   errors.push("Flash");

errors   errors   errors

- empty -   "hello"   "Flash"

errors[0]   errors[1]

In the case of this function, if the data in the **name** text field is invalid, the text "Please enter a valid name" is "pushed" into the errors array.

Next, we'll create a function to retrieve this error from the array (if name is not valid and it's pushed into the array) and display it in the **errorLog** text field.

3) With the Actions panel still open, add this function definition at the end of the current script:

```
function validateForm () {
  errorLog.text = "";
  errors.length = 0;
  validateName();
  if (errors.length > 0) {
    errorLog.htmlText = "<b>These errors were found:</b><br>";
    var i = -1;
    while (++i < errors.length) {
      errorLog.htmlText += errors[i] + newline;
    }
  } else {
    gotoAndStop ("Confirm", 1);
  }
}
```

In the previous step, we created a validation function to check the data entered into the **name** text field. As we progress through this lesson, we'll create several more validation functions to validate the data entered into our other form fields. However, the function you'll create in this step—validateForm()—is really the mother of all these other functions because eventually it will be used to call all of the individual validation functions and then finalize the validation process, including outputting error messages to the **errorLog** text field. Take special note of the sequence of actions in this function: This flow plays an important role in how the function works.

The first two actions in this function clear the **errorLog** text field as well as any messages that may exist in the errors array. Obviously, the first time the form is validated, these actions are worthless because both begin empty anyway. Any subsequent validation of the entered data will require that the **errorLog** text field begin the process empty of any text and that any error messages in the errors array be erased.

The next line contains a function call to the validateName() function we defined in the previous step. This will cause that function to execute and thus validate the data in the **name** text field. As a result, an error message is either pushed into the errors array (if data is invalid) or it is not.

The next action in this function is an `if` statement, which is evaluated only *after* the `validateName()` function has completed its job. This is where the sequence of actions becomes important. If an error message gets pushed into the `errors` array as a result of calling the `validateName()` function, the `length` property of the `errors` array gets changed to 1, indicating that it contains at least one error message. This `if` statement then looks at the `length` property of the `errors` array and acts accordingly. If the `length` property has a value greater than 0 (indicating error messages within the array), the resulting actions output those messages to the **errorLog** text field. If `errors.length` is 0, this means there are no error messages and the data is valid; thus, a `gotoAndStop()` action sends the timeline to the scene named Confirm.

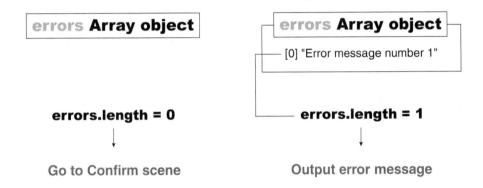

The actions used to output the error messages are pretty straightforward: The first creates the line that appears initially. Using a couple of HTML bold tags (`<b></b>`), the text "These errors were found:" is displayed in bold, followed by a line break (`<br>`). Next, a looping statement is used to loop through the `errors` array to add the error messages stored there to the **errorLog** text field (using ActionScript you're by now familiar with). When this process is complete, the **errorLog** text field will display any messages within the `errors` array.

Although you're by now familiar with the `text` property of text fields, you'll notice that the above script uses `htmlText` in relation to the **errorLog** text field. You can use this text field property in two ways (similar to the `text` property): to retrieve the HTML representation of text displayed in a text field, or to set the text displayed (rendered in HTML) in a text field. To better understand this, take a look at the following example:

```
message.text = "<b>Hello there!</b>";
```

The above script will display Hello there! in a text field named **message**. Because we're setting the `text` property, the displayed text is an exact representation of the string value. In contrast, take a look at the following:

```
message.htmlText = "<b>Hello there!</b>";
```

The above script will display **Hello there!** in the text field. In the above, we simply changed the script so that it sets the text to be rendered in HTML, as it should be. When setting HTML text in a text field using the `htmlText` setting, you're telling the field to be aware that the incoming text has HTML tags and thus should be rendered as such.

A text field must be HTML-aware to properly render a string of text containing HTML tags. You can indicate that a text field is an HTML text field by pressing the "Render text as HTML" button in the Property inspector, or by setting the text field's `html` property to `true`. For our project, we simply selected the option (for the **errorLog** text field) on the Property inspector.

4) With the Actions panel still open, select the Submit button at the bottom of the screen and add this script:

```
on (release) {
  validateForm();
}
```

This script calls the `validateForm()` function we just defined, causing the actions within that function to be executed when the button is released.

5) Choose Control > Test Movie to test the project up to this point.
Enter an invalid name into the **name** text field to see what the validation process turns up. Pressing the Clear button will reset the scene's the visual and data elements.

6) Close the test movie to return to the authoring environment and save this file as validate3.fla.
We'll build on this file in the following exercise.

VALIDATING SEQUENCES

A sequence is a string of characters (letters, numbers, and special characters) placed in a specific order or formatted in a special way. Some example sequences might include the following:

- Telephone numbers (xxx-xxxx)
- Credit card numbers (xxxx xxxx xxxx xxxx)
- Dates (xx/xx/xxxx)
- URLs (http://www.xxxxxx.xxx)

Although the characters within sequences may change, they must still follow certain formatting rules. Sequence validation is typically a bit more involved then other types of data validation—primarily because there are numerous validation points to check. By breaking the process down, you can more readily understand how it works. The following are some validation points for a typical email address:

1) It cannot contain more than one @ symbol.

2) It must include at least one period (separating the actual domain name from the domain extension, such as in mydomain.com or mydomain.net).

3) The last period must fall somewhere after the @ symbol, but it can't be either of the last two characters.

4) The @ symbol may not be the first or second character.

5) There must be at least two characters between the @ symbol and the first period that proceeds it.

6) The email address must include at least eight characters (aa@bb.cc)

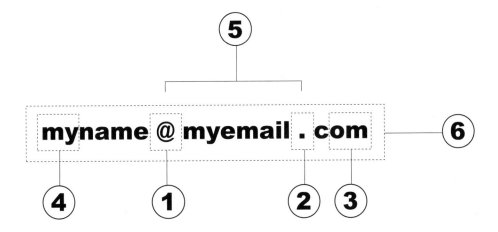

If an email address has been checked for the six points listed above, you've performed a reasonable validation check. Although we could add many more validation points (for example, characters following the last period must be com, net, org, *or something similar), your code would become extremely long and you would need to update it frequently to keep pace with changing Internet standards. Thus, it's important to determine the most important validation points and just check for them.*

In this exercise, we'll use only the following three validation points for text entered into the email text field of our registration form:

1) The @ symbol must be included somewhere after the second character.

2) The email address must include a period at least two characters following the @ symbol.

3) The email address must include at least eight characters.

Be sure to provide your user with clear instructions about how to format data. It's common practice to provide an example of correctly formatted data either above or below the text box where it's to be entered, providing a quick reference for the user.

Phone: _____
(e.g., 123-456-7890)

Date: _____
(e.g., 07/27/1966)

SS#: _____
(e.g., 123-45-6789)

1) Open validate3.fla in the Lesson13/Assets folder.
We will continue building on the project from the last exercise.

2) With the Actions panel open, select Frame 1 on the Actions layer and add this function definition at the end of the current script:

```
function validateEmail () {
  if (email.text.indexOf("@") < 2) {
    errors.push(" \"@\" missing in email or in the wrong place.");
  }
  if (email.text.lastIndexOf(".") <= (email.text.indexOf("@") + 2)) {
    errors.push(" \".\" missing in email or in the wrong place.");
  }
  if (email.text.length < 8) {
    errors.push("Email address not long enough.");
  }
}
```

This function, `validateEmail()`, validates the text entered into the **email** text field and is made up of three conditional statements, each of which checks one of the individual validation points we outlined at the beginning of this exercise. Because these are separate `if` statements (rather than `if/else`, `if/else if` groupings), *all* of them will be evaluated. Let's look at each a bit more in depth. The first statement reads as follows:

```
if (email.text.indexOf("@") < 2) {
  errors.push("@ missing in email or in the wrong place.");
}
```

You'll remember from previous exercises that the `indexOf()` method of the String object returns the character number where the value in parentheses is first found in a string. Using this method, the above statement determines whether the first @ symbol appears before the third character in the **email** text field. Because the first character in a string has an index number of 0, this statement evaluates to `true` and an error message is pushed into the `errors` array if the @ symbol is found at position 0 or 1. If the @ symbol doesn't occur anywhere within the **email** text field, this statement returns a value of –1, which is still less than 2 and thus also causes the statement to evaluate to `true` and the error message to be pushed into the array.

TIP *Using the `indexOf()` method, you can also check for stings longer than one character. For instance, you can check for "`http://`" in a string using something similar to the following syntax: `string.indexOf("http://")`. The number returned is the character number of the first letter in the string.*

Let's look at the second statement in this function, which reads as follows:

```
if (email.text.lastIndexOf(".") <= (email.text.indexOf("@") + 2)) {
  errors.push(". missing in email or in the wrong place.");
}
```

This statement uses the `lastIndexOf()` method of the String object—similar to the `indexOf()` method except that it returns the character number of the *last* occurrence of the character in the parenthesis. For example, if `email.text = "derek.franklin@derekfranklin.com,"` `email.text.lastIndexOf(".")` returns 27. Using this method, the above statement looks at the position of the last period in relation to the @ symbol. If the period is less than two characters to the right of the @ symbol, this statement proves `true` and an error message is pushed into the `errors` array.

```
if (email.text.lastIndexOf(".") <= (email.text.indexOf("@")+2))
```
⬇
```
if (9 <= (7+2))
```
⬇
```
if (9 <= 9)
```
⬇

true

The third statement in this function is the easiest one to comprehend. It reads as follows:

```
if (email.text.length < 8) {
  errors.push("Email address not long enough.");
}
```

As already mentioned, the smallest reasonable email address is aa@bb.cc—eight characters, including the @ symbol and the period. If the `length` of the data entered into the **email** text field is less than eight characters, an error message stating the email address is too short is pushed into the `error` array.

After all of these statements have been evaluated, you may find that the information entered into the **email** text field is invalid on all counts. In this case, three different error messages would be pushed into the `errors` array.

3) Add the following function call just below the `validateName()` **function call in the** `validateForm()` **function definition:**

```
validateEmail();
```

This is a call to the function we just defined. Placing this function call here adds email validation capability to the main `validateForm()` function. This function call is placed just above the statement that checks the length of the `errors` array because the `validateEmail()` function is able to push error messages into the array, thus affecting its length and the way the statement is evaluated. In the end, if either the `validateName()` or `validateEmail()` functions find errors, their corresponding messages will be displayed in the **errorLog** text field.

NOTE *The Submit button in our scene already has a function call to the* `validateForm()` *function. Therefore, any new functionality we add to that function (as we have just done) is automatically executed when the button is released.*

4) Choose Control > Test Movie to test the project up to this point.
Enter an invalid email into the **email** text field or an invalid name into the **name** text field to see what the validation process turns up. Pressing the Clear button resets the visual and data elements in the scene.

5) Close the test movie to return to the authoring environment and save this file as validate4.fla.
We will build on this file in the following exercise.

VALIDATING AGAINST A LIST OF CHOICES

There are times when a value entered into a form must match one of several choices. For example, if a form asks the user to enter a specific color (for example, "red," "yellow," or "blue"), and the user accidentally enters "rod" or "yullow" instead, it's important to be able to detect that error when validating the form.

If you're going to compare data entered against a list of choices, you must obviously define that list first. In ActionScript, an array can include a list of choices. The validation process is simply a matter of comparing the data entered against the values in the array to see if there's a match.

In this exercise, we'll create another validation routine—this one to compare what's entered in the **state** text field against an array of state names.

TIP *It's best to have users do as little manual data entry as possible. Thus, instead of requiring that the user input data that matches one of several choices, you would be better off providing a drop-down list from which he or she could choose a value—a method that eliminates the need for data validation. In some applications, however, this is not possible— say for a quiz application that contains a list of answers you don't want users to be able to access. In such cases, there's no way to avoid manual validation.*

Method 1

State: Indianer|

Method 2

State: Indiana
Illinois
Kentucky

1) Open validate4.fla in the Lesson13/Assets folder.
We will continue building on the project from the last exercise.

2) With the Actions panel open, select Frame 1 on the Actions layer and add this function definition at the end of the current script:

```
function validateState () {
  states = ["California", "Indiana", "North Carolina", "Oklahoma"];
  matchFound = false;
  i = -1;
  while (++i < states.length) {
    if (state.text == states[i]) {
      matchFound = true;
    }
  }
  if (!matchFound) {
    errors.push("Please enter a valid state.");
  }
}
```

This function, `validateState()`, validates the data entered into the **state** text field.

The first action in this function creates an array named `states`, which will hold all of the possible choices. To keep this as short as possible, we've only included four state names, though you could easily add all 50.

The next action creates a variable named `matchFound` and assigns it an initial value of `false`. The importance of this variable will become evident in a moment.

The next several lines in this function are part of a looping statement, which is used to loop through all of the values in the `states` array, comparing each to the value entered in the **state** text field. If a match is found, `matchFound` is set to `true`. If a match is not found, the value of this variable remains `false` (its initial state), indicating an error.

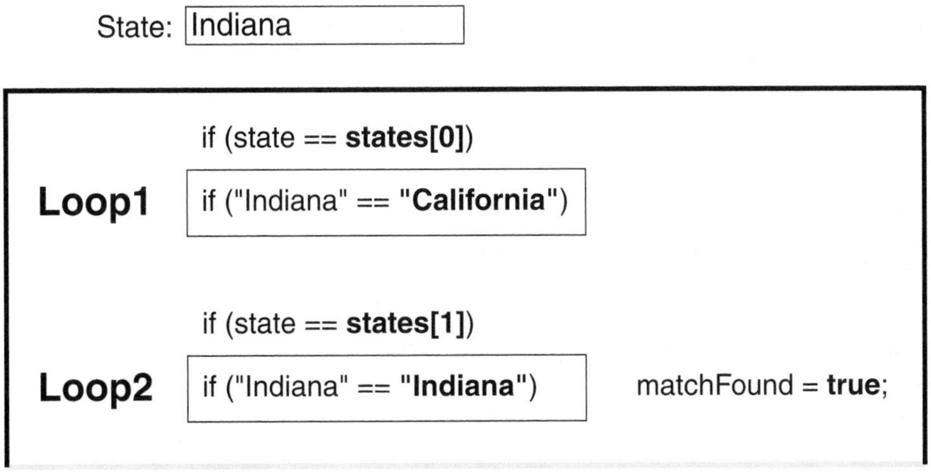

State: Indiana

if (state == **states[0]**)

Loop1   if ("Indiana" == **"California"**)

if (state == **states[1]**)

Loop2   if ("Indiana" == **"Indiana"**)   matchFound = **true**;

The last part of the function contains an `if` statement that's executed after the looping statement has completed its job. It says that if `matchFound` is `false` (which it will be if a match is not found), an appropriate error message should be pushed into the `errors` array (as with the other functions we've created thus far).

3) Add the following function call just below the `validateEmail()` function call:

```
validateState();
```

This is a call to the function we just defined. Placing this function call here adds state-name validation capability to the main `validateForm()` function. This function call is placed just above the statement that checks the length of the `errors` array because that function is able to push error messages into the array, thus affecting its length and the way this statement is evaluated. In the end, if the `validateName()`, `validateEmail()`, or `validateState()` functions find errors, their corresponding messages will be displayed in the **errorLog** text field.

4) Choose Control > Test Movie to test your project thus far.
Enter an invalid state name (anything other than the four state names in the array) into the **state** text field to see what the validation process turns up. Pressing the Clear button resets the visual and data elements in the scene.

5) Close the test movie to return to the authoring environment and save this file as validate5.fla.
We will build on this file in the following exercise.

VALIDATING NUMBERS

Validating numbers is not much different than validating strings, which we've already discussed.

In this exercise, we'll create one last validation function to validate the data entered into the **zip** text field. As a valid U.S. Zip code, the data entered must meet two requirements:

- **Length.** It must include exactly five characters.
- **Type.** It must contain numbers; text is invalid

> **TIP** *When validating numbers, you may need to call for the number entered to be more or less in value than another number—which by now you should be able to do easily!*

1) Open validate5.fla in the Lesson13/Assets folder.

We will continue building on the project from the last exercise.

2) With the Actions panel open, select Frame 1 on the Actions layer and add this function definition at the end of the current script:

```
function validateZip () {
  if (zip.text.length != 5 || isNaN(zip.text) == true) {
    errors.push("Please enter a valid zip.");
  }
}
```

When called, this function checks that the data entered into the **zip** text field meets two conditions regarding length and type—the validation points we defined at the beginning of this exercise. The conditional statement here states that if the **zip** text field does not contain five characters, or if it consists of text (rather than numbers), the following text string should be pushed into the `errors` array: "Please enter a valid zip."

NOTE *To refresh your understanding of* isNaN() *, review the information in the Validating Strings exercise.*

3) Add the following function call just below the validateState() **function call:**

```
validateZip();
```

This is a call to the function we just defined. Placing this function call here adds Zip code validation capability to the main `validateForm()` function. This function call is placed just above the statement that checks the length of the `errors` array because that function is able to push error messages into the array, thus affecting its length and the way this statement is evaluated. In the end, if the `validateName()`, `validateEmail()`, `validateState()`, or `validateZip()` functions find errors, their corresponding messages will be displayed in the **errorLog** text field.

4) Choose Control > Test Movie to test the project up to this point.

Enter an invalid Zip code in the **zip** text field to see what the validation process turns up. Pressing the Clear button resets the visual and data elements in the scene.

5) Close the test movie to return to the authoring environment and save this file as validate6.fla.

This completes the validation portion of this lesson. The great thing about the way we've set up this project's validation process is that it's dynamic. To analyze additional rules, or validation points, for any of the text fields, all you have to do is add more conditional statements to the appropriate function. The validation process can grow as your needs grow.

If the validation process determines that all of the user-entered data is valid, the timeline is sent to the Confirm scene. This scene then displays a custom message based on the validated data—and to add some style to it, we'll take advantage of Flash's ability to format text using HTML.

DYNAMIC TEXT FORMATTING WITH HTML

Dynamic- and input-text fields within Flash can be set up to interpret basic HTML code—which means you can display text containing hyperlinks and various colors and styles. Flash is able to interpret the HTML tags in the following table.

TAG	DESCRIPTION
<a>	For setting an anchor (hyperlink) value
<b>	For bolded text
 	For creating a break (starting a new line)
<font color>	For setting text color
<font face>	For setting text font style
<font size>	For setting text size
<i>	For italicized text
<p>	For starting a new paragraph
<u>	For underlined text

To be able to display HTML-rendered text, a text field must be made HTML-aware (as described in Step 3 of the "Validating Strings" section of this lesson). Once you've set a text field to render HTML text, you would use the following syntax to display formatted HTML:

```
myText.htmlText = "<b>Hello! </b><br>Thank <u>you</u> for visiting our
site.";
```

This script tells the **myText** text field instance to display the string shown as rendered HTML-formatted text. The rendered HTML is simply a string of text containing the aforementioned supported HTML tags.

Hello!
Thank <u>you</u> for visiting our site.

NOTE *You cannot type HTML-based code directly into a text field and expect Flash to interpret it.*

The `htmlText` property represents the actual HTML code that a text field contains, thus using the example from above, the following:

```
myVariable = myText.htmlText;
```

would set `myVariable` to contain a string value of "Hello!
Thank <u>you</u> for visiting our site." Whereas the following:

```
myVariable = myText.text;
```

would set `myVariable` to contain a string value of "Hello! Thank you for visiting our site." Same text, but because we referenced the `text` property, the string value returned does not include HTML tags.

You can use variable values in conjunction with HTML tags to create truly dynamic text messages. Take, for example, the following:

```
myText.htmlText = "<b>Hello " + name + "!</b><br>Thank <u>you</u> for
visiting our site.";
```

If `name` has a value of "Jack," the above line would look like the following:

```
myText.htmlText = "<b>Hello Jack!</b><br>Thank <u>you</u> for visiting our
site.";
```

You can even set which tags are used dynamically. For example:

```
tagToUse = "u";
myText.htmlText = "<" + tagToUse + ">Hello Jack!</" + tagToUse + ">";
```

The above would be rendered as the following:

```
<u>Hello Jack!</u>";
```

This will cause "Hello Jack!" to appear with an underline. Now take a look at the following:

```
tagToUse = "b";
myText.htmlText = "<" + tagToUse + ">Hello Jack!</" + tagToUse + ">";
```

This would be rendered as the following:

```
<b>Hello Jack!</b>";
```

Thus, "Hello Jack!" will appear bold.

NOTE *Once you've selected a dynamic or input text field, you can assign a variable reference to that text field from the Property inspector. This means that the value contained by that variable will automatically be displayed in the text field. If the variable value is a string of text containing HTML tags, the field will automatically render the text properly—if, that is, you've selected the "Render text to HTML" option for the field. Because the text field references the value of a variable, the contents of that text field (that is, what's displayed there) will change whenever that value changes. This is different than assigning a text field an instance name and then using the* htmlText *property (as shown above) to display formatted text in the field. The former method exists primarily to make MX's implementation of displaying HTML-formatted text compatible with Flash 5 (because this is the way it was accomplished in that version); the latter is the preferred way.*

In the following exercise, we'll use some of the validated values entered into the form in the previous exercises to generate a custom confirmation page.

1) Open validate6.fla in the Lesson13/Assets folder.

We will continue building on the project from the last exercise. While most of the work in this exercise will take place in the Confirm scene, we must first make several simple additions to the validateForm() function (on the Registration scene) we've been working on.

2) With the Actions panel open, select Frame 1 of the Actions layer and insert the following lines of script after where it says `}else{` **but just above where it says** `gotoAndStop ("Confirm", 1);` **in the** `validateForm()` **function definition:**

```
name = name.text;
email = email.text;
state = state.text;
zip = zip.text;
```

You'll remember that the `else` part of this statement deals with what happens if all of the entered data is valid. Prior to the addition of the above lines of script, this statement had just a `gotoAndStop()` action that sent the movie to the Confirm scene. These lines of script create four variables *before* the movie is sent to that scene. The values assigned to these variables represent the text values entered into the form's text fields. The reason for creating variables to hold the various text values is because we want to use those values in the next scene, and while variables and their value persist in a timeline even when moving between scenes, text field property values do not. Thus, the variables are used as a way of transferring the text values from the Registration scene to the Confirm scene.

3) With the Scene panel open, navigate to the Confirm scene.

This scene contains four layers, named according to their content. The Background layer contains the scene's graphical content—with the exception of buttons, which exist on the Buttons layer. The Text Fields layer contains one text field, **confirmText**, which is placed in the middle of the scene. This text field will display a custom confirmation message about the registration process.

4) With the Property inspector open, select the *confirmText* **text field in the middle of the stage.**

If you look at this text field's settings, you'll note this is a dynamic text field. Because the Multiline option is selected, this field will be able to display more than a single line of text. You'll also note that the "Render text as HTML" option has been selected for this field. By selecting this option, you tell Flash to let this text field *interpret* HTML sent to it rather than display the actual code.

You will also notice the following character settings:

- **Font** - _sans
- **Size** – 12
- **Color** – Black

These are the default settings for this text field. In the absence of any HTML font tags to style it, text displayed in this field will appear with these characteristics. However, you can override these settings at any time, using the `<font face>`, `<font size>`, or `<font color>` tags—which we'll do in this exercise.

Let's begin the scripting process.

5) With the Actions panel open, select Frame 1 on the Actions layer and add this script:

```
confirmMessage = new Array();
```

This action creates a new array, named `confirmMessage`, which will hold the sentences that make up our confirmation message.

This action—along with all of the other actions created in this exercise—will be placed on Frame 1 of this timeline so that it will execute as soon as the movie reaches this scene.

6) Add this script just below the current line of script:

```
confirmMessage.push("<font size = \"15\" color = \"#FF9900\"><b>Thank you " +
name + "!</b></font><br>");
```

This action pushes a coded sentence into the `confirmMessage` array, making it the first element in that array. This sentence is simply a string of text that contains a reference to the `name` variable created in Step 2, as well as various HTML tags.

You may find this string's use of quotation and backward-slash (\) marks confusing. To better understand this text string, let's break it into sections—the first of which contains font and bold tags as well as the text "Thank you," all within quotes:

```
"<font size = \"15\" color = \"#FF9900\"><b>Thank you "
```

The important thing to note here is the use of \" in the code (in four places). This is known as an *escape sequence* and is necessary to differentiate HTML code from ActionScript code. Normally, the above code would be written as the following:

```
"<font size = "15" color = "#FF9900"><b>Thank you "
```

Here, regular quotes are used in the size and color settings. However, because ActionScript also uses regular quotes to define string values (as shown on either side of the string), you need a syntactical mechanism to differentiate between the two—without one, you'll get an error when Flash reads the code as the following:

```
("<font size = ") (15) (" color = ") (#FF9900) ("><b>Thank you ")
```

Using the escape sequence as shown, Flash knows to convert \" first to regular quotes when the code is rendered in the text field. Doing so will render that section of code as the following:

```
"<font size = "15" color = "#FF9900"><b>Thank you "
```

Following this section of code in the push() action above, you will see the following code:

```
+ name +
```

Using concatenation, this inserts the value of name into the middle of this string of HTML code. This is followed by the ending section of the script, which reads as follows:

```
"!</b></font><br>"
```

This section contains the closing font and bold tags, as well as a break tag.

Assuming the value of name is "Jill," the complete string would be rendered as follows:

```
<font size = "15" color = "#FF9900"><b>Thank you Jill!</b></font><br>
```

In an HTML-enabled text field, the text "Thank you Jill!" would be displayed in orange at a font size of 15.

7) Add the following script just below the current line of script:

```
confirmMessage.push("This product has been registered to <font color =
\"#3399CC\"><u><a href = \"mailto:" + email + "\">" + name +
"</a></u></font>. ");
```

This action pushes another coded sentence into the confirmMessage array, making it the second element in that array. This sentence is a string of text that contains a reference to both the email and name variables created in Step 2, as well as various HTML tags.

If name had a value of "Jill" and email had a value of "jill@mydomain.com", this line would be rendered as follows:

```
This product has been registered to <font color = "#3399CC"><u><a href =
"mailto:jill@mydomain.com">Jill</a></u></font>.
```

In an HTML-enabled text field, the text would read, "This product is registered to Jill." In the preceding, *Jill* would appear as a blue, underlined hyperlink, linked to her e-mail address.

8) Add the following script just below the current line of script:

```
confirmMessage.push("We hope you enjoy using <b><i>NotSoSoft LastPage</i></b>
as much as we enjoyed developing it for you.<br>");
```

This action pushes another coded sentence into confirmMessage array, making it the third element in the array. This text string does not contain any references to variables.

In an HTML-enabled text field, the text would read, "We hope you enjoy using NotSoSoft Last Page as much as we enjoyed developing it for you," with *NotSoSoft LastPage* in bold and italics, followed by a line break.

424

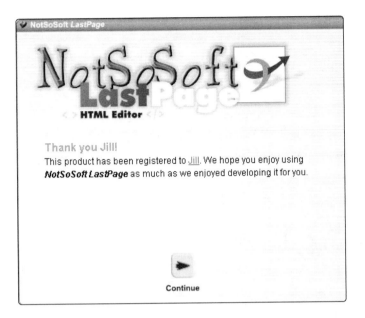

9) Add the following script just below the current line of script:

```
confirmMessage.push("There are many users in the state of <b>" + state +
"</b> that have had great success with our product.<br>");
```

This action pushes another coded sentence into confirmMessage array, making it the fourth element in the array. This text string contains a reference to the state variable, as well as various HTML tags.

If the state variable contained a value of "Indiana", this line would be rendered as follows:

```
There are many users in the state of <b>Indiana</b> that have had great
success with our product.<br>
```

In an HTML-enabled text field, that text would read, "There are many users in the state of Indiana that have had great success with our product," with *Indiana* appearing in bold, followed by a line break.

10) Add the following script just below the current line of script:

```
confirmMessage.push("For more information about this product, please visit
our website at <font color = \"#3399CC\"><u><i><a href
=\"http:\\www.notsosoft.com\">www.notsosoft.com</a></i></u></font>.");
```

This action pushes another coded sentence into confirmMessage array, making it the fifth element in the array. This text string does not contain any references to variables.

This line is rendered as follows:

```
For more information about this product, please visit our site at <font
color = "#3399CC"><u><i><a href ="http:\\www.notsosoft.com">
www.notsosoft.com</a></i></u></font>.
```

In an HTML-enabled text field, this text would read, "For more information about this product, please visit our site at www.notsosoft.com," with *www.notsosoft.com* appearing as a blue, underlined hyperlink, linked to http://www.notosostoft.com.

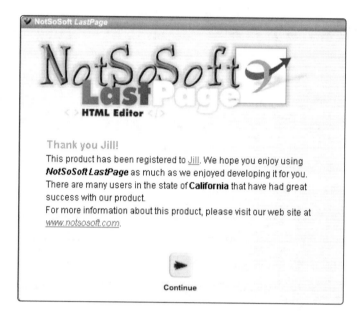

TIP *As you have seen, using an array, then pushing individual sentences into it, is a great way to limit the confusion that comes with entering too much information into a single line of script.*

11) Add the following script just below the current line of script:

```
i = -1;
while (++i < confirmMessage.length) {
  confirmText.htmlText += confirmMessage[i];
}
```

This part of the script is used to loop through the confirmMessage array, adding each sentence in the array to the **confirmText** text field using by-now-familiar ActionScript. Because the array contains strings of text with HTML tags, you must use htmlText to output the message so that it's rendered with the appropriate HTML formatting.

12) Choose Control › Test Movie to test the project up to this point.

Complete the registration form with valid data, then press the Submit button to move the timeline to the Confirm scene, where the confirmation message we scripted appears in the middle of the page. You can see how the various HTML tags affect the look of the text.

13) Close the test movie to return to the authoring environment and save this file as validate7.fla.

This completes this exercise. As you've seen, mixing dynamic data with HTML syntax enables you to provide your user with more pleasing and interesting textual information. You can also use this mix to highlight portions of text in various ways.

CREATING AND CONTROLLING TEXT FIELDS WITH ACTIONSCRIPT

Although you're presented with a variety of options when creating and configuring text fields in the authoring environment, being able to create text fields on the fly—*while* your movie is running—gives you even greater control over the way your project handles text. Let's take a look at the dynamic creation process.

To create a text field using ActionScript, you would use the `createTextField()` method, as follows:

```
_root.createTextField(instanceName, depth, x, y, width, height);
```

Now take a look at the following example, which uses the `createTextField()` method to create a text field:

```
_root.createTextField("myField", 10, 20, 50, 200, 30);
```

The above script creates a text field named **myField** on the root timeline, with its initial `depth`, `x`, `y`, `width`, and `height` properties set as shown. Although the above syntax creates a text field on the root timeline, keep in mind that you can create text fields in any timeline as long as you add the proper target path:

```
_root.myMovieClip.createTextField("myField", 10, 20, 50, 200, 30);
```

Every text field, whether placed on the stage while authoring the movie or created dynamically, is considered an instance of the Text Field object. As such, text fields can be treated similarly to movie clip instances in several ways. First, individual text fields are given instance names from the Property inspector (or when created dynamically, as shown above). When targeting a text field instance with a script, you use its target path (which includes its instance name).

Although you won't necessarily be able to tell by looking at the Actions toolbox in the Actions panel, several methods (similar to Movie Clip object methods) are available to text field instances. For example:

```
startDrag("myField", true);
```

will make the **myField** text field draggable. Because text fields—unlike movie clips—are not timelines, certain methods (for example, `prevFrame()`, `attachMovie()`, `loadMovie()`, and so on) have no meaning when used in the context of a text field instance.

Several properties (similar to movie clip properties) exist for text field instances as well. For example:

```
myField._alpha = 50;
```

will make the **myField** text field 50 percent transparent. With a little bit of experimentation, you'll be able to see which methods and properties movie clip and text field instances share.

In addition to the properties and methods discussed thus far, text fields have numerous *unique* methods and properties for manipulating and controlling text *within* the text field (rather than the text field itself, as previously discussed). Several of these methods are employed to format text-field text using TextFormat objects—we'll save our discussion of those for the next section, "Using the TextFormat Object." In the meantime, let's take a look at a couple useful methods that *do not* pertain to formatting.

To remove a text field instance that was created dynamically, you would use the `removeTextField()` method in the following manner:

```
myField.removeTextField();
```

The above script will remove the text field named **myField**.

NOTE *Only text fields created dynamically can be removed using this method. Text fields placed on the stage while authoring your movie cannot.*

Two of the most common things you do in conjunction with text fields are add and delete text—both of which you can use the `replaceSel()` method for. You can invoke this method to replace the currently selected text with anything you define.

In the following example, assume that the **myField** text field contains the text, "I love my dog and cat very much!" Then, assume that the "dog and cat" portion of text has been selected. Now use the `replaceSel()` method, as shown in the following, to replace that text:

```
myField.replaceSel("bird and snake");
```

The **myField** text field will now read "I love my bird and snake very much!"

The value placed within the `replaceSel()` method when it is invoked can be a string of text, an empty string (`""`), or even a variable.

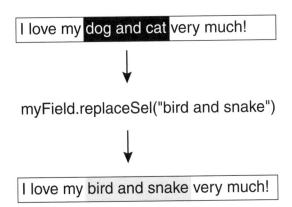

As mentioned earlier, text fields have numerous properties that you can configure while the movie is playing using ActionScript. These properties affect not only the way the field looks and reacts to text but also how it functions. Some of these properties will be familiar because we've already used and discussed them; others don't warrant much discussion because they do the same thing as the corresponding properties that you set with the Property inspector when creating a text field in the authoring environment. Take, for example, the bold property—you would use the following to make the text in the **myField** text field instance appear bold:

```
myField.bold = true;
```

Now let's take a look at some of the less obvious properties of text field instances.

- `autoSize`. This property determines whether a text field will expand and contract its borders automatically to accommodate the amount of text it contains. Normally, a text field's width and height are set using static (nonchanging) values. This property allows a text field's size to be dynamic—that is, determined by the text that's typed into it.

- `borderColor`. This property represents the color of the border around a text field. You can set it using a hex value, such as `myField.borderColor = 0x336699;`. Setting the border color has no visible affect unless the border itself is visible (`myField.border = true;`). The same logic applies to the `background` and `backgroundColor` properties.

429

- **bottomScroll.** This property represents the line number of the bottommost visible line of text in a text field. This is a read-only property.

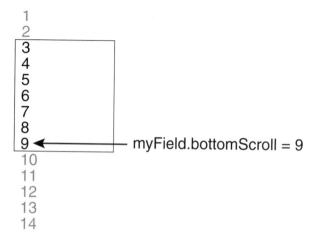

myField.bottomScroll = 9

- **hScroll.** This property is a numeric value representing the current horizontal scrolling position, in points. If the hscroll property of a text field is set to anything greater than 0, say 10, all the text will be shifted to the left 10 points. This property cannot be set to a value higher than the maxhscroll (see below) property value for the same field and is only useful if the text field has had word-wrapping disabled (thus requiring horizontal scrolling in order to see text that exists beyond the right boundary of the field).

- **maxhscroll.** This property represents the maximum value that text can be scrolled horizontally. This is a read-only property.

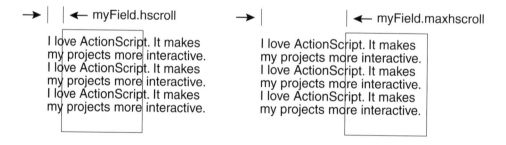

- **maxscroll.** This read-only property represents the highest line number that text can be scrolled vertically in a field. To understand this property better, imagine that a particular text field can display 7 lines of text at once but contains 14. Since you don't want the user to be able to scroll beyond Line 14, you would set the maxscroll property value to 8—a value that can change if additional lines are added.

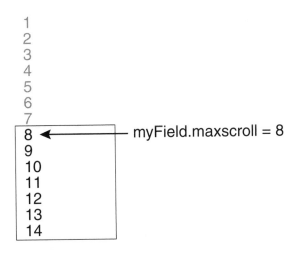

1
2
3
4
5
6
7
8 ← myField.maxscroll = 8
9
10
11
12
13
14

- `restrict`. This property determines which characters can be entered into the field. A value of `null` (`myfield.restrict = null;`), or `""`, indicates that any character can be entered into the field. A specified string of text (`myField.restrict = "meatloaf";`) means only characters included in that string can be entered into the field. A range of characters may be indicated using a dash (`myField.restrict = "A-Z 0-9 a-z";`). Using the caret symbol (^), you can specify a range of characters to accept, with exceptions. For example, `myField.restrict = "0-9^567";` will allow numbers 0, 1, 2, 3, 4, 8, and 9 but not 5, 6, or 7. To include all characters with some exceptions, use the caret in the following manner: `myField.restrict = "^bug";`. In the preceding example, all characters except b, u, and g are allowed. The `restrict` property only applies to text entered by the user; ActionScript can place any text in the field regardless of this property's setting.

- `scroll`. This property represents the number of the top line displayed in the text field. For example, if you wanted to scroll the text in a field so that the fourth line was the highest displayed in the field, you would use the following syntax: `myField.scroll = 4;`. This property's value cannot exceed the `maxscroll` property value for the same field (see `maxscroll` description above).

- `tabEnabled`. This property determines whether the field is included for selection when using the Tab key to select elements in the scene. A value of `true` or `undefined` will include the field. A value of `false` will cause the field to be skipped.

- `tabIndex`. If a field's `tabEnabled` property is set to `true` or `undefined` (allowing the field to be included in tab selecting), this property value indicates the field's selection position in the process.

- `textHeight`. This read-only property determines the height of text in a field (not the height of the field itself, which can be different).

- **textWidth.** This read-only property represents the width of text in a field (not the width of the field itself).

- **type.** This property determines whether the field is an input or dynamic text field. `myField.type = "input";` makes **myField** an input text field.

- **variable.** This property represents the name of the variable associated with the text field. As mentioned in the previous section, associating a variable with a text field will cause that variable's value to be displayed in the field. (You can change it at any time to display a different variable's value.)

Most of these property values can be set, or retrieved for use in other scripts.

When a text field is created, it has the following default property settings:

```
type = "dynamic";
border = false;
background = false;
password = false;
multiline = false;
html = false;
embedFonts = false;
variable = null;
maxChars = null;
```

In the following exercise, we'll dynamically create, configure, and control a couple of text fields as we build an interactive typing application.

1) Open flashWriter1.fla in the Lesson13/Assets folder.

This project contains five layers named according to their content: The Background layer contains the scene's graphical content—with the exception of the buttons, which reside on the Buttons layer. The Components layer contains the Checkbox component (named **applyToAll**) that appears at the top left of the stage. The Box layer contains the movie clip instance named **box**, just to the left of the stage, which looks like a transparent-white box with a white border. Other than some ActionScript, which will be placed on Frame 1 of the Action layer, the white box will be the only element in the scene used in this exercise. The buttons and Checkbox component will be used and scripted in the next exercise.

The goal of this exercise will be to dynamically create a couple of text fields as the movie plays. One field will be larger than the other and will be used for entering text. The smaller one will be used to keep a running total of the number of characters currently in the larger field. Both fields will move from left to right as text is typed into the larger field. In addition, the white box will mimic the movement and size of the larger text field in order to act as its background (this box is partially transparent; transparent backgrounds behind text fields are not inherently possible).

2) **With the Actions panel open, select Frame 1 of the Actions layer and add this script:**

```
_root.createTextField("movingField", 10, 150, 80, 200, 20);
with (movingField){
  autoSize = true;
  html= true;
  multiline = true;
  text = "Enter text here";
  type = "input";
  wordWrap = true;
}
```

The first line of script creates a text field named **movingField**, which will be placed initially at x = 150 and y = 80 and have a width of 200 and a height of 20. Using a `with` statement that references **movingField**, the initial property settings are configured for this field. Initially, this field—which is set to autosize text as it's entered—will display the text "Enter text here." You'll also notice that **movingField** has been set up as an input text field and can wrap lines of text. It is the larger of the two text fields this project will contain.

> **TIP** *As you can see, a `with` statement provides a quick and easy way to address an object (Text Field, Movie Clip, and so on) when several lines of script need to reference it.*

3) Add the following script just below the end of the script added in the previous step:

```
_root.createTextField("statusField", 20, 150, 80, 100, 20);
with (statusField){
  autoSize = true;
  background = true;
  html = true;
  multiline = false;
  selectable = false;
  text = "0";
  type = "dynamic";
  wordWrap = false;
}
```

The first line of script creates a text field named **statusField**, which will be placed initially at x = 150 and y = 80, and have a width of 100 and a height of 20. Using a `with` statement that references the newly created **statusField**, the initial property settings are configured for this field. The field—which is set up to auto-size—will initially display the text "0." You'll also see that **statusField** has been set up as a dynamic text field and can't wrap lines of text. As the smaller of the two text fields, it will mimic the larger field's movement. Let's next script a function that will accomplish that.

4) Add the following function definition just below the end of the script added in the previous step:

```
function updateStatus(){
  statusField._x = movingField._x;
  statusField._y = (movingField._y + movingField._height) + 10;
  statusField.text = movingField.length;
}
```

Remember that in a moment we'll be scripting the **movingField** to move as text is typed into it.

This function accomplishes two things when called: It keeps **statusField** at a specific relative distance from the **movingField** text field as it moves, and it updates the text displayed in the **statusField** text field.

The first line sets the *x* position of the **statusField** to match that of the **movingfield**. The next line is used to place the top of the **statusField** (its *y* position) 10 pixels below the **movingField**. It does this by adding the **movingField** *y* position to its height (which gives us the coordinate of its bottom boundary) and then adding 10 to that result.

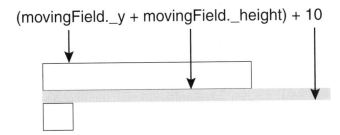

(movingField._y + movingField._height) + 10

The last action updates the text in the **statusField** to indicate the number of characters in the **movingField**. In a moment, we'll script this function to be called every time text is added or removed from **movingField**.

5) Add the following function definition just below the end of the script added in the previous step:

```
function reshapeBox(){
  with(box){
    _x = movingField._x;
    _y = movingField._y;
    _width = movingField._width;
    _height = movingField._height;
  }
}
```

When called, this function will cause the **box** movie clip instance to mimic the position and size of the **movingField** text field, using by-now-familiar actions. As with the function defined in the previous step, we'll soon script this function to be called every time text is added to or removed from **movingField**, making the **box** movie clip instance act as the background for that text field.

6) Add the following function calls just below the end of the script added in the previous step:

```
updateStatus();
reshapeBox();
```

These two lines of script call the functions we just defined so that the **statusField** text field and **box** movie clip instance can be configured (as defined in the function definitions) as soon as the movie begins to play. These same function calls will be made repeatedly.

7) Add the following script just below the function calls added in the previous step:

```
movingField.onChanged = function(){
  movingField._x += 4;
  if (movingField._x + movingField._width > 500){
    movingField._x = 150;
  }
  reshapeBox();
  updateStatus();
}
```

This section of script uses the onChanged event handler method (available to text field instances) to deal with what happens each time text is added or removed from the **movingField** text field.

The first line moves **movingField** 4 pixels from its current position, causing the text field to move to the right each time a character is added to or deleted from the field. The if statement that follows prevents the field from moving off the stage when it moves to the right: It does this by comparing the right side of the field's position (achieved by adding the x position to the width of the field) with the value of 500— the farthest right we want to allow the field to move. If the right side of the field exceeds this amount, the field is set back to its starting x position of 150.

The last two lines call the functions we defined earlier, updating the **statusField** text field and **box** movie clip instance immediately each time text is added to or removed from the **movingField** text field.

8) Choose Control > Test Movie to view the project up to this point.

As soon as the movie begins to play, two text fields are created and their properties set. The **statusField** appears below the **movingField**, and the **box** movie clip instance has the same position and size as the **movingField** text field. As text is typed into the **movingField** text field, it moves to the right, as the **statusField** follows it in a relative position, displaying the current number of characters in the **movingField** text field. Once **movingField** moves too far to the right, it's moved back to its original position.

9) Close the test movie and save your work as flashWriter2.fla.

We'll continue building on this file in the next exercise.

As you've seen, creating and controlling text fields dynamically is a straightforward process that enables you to add a new dimension of interactivity to your projects.

USING TEXTFORMAT OBJECTS

Using HTML tags in strings of text is not the only way to style text dynamically: TextFormat objects afford you all of the formatting power of HTML—and more!

As nothing more than special objects containing formatting properties for character and paragraph styles, TextFormat objects offer similar functionality to cascading style sheets (CSS). Once a TextFormat object has been defined, that object is then "applied" to a text field or section of text in a field, causing the affected text to take on the formatting style described by the object. A TextFormat object can be created and defined in one of two ways. Take a look at the following syntax:

```
myStyle = new TextFormat(nameOfFont, size, color, bold, italic);
```

In this syntax, a TextFormat object is created and its formatting settings configured simultaneously. An example use of this syntax looks like the following:

```
myStyle = new TextFormat("Arial", 12, 0x336699, true, true);
```

437

NOTE *You can configure many additional formatting settings using the constructor function.*

The preceding syntax creates a TextFormat object named myStyle. This object represents a format that uses the Arial font at a point size of 12, the color blue, and in bold and italic. To create the same TextFormat object using the alternative syntax, you would use the following:

```
myStyle = new TextFormat();
with(myStyle){
  font = "Arial";
  size = 12:
  color = 0x336699;
  bold = true;
  italic = true;
}
```

The above syntax uses a with statement to configure various formatting properties of the newly created object. Either way works, but the latter is generally easier to read and use.

Once you've created a TextFormat object, you can apply it to text in a field in several different ways—to all of the current text in the field, to a portion of the current text in the field, or to any new text entered into the field. Take a look at the following examples:

```
myField.setTextFormat(myStyle);
```

The above script will cause all text in the **myField** text field to be displayed in the formatting style described by the myStyle TextFormat object. Even if the text had been previously styled (using a different TextFormat object), that style would be overwritten with the newly applied style. To apply a TextFormat object to a single character in a text field, you would use the following syntax:

```
myField.setTextFormat(27, myStyle);
```

This script will cause the character at index position 27 to take on the style defined by the myStyle TextFormat object. To style a range of characters in a field, you would use the following syntax:

```
myField.setTextFormat(10, 50, myStyle);
```

This script will cause the characters between index positions 10 and 50 to take on the formatting style described by the myStyle TextFormat object.

| Macromedia Flash is a very powerful program. Not only is it powerful, but it is easy to use as well. | Original |

| **Macromedia Flash is a very powerful program. Not only is it powerful, but it is easy to use as well.** | setTextFormat(style1) |

| Macromedia Flash is a very **p**owerful program. Not only is it powerful, but it is easy to use as well. | setTextFormat(27, style1) |

| Macromedia Flash is a very **powerful program. Not on**ly is it powerful, but it is easy to use as well. | setTextFormat(27, 50, style1) |

If you want the *current* text in the field to maintain its formatting while styling any *new* text entered into the field, you would use the `setNewTextFormat()` method instead. Take a look at the following syntax:

```
myField.setNewTextFormat(myStyle);
```

Using the above script, nothing in the **myField** text field will change initially, but any new text entered into it (either by the user or via ActionScript) will take on the character and paragraph formatting defined by the `myStyle` TextFormat object. This applies to new text entered at the *end* of any text currently in the field. If the insertion point is moved somewhere in the middle of the text, then that text will take on the same formatting as the character just to the right of the insertion point.

You may sometimes need to know what formatting has been applied to a specific character or an entire text field (that is, which TextFormat objects have been applied), so that you can copy and apply that formatting elsewhere. You can get this information by using the `getTextFormat()` and `getNewTextFormat()` methods. To understand how these methods work, keep in mind that when you apply a TextFormat object to text in a field, Flash keeps a record of it, so to speak. For example, take a look at the following script, which assigns the `myStyle` TextFormat object to the **myField** text field:

```
myField.setTextFormat(myStyle);
```

Later, if you wanted another text field to be styled in the same way but weren't sure what style had been applied, you could use the following script to find out:

```
newStyle = myField.getTextFormat();
```

The above script creates a new TextFormat object named newStyle that's automatically defined with the same formatting and character settings as the TextFormat object currently applied to **myField**. The newStyle TextFormat object can then be applied to text fields in the manner described above. Just as the setTextFormat() method allows you to apply a format to a specific character or range of characters (as opposed to an entire field), the getTextFormat() method allows you to retrieve formatting data that exists at a specific character index or range of characters. Take a look at the following:

```
newStyle = myField.getTextFormat(27);
```

This script creates a new TextFormat object named newStyle that's automatically defined with the same formatting and character settings as the TextFormat object currently applied to the character at index position 27. If you want to retrieve the formatting that is being applied to *new* text entered into a field (as set with the setNewTextFormat() method), you would use the following syntax:

```
otherStyle = myField.getNewTextFormat();
```

This script creates a TextFormat object named otherStyle that's automatically defined with the same formatting and character settings as the TextFormat object currently set to *new* text entered into the **myField** text field.

NOTE *The setTextFormat(), setNewTextFormat(), getTextFormat(), and getNewTextFormat() methods are actually Text Field object methods. We're discussing them here because you need to understand TextFormat objects to understand and use those methods.*

TextFormat objects have numerous properties that can be set to describe the formatting the object represents. Many are self-explanatory, including align, bold, color, left margin, right margin, and so on. The following describes a few properties that you might *not* be familiar with.

- font. This property—which represents the font face used by the object—is a string value such as "Arial" or "Times New Roman." Using the getFontList() method of the Text Field object, you can apply virtually any font face the user currently has installed on his or her machine. (We'll demonstrate the use of this property in the following exercise.)

- `tabStops`. This property represents the distance (in points) the caret will move within a field when the Tab key is pressed. This property's value is set by referencing the name of an array that contains positive numbers. For example, the following creates an array with five numbers: `myTabStops = [4, 20, 36, 52, 70];`. To use the values in this array to set the `tabStops` property of the `style1` TextFormat object, you would use the following syntax: `style1.tabStops = mytabStops;`. Any field that uses this TextFormat object will tab at 4, 20, 36, 52, and 70 points.

- `target`. This property—which is used in conjunction with the `url` property (see below)—represents the window in which a URL will open when requested. This is similar to the target setting used with HTML.

- `url`. This property represents a URL to which the text formatted as a TextFormat object is hyperlinked. This is a string value such as, "http://www.macromedia.com."

TextFormat objects also have a method available to them: `getTextExtent()`. This method is used to determine the width and size a string of text will be if it is styled in the specified TextFormat. Take a look at the following example:

```
sizeInfo = myStlye.getTextExtent("I have GOT to quit eating donuts!");
```

This creates a generic object named `sizeInfo` with two properties, `width` (`sizeInfo.width`) and `height` (`sizeInfo.height`), which contain the respective size values of the specified text *if* styled using the `myStyle` TextFormat object. This data can be compared against the size of a particular text field to see if the specified text can be placed and displayed in that text field without scrolling.

sizeInfo.height

sizeInfo.width

In the following exercise, we'll access your computer's fonts to create TextFormat objects and apply them in various ways to the **movingField** text field that we created in the previous exercise.

1) Open flashWriter2.fla in the Lesson13/Assets folder.

We will continue to build on the file you used in the previous exercise.

In this exercise, you'll add script to Frame 1 of the Actions layer, script our buttons, and use the Checkbox component to facilitate part of our project's functionality.

2) With the Property inspector open, select the Checkbox component.

The most important thing to know about this component is that its instance is **applyToAll**. Knowing this, we can use the `getValue()` method (available to Checkbox components) to determine whether it's currently checked (`true`) or not (`false`), then act accordingly. For example, if this component were currently checked, the following script would place a value of `true` into the `currentValue` variable:

```
currentValue = applyToAll.getValue();
```

3) With the Actions panel open, select Frame 1 of the Actions layer and add this script to the end of the current script:

```
myFonts = TextField.getFontList();
```

This script creates an array named `myFonts`, which contains the names (as string values) of all fonts on the Flash Player host system (including fonts in the SWF file and any loaded asset SWF files). For example, on my machine, after running the script above, `myFonts[3]` has a value of "Arial." You can work with this array in the same manner you would any other array. The various values in this array will be used to randomly set font face styles for several TextFormat objects we will create.

> **NOTE** *When using the `getFontList()` method, you don't reference a particular text field instance name (as you might think). Instead, you simply use `TextField` (see example script above).*

4) Add the following lines of script just below the current script:

```
styleStatus = new TextFormat()
with(styleStatus){
  font = myFonts[random(myFonts.length)];
  color = 0x858273;
  size = 16;
  bold = true;
}
```

The first line of the above script creates a new TextFormat object named `styleStatus`. In a moment, you'll see how this object dictates the appearance of the text in the **statusField** text field. The `with` statement that follows the object's creation is used to define several of its formatting parameters. Although most of the settings are fairly easy to understand, let's take a look at the line that sets the `font` property. The value of this property is set based on a random index value of the `myFonts` array. The expression uses the length of the `myFonts` array to generate a random number from all possible index values in the array. Thus, if the array has a length of 200, the number generated will be between 0 and 199. That random number is then used to set the index value of one of the font names in the `myFonts` array. If, for example, the number generated is 37, the expression would be evaluated as follows:

```
font = myFonts[37];
```

If the string value at that index is "DiscoMonkey," that's the name of the font face assigned to this TextFormat object.

To apply the formatting of this new TextFormat object to the **statusField** text field, we need to use the `setTextFormat()` method, which we'll do in the following step.

5) **Modify the** `updateStatus()` **function definition as shown:**

```
function updateStatus(){
  statusField._x = movingField._x;
  statusField._y = (movingField._y + movingField._height) + 10;
  statusField.text = movingField.length;
  statusField.setTextFormat(styleStatus);
}
```

Note the last line of script that we added to this function definition: You'll remember that this function is used to update the position and text displayed in the **statusField** text field. The last line of script uses the `setTextFormat()` method to set the format of the **statusField** text field to that described by the `styleStatus` TextFormat object. By placing this line of script in the function definition, should the format description of the `styleStatus` object ever change, those changes would be reflected in the **statusField** when the function is called.

6) **Add the following script to the end of the current script on Frame 1:**

```
style1 = new TextFormat()
with(style1){
  align = "left";
  bold = false;
  color = 0x1A1917;
  font = myFonts[random(myFonts.length)];
  indent = 0;
  italic = true;
  leading = 0;
  leftMargin = 20;
  rightMargin = 20;
  size = 20;
  target = null;
  underline = false;
  url = null;
}
```

This script creates another TextFormat object named `style1`. The `with` statement that follows defines the formatting properties of that object. Note that the properties `bold`, `indent`, `leading`, `target`, `underline`, and `url` are set to `false`, `0`, or `null`—in essence indicating that this TextFormat object should not use these properties. Although the TextFormat object could be defined even if we removed these lines of script, we've set them as shown for a reason. Assume you applied a TextFormat object (whose `bold` property was set to `true`) to a text field. The text in that field would appear in bold—simple enough. Now assume you applied a different TextFormat object (whose `bold` property was not explicitly set as shown above) to that same field. In this case, the text in that field would still appear bold, although it would take on the other characteristics of the newly applied TextFormat object. In order for a formatting characteristic to change when applying a *new* TextFormat object, that new object must specifically define a different value—otherwise the old value (and its affect) remains. This same principle applies when using the `setNewTextFormat()` method as well. Thus, it's good practice to always define *something* to property values so that you get the results you intended.

7) Add this script to the end of the current script on Frame 1:

```
style2 = new TextFormat()
with(style2){
  align = "center";
  bold = false;
  color = 0xCC0000;
  font = myFonts[random(myFonts.length)];
  indent = 0;
  italic = false;
  leading = 15;
  leftMargin = 0;
  rightMargin = 0;
  size = 14;
  target = null;
  underline = false;
  url = null;
}
```

This script creates another TextFormat object named `style2`.

NOTE *The accompanying source file for this exercise has defined two additional TextFormat objects, `style3` and `style4`. To avoid redundancy (since these objects are very similar to the ones already defined) as well as to save trees, we're not including the syntax for these two objects here.*

We've now defined all of the TextFormat objects that our project will use. Before we put them to use, however, we need to tweak the script's flow in Frame 1 just a bit.

8) Move the `updateStatus()` and `reshapeBox()` function calls from just above where it says `myFonts = TextField.getFontList();` to the end of the script on Frame 1.

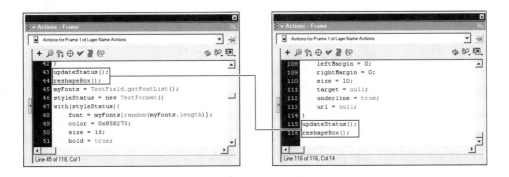

As always, it's a good idea to put all initial function calls at the end of a script—here, there's an especially good reason. You'll remember that in Step 5 we modified the updateStatus() function to include a line of script that uses the styleStatus TextFormat object. If we had left that function call where it was, the updateStatus() function would have been called just a split-second before the script that creates and defines the styleStatus TextFormat object—resulting in a minor bug, since you can't use something before it's been created. By moving the function calls to the end of the script, we're assured that all objects are created and defined *first*.

The last thing we need to do is script our buttons.

9) With the Actions panel open, select Button 1 and add this script:

```
on(release){
  if (_root.applyToAll.getValue()){
    movingField.setTextFormat(style1);
    movingField.setNewTextFormat(style1);
  }else{
    movingField.setNewTextFormat(style1);
  }
  updateStatus();
  reshapeBox();
}
```

This script takes one of two actions, depending on whether the Checkbox component (named **applyToAll**), discussed earlier, is checked or unchecked when the button is clicked. The if statement says that if its value is true (it is checked), apply the style1 TextFormat object to all currently displayed text in the **movingField** text field (setTextFormat()), as well as any new text entered into that field (setNewTextFormat()). This will cause the text in that field to immediately reflect the new formatting style. If the checkbox's value is false (else), the style1 TextFormat will only be applied to *new* text entered. After either one of these sets of actions has executed, the updateStatus() and reshapeBox() functions are called to handle any changes that need to be made to the **statusField** text field and the **box** movie clip instance as a result of the new formatting applied.

10) To avoid redundancy, place similar scripts on Buttons 2, 3, and 4, but modify them where it says style1 to read style2, style3, and style4, respectively.

11) Choose Control > Text Movie to test the project.
When the movie appears, test the various buttons in conjunction with the checkbox to see the effect that it has on the text in the **movingField** text field. All the functionality from the previous exercise should be retained as well.

12) Close the test movie and save your work as flashWriter3.fla.

This completes the exercise and the lesson! As you've learned, you can work with and manipulate text input by the user in numerous ways. ActionScript provides the means to validate many types of data as well as to format it using HTML and TextFormat objects. With the skills you've learned here, you're ready to make text and user input a greater part of your project's interactivity.

WHAT YOU HAVE LEARNED

In this lesson, you have:

- Learned why validation is important (page 398)
- Defined validation requirements and used them to create conditional statements (pages 399–401)
- Set up a method to handle errors detected in the validation process (pages 401–403)
- Created several functions for validating strings, numbers, and sequences (pages 403–418)
- Formatted dynamic data in a custom confirmation message using HTML (pages 418–427)
- Dynamically created, configured, and controlled several text fields (pages 427–437)
- Used TextFormat objects to dynamically style the text in a field (pages 437–447)

controlling movie clips dynamically

In the lessons leading up to this, you learned how to use frame events, clip events, and button events to make things happen—often to manipulate a movie clip instance. In this lesson, you'll learn how to manipulate movie clip instances—duplicating, attaching, coloring, scaling, and positioning them—based on *dynamic input*. We'll also show you how to control movie clip instances based on the continuous feedback of a pressed button, as well as introduce you to Flash's drawing methods. By the end of the lesson, you will have created a simple drawing application and a dynamically generated scrolling list.

This drawing application is one of the projects you will create in this lesson in order to learn about the various ways you can control movie clip instances dynamically.

WHAT YOU WILL LEARN

In this lesson, you will:

- Build a scrolling list.

- Duplicate and attach movie clip instances.

- Create continuous-feedback buttons to move a movie clip instance

- Create empty movie clip instances dynamically

- Learn to how to draw lines and filled shapes dynamically

- Change the stacking order of movie clip instances dynamically

- Script drag and drop functionality

- Remove movie clip instances dynamically

APPROXIMATE TIME

This lesson takes approximately 1 hour to complete.

LESSON FILES

Media Files:

None

Starting Files:

Lesson14/Assets/scrollingList1.fla

Lesson14/Assets/draw1.fla

Completed Project:

scrollingList3.fla

draw5.fla

CREATING MOVIE CLIP INSTANCES DYNAMICALLY

You can dynamically create a movie clip instance by using one of the following three methods of the movie clip object:

- `duplicateMovieClip()`: Using this method, you can duplicate an already existing movie clip instance on the stage to create a new instance of that movie clip.

- `attachMovie()`: This method creates a new instance of a movie clip directly from the library.

- `createEmptyMovieClip()`: This method creates an empty movie clip instance—that is, one that contains no data or graphical content.

You will use each of these methods in the course of the exercises for this lesson.

DUPLICATEMOVIECLIP()

Although we introduced you to this method in Lesson 10, Automating Scripts With Loops, we didn't cover it in detail there. Now, at last, you get to learn everything you need to know about the powerful `duplicateMovieClip()` method!

Using the `duplicateMovieClip()` method, you can direct Flash to duplicate a movie clip instance that is currently on the stage and give it a new instance name. If the movie clip instance is not on the stage (that is, it's in a previous frame or in a frame not yet visited), Flash cannot duplicate it. In addition, the movie clip instance can only be duplicated into the same timeline as the original, and it will exist in the same relative hierarchical position as the original. (To dynamically generate a movie clip instance that also allows dynamic timeline insertion, you would use `attachMovie()`, which we'll discuss later in this lesson.)

When a movie clip instance is duplicated, the duplicate inherits all of the instance's current physical properties.

A duplicated movie clip instance inherits the following from the original:

- Position
- Scale
- Alpha
- Rotation
- Color
- Clip events attached to the movie clip instance

A duplicated movie clip does not inherit the following:

- Variables, arrays, objects
- Name
- Visibility
- Current frame

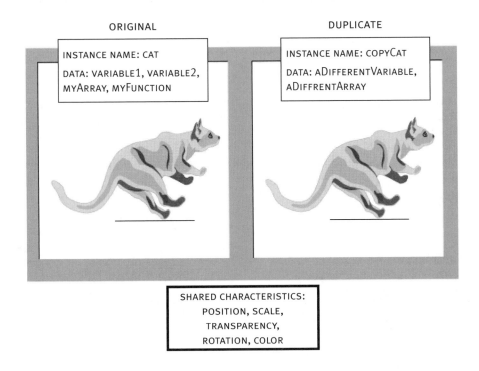

> **NOTE** *A duplicated movie clip instance starts playing at Frame 1, even if the original from which it was copied was at another frame at the time the duplicate was created.*

The following is the syntax for duplicating a movie clip instance:

```
myClip.duplicateMovieClip(name, depth, object);
```

This line of ActionScript starts with the instance name (target path) of the movie clip to be duplicated and then invokes the duplicateMovieClip() method of the MovieClip object to create a new instance called the value of name at a depth of depth. The object parameter is optional. For example:

```
name = "ball2";
depth = 100;
ball.duplicateMovieClip(name, depth);
```

These three lines of ActionScript, duplicate the **ball** movie clip instance, name the new instance **ball2**, and place it into a depth of 100.

When we talk about depth *here, we're referring to the stacking order of movie clip instances in a particular timeline. If two movie clip instances overlap in Flash, one must appear to be above the other, with the top instance having a higher depth. Every movie clip instance has a unique depth in relation to other objects on the stage. When a movie clip instance is duplicated, you can assign it a numeric depth of any positive integer. The higher the integer, the higher the depth in that timeline. Although you may not be aware of it, any movie clip instances that you manually place in a particular timeline while authoring a movie are placed at a depth starting from -16384. This means that if a dynamically created instance is placed in a timeline at a depth of 1, it will appear above any manually placed instances.*

Each timeline has its own range of depths, from -16384 to 1048575. These depths are relative to the depth of the parent timeline. In other words, instance1 contains child instances at levels on its timeline from -16384 to 1048575. But instance1 is below instance2, so that even the highest placed child instance in the timeline of instance1 is still lower than the lowest placed child instance in instance2.

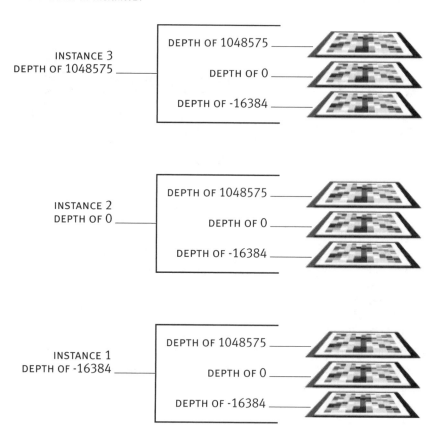

A *depth can only contain one movie clip instance at a time. If you duplicate a movie clip instance into a depth that already contains another movie clip instance, you will destroy the movie clip instance that is already there.*

Movie clip instances can be placed in a total of 1064960 (-16384 to 1048575) depths in a single timeline. Every timeline in a movie has its own set of depths that do not interfere with any other timelines. This means, for example, that you can duplicate instances into a depth of 10 in as many timelines as you like.

The third parameter in the `duplicateMovieClip()` method, `object`, is optional though useful. The properties of any object specified in that parameter are used to populate the newly duplicated movie clip instance. If the parameter is left blank, it's ignored. To extend the above example, take a look at the following:

```
myObject = new Object();
myObject.ballColor = "red"
name = "ball2";
depth = 100;
ball.duplicateMovieClip(name, depth, myObject);
```

When the new instance of **ball** is created, it will contain all of the properties of the `myObject` object. In this case, that means that a variable `ballColor` with a value of "red" is created in the new instance.

TIP *To copy the variables from the original instance into the duplicate, use the instance name of the original as the initializing object. For example:*

```
ball.duplicateMovieClip(name, depth, ball);
```

ATTACHMOVIE()

Using `attachMovie()`, you can actually pull a movie clip out of the library dynamically and "attach" an instance of it to *any* timeline currently available on the stage—in essence adding the content of the attached movie clip instance to the content of the movie to which it's attached. The attached movie becomes a *child* of the timeline to which it's attached. As such, the attached movie takes on any graphical transformations performed on its parent (size, rotation, transparency, and so on) yet remains separate with respect to data, visibility, current frame, and so on (for more information on parent/child relationships, see Lesson 3, Understanding Target Paths).

FACE.ATTACHMOVIE("GLASSES", "MYGLASSES", 1)

FACE.ATTACHMOVIE("MOUTH", "MYMOUTH", 2)

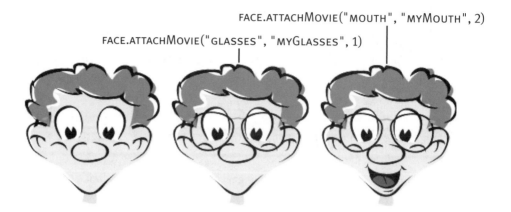

TRANSFORMATIONS TO FACE

So what are the main differences between this method and the `duplicateMovieClip()` method? As mentioned earlier, you can use `attachMovie()` to attach a movie clip instance from the library to any timeline currently in the scene. Because this method attaches clip instances from the library (and the library contains all of your movie clips), the movie clip to which you attach the instance doesn't have to be on stage when you attach it. With `duplicateMovieClip()`, on the other hand, an instance of the movie clip that you wish to duplicate does need to exist on the stage. What's more, you must place the duplicate inside the same timeline as the original—you can't duplicate it to another timeline. In addition, if the instance you're duplicating has any attached clip events (`data`, `enterframe`, `mouseDown`, and so on), the duplicate will automatically inherit those same clip events. Although there are ways to add clip events to an attached movie clip instance, the process is not as straightforward as in the duplication process.

In the simplest terms, attaching movie clip instances allows you to add virtually any timeline to any other timeline. Duplicating movies, in contrast, enables you to make exact replicas of movie clip instances for inclusion in the same timeline as the original.

ATTACHING AN INSTANCE

ATTACH   ATTACH   ATTACH

DUPLICATNG AN INSTANCE

DUPLICATE   DUPLICATE

There are several steps you'll need to follow to use the `attachMovie()` method in a project—the first of which is to specify, in the library, which movie clips you want to make available for attaching. This is called *linkage*. *Linkage* may not seem to be the best term to describe identifying movie clips in the library that can be attached. However, the term also pertains to sharing libraries—in which assets in one SWF's library are *linked*, or shared, by another SWF. When specifying movie clips to make available for attaching, or when sharing assets between two SWFs, the movie clips involved must be given identifier names. Macromedia therefore considers any process that involves giving a movie clip in the library an identifier name to be *linkage*.

To add the most common type of linkage to a movie clip:

1. Open the library.

2. Right-click the movie clip of interest.

3. Select Linkage.

4. Select the Export for ActionScript checkbox.

5. Enter the Identifier name. (The identifier is how you refer to this library-based movie clip with ActionScript.)

TIP *You can also set the linkage when creating a movie clip in the Convert to Symbol pop-up window by pressing the Advanced button.*

Convert to Symbol

Name: `Symbol 1` | **OK**

Behavior: ● Movie Clip   Registration: ⣿   **Cancel**
○ Button
○ Graphic   **Basic**   **Help**

Linkage

Identifier: `myClip`

Linkage: ☑ Export for ActionScript
☐ Export for runtime sharing
☐ Import for runtime sharing
☑ Export in first frame

URL:

Source

☐ Always update before publishing

File: **Browse...**

Symbol Name: Symbol 1   **Symbol...**

NOTE *When setting linkage, there is one other option to note: "Export in first frame," which is checked by default. This option is used to determine when a linked (or attachable) movie clip is downloaded when your project is viewed over the Web. If this box is left checked, that movie clip will be downloaded before Frame 1 of your movie so that the clip's content is available before your first opportunity to attach it (that is, Frame 1). If you're using large movie clips (say ones that contain many other movie clips or sounds), Flash may appear to hang. Don't worry: It's just preloading the contents of all linked movie clips. If you uncheck the "Export in first frame" option, the movie clip will not be preloaded before the first frame (as just described). If you choose this option, you must place an instance of that movie clip on the stage at some point before it can be attached (so that Flash knows when to load it). After it is instantiated (seen or placed in your movie) on some frame, you can attach it anywhere. For example, if there is an action on Frame 25 that attaches the movie clip, then an instance of that clip must have been placed on Frame 24 or lower in order for the* `attachMovieClip()` *action to work. Any frames after Frame 24 can attach the instance, since it has been loaded into memory.*

Here is the syntax to attach an instance of a movie clip in the library to a timeline:

```
path.attachMovie(identifier, newName, depth, object)
```

For example:

```
_root.wall.attachMovie("paint", "paint2", 10)
```

This script will attach the movie clip in the library with the identifier name of "paint" to the _root.wall movie clip instance. The newly attached movie is given an instance name of **paint2** and placed on a depth of 10. Since an attached movie becomes a child of the movie clip instance to which it's attached, the newly attached instance will have a target path of _root.wall.paint2. Notice in the above syntax (first line) that, again, the option is available to populate the newly created clip with the properties and variables of an object. However, as with duplicateMovieClip(), this parameter is optional and thus we left it out in the example above (second line).

> **TIP** *The easiest way to dynamically assign a clip event to an attached (or duplicated) movie is to define the assignment immediately after the attachment (or duplication) action, as the following shows:*
>
> ```
> _root.attachMovie("box", "dynamicBox", 1);
> dynamicBox.onEnterFrame = function (){
>   dynamicBox._rotation += 15;
> }
> ```
>
> *In this example, an instance of the movie clip named **box** (its identifier name in the library) is dynamically attached to the root timeline. The attached instance is given a name of **dynamicBox**. On the next few lines, after the attach action, a clip event is assigned to this newly attached instance.*

CREATEEMPTYMOVIECLIP()

Using the createEmptyMovieClip() method, you can dynamically create (in any timeline) a new instance of an empty movie clip instance. Why would you want to do such a thing? Take a look at the following examples:

- With this method, once you've created an empty instance, you can attach other movie clip instances to it—useful for dynamically generating a list of movie clip instances for use as menu choices. Once you create this type of "main" movie clip instance, you can move it around as a whole rather than move each menu item individually.

- You can create an empty movie clip instance and then dynamically load in music or an image.

- An empty movie clip instance makes a nice storage area for lines, fills, and gradient fills created using Flash's drawing capabilities.

Here is the syntax for creating an empty movie clip instance in a timeline:

```
Path.createEmptyMovieClip(name, depth);
```

For example:

```
_root.createEmptyMovieClip("box", 1);
```

The first parameter is the instance name that you want to assign to the empty movie clip instance you create; the second parameter is the depth at which you want to place that movie clip instance. If you were to test this action, you wouldn't get a visual result because you're creating an empty movie clip instance. Later in this lesson you'll learn how to use `createEmptyMovieClip()` to hold drawn lines.

USING ATTACHMOVIE()

With `attachMovie()`, you can create a new instance of a movie clip in the library. In this exercise, you'll begin a project that when complete will be a scrolling list of items. You will create the items in the list by attaching movie clip instances dynamically.

1) Open scrollingList1.fla in the Lesson14/Assets folder.

On the main timeline, you'll see three layers: Actions, Window, and Background. The Background layer contains the main graphics for the project; the Actions layer will contain most of the project's ActionScript, and the Window layer contains a movie clip instance called **display**.

Inside **display's** timeline you'll find four layers: Mask, Fields, Scroll Buttons, and Window Graphics. The Window Graphics layer contains the border and background graphics of the window; the Scroll Buttons layer contains a movie clip instance that holds the Up and Down scroll buttons that you will work with in the next exercise; and the Fields layer contains an empty movie clip instance called **list**, which will contain instances that are dynamically created using `attachMovie()`. These attached instances will appear as items on a list, one on top of the other. When the **list** movie clip instance is filled with these attached instances, it will become quite long. Thus, **list** is masked by a rectangular shape in the Mask layer (of its own timeline) so that only the area of **list** over the window graphics will be visible.

CONFIGURATION   RESULT

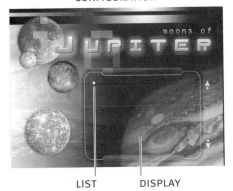

LIST   DISPLAY

2) Open the library and locate the movie clip named *score list info bar*. Right-click (or Control-click on a Mac) it and select Linkage from the menu that appears. Select Export for ActionScript in the Linkage Properties dialog box that appears and enter *infoBar* into the Identifier field.

This movie clip is now available for use with the `attachMovie()` method.

One instance of this movie clip will be attached to the **list** instance for every line of information in the scrolling list (16 lines, 16 attachments). Inside this attached movie clip are two dynamic text field instances, **moonName** and **moonNum**, which will be used in the attached instances to display the various names of the moons as well as an associated moon number.

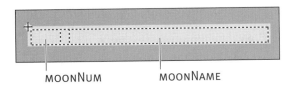

MOONNUM   MOONNAME

3) Select Frame 1 in the Actions layer on the main timeline. Open the Actions panel and enter this ActionScript:

```
list =
["Adrastea","Amalthea","Ananke","Callisto","Carme","Elara","Europa","Ganymede",
"Himalia","Io","Leda","Lysithea","Metis","Pasiphae","Sinope","Thebe"];
```

The object of this exercise is to create a list of items by attaching movie clip instances. To this end, we've created an array of names: the 16 most well-known moons of Jupiter. For each name in this array, an instance of the movie clip in the library (that we previously gave an identifier name to) will be attached to the **list** instance.

Now it's time to begin defining the function that will be used to create the list of movie clip instances.

459

4) With Frame 1 still selected, add the following code:

```
function buildList () {
  spacing = 30;
}
```

The buildList() function will ultimately contain all of the ActionScript needed to attach, position, and populate the entire list with movie clip instances. To position the vertical list properly, a variable called spacing is created and given a value of 30, which will be used to set the vertical (y) distance between the center of one attached movie clip instance and the center of the one placed below it.

5) To attach and position the list items, add the following ActionScript to the function definition:

```
var i = -1;
while (++i < list.length) {
  name = "infoBar" + i;
  y = i * spacing;
  display.list.attachMovie("infoBar", name, i);
  display.list[name]._y = y;
  display.list[name].moonName.text = list[i];
  display.list[name].moonNum.text = i + 1;
}
```

Using by-now-familiar ActionScript, this part of the function uses a while loop to loop through every element in the list array. For each element in the array, the loop attaches an instance of the **infoBar** movie clip to the **list** instance (to build the list).

The first action in the loop creates a variable called name whose value is set using an expression that concatenates the string "infoBar" with the current value of i. Since the value of i is incremented with each loop, the value of name will be "infoBar0", "infoBar1", "infoBar2", and so on, with each successive iteration of the loop. Further down in the loop, the current value of name is used to assign a name to each successive attached instance of **infoBar**. Next in the loop, a variable called y is created to store the intended y position of the movie clip instance that's being attached. The value of this variable is based on an expression that multiplies the current value of i with the value of spacing. Since the value of i increases with each iteration, so too does the value of y. This results in successive attached instances being placed in a y position below the previous one created.

The last four actions in the loop attach and populate (with data) the dynamic text fields in each attached instance. First, an attached instance of the **infoBar** movie clip is created with an instance name and depth based on the current value of name and i, respectively. Next, this attached instance's *y* position is set based on the current value of the variable named y. Since each attached instance contains the same graphical elements as the original, each has two text fields: **moonName** and **moonNum**. The last two actions in the loop populate those fields with the appropriate data. First, using the current value of i, the text value of **moonName** in the attached instance is set to the appropriate string value in the list array. Since the value of i is incremented with each loop, the **moonName** text field in each successively attached instance will display the successive string elements (moon names) in the list array. Lastly, the **moonNum** text field in each attached instance is set to a numerical value of i plus 1. This will result in numerical values of 1, 2, 3, and so on appearing in the **movieNum** text fields of successive attached instances.

Once this loop has been completed, each element in the list array has an attached movie clip instance that's populated with information and appears in an ordered vertical fashion.

6) **To have the function execute, add** `buildList();` **at the end of the current script on Frame 1 (below the function definition).**

```
1  list=["Adrastea","Amalthea","Ananke","Callisto","Carme'
2  function buildList() {
3      spacing=30;
4      var i=-1;
5      while (++i<list.length) {
6          name="infoBar"+i;
7          y=i*spacing;
8          display.list.attachMovie("infoBar",name,i);
9          display.list[name]._y=y;
10         display.list[name].moonName.text=list[i];
11         display.list[name].moonNum.text=i+1;
12     }
13 }
14 buildList();
15
```

Line 14 of 15, Col 1

After the function has been defined in Frame 1 of the movie, this line of script will execute all of the actions we set up in the previous steps.

7) Choose Control > Test Movie to test what you've created.

When the movie initializes, your list of items will appear. Remember: Because you've used a mask to limit the number of items that can be displayed simultaneously, you'll only see a partial list.

8) Close the test movie and save your work as scrollingList2.fla.

You've completed the hardest part of this lesson: You've written ActionScript that dynamically attaches instances of a movie clip from the library in order to build a list of items. In the next exercise, you'll be working with the same file to make the window scrollable.

BUILDING CONTINUOUS-FEEDBACK BUTTONS

You'll find that it's sometimes useful to have actions continually executed while a button is being pressed. A button set up to enable this is known as a *continuous-feedback button*—and scroll buttons (the focus of this exercise) provide a perfect example of such.

NOTE *The Scrollbar component makes implementing scrolling functionality easy, in many cases. This exercise is intended to show some of logic behind the way scrollbars work, so you can implement your own custom scrolling solutions.*

If you wanted to scroll through a list of information in a window, you would quickly become frustrated if you had to click a button every time you wanted to make the information scroll up (or down). Far less frustrating is a button that needs to be pressed just once to scroll continuously until it's released. In Flash, you can create this type of functionality by using the `enterFrame` or `mouseMove` clip events with a button (as we'll soon demonstrate).

In this exercise, you'll add scrolling buttons to the list you built in the previous exercise.

1) Open scrollingList2.fla in the Lesson14/Assets folder.

You'll pick up where you left off with this file in the previous exercise; thus, you should be familiar with its layout. In this exercise, you'll add ActionScript to Frame 1 of the Actions layer in the main timeline, to the scroll buttons themselves, and to the clips that contain the scroll buttons. First, you'll build the function that performs the actual scrolling; then you'll add the commands to the required areas so that the function is called.

462

You'll remember that there's a movie clip instance called **list** inside the **display** clip. All of the attached movie clip instances that we create (of **infoBar**) will exist inside of the **list** instance. Thus, we'll set up our scrolling function to vertically move the **list** movie clip instance up and down to achieve the effect of scrolling through the list of items.

NOTE *When we use the term* scrolling *in this exercise, we're talking about increasing or decreasing the* _y *property value of the* **list** *movie clip instance to move it up or down on the screen.*

2) With the Actions panel open, select Frame 1 of the Actions layer and add the following line of script just below the line that creates the `list` array:

```
startingY = display.list._y;
```

With scrolling, you must establish maximum and minimum vertical locations (y) to which the list can scroll: These represent the boundaries for scrolling (or continued vertical movement). In any application where scrolling is allowed, you're prevented from scrolling beyond the top or bottom borders of the document. The above line of script is used to establish the edge of one of these vertical boundaries: The movie clip instance **list** (which will contain the list of attached instances) should not continue scrolling if its *y* position exceeds its *starting y* position. In a moment, we'll use the value of the `startingY` variable to accomplish this.

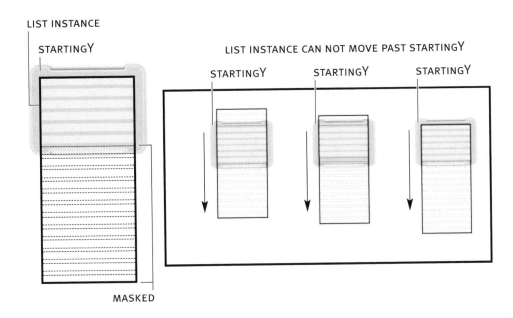

LIST INSTANCE

STARTINGY

LIST INSTANCE CAN NOT MOVE PAST STARTINGY

STARTINGY   STARTINGY   STARTINGY

MASKED

3) To set part of the other scrolling boundary, add `bottom=120;` **to Frame 1, just below the line of script you added in the previous step.**

As mentioned in the previous step, the highest possible *y* value that the **list** movie clip instance can scroll to is its starting position. The `bottom` variable, as defined in this step, will be used as an offset to the upward extreme of scrolling so that the bottom of the list does not go all the way to the top of the window. (Our reasons for using this variable will become more obvious in coming steps.)

4) Start defining the function that will be used to scroll the movie clip instance. To do this, add the following ActionScript to Frame 1, just below the `buildList()` **function definition:**

```
function scroll (direction) {
  speed = 10;
}
```

Soon, we'll set up our project to call this function via an `enterFrame` clip event attached to the movie clip instance that contains the scroll buttons. One of the scroll buttons will be used to scroll up; the other will be used to scroll down. The `direction` parameter will be used to send a string value of "up" or "down" to this function. A conditional statement in the function (which we'll soon add) will evaluate this value so that the function knows which direction to scroll the **list** instance. The variable `speed` is just that—the scrolling speed. When the scroll button is held down, the **list** instance will scroll up or down. Its rate of movement will be determined by the value of this variable. (Keep in mind that there's nothing magic about the number 10; you can adjust it to anything that looks good.)

5) Add this `if/else if` **statement inside the function definition, just below** `speed = 10`**:**

```
if (direction == "up") {
} else if (direction == "down") {
}
```

As mentioned in the previous step, the `direction` parameter is used to send a string value of "up" or "down" to the function. The above conditional statement determines how this function works, based on that value. Over the next few steps, you'll be adding actions to this conditional statement so that if the intended scrolling direction is "up," a certain list of actions will be performed, and if the scrolling direction is "down," another set of actions will be performed.

6) Nest this `if/else` statement in the "up" leg of the `if` statement just entered:

```
if (display.list._y – speed + display.list._height > (startingY + bottom)) {
  display.list._y -= speed;
} else {
  display.list._y = (startingY + bottom) – display.list._height;
}
```

Since this statement is nested within the "up" leg of the previous statement, it is evaluated if a string value of "up" is sent to the function (as will occur when the Up scroll button is pressed, as we'll soon set up) to determine if upward scrolling of the **list** movie clip instance will occur.

The first part of the expression in the statement is used to determine what the *bottom* position of the **list** instance would be if it were to move 10 pixels upward. The expression does this by looking at the **list** instance's current *y* position, then subtracting the value of `speed` and adding the height of the instance. That bottom position of the instance is then compared against one of the scrolling boundaries (as established by adding the value of `bottom` to the value of `startingY`). If moving the **list** instance up doesn't cause the bottom of the instance to exceed the boundary, the first action in the statement is executed and the list is moved up. However, if moving the instance up would make it exceed the boundary, the `else` part of the statement would be executed, simply snapping its vertical position to the maximum allowable.

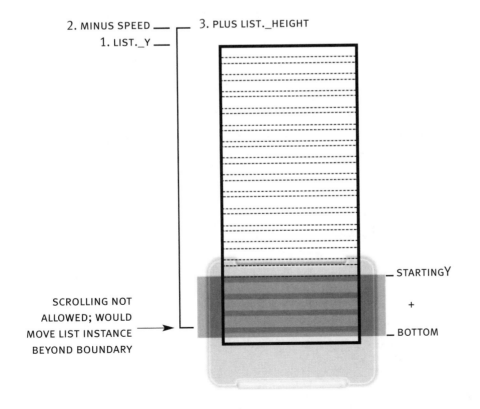

2. MINUS SPEED —— —— 3. PLUS LIST._HEIGHT

1. LIST._Y ——

SCROLLING NOT ALLOWED; WOULD MOVE LIST INSTANCE BEYOND BOUNDARY

— STARTING Y

+

— BOTTOM

If you're confused, don't worry: Let's take a look at an example to see how this works. For this demonstration, we'll assume the following values for various elements:

```
speed = 10
startingX = 100
bottom = 120
display.list._height = 400 //vertical height of the list instance
display.list._y = -165 //current vertical position of list instance
```

Using these values, the expression in the if statement is evaluated as follows:

```
if (-165 - 10 + 400 > (100 + 120))
```

Which further evaluates to:

```
if (225 > 220)
```

In this case, 225 is greater than 220, so the following action is executed:

```
display.list._y -= speed;
```

This moves the **list** instance up 10 pixels, and its *y* position now equals -175. With this in mind, if the statement were evaluated again, it would look like the following:

```
if (-175 - 10 + 400 > (100 + 120))
```

Which further evaluates to:

```
if (215 > 220)
```

In this case, 215 is less than 220, so the following action (the else part of the statement) is executed:

```
display.list._y = (startingY + bottom) - display.list._height;
```

Here, the **list** instance's *y* position is set based on what the expression to the right of the equals sign evaluates to. Using the values established for this example, this expression would be evaluated as follows:

```
(startingY + bottom) - display.list._height
```

Which further evaluates to:

```
(100 + 120) - 400
```

Which further evaluates to:

```
220 - 400
```

Which further evaluates to:

```
-180
```

This means that the **list** instance would be snapped into a vertical position of -180, placing the bottom of the instance at the edge of the upper scrolling boundary. This statement is set up so that the bottom of the **list** instance never scrolls beyond this point.

NOTE *This can be a tricky concept: You may want to review this information several times.*

Next, let's set up the function to handle downward scrolling.

6) Nest this `if/else` **statement in the "down" portion of the outer** `if/else if` **statement:**

```
if (display.list._y + speed < startingY) {
  display.list._y += speed;
} else {
  display.list._y = startingY;
}
```

```
1  list=["Adrastea","Amalthea","Ananke","Callisto","Carme","Elara","Europa","Ganyn
2  startingY=display.list._y;
3  bottom=120;
4  function buildList() {
5      spacing=30;
6      var i=-1;
7      while (++i<list.length) {
8          name="infoBar"+i;
9          y=i*spacing;
10         display.list.attachMovie("infoBar",name,i);
11         display.list[name]._y=y;
12         display.list[name].moonName.text=list[i];
13         display.list[name].moonNum.text=i+1;
14     }
15 }
16 function scroll(direction) {
17     speed=10;
18     if (direction=="up") {
19         if (display.list._y-speed+display.list._height>(startingY+bottom)) {
20             display.list._y-=speed;
21         } else {
22             display.list._y=(startingY+bottom)-display.list._height;
23         }
24     } else if (direction=="down") {
25         if (display.list._y+speed<startingY) {
26             display.list._y+=speed;
27         } else {
28             display.list._y=startingY;
29         }
30     }
31 }
32 buildList();
```

Line 24 of 33, Col 1

467

This part of the statement serves to scroll the movie clip instance downward. Similar to the statement in the previous step, this statement looks to see if moving the **list** instance down by the value of speed (display.list._y + speed) will keep the instance within the lower scrolling boundary (startingY). If it does, the first action in the statement is executed, moving the instance down. Otherwise (else), if moving the instance by the value of speed causes it to exceed the lower boundary, the action within the else part of the statement is executed, snapping the instance into vertical alignment with the lower boundary.

Now that you've defined this function, it's time to begin working with the scroll buttons.

7) With the library open, double-click the movie clip instance named *list arrow* in the library window.

Included on this movie clip's timeline is the Arrow button that appears in the middle of the screen. As you will soon see, this button (as well as the **list arrow** movie clip it's part of) will be used for both up and down scrolling.

8) With the Actions panel open, select the button and add this script:

```
on (press) {
  buttonPressed = "yes";
}
on (release, releaseOutside, dragOut) {
  buttonPressed = "";
}
```

This button simply sets the buttonPressed variable to either "yes" or "" based on user interaction. If the user presses the button, buttonPressed is set to "yes". If the user releases the button, drags out, or releases outside of the button, the buttonPressed variable is set to "". We'll show you how this variable is used in the next step.

9) With the library open, double-click the movie clip named *scroll* in the library window.

This movie clip's timeline includes two instances of the **list arrow** movie clip that contains the Arrow button to which we added ActionScript in the previous step. One of the instances has been rotated 180 degrees. The top clip has an instance name of **down** and the bottom one has an instance name of **up**.

You'll remember that the button in this movie clip instance sets a variable named buttonPressed to "yes" when pressed. Note that the two instances of the movie clip in use here are considered separate timelines. Pressing the button in one of the instances will set the variable to "yes" in that timeline only. Pressing the button in the other instance will set the variable to "yes" in that timeline. It will be important that you understand this concept as you go through the following steps.

10) With the Actions panel open, select the *down* movie clip instance and add this script:

```
onClipEvent (enterFrame) {
  if (buttonPressed == "yes") {
    _root.scroll("down");
  }
}
```

Using an `enterFrame` event, this ActionScript will continuously call (24 times a second) the `scroll()` function on the root, or main, timeline when the variable `buttonPressed` (in this timeline) has a value of "yes". This is the heart of a continuous-feedback button. A Boolean value is set by the button itself—here, we've chosen "yes" or "" as our Boolean. As long as `buttonPressed` has a value of "yes" (which it will as long as the button inside this instance is pressed), scrolling will occur. The parameter of "down" is passed into the `scroll()` function so that it knows which direction to scroll (as described earlier).

11) With the Actions panel still open, select the *up* movie clip instance and enter the following:

```
onClipEvent (enterFrame) {
  if (buttonPressed == "yes") {
    _root.scroll("up");
  }
}
```

Other than the parameter passed to the `scroll()` function, "up", this is identical to the ActionScript created in the previous step.

12) Choose Control > Test Movie to test this movie.
Give your buttons a try to test your ActionScript. You can press and hold a button down to make scrolling occur. When the **list** movie clip instance reaches its upper or lower maximum, it will stop scrolling.

13) Close the test movie and save your work as scrollingList3.fla.
You've now created the ActionScript required to scroll a list of dynamic items between upper and lower boundaries using continuous-feedback buttons.

USING ACTIONSCRIPT TO DYNAMICALLY DRAW LINES

Using ActionScript, you can dynamically draw lines in a movie as it plays—a capability that arises from a number of drawing methods available to the Movie Clip object.

Using these drawing methods, you can:

- Draw a line from the current "drawing position" to a point you specify
- Move the current drawing position without drawing
- Specify the line style for a timeline
- Fill a shape with a color
- Fill a shape with a gradient
- Curve a line between two points
- Clear a timeline of drawn lines and gradients

In this section, we'll show you how to draw lines, move the drawing position, set the line style, and clear a movie clip instance. In the next section, we'll briefly touch on using flat and gradient fills. Although we're not going to cover the `curveTo()` method (which allows you to dynamically draw curved lines) here, you should understand enough about Flash drawing fundamentals by the end of the lesson that you'll be able to implement it in your own drawing applications, if you wish.

LINESTYLE()

Before drawing any lines in a timeline, you must set the line style for that timeline. This is what Flash uses to determine:

- Line thickness
- Line color
- Line alpha

Here's the syntax,

```
path.lineStyle(thickness, color, alpha)
```

Line thickness must be a value between 0 and 255 (with a thickness of 0 representing a hairline); line color must be a hex color value. Line alpha represents the transparency level for a line (where 0 is transparent and 100 is opaque). Take a look at the following example:

```
_root.myClip.lineStyle(10, 0x009900, 100);
```

That line of ActionScript sets the line style in **myClip** so that all lines drawn will be green and opaque, and have a thickness of 10.

MOVETO()

All movie clip instances have a *drawing position* that indicates the coordinate at which a line would start if `lineTo()` (see next sub-section) were used—in other words, the beginning point of a line. When a movie clip instance is created, the drawing position is set to x = 0 and y = 0. However, you can move the drawing position at any time using `moveTo()`. When a line is drawn, the drawing position is updated to the end point of the drawn line.

The following is the syntax for using `moveTo()`:

```
path.moveTo(x, y);
```

All you need to do is specify the *x* and *y* positions of your drawing position. For example:

```
_root.myClip.lineStyle(10,0x009900,100);
_root.myClip.moveTo(100,100);
```

The above ActionScript sets the line style and then moves the drawing position.

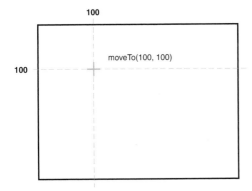

LINETO()

The `lineTo()` drawing method of the Movie Clip object simply draws a line of the destination timeline's `lineStyle` format from the drawing position to the end position specified in the method.

The following is the syntax for `lineTo()`:

```
myClip.lineTo(x,y);
```

The x and y parameters specify the end point of the line to be drawn.

TIP *After the line is drawn, the drawing `moveTo()` position is updated to the end point of the line.*

The following shows how you would use the methods we've described to draw a line:

```
_root.createEmptyMovieClip("canvas",1);
_root.canvas.lineStyle(2,0x009900,100);
_root.canvas.moveTo(100,100);
_root.canvas.lineTo(200,150);
```

This ActionScript draws a line between the points (100, 100) and (200, 150).

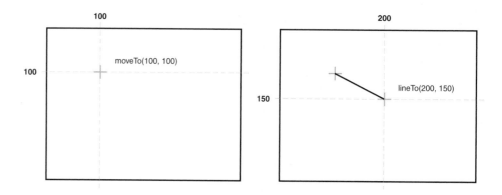

USING THE DRAW METHODS

In this exercise, you will use the drawing methods of the Movie Clip object to start a simple drawing application.

1) Open draw1.fla in the Lesson14/Assets folder.

The main timeline includes five layers, which are named according to their contents. The Background layer contains the project's main graphics. The Canvas layer contains a movie clip instance, **canvas**, which will be used to define an allowable area in which to draw. The Icon layer contains the movie clip instance that appears as a bug, just to the left of the stage. This instance is named **icon**, and in a later exercise, we'll duplicate it to provide the user with several icons to drag onto the canvas or draw over. The Controller layer contains a special movie clip instance known as a *controller clip*, which has an instance name of **controller**. (A controller clip is simply an instance that will contain most of the ActionScript that makes the project work.) Finally, the Windows layer contains two instances, **window1** and **window2**, which appear to the right of the canvas and will be addressed in a later exercise.

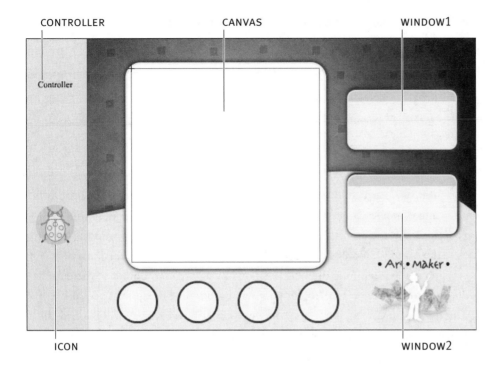

CONTROLLER   CANVAS   WINDOW1

Controller

ICON   WINDOW2

• Art • Maker •

The main focus of this exercise is creating ActionScript that will enable you to draw on the canvas. You will use clip events in concert with the `hitTest()` method to determine whether the mouse is pressed while over the **canvas** instance; you will then use the `mouseMove` clip event to draw. Every time the `mouseMove` event is fired, the mouse's positions are recorded and a line is drawn between its last and current position—resulting in a drawing.

2) With the Actions panel open, select the *controller* movie clip instance on the main timeline and add the following script:

```
onClipEvent (mouseUp) {
  down = false;
}
```

As mentioned earlier, most of the actions for this project will be added to the **controller** instance. This script creates a variable named `down` that will be used to store the current state of the mouse. Using the `mouseUp` event, this variable's value is set to `false` whenever the mouse is released, indicating that the mouse button is not pressed down.

3) Add this `mouseDown` **clip event at the end of the current script:**

```
onClipEvent (mouseDown) {
  if (_root.canvas.hitTest(_root._xMouse,_root._yMouse)) {
    x = _root._xMouse;
    y = _root._yMouse;
    _root.holder.moveTo(x,y);
    down = true;
  }
}
```

On `mouseDown`, we use a conditional statement to determine whether the mouse is over the **canvas** movie clip instance when the mouse is pressed. If it is, several things occur. First, the current *x* and *y* positions of the mouse are recorded as the values of the x and y variables, respectively. Next, these values are used in a `moveTo()` action to move the beginning drawing position of a clip named **holder** to the current coordinates of the mouse. The **holder** clip is an empty movie clip instance that will be created dynamically (as scripted in the next step). This instance will contain all the drawn lines. The last action in this script sets the `down` state variable to `true`, indicating that the mouse is pressed down.

4) Add this `onLoad` **event at the end of the current script:**

```
onClipEvent (load) {
  currentColor = "7F6696";
  _root.createEmptyMovieClip("holder",100);
}
```

In our application, as lines are drawn, their color will be based on the current value of `currentColor`. The value entered in the above script represents its *initial* value—that is, its value when the project first plays. In the next exercise, you'll change this variable's value dynamically based on button actions in one of the window movie clip instances, enabling coloring of lines using different colors.

The next line of this script creates an empty movie clip instance, **holder**. As mentioned earlier, this clip will contain all of the lines that are drawn. It is given a depth of 100 so that drawn lines will appear above any icons dragged onto the canvas.

5) Start defining the `draw()` **function by adding the following script to the** `load` **event:**

```
function draw() {
  _root.holder.lineStyle(0, parseInt(currentColor,16), 100);
  x = _root._xmouse;
  y = _root._ymouse;
  _root.holder.lineTo(x, y);
}
```

This function will eventually be called by a mouseMove clip event not yet defined. When called, the first thing it does is set the line style for the lines to be drawn. As you can see, the lines drawn will be hairlines; their color will be based on the currentColor variable; and their alpha setting will be 100. The last three lines of this script are used to complete the drawing of a line. A line is drawn from the current *drawing* position (as set with moveTo() when the mouseDown event occurs, as scripted earlier) to the *current* mouse position (x and y values in this script) using lineTo().

6) Add this mouseMove clip event to the end of the current script:

```
onClipEvent (mouseMove) {
  updateAfterEvent();
  if (down && _root.canvas.hitTest(_root._xmouse, _root._ymouse)) {
    draw();
  }
}
```

The mouseMove event is fired whenever the mouse changes positions. The updateAfterEvent() function is a predefined Flash function that tells Flash to update the stage after this event is fired (that is, do not wait until the next frame). The if statement checks to see that the down variable state is true and that the mouse is indeed over the canvas. If both are true, the draw() function is called. Calling the function repeatedly with this event will emulate the effect of drawing while the mouse is pressed and over the canvas. The if statement prevents the draw() function from being called should the mouse button be up or the mouse move outside the boundary of the **canvas** movie clip instance.

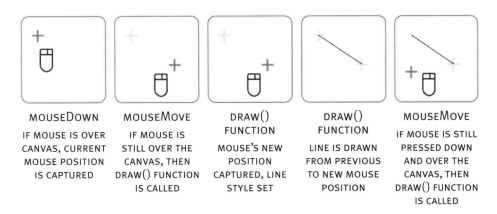

MOUSEDOWN
IF MOUSE IS OVER CANVAS, CURRENT MOUSE POSITION IS CAPTURED

MOUSEMOVE
IF MOUSE IS STILL OVER THE CANVAS, THEN DRAW() FUNCTION IS CALLED

DRAW() FUNCTION
MOUSE'S NEW POSITION CAPTURED, LINE STYLE SET

DRAW() FUNCTION
LINE IS DRAWN FROM PREVIOUS TO NEW MOUSE POSITION

MOUSEMOVE
IF MOUSE IS STILL PRESSED DOWN AND OVER THE CANVAS, THEN DRAW() FUNCTION IS CALLED

7) Choose Control › Test Movie. Start drawing.

When your mouse is pressed while over the canvas, the down variable is set to true—which means that when the mouse is moved, lines are drawn. If the mouse leaves the canvas area, drawing ceases.

8) Close the test movie and save your work as draw2.fla.

Now you're ready to make the windows to the right of the canvas active and add the drag-and-drop functionality that will allow you to add icons to the canvas.

CREATING FILLED SHAPES DYNAMICALLY

Even though we're not going to devote an exercise to the topic, drawing filled shapes is still worth discussing.

By building on the syntax you've used thus far in this lesson, you can use the drawing methods to create a shape and then fill it with a single color (a flat fill) or a gradient (a gradient fill).

To create a flat fill, you must let Flash know that the shape about to be drawn will be filled. You do this by employing the following method:

```
path.beginFill(color,alpha)
```

The path points to the timeline where the lines will exist. The color parameter accepts a hex color value. The second parameter, alpha, accepts a number between 0 and 100 to set the alpha level of the fill. To let Flash know when you're finished drawing a shape, you would use the following method:

```
path.endFill()
```

Here is an example use of this code:

```
_root.createEmptyMovieClip("box",1);
with (_root.box) {
  lineStyle(0,0x000000,100);
  beginFill(0x990000,100);
  moveTo(0,0);
  lineTo(100,0);
  lineTo(100,100);
  lineTo(0,100);
  lineTo(0,0);
  box.endFill();
}
```

The above ActionScript does the following,

1. Creates an empty movie clip instance

2. Sets the line style

3. Initiates the fill

4. Draws a shape

5. Ends the fill

It's important to note that when creating a filled shape, the starting point of the shape (as defined by `moveTo()`) must also be the ending point of the shape (as defined by the last `lineTo()`).

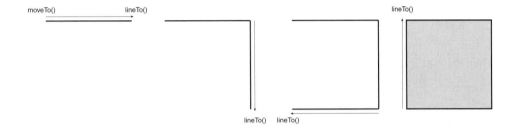

Creating a gradient fill is a little more difficult than creating a flat fill; *understanding* how the gradient fill works is much more difficult. You must first tell Flash that the shape you're about to draw is to be filled with a gradient. The syntax for this is as follows:

```
path.beginGradientFill (type, colors, alphas, ratios, matrix)
```

The first parameter, `type`, accepts the string *linear* or *radial*. The `colors` parameter is an array of hex color values that you want to use in your gradient. This array can contain two or more elements. The third parameter, `alphas`, is an array of alpha values to be applied to each respective color. This array should have the same number of elements as the `colors` array. The `ratios` parameter is an array of elements that contain values between 0 and 255. These values determine the color distribution.

The `matrix` parameter of the `beginGradientFill()` method deserves some attention. This object contains values that are used to move, skew, and rotate the gradient.

There are two ways to configure the `matrix` object—the more common of which contains the following properties:

- `matrixType`: This is a variable with a value of "box". You must set it so that Flash knows which type of matrix you're using.

- `x`: This is the *x* position at which to start the gradient. Flash uses the upper left-hand corner of the overall gradient to place this gradient.

- `y`: This is the *y* position at which to start the gradient. Flash uses the upper left-hand corner of the overall gradient to place this gradient.

- `w`: This is the width of the gradient.

- `h`: This is the height of the gradient.

- `r`: This is the rotation of the gradient (in radians).

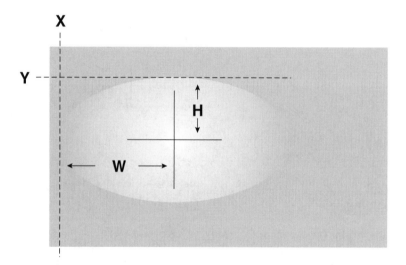

Here is an example of the syntax used to create a gradient-filled shape:

```
_root.createEmptyMovieClip("holder", 1);
with (_root.holder) {
  lineStyle(0, 0x000000, 0);
  rotation = 90 * (Math.PI/180);
  colors = [ 0x6666FF, 0xFF6600 ];
  alphas = [ 100, 100 ];
  ratios = [ 0, 255 ];
  matrix = { matrixType:"box", x:0, y:150, w:200, h:100, r:rotation };
  beginGradientFill( "linear", colors, alphas, ratios, matrix );
  moveTo(0,0);
  lineTo(550,0);
  lineTo(550,300);
  lineTo(0,300);
  lineTo(0,0);
  endFill();
}
```

The above ActionScript creates a square and then fills it with a gradient. The lines of the square have an alpha of zero so you cannot see them.

You'll probably need to test `beginGradientFill()` a few times to feel comfortable using it.

Z-SORTING MOVIE CLIP INSTANCES

Changing the depth of movie clip instances is known as *z-sorting*. The letter *z* is used in the name because changing the depth gives the effect of a third dimension in Flash: *z* (in addition to *x* and *y*). You can use `duplicateMovieClip()` or `attachMovie()` to set the depth of movie clip instances when you create them, or you can change the depth dynamically using the `swapDepths()` method of the Movie Clip object. With `swapDepths()` you can exchange the depth of any two movie clip instances or move an instance to a specified depth.

Here is the syntax for swapping the depths of two movie clip instances:

```
movieClip1.swapDepths(movieclip2);
```

If `movieClip2` were above `movieClip1`, the above script would swap their depths, causing `movieClip1` to appear above `movieClip2`.

Here's the syntax for sending any movie clip instance—even one created using `duplicateMovieClip()` or `attachMovie()`—to a specific depth:

```
movieClip1.swapDepths(anyDepth);
```

The `swapDepths()` method is easy to use and can add a nice effect to applications and games. In this exercise, you'll make the two windows in the drawing application draggable, use `swapDepths()` to bring the window of interest to the top of the stack, and add actions to some of the buttons.

1) Open draw2.fla in the Lesson14/Assets folder.

This is the file as you left it at the end of the previous exercise. In this exercise, you'll add some more ActionScript to the **controller** movie clip instance and work with the window clips.

2) With the Actions panel open, select the movie clip instance named *window1* and add this script:

```
onClipEvent (load) {
  this.gotoAndStop("color");
}
```

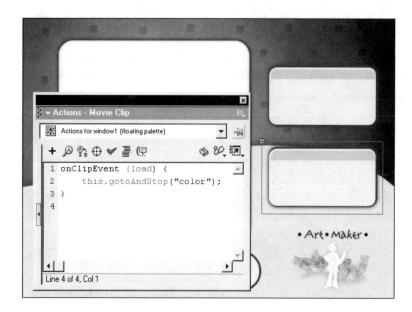

Both **window1** and **window2** are instances of the same movie clip—they just have different names. The above script is used to direct the **window1** instance to the frame labeled color as soon as the movie loads. At this frame are several buttons that will eventually be set up to change the color of the line used in drawing.

3) With the Actions panel still open, select the movie clip instance named *window2* and add the following script:

```
onClipEvent (load) {
  this.gotoAndStop("admin");
}
```

This script instructs this instance to go to the frame labeled admin immediately upon loading. At this frame are a couple of buttons that will allow for clearing and printing of what appears on the canvas.

4) Double-click *window1* and move to the color frame label. Add this button action to the first button on the left (at the tip of the first pencil on the left):

```
on (release) {
  _parent.controller.currentColor = "7F6696";
}
```

You may remember that the currentColor variable (in the **controller** movie clip instance) stores the color that the drawn lines will become. This script changes the value of currentColor to the hex value shown.

5) Select the remaining buttons (from left to right) and add the following scripts to them:

Add to 2nd button:

```
on (release) {
  _parent.controller.currentColor = "FAC81C";
}
```

Add to 3rd button:

```
on (release) {
  _parent.controller.currentColor = "E72638";
}
```

Add to 4th button:

```
on (release) {
  _parent.controller.currentColor = "1091CB";
}
```

Add to 5th button:

```
on (release) {
  _parent.controller.currentColor = "1FA900";
}
```

Add to 6th button:

```
on (release) {
  _parent.controller.currentColor = "BC0077";
}
```

The ActionScript on each of these buttons does the same thing as the ActionScript in the previous step—except for the color value that is set.

Now let's make the window draggable.

6) With the Actions panel still open, select the orange dragbar button at the top of this window and add the following script:

```
on (press) {
  startDrag (this);
  _root.controller.swap(_name);
}
```

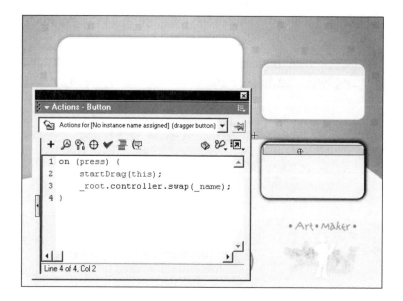

Because the button is on the window movie clip's timeline, the window itself (`this`) becomes draggable when that button is pressed.

The second action calls a function (not yet written) in the **controller** called `swap()`—the purpose of which is to change the z-order of the window to bring it to the front of the stack. When the function is called, you'll see that it's passed the `_name` property (which represents the name of the instance) of the current movie. Because our project contains two instances of the same movie clip—**window1** and **window2**—the actions on this button will work as follows: When the button is pressed in the **window1** instance, that instance becomes draggable and a value of "window1" is sent to the `swap()` function. When the button in **window2** is pressed, that instance becomes draggable and a value of "window2" is sent to the `swap()` function.

7) Now add the following script to the button:

```
on (release) {
  stopDrag ();
}
```

This stops the dragging process when the button is released.

482

8) Return to the main timeline. With the Actions panel open, select the *controller* movie clip instance and add the following action to the `load` event:

```
topDog = "window1";
```

We will be using `swapDepths()` to swap the depths of the **window1** and **window2** movie clip instances . The `topDog` variable is used to store the name of which instance is currently at the higher depth. When the movie is generated, **window1** is at a higher depth so that's how we initialize this variable's value.

9) Add the following function definition to the `load` event:

```
function swap (name) {
  _root[name].swapDepths(_root[topDog]);
  topDog = name;
}
```

This function accepts a parameter of `name` and uses it to swap the value of `name` (the parameter value sent to the function) with the value of `topDog`. The variable `topDog` is then modified to contain the name of the instance that is *now* the highest in the stacking order. As shown in Step 6, when this function is called, it is sent the `_name` property of the current movie (which will be either **window1** or **window2**). Assuming `topDog` currently has a value of "window1", pressing the dragbar in **window2** (thus calling this function and passing it a value of "window2") would result in the function being evaluated in the following manner:

```
function swap ("window2") {
  _root.window2.swapDepths(_root.window1);
  topDog = "window2";
}
```

10) Choose Control > Test Movie to test the movie. Click on the windows and drag them around. Change the color of the lines.

When you press the button at the top of one of the windows, its depth is set to the highest in the stacking order and a drag is initiated.

The only thing that happens when you click the color buttons is that the value of the `currentColor` variable on the **controller** movie clip instance changes, allowing you to draw lines of different colors.

11) Close the test movie and save your work as draw3.fla.

You've now used `swapDepths()` to bring the window of interest to the front of the window stack—but you're not finished yet! You still need to script the functionality to clear the canvas and add drag-and-drop functionality to the icons.

DRAGGING AND DROPPING MOVIE CLIP INSTANCES

In user interfaces, it's sometimes useful to add *drag-and-drop* behaviors to movie clip instances—a term that refers to the process of clicking and dragging movie clip instances around the stage, so that when they're released (dropped), they'll perform a set of actions (determined by the location where they're dropped). The easiest way to conceptualize this type of behavior is by thinking of the trashcan on your computer desktop: If you drag a file over the trashcan and let go of it, that file is deleted; however, if you're not over the trashcan when you let go, you've simply moved the file icon.

The most common way to create drag-and-drop items in Flash is by using _droptarget or hitTest(). Checking the _droptarget property of a movie will return the path in slash syntax to the highest movie clip instance that the currently dragged movie clip instance is over. Using the hitTest() method, you can determine whether the bounding box of one instance is touching the bounding box of another (for more on this, see Lesson 9, Using Conditional Logic) and take action accordingly. The hitTest() method is used more frequently because it's more versatile than the _droptarget property.

In this exercise, you'll extend our project to dynamically create a row of icons (simple graphical movie clip instances) that can be dragged and dropped onto the canvas using hitTest(). When dropped, a copy of the movie clip instance will be created using duplicateMovieClip() and the original will be sent back to its initial position.

1) Open the draw3.fla file in the Lesson14/Assets folder.

This file is as you left it at the end of the previous exercise. You will add ActionScript to the **controller** and **icon** movie clip instances. First, you'll create a function that creates the row of icons below the canvas. Then, you'll add the ActionScript that makes them draggable and the ActionScript that detects if they were dropped onto the canvas.

2) With the Actions panel open, select the *controller* movie clip instance and add this function definition to the load event:

```
function buildIconList () {
  spacing = 85;
  iconY = 360;
  iconX = 70;
  var i = -1;
  while (++i < _root.icon._totalFrames) {
    newName = "icon" + i;
    _root.icon.duplicateMovieClip(newName, 10000 + i);
    _root[newName]._x = iconX + i * spacing;
    _root[newName]._y = iconY;
    _root[newName].gotoAndStop(i + 1);
  }
}
```

There's nothing in this function you haven't seen before. The **icon** movie clip instance contains a certain number of frames on its timeline, each of which includes a different icon graphic. This ActionScript will duplicate the **icon** clip one time for every frame in that movie clip. It will send each duplicated movie clip instance to a unique frame and align it along the bottom of the screen. The result is a row of icons at the bottom of the screen. You can add or remove icons (that is, add or remove frames) in the **icon** movie clip instance, and this ActionScript loop will adapt based on the `_totalFrames` property (used in the `while` loop). The `spacing` variable represents the vertical space between the duplicated icon. `iconY` and `iconX` represent the coordinates of the first duplicate.

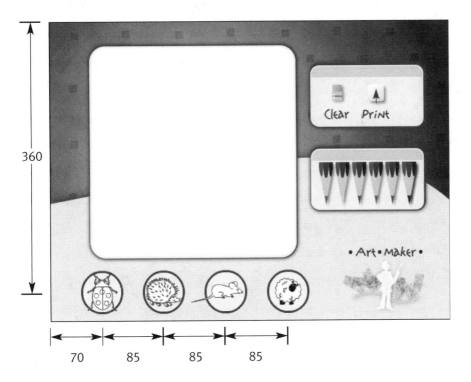

3) Add `buildIconList();` to the bottom of the `load` event.

This will call the function you created in the previous step to create the icon list.

4) Double-click the *icon* movie clip instance to edit it in place. With the Actions panel open, select the invisible button and add this script:

```
on (press) {
startDrag (this);
}
```

485

As you saw in the previous two steps, the **icon** movie clip instance (which contains the button to which this script is attached) will be duplicated four times, and each of those duplicates will be moved to one of the four frames on its timeline. This will place four icons (with different graphics) just below the canvas. Each of these icons must be able to be dragged onto the canvas, where on release, a copy (yes, a duplicate of a duplicate) will be placed on the canvas—producing the effect of dragging a copy of the icon onto the stage in order to color over it. The invisible button triggers the dragging process when pressed, as you can see by the `startDrag()` action that's attached to it.

It's important to note that this invisible button has an instance name of **iconButton**. Here's why. When the icon is dropped onto the canvas for duplication, the duplicate will inherit the invisible button as well as the actions it contains. This means that the duplicate (which would appear on the canvas) would also be draggable, which is not what we want. We want the duplicates to remain stationary once they've been dropped onto the canvas). Giving the button an instance name allows you to disable it in duplicates placed on the canvas. The function that handles the drag-and-drop functionality will be set up so that when the duplicate is created, the button inside of it is disabled, preventing it from executing the `startDrag()` action. This button will only be enabled (the default behavior for all buttons) on the instances of this clip *below* the canvas—which means those instances can be dragged, facilitating the first part of the drag-and-drop functionality.

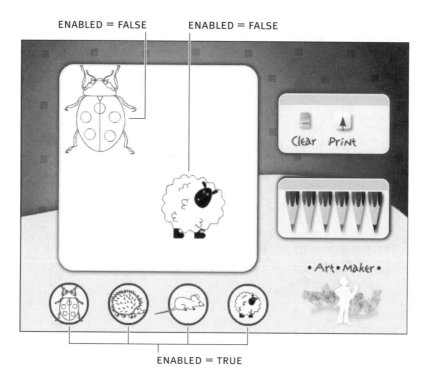

5) With the Actions panel still open, add the following script to the button:

```
on (release) {
stopDrag ();
  _root.controller.iconReleased(_name);
}
```

The first action in this script simply stops the drag action when the button is released, making it appear to be "dropped." The second action calls the `iconReleased()` function (which we have yet to define) on the **controller** movie clip instance. This function will duplicate the instance that has been dragged onto the canvas and place it back in its original position (just below the canvas), where it's ready to be dragged and dropped again. You'll notice that the function call sends the `_name` property of the dropped instance to the function: This tells the function which of the four icons has been dragged onto the canvas—and thus which one needs to be duplicated.

6) Navigate back to the main timeline and select the *icon* movie clip instance. With the Actions panel open, add the following script:

```
onClipEvent (load) {
      homeX = _x;
      homeY = _y;
}
```

Using a `load` event, two variables, `homeX` and `homeY`, are created to store the location of the instance when first loaded. Each duplicate will inherit this script so that its original *x* and *y* positions are stored on its own timeline using these variable names. Knowing these values will let the icons that are dragged and dropped onto the canvas and duplicated be returned to their original position on the stage, so that they can be dragged and dropped again and again.

Now let's set up the function that will bring everything together.

7) Select the *controller* clip and add this function to the `load` event:

```
function iconReleased (name) {
  if (_root.canvas.hitTest(_root._xmouse, _root._ymouse)) {
    ++v;
    newName="object" + v;
    _root[name].duplicateMovieClip(newName, v);
    _root[newName].gotoAndStop(_root[name]._currentFrame);
     _root[newName].iconButton.enabled = false;
    _root[newName]._xscale = 250;
    _root[newName]._yscale = 250;
  }
  _root[name]._x = _root[name].homeX;
  _root[name]._y = _root[name].homeY;
}
```

This function is set up to receive one parameter, which is identified as name. As described in Step 5, this will be the instance name (_name property) of the icon that is dragged and dropped onto the canvas. The value of this parameter plays an important role in how the rest of the function works.

First, a conditional statement checks to see if the mouse is over the **canvas** movie clip instance when the function is called, indicating that an icon has actually been dropped *on* the canvas. If the mouse is over the canvas, a copy of the movie clip instance that is dragged and dropped is created using duplicateMovieClip(). The name given to the duplicate is derived by concatenating "object" with the current value of v (which is incremented with each new duplicate created). Based on this functionality, the current value of v will always reflect the number of duplicate icons that have been dragged and dropped onto the canvas—an important thing to remember for the next exercise.

Once created, the duplicate is sent to the same frame as the original instance (so that the same icon that was dragged appears on the canvas). The next action is used to disable the invisible button inside the duplicate named **iconButton** (as discussed in Step 4). In addition, the duplicate is scaled vertically and horizontally by 250 percent so that it will appear on the canvas as a larger representation of the icon instance from which it was created.

NOTE *A duplicated instance inherits the exact* x *and* y *positions of the original (at the time of its duplication). Thus, unless you use a simple script to move it, a duplicate—upon its creation—is placed right on top of the original (which means you won't even be able to tell that a duplicate has been created because nothing will have changed visually).*

The last two lines of ActionScript in this function send the dragged movie clip instance back to its original position, based on the values of homeX and homeY on its timeline. You'll notice that these actions are placed outside the conditional statement, meaning they're executed regardless of whether the statement proves true and a duplicate is created. Thus, if the user tries to drop an icon anywhere other than on top of the **canvas** movie clip instance, a duplicate will not be created and the icon will simply snap back to its original position below the canvas.

IF DROPPED, DUPLICATE WILL BE CREATED IF DROPPED, DUPLICATE WILL *NOT* BE CREATED

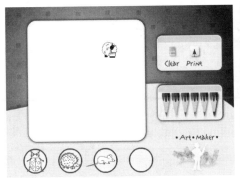 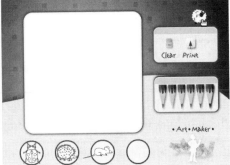

8) Choose Control › Test Movie to test your work. Drag the icons onto the canvas.

If you drag an icon and drop it anywhere other than on the **canvas** instance, it will return to its original location, *unduplicated.* If you release the icon when your mouse is over the **canvas** movie clip instance, a duplicate will be created and the *original* will be sent back to its starting position.

9) Close the test movie and save your work as draw4.fla.

You've now created a simple, medium-sized drawing application. By applying the concepts you've learned here, you can create an application that includes many more features than this one.

REMOVING DYNAMICALLY CREATED CONTENT

You can easily remove dynamically drawn lines from a timeline using the `clear()` method. Here's the syntax:

```
path.clear();
```

Movie clip instances that are created using `duplicateMovieClip()` or `attachMovie()` (such as icons that are dragged and dropped onto the canvas) can be removed using a method of the Movie Clip object called `removeMovieClip()`.

> **NOTE** *You can't use this method to remove movie clip instances that were not created using ActionScript (that is, those you've actually dragged from the library and placed on the stage).*

Removing movie clip instances can be useful for dynamically clearing the stage content, freeing up system resources, re-initializing applications, or adding functionality to some applications. As you can see from the following, the syntax is simple:

```
someMovieClip.removeMovieClip()
```

In this exercise you will create a function that will clear the canvas of all dynamically drawn lines as well as instances of the **icon** movie clip that might be dragged and dropped on the canvas.

1) Open draw4.fla in the Lesson14/Assets folder.

This is the file as you left it at the end of the previous exercise. In this exercise, you'll add a function to the **controller** that will clear the canvas of any content and you will add an action to the Clear button in the **window2** movie clip instance.

2) With the Actions panel open, select the *controller* movie clip instance and add this function definition to the load event:

```
function clearContent () {
  _root.holder.clear()
  i = 0;
  while (++i <= v) {
    name = "object" + i;
    _root[name].removeMovieClip();
  }
  v = 0;
}
```

The first action in this function clears all dynamically drawn lines from the **holder** movie clip instance. Next, a simple while loop is used to remove any instances of the **icon** movie clip instance that have been dragged and dropped onto the canvas. Since the value of v is incremented with each **icon** instance that is dragged and dropped (as shown in the buildIconList() function definition scripted in the previous exercise), its value always represents the number of **icon** instances that have been duplicated and placed on the canvas. This value is thus used in the loop to set how many iterations the removal loop should perform. After the loop finishes removing all the dragged and dropped **icon** instances, the value of v is set to 0 so that the next time an **icon** instance is dragged and dropped onto the canvas, naming of the duplicated instances can once again begin with 0.

490

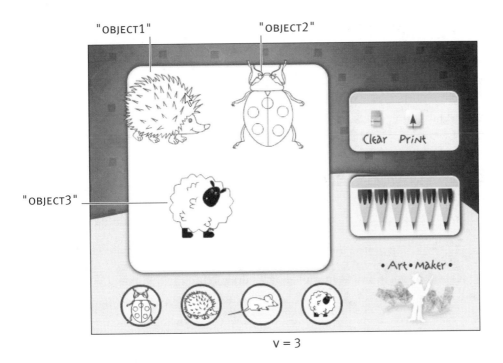

"OBJECT1"

"OBJECT2"

"OBJECT3"

Clear   Print

• Art • Maker •

v = 3

3) Double click on the *window2* instance to edit it in place. Move the admin frame label.

This frame contains two buttons, a Clear button, and a Print button. You will add ActionScript to the Clear button that will call the `clearContent()` function in the **controller** movie clip instance. While you're editing this frame, you'll also add an action to the Print button.

4) With the Actions panel open, select the Print button and add this script:

```
on (release) {
  printAsBitmap ("_root", "bmovie");
}
```

When the button is released, the graphical content of the root timeline, as well as of any of its child movies (essentially everything you see, including dynamically created instances), will be printed as a bitmap graphic at actual size.

> **NOTE** *This script is just used to demonstrate how dynamically created instances can be printed as easily as anything else. Had we wanted to get a bit more sophisticated, we might have opted to print only what was drawn on the canvas itself. However, this would require some different syntax in our various functions, and printing options are not the focus of this exercise.*

5) With the Actions panel open, select the Clear button and enter this ActionScript:

```
on (release) {
  _parent.controller.clearContent();
}
```

When this button is released, the `clearContent()` function attached to the **controller** instance will be executed.

6) Choose Control > Test Movie to test the movie. Draw a few lines and then press the Clear button.

When you press the Clear button, the clear function is executed and the `while` loop loops through and deletes every created movie clip instance.

7) Close this movie and save your work as draw5.fla.

This completes the exercise and the lesson. As you have learned, the dynamic removal of content is even easier than its creation. However, knowing how to do both allows your projects to scale and change in many ways based on user input and interaction. Isn't ActionScript the best?!

WHAT YOU HAVE LEARNED

In this lesson, you have:

- Duplicated and attached movie clip instances dynamically (pages 450–457)

- Created empty movie clip instances (pages 457–458)

- Created a scrolling window that uses continuous-feedback buttons (pages 458–469)

- Drawn lines using Flash's drawing methods (pages 470–476)

- Learned how to fill shapes with colors and gradients (pages 476–479)

- Changed the z-order of instances dynamically (pages 479–483)

- Created drag-and-drop movie clip instances (pages 484–489)

- Removed movie clip instances and drawn lines dynamically (pages 489–492)

time- and frame-based dynamism

Your Macromedia Flash movie need not always depend on user actions (such as moving the mouse or pressing a button) to trigger a response; it can also respond to the passage of time and frames—elements that can be set in motion independently of the user. And by combining these elements *with* user interaction, you can create even more powerful and interactive projects. In this lesson, we'll show you how time and frames work in Flash, and then demonstrate ways you can use them to enhance your projects.

Part of the Make My Day project that we'll build in this lesson.

WHAT YOU WILL LEARN

In this lesson, you will:

- Learn how to use the element of time in Flash projects

- Create and use a Date object to display the current date

- Use the `getTimer()` function to create a Flash-based timer and alarm so that you can accurately track the progression of time in your Flash project

- Control a timeline dynamically using play, stop, fast-forward, and rewind controls

- Create a percentage-based preloader

APPROXIMATE TIME

This lesson takes approximately 1 hour to complete.

LESSON FILES

Media Files:

None

Starting Files:

Lesson15/Assets/makeMyDay1.fla

Lesson15/Assets/preloader1.fla

Completed Projects:

makeMyDay4.fla

preloader2.fla

Bonus Files:

preloaderBytes.fla

THE USE OF TIME IN FLASH

Flash uses several methods to measure the passage of time in projects. The following are the most common:

- **Date object.** A pre-built object in Flash useful for interactivity that is dependent on dates, days, months, and years.
- **getTimer() function.** This special Flash function is useful for measuring the passage of time in milliseconds.
- **Frames.** Representing divisions of time as they relate to animation, sounds, and other interactivity on timelines, frames provide the most common way of measuring the passage of time in Flash. The movement of one frame to the next (or previous) one represents the movement of time in your project, either forward or backward. As the timeline moves forward, a progression of events occurs—a streaming sound plays, for example, or a character moves across the stage.

Once you understand these elements, you'll be able to make your projects do the following:

- Play forward or backward, depending on user interaction
- React based on the current date, time, or frame number
- Display percentage-based information and download status
- More

There's also a special ActionScript tool—setInterval()—that allows a function to be called at a regular specified interval (measured in milliseconds). To understand this, take a look at the following:

```
function rotateClip() {
  myMovieClip._rotation += 10;
}
setInterval (rotateClip, 1500);
```

The first three lines of the above script define the function that will be used. Next, the setInterval() action is set up to call the rotateClip() function every 1.5 seconds (1000 equals 1 second).

If you wish to pass arguments to the called function, simply add them to the setInterval() action, as follows:

```
setInterval (updateMessageFunction, 20000, "Hello", arg2, arg3)
```

A setInterval() action can be turned on and off by assigning it a variable name, as in the following example:

```
myVariable = setInterval(rotateClip, 1500);
```

This will assign the name `myVariable` to the `setVariable()` action. To remove the functionality of the `setVariable()` action, you would use the following syntax:

```
delete myVariable;
```

The `setInterval()` action can be initiated any time, calling any function using the syntax shown. (In the next lesson, you'll learn how you can use this action to create a rotating banner ad system.)

DETERMINING CURRENT DATE AND TIME

All of us have used a calendar; in fact, most of us use one on a daily basis—to plan our days, to remind ourselves of certain events, and more. In Flash, too, it's useful to be able to access date information—to display it, to make your movie do specific things on certain dates, to create countdown timers, and to display the day of the week for a particular date in history, to name just a few.

To use dates in Flash, you must create an instance of the Date object using the following syntax:

```
myDate = new Date(year, month, date);
```

The above syntax creates a new Date object named `myDate`. The parameters in parenthesis associate the date object with a specific date. For example:

```
myDate = new Date(66, 6, 27);
```

This creates a Date object associated with July 27, 1966. The first parameter represents the year; the second represents the month; and the third represents the date. You may be wondering why July, which we consider the seventh month in the year, is actually defined as the sixth in the script above. This is because in ActionScript both months and days of the week are referenced by numbers, beginning with 0. Thus, January is the "zero" month, February is the first month, March is the second month, and so on—up to December, which is the eleventh month. Likewise, days of the week begin with Sunday as the "zero" day, Monday the first day, and so on. The following exercise will demonstrate the usefulness of this numbering system.

Months

0	1	2	3	4	5	6	7	8	9	10	11
January	February	March	April	May	June	July	August	September	October	November	December

Days of Week

0	1	2	3	4	5	6
Sunday	Monday	Tuesday	Wednesday	Thursday	Friday	Saturday

497

NOTE *Dates and years are recognized by their true values. Thus, 66 refers to 1966, while 27 refers to the 27th day in the month.*

TIP *You can continue to add parameters for the hour, minute, second, and millisecond, though you can leave them out if your application doesn't require that precision.*

If you want to create a Date object that references the current point in time (as indicated by the user's system clock), you can leave the parameter settings blank. For example, take a look at the following:

```
myDate = new Date();
```

After you've created the Date object, you can use methods of it to retrieve all sorts of information about that date. For example, the previous line of script would create a Date object that references today's date. To discover the current month, you would use the following syntax:

```
currentMonth = myDate.getMonth();
```

After executing, currentMonth would have a value of, for example, 5, which represents the month of June. To find out the current day of the week, we would use the following syntax:

```
currentDay = myDate.getDay();
```

After executing, currentDay would have a value of, for example, 4, which represents Thursday (assuming that is the current day as set on the computer executing the script).

NOTE *Your project can contain numerous Date objects, each used for a different purpose.*

In the following exercise, we'll create a Date object, as well as use various methods to display the current date.

1) Open makeMyDay1.fla in the Lesson15/Assets folder.

This project contains two scenes, Alarm and Messages. In this lesson, we'll work solely in the Alarm scene, focusing on the calendar portion, which is located on the left side of the stage. We'll work on the other side of the stage in the next lesson. The layers in this scene are named according to their contents.

Just below the text that reads, "Today is:" you'll see four text fields named (from top to bottom) **currentDay**, **currentMonth**, **currentDate**, and **currentYear**. These will be used to dynamically display various portions of the date:

- **currentDay.** Displays the current day of the week (for example, "Saturday").
- **currentMonth.** Displays the current month (for example, "April").
- **currentDate.** Displays the current day of the month (for example, "27").
- **currentYear.** Displays the current year (for example, "2002").

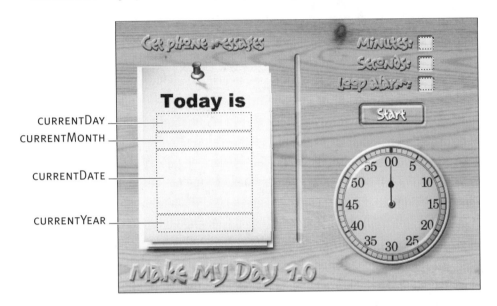

We've used a slightly different character setting for each of these text fields to create a nice balance for our design.

2) With the Property inspector open, select the top text field, *currentDay*. Press the Character button that appears on the Property inspector to bring up the Character Options dialog box.

At the bottom of this panel you'll see a bunch of jumbled text. These characters represent the specific font outlines we want to embed for this text field. These characters are all of the characters necessary to spell out the days of the week, nothing more. Because this text field will contain dynamically generated text, embedding these fonts will allow the text displayed in this field to appear antialiased, or smooth.

The text fields below this one also have specific font outlines embedded (depending on what they will be used to display).

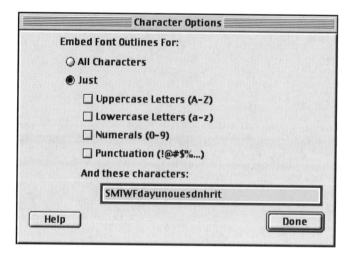

3) **With the Actions panel open, select Frame 1 on the Actions layer and add the following script:**

```
stop();
today = new Date();
```

The first action prevents the timeline from moving forward until we instruct it to.

The next line of script creates a new Date object named today as soon as the movie begins to play. Since we haven't specified any date parameters within the parentheses, this Date object references the current time on the user's computer (that is, the time when the movie is played).

4) **Add the following two lines of script to the end of the current script:**

```
nameOfDays = ["Sunday", "Monday", "Tuesday", "Wednesday", "Thursday",
"Friday", "Saturday"];
nameOfMonths = ["January", "February", "March", "April", "May", "June",
"July", "August", "September", "October", "November", "December"];
```

The first line is used to create an array called nameOfDays; the second line is used to create an array called nameOfMonths. Each of these arrays contains several string values representing the names of days and months, respectively. These arrays are necessary because although humans assign names to months and days of the week, ActionScript does not. Instead, it references with a number aspects of dates that we normally associate with a name. As you'll see in a moment, the trick to making this part of the

500

project work is associating the proper name (based on its index value in the array) with the numbers ActionScript returns as the current day and month, respectively.

5) Add the following line of script at the end of the current script:

```
currentDay.text = nameOfDays[today.getDay()];
```

This action is used to set the information displayed in the **currentDay** text field. Here's how it works.

The `getDay()` method (inside the brackets) is used to determine the day of the week for the `today` object. This method will return a value between 0 and 6, with 0 representing Sunday and 6 representing Saturday. Thus, if this method determines that the day of the week is 3, that value is inserted into the brackets within the expression, making it look like this:

```
currentDay.text = nameOfDays[3];
```

At this point, you can see that **currentDay** will display the value residing at index position 3 of the `nameOfDays` array: the string value of "Wednesday". Knowing that the `getDay()` method will return a value between 0 and 6, we created an array (in the previous step) with the names of the days at corresponding array index positions of 0 through 6. Thus, when the script is executed, the appropriate day name is used based on the numerical value returned by the `getDay()` method.

6) Add the following line of script at the end of the current script:

```
currentMonth.text = nameOfMonths[today.getMonth()];
```

This action is used to set the information that's displayed in the **currentMonth** text field. It works in the same way as the action discussed in the previous step—except that the `getMonth()` method used here will return a numerical value between 0 and 11 (for January through December). The `nameOfMonths` array has appropriate string values at corresponding index positions.

7) Add the following line of script at the end of the current script:

```
currentDate.text = today.getDate();
```

This action is used to set the information that's displayed in the **currentDate** text field. It uses the `getDate()` method, which will return a numerical value between 1 and 31, depending on the date associated with the Date object. Since we want to use the numerical value returned in this circumstance, we don't need to use an array to convert the information to a string value (as discussed in the previous two steps).

501

8) Add the following line of script at the end of the current script:

```
currentYear.text = today.getFullYear();
```

This action is used to set the information that's displayed in the **currentYear** text field. It uses the `getFullYear()` method, which will return a numerical value representing the full year of the date associated with the Date object (for example, 2002). Once again, since we want to use the numerical value returned in this circumstance, we don't need to use an array to convert it to a string value.

9) Choose Control > Test Movie to view the project to his point.

As soon as the movie appears, the text fields in the calendar section of the screen are populated with the appropriate data, displaying the full date.

10) Close the test movie and save your project as makeMyDay2.fla.

We will continue building on this exercise in the lessons that follow.

DETERMINING THE PASSAGE OF TIME

The `getTimer()` function is used to return (in milliseconds) the length of time that's elapsed since the movie was first opened and played. Thus, if your movie has been open for six seconds, the following script:

```
playBackTime = getTimer();
```

would assign `playBackTime` a value of 6000 (1000 for each second). This is an accurate and precise representation of time based on the user's system clock and is not dependent on the movie's frame rate, the user's processor speed, or whether or not the movie is playing. This is also a universal value, which means it represents the playback of the movie as a whole; you cannot track the length of time that individual timelines have been present.

By setting a variable's value based on the value returned by the `getTimer()` function, then comparing that value to the value returned by the function at a later point in time, you can evaluate the amount of time (too much or too little) that's passed within the span and take appropriate action. To better understand this, take a look at the following example:

```
// Place on button A
on (release) {
  startTime = getTimer();
}
// Place on button B
on (release) {
  nowTime = getTimer()
  if (nowTime - startTime < 1000) {
    message.text = "You press buttons pretty quickly";
  } else {
    message.text = "You're pretty slow";
  }
}
```

Here, the action on one button (button A) establishes a starting point by capturing the time when the button is pressed and released. When button B is pressed and released, the time is captured once again. A conditional statement is then used to determine whether the amount of time between these two button-presses was more or less than a second—and then acts accordingly. Similarly, by placing the following script on a single button, you can facilitate double-clicking functionality for that button (that is, the script will only take action if separate clicks occur within a half-second of each other):

```
on (release) {
  if(getTimer() - lastClick < 500) {
    // Actions
  }
  lastClick = getTimer();
}
```

By integrating the getTimer() function with the enterFrame event and some conditional statements, you can create a mechanism that triggers actions at specific times—independently of the timeline and with much greater accuracy. Take a look at the following example:

```
onClipEvent (enterFrame) {
  if (getTimer() > 5000) {
    // Actions
  }
  if (getTimer() > 10000) {
    // Actions
  }
  if (getTimer() > 150000) {
    // Actions
  }
}
```

This script will trigger actions every five seconds while the movie plays—often the most accurate way of executing actions at specific points in time during your movie's playback.

In the following exercise, we'll use the getTimer() function to create a timer/alarm.

NOTE *The getTimer() function can be found under Functions, of the Toolbox list window in the Actions panel.*

1) Open makeMyDay2.fla in the Lesson15/Assets folder.

We will continue to build on the project from the last exercise. You'll remember that this file has two scenes, Alarm and Messages. As in the previous exercise, we'll be working solely in the Alarm scene—this time focusing on the timer portion of the scene, which is on the right side of the stage. This section of the project contains three text fields at the top-right corner of the stage: **minutesToAlarm**, **secondsToAlarm**, and **numberOfLoops** (from top to bottom). These are input text fields used to set when the alarm should go off as well as how many times the alarm sound will play.

Just below these text fields is a Start button, which will be used to start the timer/alarm.

Below this button is a movie clip instance named **clock**, which includes several moving elements (just like a real timer); let's take a look at those.

MINUTETOALARM
SECONDSTOALARM
NUMBEROFLOOPS

2) Double-click the *clock* movie clip instance to edit it in place.

This timeline contains two layers: The Clock layer contains the main clock graphic, and the Hands layer contains three movie clip instances that represent various indicators on the clock face. One of these movie clip instances, **secondHand**, represents the clock's second hand, which will rotate, simulating a tick each second the timer is on. Just below this instance is a movie clip instance named **minuteHand**, which will rotate as well—only at one-tenth the speed of the second hand (just as on a real clock). The third movie clip instance appears as a small, red tick mark at the top of the clock. Named **alarmHand**, this instance will rotate when the timer is started to indicate when the alarm is set to go off.

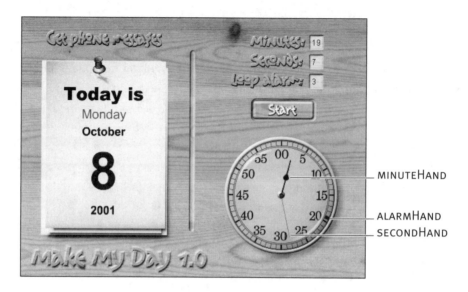

3) **Return to the main timeline. With the Actions panel open, select the Start button and add the following script:**

```
on (release) {
  clock.alarmOn = true;
  clock.startingTime = getTimer();
}
```

When this button is pressed and released, it will set the value of two variables in the **clock** movie clip instance. As you will see in a moment, the alarmOn variable being set to true will "turn on" a script attached to that instance. Using the getTimer() function, the startingTime variable's value is set to a numerical value representing the length of time (in milliseconds) that has elapsed since the movie was first opened and played. Capturing the exact time at which the timer was started is critical to making this part of the project work properly—we'll explain why in a moment.

4) **With the Actions panel still open, select the *clock* movie clip instance and add this script:**

```
onClipEvent (enterFrame) {
  if (alarmOn) {
}
```

With the above script, a conditional statement is analyzed every time the enterFrame event occurs. This statement determines whether alarmOn has a value of true. (And you'll remember that in the last step we added an action to the Start button that will set it to true when that button is clicked.) Over the course of the next several steps, we'll add some actions to this statement that will only be executed when that value is true. These actions will move the hands on the timer as well as detect when the alarm should go off. So essentially, clicking the Start button will turn on the timer.

5) Add the following line of script within the conditional statement:

```
totalTimeToAlarm = (Number(_root.minutesToAlarm.text) * 60) +
Number(_root.secondsToAlarm.text);
```

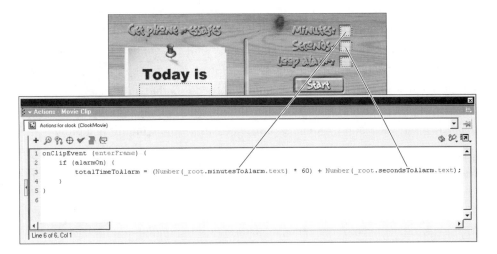

You'll remember that our scene contains one input text field for entering minutes and another for entering seconds: Used together, they determine how much time should elapse before the alarm goes off. The above line of script is used to convert the minutes entered to seconds and then add that figure to the seconds entered to come up with the total time (in seconds) that must elapse before the alarm sounds.

Using parentheses in the expression, we've sectioned it off into two parts: `(Number(_root.minutesToAlarm.text) * 60)` gets added to `Number(_root.secondsToAlarm.text)` to determine the value of `totalTimeToAlarm`. We've used the `Number` function in both parts of the expression to ensure that the values of `minutesToAlarm.text` and `secondsToAlarm.text` are treated as numbers (not strings) before any mathematical processes occur. In a moment, you'll see why this is necessary. To understand how this expression works, let's look at an example. Assume the user has entered a value of *5* into the **minutesToAlarm** text field and *37* into the **secondsToAlarm** text field. Using these values, the expression would initially look like this:

```
(Number("5") * 60) + Number("37")
```

507

As you can see, these values are initially recognized as strings—which would normally prevent this expression from evaluating properly. By using the `Number` function, however, the values are converted to numbers so that the expression ends up looking like this:

```
(5 * 60) + 37
```

NOTE *Values from the `text` property of a text field (as in `minutesToAlarm.text`) are always considered string values unless you convert them to numbers as shown.*

Since there are 60 seconds in a minute, you can get the seconds equivalent of the minutes entered by multiplying the value entered for minutes by 60. In this case, that value comes out to be 300. This value is then added to the actual seconds entered to give a final total of 337 (seconds)—which is assigned to `totalTimeToAlarm`. Eventually our script will compare the number of seconds that have passed since the timer was started with this value. Once the seconds that have passed *exceed* this value, the script will know it's time to sound the alarm—more on this in a bit.

TIP *Although the timer would work just fine if the value of `totalTimeToAlarm` was set just once, by placing this line of script within the `enterFrame` event, we enable the variable's value to be updated 24 times a second (the frame rate of the movie) if necessary. This allows the user to reset the minute and second settings of the timer dynamically—that is, while the timer is on—and have the value of `totalTimeToAlarm` be automatically updated, affecting when the alarm will sound.*

6) Add the following line of script just below the one you added in the last step:

```
secondsElapsed = Math.round((getTimer () - startingTime) / 1000);
```

It's critical that our script track the amount of time that has elapsed since the user clicked the Start button and activated the timer. That's what the above line of script does. Understanding the precedence in this expression, we know that it's evaluated in the following manner:

Using the `getTimer()` function, the current time (which is checked 24 times a second since this line of script is executed using an `enterFrame` event) is subtracted from the value of `startingTime`:

```
getTimer() - startingTime
```

You'll remember that the value of startingTime is set to the current time at the point when the Start button is clicked. By constantly checking and subtracting the current time from that value, the script can determine how many milliseconds have elapsed between the current time and the time the Start button was pressed. As mentioned, this part of the expression will result in a millisecond value, such as 29349. If you were to divide this value by 1000, as the next part of the expression does:

```
/ 1000
```

you would get a result of 29.349—equal to 29.349 actual seconds. The last part of the expression is used to off round the value:

```
Math.round()
```

In the end, secondsElapsed will be assigned a value of 29. Remember, though, that this value continues to increment as long as the script executes (because the difference between the current time and the time the Start button was pressed continues to increase). Also, since the Math.round() method is used in the expression, its value will increment only in whole numbers (29, 30, 31, and so on). This will provide us with the amount of time that has elapsed—accurate to $1/24^{th}$ of a second, since that's how often the line of script is executed.

At this point, we have two variable values that will facilitate the rest of the actions in this script.

7) Add the following line of script just below the one you added in the last step:

```
alarmHand._rotation = totalTimeToAlarm / 10;
```

You'll remember that **alarmHand** is the instance name of the hands (red tick mark) inside the **clock** movie clip instance that indicate (on the clock's face) when the alarm is set to go off. This line of script is used to set the **alarmHand**'s rotation so that it can perform this functionality. For example, if the alarm is set to go off in 20 minutes, the **alarmHand** instance needs to be rotated so that the red tick mark in the instance appears at the 20-minute mark on the clock's face. Let's look at how this expression accomplishes that.

A full circular rotation is 360 degrees. By breaking this rotation into the 60 points on a clock's face that represent minutes, we can determine that each minute needs to represent a rotation of 6 degrees (6 x 60 = 360). Thus, to rotate the **alarmHand** movie clip instance to the 20-minute point, it needs to be rotated 120 degrees (6 degrees per minute x 20 minutes). Using the expression that sets the value of totalTimeToAlarm (as shown in Step 5), 20 minutes would be converted to 1200

509

seconds. Dividing this value by 10, as the expression in this line of script does, results in **alarmHand** being rotated 120 degrees—right to where it needs to be to indicate that the alarm will go off in 20 minutes.

$$\text{TOTALTIMETOALARM} = 1200$$
$$\text{ALARMHAND.\_ROTATION} = \text{TOTALTIMETOALARM} / 10$$
$$1200 / 10$$
$$120$$

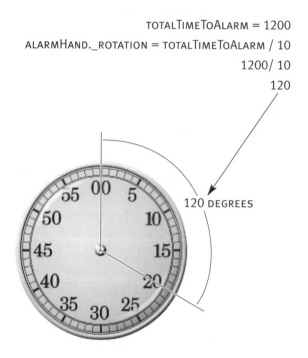

120 DEGREES

NOTE *Since the minute and second values that the user sets can be changed while the timer is on, and this script uses that total time to rotate this instance, changing those values will change its rotation to reflect the updated values.*

8) Add the following lines of script just below the one you added in the last step:

```
secondHand._rotation = secondsElapsed * 6;
minuteHand._rotation = secondsElapsed / 10;
```

These two lines are used to rotate the **secondHand** and **minuteHand** movie clip instances, based on the continually updated value of secondsElapsed. The logic that makes this occur is once again based on the fact that a full circular rotation is 360 degrees, and the clock face is split into 60 graduations (both minutes and seconds) of 6 degrees each. For each second that elapses, the second hand needs to move 6 degrees, representing one second. Knowing this, the first action above sets the rotation of the **secondHand** movie clip instance to the value of secondsElapsed *multiplied* by 6. Thus, at one second it will be rotated 6 degrees, at two seconds it will be rotated 12 degrees, and so on, making it appear to tick like a real clock.

The minute hand functionality requires a slightly different approach. The minute hand on a clock usually rotates at $\frac{1}{60}$th the pace of the second hand. For example, if 60 seconds have ticked away, the second hand has made a full rotation. At this point, the minute hand should have rotated just 6 degrees on the clock face, indicating that one minute has passed. Knowing this, the second action above sets the rotation of the **minuteHand** movie clip instance based on the value of `secondsElapsed` *divided* by 10. Thus, if 60 seconds pass, this expression will evaluate to a value of 6, which is the amount **minuteHand** is rotated.

In the end, the **secondHand** movie clip instance is rotated six times the value of `secondsElapsed,` while the **minuteHand** instance is rotated one-tenth that same value. Thus, the **minuteHand** instance rotates $\frac{1}{60}$th as much as the **secondHand** instance, just like on a real clock.

Since the value of `secondsElapsed` is constantly being updated, both of these hands are in constant motion while the timer (the entire script we've been working on) is "on."

9) Add the following conditional statement just below the actions added in the last step:

```
if (secondsElapsed == totalTimeToAlarm) {
  activateAlarm();
}
```

```
1  onClipEvent (enterFrame) {
2      if (alarmOn) {
3          totalTimeToAlarm = (Number(_root.minutesToAlarm.text) * 60) + Number(_ro
4          secondsElapsed = Math.round((getTimer () - startingTime) / 1000);
5          alarmHand._rotation = totalTimeToAlarm / 10;
6          secondHand._rotation = secondsElapsed * 6;
7          minuteHand._rotation = secondsElapsed / 10;
8          if (secondsElapsed == totalTimeToAlarm) {
9              activateAlarm();
10         }
11     }
12 }
13
```

This conditional statement, which is executed 24 times a second like all the other actions in this script, compares the value of `secondsElapsed` to the value of `totalTimeToAlarm`. Once they both have the same value (indicating that it's time for the alarm to sound), this statement becomes `true` and the action within it is executed. The action within the statement calls the `activateAlarm()` function, causing the action of that function to be executed. This function will be defined next.

10) Add the following script just below the current script:

```
onClipEvent (load) {
  function activateAlarm () {
    alarmOn = false;
    secondHand._rotation = 0;
    minuteHand._rotation = 0;
    alarmHand._rotation = 0;
    alarmSound = new Sound();
    alarmSound.attachSound("annoying");
    alarmSound.start( 0, _root.numberOfLoops.text );
  }
}
```

```
▽ Actions - Movie Clip                                          ☰

  [⚙] Actions for clock (ClockMovie)                      [▲▼] [⊶]

  +  ⊘ ⅋ ⊕ ✔ ≣ (⊡                              ⊙ ⅋ ⊡

   1 onClipEvent (enterFrame) {
   2     if (alarmOn) {
   3         totalTimeToAlarm = (Number(_root.minutesToAlarm.text) * 60) + Number(_
   4         secondsElapsed = Math.round((getTimer () - startingTime) / 1000);
   5         alarmHand._rotation = totalTimeToAlarm / 10;
   6         secondHand._rotation = secondsElapsed * 6;
   7         minuteHand._rotation = secondsElapsed / 10;
   8         if (secondsElapsed == totalTimeToAlarm) {
   9             activateAlarm();
  10         }
  11     }
  12 }
  13 onClipEvent (load) {
  14     function activateAlarm() {
  15         alarmOn = false;
  16         secondHand._rotation = 0;
  17         minuteHand._rotation = 0;
  18         alarmHand._rotation = 0;
  19         alarmSound = new Sound();
  20         alarmSound.attachSound("annoying");
  21         alarmSound.start( 0, _root.numberOfLoops );
  22     }
  23 }
  24
  Line 3 of 24, Col 55
```

This script defines the `activateAlarm()` function when the **clock** movie clip instance (to which this script is attached) is first loaded. The first thing this function does is set the value of `alarmOn` to `false`. This will "turn off" the script being executed by the `enterFrame` event, causing the timer to stop functioning. The next three actions in the function reset the rotation of the various hands on the clock to their starting

512

positions. After that, a Sound object is created and given a name of `alarmSound`. Obviously, this Sound object represents the alarm sound. The next action attaches the sound in the library named "annoying" to the newly created Sound object. The last action uses the `start()` method to play that sound. The first parameter determines how many seconds *into* the sound it should begin to play; the second parameter determines how many times the sound should loop. Because we want the sound to start playing at its beginning, we set the first parameter to 0. The value of the second parameter is set based on what the user inputs into the **numberOfLoops** text field on the main timeline.

11) Choose Control › Test Movie to view the project to this point.

When the movie appears, enter values into the appropriate input text fields for the timer, then press the Start button. The various hands on the clock should go into action. When the time the alarm is set to go off is reached, the timer will turn off, its hands will be reset, and the alarm will sound and continue to loop based on the value entered into the **numberOfLoops** text field.

12) Close the test movie and save your project as makeMyDay3.fla.

As you've seen in this lesson, the `getTimer()` function plays a vital role in interactivity that requires an accurate measurement of time in order to function properly.

We will continue building on this exercise in the next lesson.

CONTROLLING THE PLAYBACK SPEED AND DIRECTION OF A TIMELINE

Normally, a movie's timeline plays in a forward direction at a pace dictated by the fps (frames-per-second) setting in the Movie Properties dialog box. However, *you* can control the direction in which your timeline moves as well as its speed by using ActionScript. In fact, you'll find that by combining scripting elements (which control direction) with the `enterFrame` event, you can gain incredible control over your project's timeline.

The first two scripting elements we'll discuss here are the `nextFrame()` and `prevFrame()` methods of the Movie Clip object. You use these methods to move a timeline to the next or previous frame by employing the following syntax:

```
on(release) {
  myMovieClip.nextFrame();
}
```

or

```
on(release) {
  myMovieClip.prevFrame();
}
```

By placing the above scripts on buttons, you can easily create navigation controls that will automatically advance or rewind a timeline a frame at a time with each click of the button.

Even more powerful is a timeline's `_currentframe` property (a read-only property): Its value represents the frame number at which the playhead currently resides. For example, if the main movie were being played, the following script would place the numerical value of the playhead's current frame position into a variable named whereAreWe:

```
whereAreWe = _root._currentframe;
```

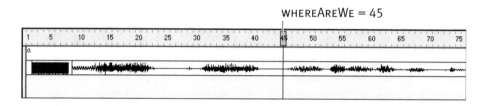

WHEREAREWE = 45

You can also use this property in conjunction with a conditional statement to determine when the playhead is within a specific range of frames and make it act accordingly:

```
onClipEvent (enterFrame) {
  if(_root._currentframe >= 50 && _root.currentframe <= 100)
    // Perform these actions
  }
}
```

In the above script, the actions within the conditional statement are only executed when the playhead on the main timeline is between Frames 50 and 100.

Using the `_currentframe` property in conjunction with a `gotoAndPlay()` action allows you to control the direction in which the timeline moves as well as the pace. Take a look at the following example:

```
_root.gotoAndPlay (_currentframe +10);
```

This will cause the playhead on the main timeline to advance 10 frames from its current position. In the same way, you can use the following script to make the timeline moved backward 10 frames:

```
_root.gotoAndPlay (_currentframe -10);
```

As you will see in this exercise, by using the `enterFrame` event to execute a line of script like the above, you can create fast-forward and rewind buttons to control a timeline's playback.

514

1) Open makeMyDay3.fla in the Lesson15/Assets folder.

We will continue to build on the project from the last exercise. Most of our work for this exercise will take place in the Messages scene. However, before we do anything, we need to give our project the ability to navigate to that scene when it is played—which is where the button with the text "Get phone messages" (at the top-left corner of the Alarm scene) comes into play. To do this, we'll place a navigation script on this button.

2) With the Actions panel open, select the "Get phone messages" button and add this script:

```
on (release) {
  nextFrame();
}
```

When the user presses and releases this button, the main timeline will advance to the next frame. Because there's only one frame in this scene, the next frame is actually considered to be the next scene. Thus, this action moves the timeline to the Messages scene, where we will be working next.

3) With the Scene panel open, select the Messages scene in the scene list to make it visible in the authoring environment.

This scene consists of four layers. The Background layer contains the main graphics. The Buttons layer contains the scene's four buttons: Play, Stop, FF, and Rew. The Flashing Indicator layer contains a movie clip instance of a flashing *4*. The Sound Clip layer contains a graphically empty movie clip instance that appears just above the stage, on the left. This instance is named **messages**; let's take a closer look at it.

MESSAGES

4) Double-click the *messages* movie clip instance to edit it in place.

This movie clip's timeline contains two layers, Sound Clips and Actions. Frame 1 of the Actions layer contains a `stop()` action to prevent the timeline from moving forward until we instruct it to. The Sound Clips layer has a series of streaming sound clips that stretches across 700 frames. (Dragging the playhead will allow you to hear the various clips.) In this exercise, we'll set up the buttons on the main timeline that the user can employ to navigate this timeline forward and backward.

5) Return to the main timeline. With the Actions panel open, select the *messages* movie clip instance and add the following script:

```
onClipEvent (enterFrame) {
  if (action == "ff") {
    gotoAndStop (_currentframe + 3);
  } else if (action == "rew") {
    gotoAndStop (_currentframe - 10);
  } else if (action == "play") {
    play ();
  } else if (action == "stop") {
    stop();
  }
}
```

This script is executed with an `enterFrame` event, meaning that the conditional statement is analyzed 24 times per second. This statement is set up to do various things based on the value of a variable named `action`. As you will soon see, pressing the Play, Stop, FF, and Rew buttons in the scene will change this variable's value accordingly.

The first part of this statement says that `if action` has a value of `"ff"` (which it will when the FF button is pressed), the current movie (the **messages** movie clip) should advance three frames from its current frame and stop. Since this script is executed 24 times a second, as long as `action` equals `"ff"` (that is, as long as the FF button is pressed), the timeline will continue to advance, always skipping ahead three frames, and simulating the process of fast-forwarding.

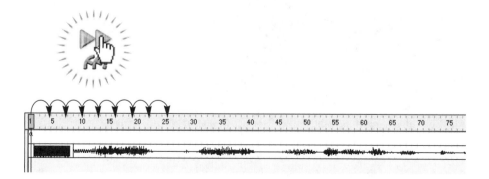

The next part of the statement has just the opposite effect. It says that if `action` has a value of `"rew"` (which it will when the Rew button is pressed), the current movie should start at its current frame then go to the frame that's 10 frames back and stop there. Once again, since this script is executed 24 times a second, as long as `action` equals `"rew"` (that is, as long as the Rew button is pressed), the playhead on the timeline will continue to move backward, always subtracting 10 more frames from the new current frame, which simulates the process of rewinding.

The third part of the statement says that if `action` has a value of `"play"` (as it will when the Play button is clicked or the FF or Rew buttons are released), the current movie should play.

The last part of the statement says that if `action` has a value of `"stop"` (which it will when the Stop button is pressed and released), the current movie should be halted.

Next, let's set up our buttons.

6) **With the Actions panel open, select the Play button and add the following script:**

```
on (release) {
  messages.action = "play";
}
```

When the user presses and releases this button, the value of `action` (in **message**'s timeline) is set to a value of `"play"`. This will cause the script attached to that instance to take the appropriate action (as described in the previous step).

7) **With the Actions panel open, select the Stop button and add the following script:**

```
on (release) {
  messages.action = "stop";
}
```

When the user presses and releases this button, the value of `action` (in **message**'s timeline) is set to `"stop"`. This will cause the script attached to that instance to take the appropriate action, as described in the Step 5.

8) **With the Actions panel open, select the FF button and add this script:**

```
on (press) {
  messages.action = "ff";
  fastSound = new Sound();
  fastSound.attachSound("rewind");
  fastSound.start(0, 50);
}
on (release) {
  messages.action = "play";
  fastSound.stop();
}
```

517

This button responds to two events: pressing and releasing. When the user presses this button, the value of `action` (in **message**'s timeline) is set to `"ff"`, causing the script attached to that instance to take appropriate action (as described in Step 5). In addition, a Sound object is created to simulate the sound of fast-forwarding (and the "rewind" sound from the library is attached to it), and the sound itself starts, set to loop 50 times.

> **NOTE** *To avoid confusion, its important to note that the "rewind" sound is used both to simulate the sound of fast-forwarding (here) and rewinding (next step), since they are very similar in nature.*

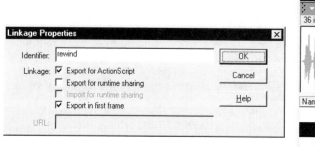 

When the button is released, the value of `action` is set to `"play"`, thus halting the fast-forwarding process. In addition, the `fastSound` Sound object is instructed to stop.

9) With the Actions panel open, select the Rew button and add this script:

```
on (press) {
  messages.action = "rew";
  fastSound = new Sound();
  fastSound.attachSound("rewind");
  fastSound.start(0, 50);
}
on (release) {
  messages.action = "play";
  fastSound.stop();
}
```

This button is set up in exactly the same way as the last one—except that when pressed, it sets the value of `action` to `"rew"`.

10) Choose Control › Test Movie to view the project to this point.

When the movie appears, press the "Get phone messages:" button to advance the movie to the next scene. When the scene appears, use the various buttons to control

518

the playback of the **messages** movie clip instance. Pressing the FF button moves that timeline quickly forward; pressing the Rew button moves it quickly backward (as is evident from the points where the various sound clips in the instance are heard).

11) Close the test movie and save your project as makeMyDay4.fla.

Playback control buttons like the ones we set up here have a wide range of uses—not just for streaming sounds (as demonstrated) but for any kind of project whose timeline contains hundreds of frames of content. By making use of them, you enable users to control the way they view your projects—a powerful capability.

TRACKING PLAYBACK AND DOWNLOADING PROGRESSION

The number of frames in a movie and the file size of their contents determine a movie's overall length and size—a fact made evident by looking at the main timeline, where these factors represent the length and size of the entire SWF. The total number of frames in a movie is a represented by the `_totalframes` property. Thus, if the main timeline has 400 frames that span several scenes, you could state that as follows:

```
_root._totalframes = 400;
```

You can use this property in your scripts to determine the overall length of your movie (based in frames).

> **NOTE** *Because it is a read-only property, the value of _totalframes is automatically set by Flash (based on the number of frames on a timeline). Thus, not only does it not make sense to attempt to reset this value, it's not even possible!*

If you know this value, you can use it in conjunction with other movie properties to make comparisons during downloading and playback. For example, by comparing the value of the `_currentframe` property with the value of the `_totalframes` property, you can determine how much longer the movie will play:

```
framesLeft = _root._totalframes - _root._currentframe;
message.text = "There are " + framesLeft + " to go.";
```

Since Flash is based on streaming technology, the process of downloading and viewing a SWF from a Web site actually occurs a frame at a time. Another property, `_framesloaded`, provides the total number of frames that have been downloaded. The value of this property can be compared to the `_totalframes` property to provide information about download's progress. In the following exercise, we'll demonstrate this by creating a progress bar (known as a *preloader)* that shows the percentage of frames that have been downloaded.

1) Open preloader1.fla in the Lesson15/Assets folder.

This project contains two scenes, Preloader and Content. The Content scene simply contains several layers of graphics and animation that will be used to demonstrate how the preloader works. All of our work in this exercise will take place in the Preloader scene, which contains three layers: Background, Preloader, and Actions. The Background layer contains a square with a radial gradient. The Actions layer contains a `stop()` action to prevent the timeline from moving forward until we instruct it to. The Preloader scene contains two elements, a text label containing the text "now loading…" and a movie clip instance named **preloader**, which includes the elements that will be used to show the downloading progress. Let's take a closer look at this instance.

2) Double-click the *preloader* movie clip instance to edit it in place.

This movie clip's timeline consists of four layers named according to their contents. The most important aspects of this timeline are the text field named **info**, which resides on the Text layer, and the tweened animation on the Amount layer. The text field will be used to dynamically display the percentage of frames that have downloaded. The tweened animation represents a 100-frame progress bar that begins at 0 percent and ends at 100 percent. Among other things, our script will move this movie's timeline to the appropriate frame number based on the percentage of frames that have been downloaded. This will result in the progress bar moving accordingly.

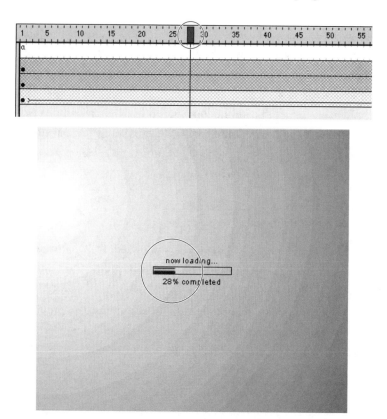

3) Return to the main timeline. With the Actions panel open, select the *preloader* **movie clip instance and add this script:**

```
onClipEvent (enterFrame) {
  framesLoaded = Math.ceil (( _parent._framesloaded / _parent._totalframes)
* 100);
  gotoAndStop (framesLoaded);
  info.text = framesLoaded + "% completed";
  if (framesLoaded >= 90) {
    _root.gotoAndPlay (2);
  }
}
```

This script is executed using an `enterFrame` event (24 times a second), which means it will instantly react to the current downloading conditions to display the most accurate representation of the process.

The first thing this script does is determine a percentage value for the number of frames that have downloaded. It then rounds that number up and assigns that value to the `framesLoaded` variable. Using precedence, the expression employed to do this is evaluated in the following manner:

```
_parent._framesloaded / _parent._totalframes
```

With this part of the expression, the number of frames on the main timeline that have *loaded* is divided by the total number of frames *on* the main timeline.

> **NOTE** *Since this script is attached to the* **preloader** *movie clip instance and that instance resides on the main timeline, the use of* `_parent` *as the target path is a reference to the main timeline. This setup allows the* **preloader** *clip to be used (and function properly) in any project—without modification.*

For demonstration purposes, let's assume that the movie has 735 frames, 259 of which have loaded. If that were the case, this part of the expression would look like the following:

```
259 / 735
```

This would result in a value of .3523. The next part of the expression is used to multiply that result by 100:

```
* 100
```

This would result in a value of 35.23. Lastly, using the `Math.ceil()` method, this value is rounded up to the next whole number, or 36—and thus `framesLoaded` is assigned a value of 36. Remember: Since this script is executed 24 times per second, this number increases as the movie is downloaded.

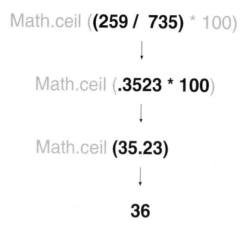

$$\text{Math.ceil} \left((259 / 735) * 100 \right)$$
$$\downarrow$$
$$\text{Math.ceil} (.3523 * 100)$$
$$\downarrow$$
$$\text{Math.ceil} (35.23)$$
$$\downarrow$$
$$36$$

TIP *The _framesloaded and _totalframes properties used in this script can be replaced with the* getBytesLoaded() *and* getByteTotals() *methods of the Movie Clip object if you want to make this preloader react to actual bytes loaded (rather than just frames). This is sometimes the preferred method of scripting a preloader because a frame is not considered loaded (thus the preloader will not advance) until all the data it contains is loaded. This may cause the preloader to appear stalled if the frames loaded contain numerous bytes of data. In contrast, looking at the bytes loaded will cause the preloader to move forward more smoothly, since changes in byte-data happens more frequently (as each byte of data is downloaded). See the bonus file on the CD that demonstrates this.*

The next action in the script is used to send the current movie to the appropriate frame, based on the value of framesLoaded. Because the current movie contains the tweened animation of the progress bar moving from the left to the right, this action controls the movement of that bar. As the value of framesLoaded increases, so does the appearance of progress on the progress bar.

The next action is used to set what's displayed in the **info** text field. Here, the value of framesLoaded is concatenated with the string "% completed". If framesLoaded has a value of 36, this will read, "36% completed".

The last part of the script contains a conditional statement used to determine when the preloader's work is complete. It says that once the value of framesLoaded is equal to or more than 90, the main timeline should be moved to Frame 2 (which is actually the Content scene) and play from there.

TIP *The value of* 90 *in this conditional statement could easily be changed to any value in order to specify when the preloader's work is finished and the movie can begin to play.*

4) Choose Control > Test Movie to view the project to this point. When the test movie appears, choose Debug > 56K, then choose View > Show Streaming.

This will provide a fairly accurate simulation of how the preloader will look and function when the movie is being downloaded over a 56K modem. As the movie loads, you'll see several points where the percentage of the movie downloaded changes. The progress bar reflects the ongoing status of the downloading process. As explained in the previous step, once 90 percent of the movie's frames have downloaded, the timeline moves to the Content scene and the movie plays from there.

5) Close the test movie and save your project as preloader2.fla.

This completes the exercise.

WHAT YOU HAVE LEARNED

In this lesson, you have:

- Learned how you can use time in Flash projects (page 496)
- Created and used a Date object to display current date (pages 497–502)
- Used the `getTimer()` function to create a Flash-based timer and alarm to accurately track progression of time (pages 502–512)
- Controlled a timeline dynamically using play, stop, fast-forward, and rewind controls (pages 513–518)
- Created a percentage-based preloader using the `_framesloaded` and `_totalframes` properties (pages 519–523)

scripting
for sound

LESSON 16

Few things enhance the way we experience something more than sound. Not only can sound provoke an almost instantaneous emotional response, it also provides dimension. When standing in the middle of a crowded room, you can close your eyes and easily determine the relative position of things just by listening. Thus, you can employ sound to provide your user with context as well as to create an engaging experience.

A thorough understanding of how to control sound dynamically is key to creating everything from games to custom MP3 players. In this lesson, we'll demonstrate Flash's versatile sound controls by emulating a bouncing basketball inside a gym.

Flash's sound controls will let this basketball sound like the real thing when we're done with it.

The user can drag the ball within a predefined area of the screen, and as the ball is dragged, the volume and panning of the bounce will be controlled dynamically to indicate its current location. In addition, you'll see how Flash enables you to add and control sounds in your movie without placing them on the timeline.

WHAT YOU WILL LEARN

In this lesson, you will:

- Learn how to create a Sound object
- Drag an object within a visual boundary
- Control the volume of a Sound object
- Control the panning of a Sound object
- Add sounds to your movie using the attachSound () method
- Start, stop, and loop sounds dynamically

APPROXIMATE TIME

This lesson takes approximately 1½ hours to complete.

LESSON FILES

Media Files:
None

Starting File:
Lesson16/Assets/basketball1.fla

Completed Project:
basketball6.fla

CONTROLLING SOUND WITH ACTIONSCRIPT

Although most of us can enjoy listening to music without thinking too much about what we're hearing, the vibrations that make up even the most elementary sounds are actually far from simple—a fact made evident by the processing power requirements of most audio-editing programs. However, despite the complexity of even the most simple audio clip, sounds can be broken down into just three basic characteristics:

- **Length**. A sound's length can provide sensory cues about size (the short chirp of a small-car horn compared to the roar of a semi-truck's horn) and urgency (the tinkle of a viciously shaken dinner bell compared to the long bong of a lazy Sunday church bell).

- **Volume**. A sound's volume provides clues about distance. Louder sounds give the feeling of closeness, whereas quiet sounds imply distance. A sound that gradually goes from quiet to loud, or vice versa, creates a sense of movement.

- **Panning**. Panning represents the position of the sound from left to right. As with volume, this sound characteristic allows you to determine the relative position of the element making the sound. If you were to close your eyes at a tennis match, you could accurately determine the position of the ball (left or right of the net) simply by the "pop" of the ball being smacked by the racket.

With Flash, you can control these various sound characteristics simply by editing sound instances on the timeline—a solution that works well for presentations that don't require audience or user participation. However, if you want to give your user control—allowing them to move and slide things around—you need a more dynamic solution. Fortunately, you can easily emulate and control all of these sound characteristics via ActionScript.

CREATING A SOUND OBJECT

To control sounds dynamically, you must use Sound objects. One of the most important things to realize about Sound objects is that you associate each one with a particular timeline in your movie at the time you create it. Thus, to dynamically control sound on the root timeline, you would need to create a Sound object and associate it with the root timeline. Or to dynamically control sound in a movie clip instance, you would have to create a Sound object associated with that timeline. Sound objects are also used to control sounds in movies loaded into levels. Since Flash projects can contain multiple timelines, projects can contain several Sound objects, each controlling the sound in a different timeline.

Although a particular timeline may contain several layers of sounds, it should be understood that when a Sound object is created and associated with a particular timeline, all sounds in that timeline will be controlled equally using that single Sound object. What this means is that setting the volume of that timeline's Sound object to 50 will relatively decrease all sounds on all layers of that timeline by 50 percent.

The syntax used to create Sound objects is quite simple; it looks like this:

```
soundObjectName = new Sound (Target);
```

Let's break it down: `soundObjectName` denotes the name of your new Sound object. You can assign any name you wish; just make sure it describes the sounds it controls and that you follow the same rules for naming your Sound object as you would for naming variables. This means no spaces, punctuation marks, or numbers as the first character of the name. The syntax `new Sound` is ActionScript's way of creating a new Sound object. `(Target)` is where you indicate to the timeline which target path this Sound object will be associated with.

Once you've created a timeline-associated Sound object, you control that timeline's sound (for example, volume and panning) by referencing the name of the Sound object in your scripts, *not* the target path or instance name of the timeline.

Let's look at a real example. To create a Sound object to control the sound in a movie clip instance named **myMovieClip**, you would use the following syntax:

```
mySound = new Sound ("_root.myMovieClip");
```

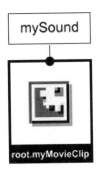

Once you've created a Sound object associated with the movie clip instance **myMovieClip**, you would use the `setVolume()` method to dynamically adjust the volume to 50 percent, as the following syntax shows:

```
mySound.setVolume (50);
```

As mentioned earlier, the goal of this lesson's project is to simulate the sound of a basketball bouncing around the court. In the exercise that follows, we'll create a Sound object—the first step in producing that bouncing ball.

1) Open basketball1.fla in the Lesson16/Assets folder.

This file contains two layers, Background and Ball. The Background layer contains the background graphics; the Ball layer contains the basketball graphic. This movie clip instance—appropriately named **basketball**—will eventually contain all of our project's interactivity.

2) Double-click the *basketball* movie clip instance to open its timeline.

This movie clip contains three layers, Shadow, Graphic, and Sound. The Shadow and Graphic layers contain a couple of tweens to emulate the look and movement of a bouncing basketball. The Sound layer simply contains a "bounce" sound on Frame 5. This sound will play at the same time the bouncing ball appears to hit the floor.

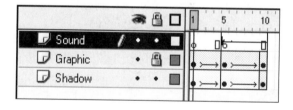

Because there are no `stop()` actions on the movie clip's timeline, playback will continue to loop, giving the effect of a continuously bouncing ball.

3) Choose Edit > Edit Document to return to the main timeline.

Now it's time to create a Sound object associated with the **basketball** movie clip instance. This will allow us to control the volume and panning of the bounce sound as the user drags the ball around the court.

4) Select the *basketball* movie clip instance, open the Actions panel, and then add the following script:

```
onClipEvent (load) {
  bounce = new Sound (this);
}
```

Because it's attached to the **basketball** movie clip instance, this script is triggered when that movie clip instance loads (that is, when it first appears in the scene). This script's only function is to create a new Sound object named **bounce** that's associated with the *this* (**basketball**) timeline. Since the "bouncing" sound is part of this timeline, by controlling the **bounce** Sound object we'll be able to dynamically control the volume and panning of that sound.

TIP *Creating Sound objects using the* `onClipEvent(load)` *event handler is an efficient way of coding. It allows you to create the Sound object only after the movie clip it controls loads into the scene—which makes managing and reading your code much easier.*

5) Choose Control ›Test Movie to see the movie play.

In its current state our project doesn't appear very dynamic. You can't drag the ball around, and the bouncing sound maintains a consistent volume and pan throughout. We'll remedy this situation as we progress through this lesson. The important thing to realize is that as soon as the ball movie clip instance appears in the scene (which is almost instantly), a Sound object is created. The bounce won't sound different until we instruct our new Sound object to do something.

6) Close the testing environment to return to the authoring environment. Save the current file as basketball2.fla.

You may want to keep this file open because we'll build on it as we progress through this lesson.

DRAGGING A MOVIE CLIP INSTANCE WITHIN A BOUNDARY

Being able to drag the ball movie clip instance around the screen is critical to our project's interactivity. This is because the ball's position on screen will determine the volume and panning of the "bounce" sound. However, if we were to allow users to freely drag the **basketball** movie clip instance on screen, our scene would not be realistic because that would mean dragging and bouncing the ball on walls, the backboard, and so forth. Thus, we need to restrict dragging to the area denoted by the court.

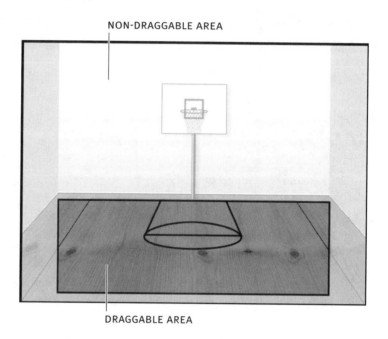

NON-DRAGGABLE AREA

DRAGGABLE AREA

There are several ways of scripting so that an object can only be dragged within a certain area. In this exercise, you'll learn how to accomplish this by tracking the mouse's movement and only allowing dragging to occur when the mouse is within a certain area on screen.

1) Open basketball2.fla in the Lesson16/Assets folder.

If you wish, you can continue using the file you were working with at the end of the previous exercise.

Before you continue, it's important to think through the problem at hand—that is, how to drag the ball movie clip instance in sync with the mouse movement, and how to constrain that dragging to a specific area on screen.

The first thing we need to do is establish the draggable area, or boundary, of our screen. In Flash you define a boundary by determining four coordinates: top, bottom, left, and right. Our script will use these coordinates to restrict movement within that area. For this exercise, the coordinates that represent the four sides of our boundary will be as follows:

Top boundary = 220

Bottom boundary = 360

Left boundary = 60

Right boundary = 490

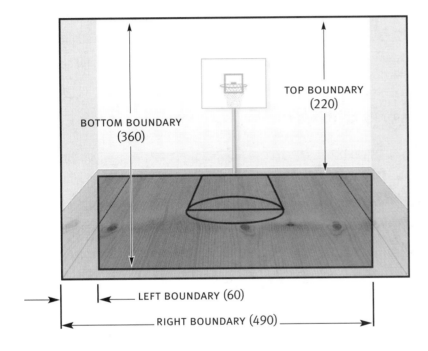

As shown by the arrows, all coordinates are based on the distance of that side from the top and left sides of the stage.

TIP *An easy and visual method of determining boundary coordinates is to draw a simple box on the stage. Resize it and position it in the area that will serve as the boundary in the scene. Select the box and then open the Info panel. Using the information in the X, Y, W, and H boxes, you can determine the four coordinates of your boundary. Y is the top boundary; X is the left boundary; Y + H is the bottom boundary; and X + W is the right boundary. Once you've determined the four coordinates of your boundary, delete the box. There are other, more dynamic ways of setting a border, but this is the most straightforward.*

Since we only want our ball to move when the mouse is within our boundary, in scripting terms this means we need to check for a condition before the ball can be dragged. Logically, this might be translated into a statement that reads as follows:

If the mouse's position is within the coordinates of our boundary, drag the **basketball** movie clip instance. Otherwise, stop dragging.

We'll need to instruct our script to check for this condition on a regular basis since the mouse is in constant motion. Using the mouseMove event handler, we can check for this condition each time the mouse is moved. This will allow our script to act instantly to allow or prevent the **basketball** movie clip instance from being dragged.

We now have all the information necessary to proceed.

2) Select the *basketball* movie clip instance, then open the Actions panel. After the line of script creating the bounce Sound object (which we created in the previous exercise), add the following lines of script:

```
leftBoundary = 60;
rightBoundary = 490;
topBoundary = 220;
bottomBoundary = 360;
```

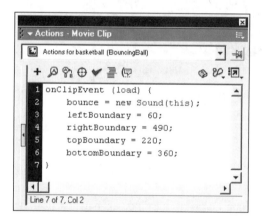

These are variables that contain the *X* and *Y* coordinates of our boundary. Since we've placed these lines within the existing load event handler, these variables won't be created until the **basketball** movie clip instance appears in the scene—a logical choice since they aren't needed until the ball movie clip instance appears in the scene.

Next, we'll add an `if` statement that constantly checks the position of the mouse and allows the ball to be dragged only if the mouse is within the boundary we just defined.

3) After the seventh line in the script—the one with the curly bracket (})—add the following:

```
onClipEvent (mouseMove) {
  if (_root._xmouse > leftBoundary && _root._xmouse < rightBoundary &&
_root._ymouse > topBoundary && _root._ymouse < bottomBoundary) {
    startDrag (this, true);
  } else {
    stopDrag ();
  }
}
```

Using a `mouseMove` event handler, our `if` statement is analyzed each time the mouse is moved.

With this `if` statement, we're checking to determine that four conditions are `true`. If they are, dragging will commence; if not, dragging will cease. We're checking the current horizontal and vertical positions of the mouse (`_root.xmouse` and `_root.ymouse`, respectively) to see how they compare to the boundaries we defined earlier.

Let's look at a couple of possible scenarios to understand the logic behind this `if` statement. Suppose that during playback of the movie, the mouse is moved to a point where its horizontal position (`_root.xmouse`) is 347 and its vertical position (`_root.ymouse`) is 285. By plugging in these values as well as the values that define our boundaries, the `if` statement would look like this:

```
if (347 > 60 and 347 < 490 and 285 > 220 and 285 < 390)
```

In this circumstance, the `if` statement would evaluate to true because all the conditions are true – 347 is greater than 60, 347 is less than 490, 285 is greater than 220, and 285 is less than 390. In this scenario, dragging is allowed.

Let's look at one more scenario. Suppose that during playback of the movie, the mouse is moved to a horizontal position of 42 and a vertical position of 370. By plugging in these values, the `if` statement would look like this:

```
if (42 > 60 and 42 < 490 and 370 > 220 and 370 < 390)
```

In this circumstance, the `if` statement would evaluate to `false` because not all the conditions are `true`—that is, 42 is *not* greater than 60 (the first condition in the statement).

When this `if` statement evaluates to true, the `startDrag()` action is triggered. This action has two parameters, separated by a comma:

```
startDrag (target to drag, lock to center)
```

Because this script resides on the **basketball** movie clip instance and we want to drag this same movie clip instance when the `if` statement evaluates to `true`, the target to drag is defined as `this`. The lock to center is set to `true` so that when dragging occurs, the center of the **basketball** movie clip instance is locked to the exact vertical and horizontal position of the mouse.

TIP *The `startDrag ()` action is not the only way to drag a movie clip instance. In our script, we could replace this action with:*

```
this._x = _root._xmouse;
this._y = _root._ymouse;
```

These two lines would cause the X and Y coordinates of the ball movie clip instance to mimic the X and Y coordinates of the mouse, essentially causing it to appear to be dragged. The advantage of this method is that it allows you to drag multiple movie clip instances simultaneously. In contrast, the `startDrag ()` action allows only a single movie clip instance to be dragged at a time. In our case, this is sufficient because the basketball is the only thing that needs to be draggable.

When the `if` statement evaluates to `false`, the `stopDrag()` action is triggered, causing the ball to stop being dragged. Since this `if` statement is evaluated with each movement of the mouse, the dragging process may be stopped and started frequently, depending on the current position of the mouse.

4) Choose Control › Test Movie to see how the movie operates.

In the testing environment, move your mouse around the court. When the mouse is moved within the boundary we defined, dragging will occur, causing the ball to appear as if it's bouncing around the court. Move the mouse outside this boundary, and dragging will stop.

5) Close the testing environment to return to the authoring environment. Save the current file as basketball3.fla.

You may want to keep this file open because we'll continue to build on it as this lesson progresses.

CONTROLLING VOLUME

Everything we've done to this point has been in preparation for the next several exercises. Although controlling the volume of a movie clip instance with an attached Sound object is pretty straightforward, we plan to take an extremely dynamic approach to the process.

You'll remember that in the first exercise in this lesson, we created a Sound object named **bounce** and associated it with the **basketball** movie clip instance. This movie clip instance contains a bounce sound that plays when the ball appears to hit the floor. To adjust the volume of this Sound object, you would use the following syntax:

```
bounce.setVolume (70);
```

This line of script uses the `setVolume()` method to set the volume of the `bounce` Sound object to 70 percent. Because this particular Sound object is associated with the **basketball** movie clip instance, the volume of all sounds on that timeline will be adjusted accordingly. Volume can be set anywhere from 0 (muted) to 100 (100 percent).

Because ActionScript is such a dynamic scripting language, we can also use a variable name to set the volume rather than hard-coding it as demonstrated above. Thus, if the value of the variable were to change, so too would the amount of the volume adjustment. Take a look at the following example:

```
bounce.setVolume (myVariable);
```

This line of script adjusts the volume of the bounce Sound object to the current value of `myVariable`. As the value of `myVariable` changes, so does the volume of the `bounce` Sound object. This dynamic approach is the one we'll be using for this exercise.

When you look at our project's background, you'll notice it was designed to provide a sense of depth, with the bottom of the basketball court giving a sense of closeness and the top of the court providing a sense of distance. The court itself is a close

535

visual representation of the boundary we scripted in the previous lesson. With this in mind, our goal is simple: We want to set the volume of the **bounce** Sound object based on the vertical position of the ball within our boundary. This means that when the ball is at the top of the boundary, the bounce sound will be at 50 percent volume, giving a sense of distance. As the ball moves toward the bottom of the boundary, the bounce sound should get louder (to a maximum of 100 percent), so that the ball sounds like it's getting progressively closer.

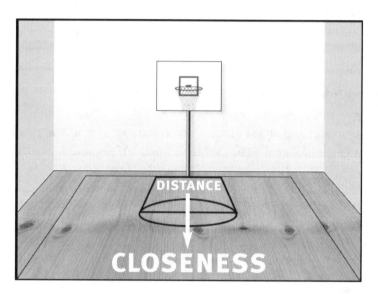

To achieve this, we need to do a couple of things: First, we want to create a variable and constantly update its value to a number between 50 and 100. We will determine this value by figuring the vertical distance (as a percentage value) between the mouse and the top side of our boundary in relation to the overall vertical size of the boundary. Sound confusing? Let's review the formula for figuring percentages as well as take a look at an example scenario. Here's the formula we'll be using:

1) Determine the overall length of an area.

2) Determine the length of the portion for which the percentage must be figured.

3) Divide the size of the portion by the overall size, then multiply by 100.

Using a sample scenario, suppose the mouse has a vertical position of 310. From the previous exercise, we know that our top boundary is 220 and our bottom boundary is 360. With the first part of our formula, we determine the overall length of an area— that is, the vertical size of our boundary. You can figure this out by subtracting 220 (the top boundary) from 360 (the bottom boundary). This gives us a value of 140

536

(360 – 220). Next, we need to determine the length of the portion for which the percentage must be figured. We get this by subtracting 220 (the top boundary) from 310 (the current position of the mouse). This gives us a value of 90 (310 – 220), which means that the mouse is currently 90 pixels from the top boundary. Lastly, we divide the size of the portion (90) by the overall vertical size of the boundary (140), then multiply that result by 100. Mathematically, our equation would look like this.

$(90 / 140) * 100 = x$

$(.6428) * 100 = x$

$x = 64.28$ or 64.28%

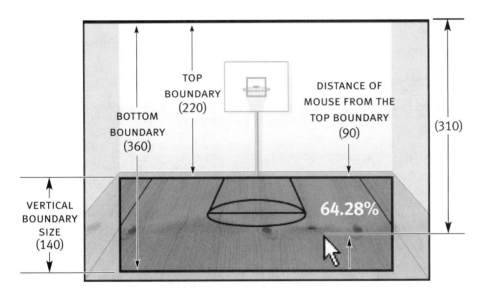

If x were a variable in our movie, we could set the volume of our **bounce** Sound object to the value of this variable by using the following syntax:

```
bounce.setVolume (x)
```

Since the value of x is currently 64.28, the volume of the **bounce** Sound object is set to that value accordingly. However, because the mouse is constantly moving, the value of x is always changing—as is the volume of the bounce.

We have one more mathematical issue to deal with. Using our current percent-generating equation, we have a percentage range between 0 and 100, with 0 indicating that the mouse is at the top of the boundary and 100 indicating that it's at the bottom. We want a percentage range between 50 and 100, where 50 is generated when the mouse is at the top of the boundary and 100 when it's at the bottom. We can easily accomplish this by dividing the percentage value generated (0 to 100) by 2, then adding 50. Take a look at the following examples to see what effect this has on 0-100 values:

$50 / 2 = 25$

$25 + 50 = 75$

Using the conversion formula, you can see how a value of 50 (normally midway between 0 and 100) is converted to 75 (midway between 50 and 100). Let's look at one more example:

$20 / 2 = 10$

$10 + 50 = 60$

Once again, while a value of 20 is one-fifth the value between 0 and 100, the converted value of 60 is one-fifth the value between 50 and100.

At this point, the overall logic we will use to accomplish volume control looks like this:

1) Each time the mouse is moved,

2) If the mouse is within the boundary,

3) Determine the vertical distance (as a percentage between 0 and100) of the mouse from the top boundary.

4) Divide this value by 2, then add 50.

5) Plug this value into a variable.

6) Use this variable's value to set the volume of the `bounce` Sound object.

It's now time to add this functionality to our movie.

1) Open basketball3.fla in the Lesson16/Assets folder.
If you wish, you can simply continue using the file you were working with for the previous exercise.

2) Select the *basketball* movie clip instance, then open the Actions panel. After the line of script defining the sides of the boundary (which we created in the previous exercise), add the following lines of script:

```
boundaryHeight = bottomBoundary - topBoundary;
```

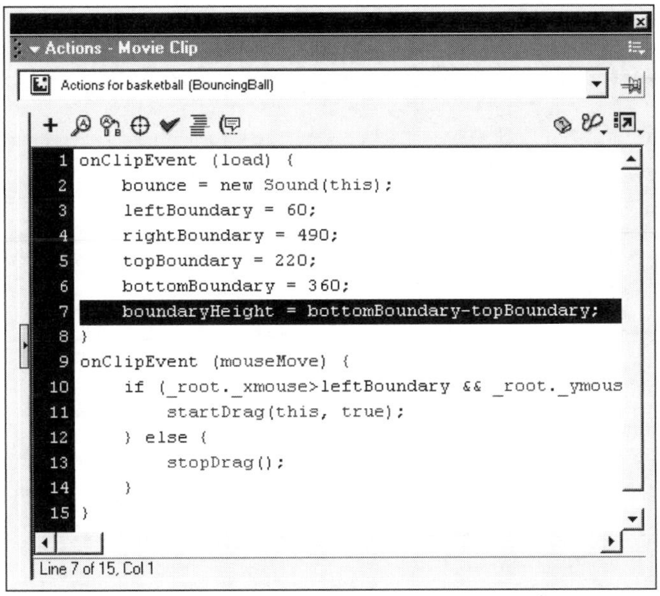

```
Actions - Movie Clip

Actions for basketball (BouncingBall)

+  🔍  🔁  ⊕  ✔  ☰  ⧼                          ◈  🕮  📥

1  onClipEvent (load) {
2      bounce = new Sound(this);
3      leftBoundary = 60;
4      rightBoundary = 490;
5      topBoundary = 220;
6      bottomBoundary = 360;
7      boundaryHeight = bottomBoundary-topBoundary;
8  }
9  onClipEvent (mouseMove) {
10     if (_root._xmouse>leftBoundary && _root._ymous
11         startDrag(this, true);
12     } else {
13         stopDrag();
14     }
15 }

Line 7 of 15, Col 1
```

This creates a variable named `boundaryHeight` and assigns it a value based on what `bottomBoundary` – `topBoundary` evaluates to. The two lines of script directly above this indicate that `bottomBoundary` = 360 and `topBoundary` = 220. Thus, this line of script written out would look like the following:

boundaryHeight = 360 – 220

or

boundaryHeight = 140

This value represents the vertical size of our boundary and will be used to determine percentage values as described previously.

TIP *Although we could have easily assigned a value of 140 to the* `boundaryHeight` *variable directly, using an expression—as we've done—is much more dynamic. This way, if you ever change the values of* `topBoundary` *or* `bottomBoundary`, *the value of* `boundaryHeight` *would automatically update accordingly. A well-thought-out script will contain few hard-coded variables; thus, be conscious of where you can use expressions.*

3) Place the following line of script after the `startDrag (this, true)` action:

```
topToBottomPercent = (((( _root._ymouse - topBoundary) / boundaryHeight) *
100) / 2) + 50;
```

```
▾ Actions - Movie Clip                                                          ⊠
   Actions for basketball (BouncingBall)                                    ▾ -⊞
+ ♦ 🔍 🐵 ⊕ ✔ ⧨ ⧦                                                        ♦ 🐦 🔟
 1  onClipEvent (load) {
 2      bounce = new Sound(this);
 3      leftBoundary = 60;
 4      rightBoundary = 490;
 5      topBoundary = 220;
 6      bottomBoundary = 360;
 7      boundaryHeight = bottomBoundary-topBoundary;
 8  }
 9  onClipEvent (mouseMove) {
10      if (_root._xmouse>leftBoundary && _root._ymouse>topBoundary && _root._xmouse<rightBoundary && _root._ymouse<bottomBoundary) {
11          startDrag(this, true);
12          topToBottomPercent = (((( _root._ymouse-topBoundary)/boundaryHeight)*100)/2)+50;
13      } else {
14          stopDrag();
15      }
16  }
Line 8 of 16, Col 1
```

This line creates the variable `topToBottomPercent` and assigns it a value based on an expression. This expression is the mathematical representation of the percent formula we discussed earlier. Three dynamic values are needed in order for this expression to be evaluated: `_root._ymouse` (the vertical position of the mouse), `topBoundary` (which currently equals 220), and `boundaryHeight` (which currently equals 140). The multiple parentheses denote the order in which each part of the expression is evaluated. The following demonstrates how this expression is evaluated:

1) `_root._ymouse - topBoundary` is evaluated.

2) The result is divided by `boundaryHeight`.

3) The result of step 2 is multiplied by 100.

4) The result of step 3 is divided by 2.

5) 50 is added to the result of step 4.

There are two unique aspects of the location of this line of script. First, you'll notice it's nested within the `mouseMove` event handler. This means the expression that determines the value of `topTopBottomPercent` is evaluated *almost* every time the mouse is moved—and thus the value of the variable is constantly changing based on the current position of the mouse. We say *almost*, because you'll notice that this line of script is also nested within our `if` statement that checks to see if the mouse is within the boundary we created. This means that this variable's value is only set/updated when the mouse is within this boundary. Since this variable's value will soon be used to set the volume of the `bounce` Sound object, you should understand that nesting it within the `if` statement will prevent changes to the volume of the sound whenever the mouse is outside of the boundary.

4) Place the following line of script after the line we just added (the one that created the `topToBottom` variable):

```
bounce.setVolume(topToBottomPercent);
```

This line simply sets the volume of the `bounce` Sound object, based on the current value of the `topToBottomPercent` variable. Since the value of this variable is being updated constantly, so too will the volume of the `bounce` Sound object.

Because this line is nested within the `mouseMove` event handler as well as in the `if` statement that looks for movement within our boundary, the volume of the `bounce` Sound object is updated each time the mouse is moved *within* the boundary.

5) Place the following line of script after the line we just added (the one that set the volume of the `bounce` Sound object):

```
this._xscale = topToBottomPercent;
this._yscale = topToBottomPercent;
```

These two lines of script add a bonus effect to our project. Using the current value of the `topToBottomPercent` variable, these lines will adjust the `_xscale` and `_yscale` properties of the **basketball** movie clip instance (`this`). Thus, the ball will be scaled in size at the same time the volume of the `bounce` Sound object is set. In other words, while the volume is being adjusted to provide an auditory sense of the ball's movement, the ball's size is being visually adjusted as well, giving the project a greater sense of reality.

50%

100%

Since these lines are nested within the `mouseMove` event handler as well as in the `if` statement that looks for movement within our boundary, the size of the ball movie clip instance is updated each time the mouse is moved *within* the boundary.

6) Choose Control > Test Movie.

In the testing environment, move your mouse around the court. As the ball is dragged upward, its size and bounce volume decrease, making it seem that the ball is moving away. As the ball is dragged downward, its size and bounce volume increase, making it seem as if the ball is moving closer.

7) Close the testing environment to return to the authoring environment. Save the current file as basketball4.fla.

You may want to keep this file open since we'll continue to build on it as this lesson progresses.

CONTROLLING PANNING

While the volume of a sound gives a sense of distance, panning helps determine its left-right position. Like setting the volume of a Sound object, setting a Sound object's panning is straightforward, as the following example demonstrates:

```
bounce.setPan (100);
```

The above code will cause the `bounce` sound to play out of the right speaker only. You can set a Sound object's panning anywhere between –100 (left speaker only) and 100 (right speaker only), with a setting of 0 causing the sound to play equally out of both speakers.

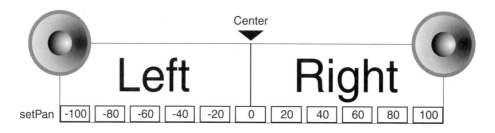

As with the `setVolume()` method, the `setPan()` method can also use the value of a variable to set a Sound object's panning more dynamically, as the following example demonstrates:

```
bounce.setPan (myVariable);
```

For our exercise, we'll use a variable to set the pan of our **bounce** Sound object. As in the previous exercise, this variable will contain a percentage value between –100 and 100 (encompassing the entire spectrum of panning values). We'll base the pan setting of the **bounce** Sound object on the horizontal distance of the mouse from the center point in either the left or right quadrant.

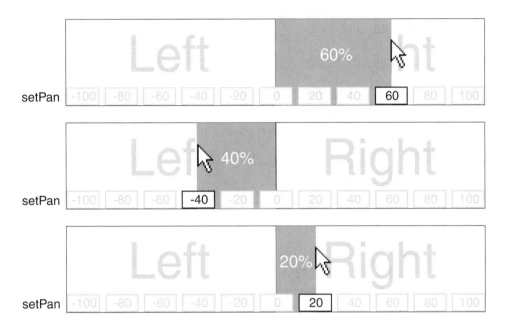

To make this work, you must:

1) Determine the horizontal size of our draggable boundary and then split it in two, essentially breaking the boundary into two "quadrants," left and right.

2) Establish the position of the horizontal center.

3) Determine the mouse's current horizontal position (at the exact center or in the left or right quadrant) each time it's moved.

If the mouse is at the exact center point, the pan will be set to 0. If the mouse is to the left of the center point (in the left quadrant), pan will be set to a value between –100 and 0. This value represents the horizontal distance (percent-based) of the mouse from the center point in relation to the overall size of the quadrant. Likewise, if the mouse is to the right of the center point (in the right quadrant), pan will be set to a value between 0 and 100, which represents the horizontal distance (percent-based) of the mouse from the center point in relation to the overall size of the quadrant.

Don't worry if you're confused. We've already discussed most of the principles for translating this logic into ActionScript; we just need to adapt them a bit.

1) Open basketball4.fla in the Lesson16/Assets folder.

If you wish, you can simply continue using the file you were working on at the end of the previous exercise.

2) Select the *basketball* movie clip instance, then open the Actions panel. After the line of script that says `boundaryHeight = bottomBoundary - topBoundary`**, add the following line of script:**

```
boundaryWidth = rightBoundary - leftBoundary;
```

This creates a variable named `boundaryWidth` and assigns it a value based on what `rightBoundary - leftBoundary` evaluates to. The lines of script directly above this indicate that `rightBoundary = 490` and `leftBoundary = 60`. Thus, this line of script written out would look like this:

boundaryWidth = 490 – 60

or

boundaryWidth = 430

This value represents the horizontal size of our boundary and will be used to determine the size of the left and right quadrants of the boundary.

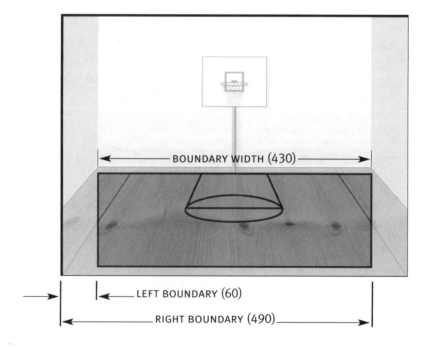

3) After the line of script that says `boundaryWidth = rightBoundary –`
`leftBoundary`, **add the following line of script:**

```
quadrantSize = boundaryWidth / 2;
```

This creates a variable named `quadrantSize` and assigns it a value based on what `boundaryWidth / 2` evaluates to. At this point, `boundaryWidth` has a value of 430. Thus, this line of script written out would look like this:

quadrantSize = 430 / 2

or

quadrantSize = 215

You need to know the size of these quadrants to determine what percentage values to use to set the pan of our `bounce` Sound object.

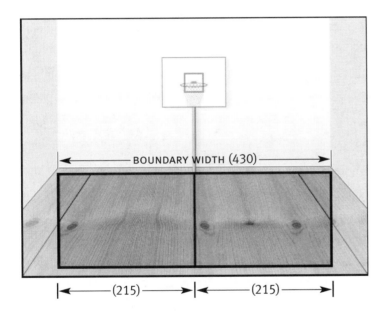

4) After the line of script that says `quadrantSize = boundaryWidth / 2`, **add the following line of script:**

```
centerPoint = rightBoundary – quadrantSize;
```

This creates a variable named `centerPoint` and assigns it a value based on what `rightBoundary – quadrantSize` evaluates to. At this point, `rightBoundary` has a value of 490, and `quandrantSize` has a value of 215. Thus, this line of script written out would look like this:

centerPoint = 490 − 215

or

centerPoint = 275

This value denotes the horizontal location of the center point of the boundary—the place where left and right quadrants meet. This variable plays a critical role in the panning process because it allows us to determine which quadrant the mouse is in—and thus whether our `bounce` Sound object should be panned left or right. If the mouse's horizontal position (`_root._xmouse`) is greater than `centerPoint` (275), we know that the mouse is in the right quadrant; if it's less than 275, we know the mouse is in the left quadrant.

5) After the line of script that says `quadrantSize = boundaryWidth / 2`**, add the following lines of script:**

```
panAmount = ((_root._xmouse − centerPoint) / quadrantSize) * 100;
bounce.setPan (panAmount);
```

In the first line the variable `panAmount` is created. The expression that sets the value of `panAmount` is based on the percent-generating equation we used to set volume.

After the value of `panAmount` has been established, this variable is used to set the pan for the `bounce` Sound object, as shown on the last line above. The expression is set up to generate a value between 100 and −100 for `panAmount`.

To help you understand the way this section of script works, we'll look at a couple of scenarios. First, let's assume that the mouse's horizontal position (`_root._xmouse`) is 374 when the expression that sets the value of `panAmount` is evaluated. By plugging in the values for `centerPoint` (275) and `quadrantSize` (215), we can break down this expression in the following way:

panAmount = ((374 − 275) / 215) * 100

or

panAmount = (99 / 215) * 100

or

panAmount = .4604 * 100

or

panAmount = 46.04

Once the value of `panAmount` has been determined, the next line we added is executed. This line sets the pan of the `bounce` Sound object based on the value that the expression assigned to the `panAmount` variable. At this point, the value of `panAmount` is 46.04. Setting the pan to this amount will cause it to sound 46.04 percent louder in the right speaker than the left, indicating that the ball is on the right side of the basketball court. Visually, the ball will appear on the right side of the court as well, since the mouse's horizontal position (374) is greater than that of `centerPoint` (275), indicating that the mouse (and thus the **basketball** movie clip instance) is 99 pixels (374 – 275) to the right of the center point.

Now let's look at one more scenario. Assume that the mouse's horizontal position is 158. Plugging all the necessary values into our expression, we can break it down as follows:

panAmount = ((158 – 275) / 215) * 100

or

panAmount = (-117 / 215) * 100

or

panAmount = -.5442 * 100

or

panAmount = -54.42

In this scenario, `panAmount` gets set to a negative number (-54.42). This is the result of subtracting 275 from 158, as is done at the beginning of the expression. Since 158 – 275 = -117 (a negative number), the expression evaluates to a negative value—ideal since we need a negative value to pan our sound to the left. Once again, after the value of `panAmount` has been determined, the next line we added is executed. This line sets the pan of the `bounce` Sound object based on the value our expression assigned to the `panAmount` variable (-54.42). This causes the bounce to sound 54.42 percent louder in the left speaker than in the right, indicating that the ball is on the left side of the basketball court. Visually, the ball will appear on the left side of the court as well, since the mouse's horizontal position (158) is less than that of `centerPoint` (275), indicating that the mouse (and thus the **basketball** movie clip instance is –117 pixels (158 – 275) to the left of the center point.

If the mouse's horizontal position is equal to that of `centerPoint` (275), the expression will set the value of `panAmount` to 0, causing sound to come out equally from both the left and right speakers. This in turn indicates that the mouse is in the center of the court.

Since these two lines of script are nested within the `mouseMove` event handler as well as in the `if` statement that looks for movement within our boundary, the sound is panned each time the mouse is moved *within* the boundary.

6) Choose Control > Test Movie to see how the movie operates.

In the testing environment, move your mouse around the court. As you drag the ball, not only does the bounce's volume change, so does the location of the sound (moving from left to right).

7) Close the testing environment to return to the authoring environment. Save the current file as basketball5.fla.

You may want to keep this file open since we'll continue to build on it.

ATTACHING SOUNDS AND CONTROLLING SOUND PLAYBACK

In non-dynamic projects, sounds are placed directly on, and controlled from, the timeline. This means that if you want a sound to play in your movie, you must drag it from the library onto the timeline and then indicate when and how long it should play as well as how many times it should loop on playback. Although this may be a fine way of developing projects for some, we're ActionScripters—which means we want control! That's why in this exercise we're going to show you how to leave those sounds in the library and call on them only when you need them. Using some more methods available to Sound objects, you'll learn how to add sounds and control their playback—all on the fly.

When you create a Sound object in Flash, one of the most powerful things you can do with it is attach a sound—in essence pulling a sound from the library that can be played or halted any time you wish.

To do this, you must assign identifier names to all of the sounds in the library. Once these sounds have identifier names, you can attach them to Sound objects and control their playback, even their volume and panning, as we discussed earlier in this lesson.

For example, let's assume there's a music soundtrack in the project library with an Identifier name of "rockMusic." Using the following code, you could dynamically employ it in your project and control its playback:

```
on (release) {
  music = new Sound ();
  music.attachSound ("rockMusic");
  music.start (0, 5);
}
```

The first line of this script shows that it's executed when the button it's attached to is released. When executed, the first line creates a new Sound object named `music`. The next line attaches the "rockMusic" sound (in the library) to this Sound object. The next line starts the playback of this Sound object, which in effect starts the playback of the "rockMusic" soundtrack (because it's attached to this Sound object). The 0 in this action denotes how many seconds into the sound to start playback. For example, if the "rockMusic" soundtrack includes a guitar solo that begins playing 20 seconds into the soundtrack, setting this value to 20 would cause the sound to begin playback at the guitar solo as opposed to its actual beginning. The second value in this action, which we've set to 5, denotes how many times to loop the sound's playback. In this case, our soundtrack will play five times before stopping.

In addition, you can set all of these values using variables or expressions—opening a world of possibilities.

In the following exercise, we'll show you how to attach a random sound from the library to a Sound object and trigger its playback whenever the mouse button is pressed. The number of times this sound loops will be random as well. We'll also set up our script so that pressing any key halts the sound's playback.

1) Open basketball5.fla in the Lesson16/Assets folder.

If you wish, you can simply continue to use the file you were working with at the end of the previous exercise.

2) Choose Window > Library to open the Library panel.

The library contains a folder called Dynamic Sounds. In this folder you'll find three sounds that have been imported into this project. These sounds only exist within the library; they have not been placed on our project's timeline yet.

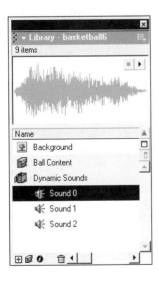

3) Click on Sound 0 to select it. From the Library Option menu, choose Linkage.

The Symbol Linkage Properties dialog box appears. This is where you assign an identifier name to the sound.

4) Choose Export for ActionScript from the Linkage options, and give this Sound an identifier name of Sound0.

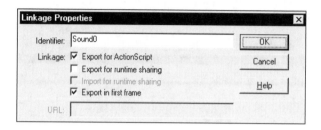

NOTE *A discussion of the settings in this dialog box can be found in Lesson 14, Controlling Movie Clips Dynamically.*

The reason we've used an identifier name ending in a number is that our script generates a random number between 0 and 2: When 0 is generated, Sound0 will play; when 1 is generated, Sound1 will play; when 2 is generated, Sound2 will play. Thus, that number at the end of our identifier name is critical.

When you've assigned an identifier name to the sound, Click OK.

5) Repeat Steps 3 and 4 for Sound 1 and Sound 2 in the library.

Give Sound 1 an identifier name of Sound1 and Sound 2 an identifier name of Sound2.

NOTE *Although library-item names can contain spaces, identifier names cannot. When assigning identifier names, follow the same naming rules that apply to variables.*

At this point, the three sounds in the Dynamic Sounds folder have been given identifier names of Sound0, Sound1, and Sound2. Next, we'll use them in a script.

6) Select the *basketball* movie clip instance, then open the Actions panel. After the line of script that creates the bounce Sound object we worked with earlier, add the following line of script:

```
dynaSounds = new Sound();
```

This creates a new Sound object called dynaSounds. As with the bounce Sound object, this Sound object is created when the **basketball** movie clip instance is loaded into the scene. When this occurs, there will be two Sound objects in our project, one that controls the bouncing sound and another (the one we just added) to randomly play the three sounds in the library.

You'll notice that when we created this Sound object, we didn't associate it with a timeline. This means that our new Sound object will be associated with the entire project—a "'universal" Sound object, so to speak.

7) Add the following lines to the end of the current script:

```
onClipEvent (mouseDown) {
  randomSound = random (3);
  randomLoop = random (2) + 1;
  dynaSounds.attachSound ("Sound" + randomSound);
  dynaSounds.start (0, randomLoop);
}
```

```
10      quadrantSize = boundaryWidth/2;
11      centerPoint = rightBoundary-quadrantSize;
12 }
13 onClipEvent (mouseMove) {
14      if (_root._xmouse>leftBoundary && _root._ymouse>topBoundary && _root._xmol
15          startDrag(this, true);
16          topToBottomPercent = ((((_root._ymouse-topBoundary)/boundaryHeight)*1(
17          bounce.setVolume(topToBottomPercent);
18          this._xscale = topToBottomPercent;
19          this._yscale = topToBottomPercent;
20          panAmount = ((_root._xmouse-centerPoint)/quadrantSize)*100;
21          bounce.setPan(panAmount);
22      } else {
23          stopDrag();
24      }
25 }
26 onClipEvent (mouseDown) {
27      randomSound = random(3);
28      randomLoop = random(2) + 1;
29      dynaSounds.attachSound("Sound"+randomSound);
30      dynaSounds.start(0, randomLoop);
31 }
```

The `mouseDown` event handler causes these lines of script to be triggered whenever the mouse is pressed down anywhere on the stage. Here's what this script does:

First, the expression `random(3);` generates one of three values between 0 and 2 and then assigns this value to the `randomSound` variable. This random value will be used further down in the script to determine which sound from the library will be attached to the `dynaSounds` Sound object and then played.

The next line in our script contains another expression for generating one of two random values. This random value is then assigned to the `randomLoop` variable. This random value will be used further down in the script to determine how many times our sound should loop. You'll notice that this expression differs slightly from the first: We've added + 1 to it. Without it, random (2) will only generate a value of 0 or 1, leaving `randomLoop` with a value of only 0 or 1. By adding + 1 to the expression, the value generated by `random(2)` will have 1 added to it, giving us the possible values of 1 (0 + 1) or 2 (1 + 1). Since this variable is used to determine how many times our sound loops, values of 1 or 2 will cause the sound to play once or twice. Zero is a useless value in this circumstance.

> ⊙ **POWER TIP** *You can use this trick whenever you wish to generate a random value between a specific range of numbers. For example, the expression `random(51) + 50;` will generate a random number between 50 and 100. Here's the formula:*
>
> *1) Determine the highest number you want generated (maybe 500)*
>
> *2) Determine the lowest number you want generated (maybe 150)*
>
> *3) Subtract the lowest number from the highest (in our example we get 350)*
>
> *4) Add 1 to this result (in our example we get 351). This step is necessary to offset the fact that the `random()` function starts generating numbers at 0*
>
> *5) Create your expression (in our example this would be `random(351) + 150`, which will generate a random number between 150 and 500)*

After its execution, the script will have generated two random numbers. These values will now be used in the remaining two lines.

```
dynaSounds.attachSound ("Sound" + randomSound);
```

Using an expression, this action attaches a sound from the library to the `dynaSounds` Sound object, based on the current value of `randomSound`. If the current value of `randomSound` is 2, this would be the same as writing this line of script as:

```
dynaSounds.attachSound ("Sound2");
```

552

With each click of the mouse, a new number is generated and thus the sound attached to this Sound object can change.

Finally, to play this Sound object, the following line is used:

```
dynaSounds.start (0, randomLoop);
```

This will play the current sound attached to this Sound object. For the two parameters of this action, 0 will cause the sound to playback from its actual beginning, and the current value of randomLoop determines how many times the sound will loop (once or twice).

8) Add the following lines to the end of the current script:

```
onClipEvent (keyDown) {
  dynaSounds.stop();
}
```

Actions - Movie Clip

Actions for basketball (BouncingBall)

```
13  onClipEvent (mouseMove) {
14      if (_root._xmouse>leftBoundary && _root._ymouse>topBoundary && _root._xmoι
15          startDrag(this, true);
16          topToBottomPercent = ((((_root._ymouse-topBoundary)/boundaryHeight) *1(
17          bounce.setVolume(topToBottomPercent);
18          this._xscale = topToBottomPercent;
19          this._yscale = topToBottomPercent;
20          panAmount = ((_root._xmouse-centerPoint)/quadrantSize) *100;
21          bounce.setPan(panAmount);
22      } else {
23          stopDrag();
24      }
25  }
26  onClipEvent (mouseDown) {
27      randomSound = random(3);
28      randomLoop = random(2) + 1;
29      dynaSounds.attachSound("Sound"+randomSound);
30      dynaSounds.start(0, randomLoop);
31  }
32  onClipEvent (keyDown) {
33      dynaSounds.stop();
34  }
```

Line 32 of 34, Col 1

The keyDown event handler causes this line of script to be triggered whenever a key is pressed. When this action is executed, playback of the dynaSounds Sound object is stopped, regardless of where it is in its playback.

9) Choose Control > Test Movie to see how the movie operates.

In the testing environment, clicking the mouse causes a random sound from the library to play. If you press a key while the sound is playing, the sound will stop.

10) Close the testing environment to return to the authoring environment. Save the current file as basketball6.fla.

This completes the project! You should now be able to see how dynamic sound control enables you to add realism to your projects—and in the process makes them more memorable and enjoyable. You can do all kinds of things with sounds, including loading them from an external source (which we'll describe in Lesson 17, Loading External Content.

WHAT YOU HAVE LEARNED

In this lesson, you have:

- Learned how and why to create Sound objects (pages 526–529)

- Controlled an object's movement within a visual border (pages 530–535)

- Used percentages in expressions to create powerful interactivity (pages 535–548)

- Controlled the volume of a Sound object based on the vertical position of the mouse (pages 535–542)

- Controlled the panning of a Sound object based on the horizontal position on the mouse (pages 542–548)

- Added random sounds to your project (without first adding them to the timeline) (pages 548–552)

- Controlled the playback, looping, and stopping of sounds dynamically (pages 551–555)

loading
external assets

LESSON 17

One of Flash's greatest strengths is that it allows you to dynamically load all of a project's media assets—bitmaps, sounds, even other movies, from external sources. As a result, a greater range of content can exist externally from the movie (such as on a Web server) and be loaded into the movie on an as-needed basis. This means you can now deliver more dynamic content than ever before, since your movie's content is not restricted to what is placed in it at the time it was authored!

In this lesson, we'll show you how the various types of media are loaded into a running movie, as well as how to work with and manipulate this external content once it has been loaded. As a result, you'll be able to greatly expand the content used in your own projects, without significantly increasing the time it takes for your user to download and view it.

In this lesson, we'll build the project shown here, which contains mostly dynamically loaded content.

WHAT YOU WILL LEARN

In this lesson, you will:

- Learn the benefits of using external assets

- Load a random external SWF into a target

- Create a scalable slide-show presentation using external JPGs

- Learn what an interactive placeholder is and how to use one in a project

- Create a rotating Flash banner system by loading external movies into a level

- Control a movie loaded into a level from within its own timeline as well as from another timeline

- Dynamically Load MP3s into a project while it plays

- Create and use a function that is called automatically when a sound finishes playing

- Script an MP3 playback progress bar

APPROXIMATE TIME

This lesson takes approximately 1 ½ hours to complete.

LESSON FILES

Media Files:

background0.swf

background1.swf

background2.swf

banner0.swf

banner1.swf

banner2.swf

image0.jpg

image1.jpg

image2.jpg

music0.mp3

music1.mp3

music2.mp3

Starting File:

Lesson17/Assets/virtualaquarium1.fla

Completed Project:

virtualaquarium8.fla

Bonus Files:

None

THE INS AND OUTS OF LOADING EXTERNAL ASSETS

When you load external assets into a movie, you're loading a media file (say an MP3 file, a JPG graphic, or even another SWF) into a Flash movie *as it plays*. In other words, you're *adding* assets to your movie. In fact, you can create a Flash movie that contains nothing but script set up to load text, animations, graphics, and sounds from external assets. Media that is loaded dynamically in this fashion can exist on a Web server, or even on a disk or CD if your project is distributed as a projector. Thus, a single project can load media from several sources simultaneously. All that's usually needed is the directory path to the files. It's that simple! No special server technologies required. Sometimes, as is the case when loading media files from a disk or CD, not even a server is required.

By loading external assets (rather than placing all of your project's media in a single SWF), you benefit in a number of ways:

- Your movie downloads faster over the Web.

Imagine that you have a site containing four sections—Home, Services, Products, and Contact—each of which has its own graphic and soundtrack. Together, the graphic and soundtrack add 100k to each section—a total of 400k if you place everything in a single SWF. For users connecting via 56Kbps modems, your site will take nearly two minutes to download—a sure way to turn viewers away. You're better off loading each section's graphic/soundtrack on an as-needed basis, or only when a user navigates to that section—the approach most HTML-based sites take.

- You can view multiple movies in the player window without navigating to different HTML pages.

When using a browser to navigate Web sites, you don't need to close one window and then open another just to move from page to page. Instead, the browser remains open while the window's content changes as pages are loaded and unloaded. The same thing happens when external movies are loaded into Flash's player window: The player window simply acts as a container whose contents (a Flash movie) change without the user having to close the movie window or navigate to a different HTML page.

- Your project becomes modular—and thus easy to update and reuse.

When you begin using assets loaded from external sources in your project, Flash movies become nothing more than interactive modules that you can load, or plug in, to your project at will. Any revisions to a particular module will automatically appear in any bigger project that contains it. Think once again of a standard Web site: Even though each graphic (for example, a logo) usually resides in a single location on the server, multiple pages can contain that logo simply by referencing its directory path on the server—that is, you don't need to create a separate logo graphic for each page. This means you can reuse that graphic on any number of pages, and any time you update that graphic all of the pages on which it appears will reflect those changes. The same holds true for externally loaded content in your Flash projects—a benefit that cannot be overemphasized since it's much easier to individually edit several smaller, externally loaded files than it is to open a complex project with numerous scenes, layers, tweens, movie clip instances, and scripting every time you need to make a change.

- Your project becomes more dynamic, offering each user a unique experience.

Lastly, by loading external assets, you can provide the user with a much more dynamic experience, employing a wider range of content that loads based on time of day, month, user input, or even a randomly generated number.

BACKGROUND MOVIES

ONLY ONE IS LOADED IN RANDOMLY

Although it would be next to impossible to create a single movie that could display appropriate content based on so many variables, using externally loaded assets makes this type of dynamic functionality a breeze.

You can load external assets by using the following actions.

- **External SWF files:** `loadMovie()` or `loadMovieNum()`
- **External JPGs:** `loadMovie()` or `loadMovieNum()`
- **External MP3s:** `loadSound()`

In the following exercises you'll learn how to load external SWFs and JPGs as well as external MP3 files. In addition, you'll learn how to control these assets using ActionScript.

LOADING MOVIES INTO A TARGET

When loading media from an external source, you must assign it a place to reside within your main movie (which we'll call the *receiving* movie). For externally loaded SWFs and JPGs, that location can be either a target or a level.

> **NOTE** *You cannot load an MP3 file into a target or level. It's a different process all together, as you will learn in the section, Loading MP's Dynamically, later in this lesson.*

> **NOTE** *We will discuss loading a movie into a level in the section, Loading Movies into a Level, later in this lesson.*

A target is simply an existing movie clip instance within the receiving movie. In fact, every movie clip instance in the receiving movie is a potential target for externally loaded SWFs or JPGs.

The syntax for loading a movie into a target looks like this:

```
loadMovie ("myExternalMovie.swf", "_root.myPlaceholderClip");
```

> **NOTE** *The directory path to the external asset can be written as an absolute or relative URL, depending on where the file exists.*

The above action loads **myExternalMovie.swf** into the movie clip instance with the target path of `_root.myPlaceholderClip`, thereby replacing the current timeline at that target path with the one that's loaded into it. Thus, when loading external media, you can think of movie clip instances as nothing more than shells containing timelines—either one placed there when the movie was authored (which happens automatically when a movie clip instance is placed on the stage) or one that is loaded dynamically as the movie plays.

When loading an external asset into a target, it's important to remember the following:

- The registration point of the externally loaded asset will match the registration point of the target/instance it's loaded into.

- If the target/instance that an external asset is loaded into has been transformed in any way (for example, rotated), the loaded asset will retain those transformations.

- Once an externally loaded asset has been loaded into a target, you can control it via ActionScript using the target path to the instance into which it was loaded. In other words, the externally loaded asset *becomes* that instance. For example, if an external movie is loaded into an instance with a target path of `_root.myPlaceholderClip`, you can control the externally loaded asset by referencing that target path.

NOTE *For more information about target paths, see Lesson 3.*

External SWFs that are loaded into targets can be as simple as animated banners or as complex as an entire Flash production.

1) Open virtualaquarium1.fla in the Lesson17/Assets folder.

This file (which we'll build on throughout this lesson) contains no actions, and the frame and movie clip structure have already been created so that we can focus on the ActionScript involved. Although the file looks uninspiring now, once the lesson is complete, it will contain several pieces of externally loaded content.

This file is made up of nine layers: The bottom layer, Loaded Background, contains two elements: a text field at the bottom left of the screen that says "loading background…" and an empty movie clip instance (with no graphical content) named **background**, which is placed at an *X* position of 0 and a *Y* position of 0. Soon, this movie clip instance will contain our project's background, which will be loaded from an external source. The second layer, banner back, contains a movie clip instance of a white box (named **bannerBack**) that says "loading banner…" as well as a button that's labeled Banner On/Off. We'll use these in a later exercise. The third layer, next/prev buttons, contains two arrow buttons that we will set up in the next exercise. The fourth layer, panel, contains a bitmap of a gray panel box. The fifth layer, placeholder, contains another empty movie clip instance (which will be used in the following exercise) named **placeholder** as well as a movie clip instance named **maskClip** that resembles a big, black square, just to the left of the stage. The layer above this, paneltop, contains a dynamic text field named **title** as well as a bitmap of a black rectangle, which sits at the top-right corner of the gray panel. The progress bar layer contains a movie clip instance named **progress** that we'll use in a later exercise. And finally, the logo layer contains a bitmap of our logo, and the Actions layer will contain most of the actions that make this project work.

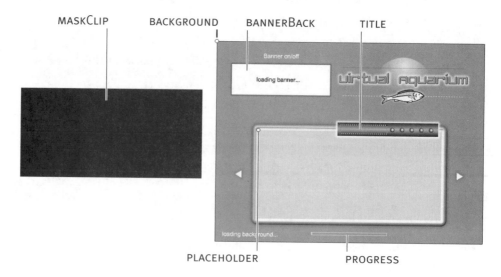

The graphic element that we're most interested in for this exercise is the empty movie clip instance named **background**, located in the top-left portion of the stage. In a moment, we'll begin scripting our project to randomly load one of three SWFs into this instance.

Before we do that, though, let's take a quick look at the external assets we'll be loading into our project in the next several exercises.

2) Using your operating system's directory exploring application, navigate to the Lesson17/Assets directory.

In this directory you'll find the files that will be loaded dynamically into our project. They include the following: background0.swf, background1.swf, background2.swf, banner0.swf, banner1.swf, banner2.swf, image0.jpg, image1.jpg, image2.jpg, music0.mp3, music1.mp3, and music2.mp3.

In this lesson, we'll work with the first three files in this list: simple, animated movies that will represent our project's background (the dimensions of which are 550 width by 400 height, the same as those of our receiving movie). You can double-click these files to view them in the Flash player. Remember their names.

Keep the directory window open and available as we progress through the following exercises since we'll be referencing it again.

3) Return to Flash. With the Actions panel open, select Frame 1 of the Actions layer and add the following script:

```
backgrounds = new Array ("background0.swf", "background1.swf",
"background2.swf");
```

This creates a new array named backgrounds, which holds the paths to our external background movies.

Now let's create a function that will randomly load one of these background movies into our project.

4) Place the following function definition below the script you just added:

```
function randomBackground() {
  randomNumber = random (backgrounds.length);
  loadMovie (backgrounds[randomNumber], "_root.background");
}
```

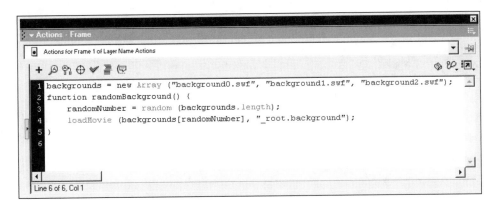

This creates a function named randomBackground(). Let's look at how this function will work.

The first line generates a random number based on the number of elements in the backgrounds array. The length of the array is analyzed to determine the range of possible random numbers to generate. Because the backgrounds array has three elements, one of three possible numbers (0, 1, or 2) will be generated and set as the value of randomNumber. The next line of the function uses the value of this variable to determine which background movie to load. If the number *1* was generated and set as the value of randomNumber, the loadMovie() action would look like this:

```
loadMovie (backgrounds[1], "_root.background");
```

563

Since the value of Element 1 of the `backgrounds` array is `"background1.swf"`, this line could be broken down further to look like this:

```
loadMovie ("background1.swf", "_root.background");
```

In this scenario, the external movie named background1.swf would be loaded into the movie clip instance with a target path of `_root.background`. You'll remember that the movie at this target path is the empty movie clip instance in the top-left portion of the stage. Because the externally loaded background movie and the receiving movie share the same dimensions (550 w by 400 h), the externally loaded background movie will cover the entire stage.

5) Place the following function call just below the function definition you previously added:

```
randomBackground();
```

Because this function call resides on Frame 1 of our movie, it will be executed as soon as the movie begins to play.

TIP *Depending on its file size, an externally loaded movie (like any other movie) may require a preloader, which you would construct and program as a regular preloader. For more information on how to create a preloader, see Lesson 15, Time and Frame-Based Dynamism.*

6) Choose Control › Test Movie.

As soon as the movie begins playing, one of the three background movies is loaded into our project.

NOTE *The **background** movie clip instance (which our external background is loaded into) resides on the bottom layer of the scene; the rest of the scene's content resides above it. When the external movie is loaded into the instance, the loaded content will appear at that same depth. In other words, it will be on the bottom layer with the rest of the scene's content above it.*

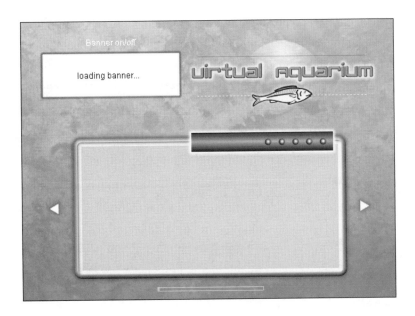

Using the above-described technique, you could construct dozens or even hundreds of background movies, though only one would be loaded when the movie plays. In this way, you can create a dynamic project without increasing download or viewing time.

TIP *With ActionScript, you could use a variation of this technique to determine the current date and then load an external background based on time of day, day of week, or month.*

7) Close the test movie. Save the file as virtualaquarium2.fla.

This completes the exercise! We'll build on this file in the following exercises.

Although our project is set up to randomly load a background movie into a target, for a typical Web site, it might make sense to create a navigation bar that loads content movies into a target. In other words, clicking on a button named Products would load products.swf into a target named *content*. There are many variations to this concept.

LOADING JPGS DYNAMICALLY

Now that you've learned how to load an external movie into a project, the process of dynamically loading a JPG should be easy: It's almost identical to that of loading an external SWF. As demonstrated in the previous exercise, the `loadMovie()` action is used to load an external SWF into a target. You'll then use the same action to load an external JPG as well—but with a twist. Take a look at the following syntax:

```
loadMovie("myBitmap.jpg", "_root.myClip");
```

This `loadMovie()` action identifies a JPG as the external asset to load, as opposed to a SWF, as shown in the previous exercise. Here, the `myBitmap.jpg` JPG is loaded into the `_root.myClip` target. Once a JPG is loaded into a movie in this fashion, Flash sees it as a movie clip instance, which means you can control it via ActionScript, rotating, resizing or making it transparent just like any other clip.

In this exercise, we'll build slide-show functionality into our project to demonstrate how we can load JPGs into a target on an as-needed basis.

1) Open virtualaquarium2.fla in the Lesson17/Assets folder.
This is the file we worked on in the previous exercise.

Note the empty movie clip instance on the placeholder layer (the small, white circle in the panel graphic's top-left corner): Called **placeholder**, this is the movie clip instance into which our external JPGs will be loaded. Also note the text field with a name of **title**, which exists at the top of the panel: We use it in our exercise as well.

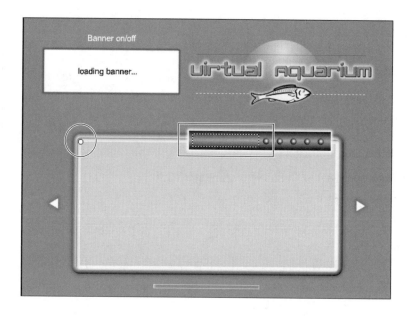

In this exercise, we'll add some script to Frame 1 of the Actions layer as well as script the two arrow buttons in the scene. Before we do this, however, let's review the contents of the directory containing our externally loaded assets.

2) Using your operating system's directory exploring application, navigate to the Lesson17/Assets directory.

Locate the following JPG images:

- image0.jpg
- image1.jpg
- image2.jpg

IMAGE0.JPG

IMAGE1.JPG

IMAGE2.JPG

NOTE *Only standard JPEG files are supported. Progressive JPEG files are not supported.*

Each of these images is 378 W by 178 H—the size at which they will be loaded into the receiving movie. Once the images are loaded, however, Flash will recognize them as movie clip instances and can thus resize and transform them in any number of ways (as we'll demonstrate in the next exercise).

3) Return to Flash. With the Actions panel open, select Frame 1 of the Actions layer and add the following line of script just below where we created the `backgrounds` **array in the previous exercise:**

```
slides = new Array(["Shark", "image0.jpg"], ["Jellyfish", "image1.jpg"],
["Seahorse", "image2.jpg"]);
```

This creates a new, two-dimensional array named `slides`. As you learned in Lesson 7, this is an array where each element in the array contains more than one item. The first part of each of these elements is simply a string description of the image; the second represents the directory path to that image.

Let's next create a function that will load these images into our project, with the functionality of a slide show.

4) Place the following function definition just below the `randomBackground()` **function definition:**

```
function changeSlide(number){
  if (number >= 0 && number < slides.length){
    currentSlide = number;
    _root.title.text = slides[number][0];
    loadMovie (slides[number][1], "_root.placeholder");
    }
}
```

```
  1 backgrounds = new Array ("background0.swf", "background1.swf", '
  2 slides = new Array(["Shark", "image0.jpg"], ["Jellyfish", "image(
  3 function randomBackground() {
  4     randomNumber = random (backgrounds.length);
  5     loadMovie (backgrounds[randomNumber], "_root.background");
  6 }
  7 function changeSlide(number){
  8     if (number >= 0 && number < slides.length){
  9         currentSlide = number;
 10         _root.title = slides[number][0];
 11         loadMovie (slides[number][1], "_root.placeholder");
 12     }
 13 }
```

This creates a function named changeSlide(). Let's look at how this function works.

First, you'll notice that the function is passed a parameter named number—a numerical value that the function will use to determine which image to load. The if statement at the beginning of the function definition dictates that the function will only execute when a number within a certain range is passed to it. The lower end of this range is 0, and the upper end depends on the number of elements in the slides array. Thus, the if statement basically states that if number is greater than or equal to 0 and less than the length of the slides array (which is 3, because the array contains three elements), the actions in the function should be executed. Under these circumstances, the function will only execute if number is 0, 1, or 2. (You'll begin to understand why we've set up the function to operate this way in a moment.)

The first action in the function sets the value of currentSlide to the value of the number parameter passed to the function. This variable's value will be used a bit later, when executing actions on our two arrow buttons.

The next line in our script sets the value of the text field **title** to whatever slides[number][0] evaluates to. The last line in the function uses a loadMovie() action to load one of our external JPG images into the instance named **placeholder**, which is on the root timeline. To make sense of this function, let's take a look at a couple scenarios:

If a value of 1 were passed to this function when called, the if statement would determine that to be an acceptable value, and thus the actions in the function would be executed—in which case they would be evaluated as follows:

```
currentSlide = 1;
_root.title.text = slides[1][0];
loadMovie (slides[1][1], "_root.placeholder");
```

Because the last two actions in the function reference elements in the slides array, you can break further break down those actions, as shown in the follwing:

```
currentSlide = 1;
_root.title.text = "Jellyfish";
loadMovie ("image1.jpg", "_root.placeholder");
```

The result is that image1.jpg is loaded into the instance named **placeholder** and the text string "Jellyfish" appears above the panel in the **title** text field.

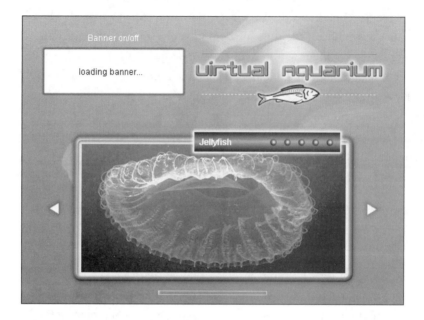

Now let's take a look at one more scenario. If, when this function was called, a value of 3 were passed to it, the `if` statement would prevent it from executing—and thus prevent our project from attempting to load content that does not exist (as defined in the `slides` array). In other words, the `slides` array does not contain an element at index number 3; thus, the function would not work properly if it were allowed to execute. Obviously, if we were to increase the number of elements in the `slides` array, the upper limit accepted by the `if` statement would dynamically increase as well.

5) Place the following function call just below the `randomBackground()` function call:

```
changeSlide(0);
```

This line of script calls the `changeSlide()` function, passes that function a value of 0, and as a result displays the initial image when the movie is played. Note that this initial function call will set the value of `currentSlide` to 0—an important thing to keep in mind as you progress through the next couple steps.

6) With the Actions panel open, select the button on the stage that points *left* and attach this script:

```
on(release){
  changeSlide(_root.currentSlide - 1);
}
```

The above script calls the changeSlide() function we defined in Step 4. The parameter value passed to that function will depend on how _root.currentSlide - 1 is evaluated. As just mentioned, when the movie initially plays, the changeSlide() function is called and passed a value of 0. Consequently, currentSlide is set to 0. Thus, pressing the button that points left, just after the movie begins to play, will result in the changeSlide() function being called and passed a value of -1 (the result of subtracting 1 from the value of currentSlide, as shown). The if statement in the changeSlide() function then evaluates that value (-1) and prevents the function from executing (see Step 4). As a result, this button does nothing until currentSlide has a value greater than 0. (This button cannot navigate the slide show beyond the initial image.) The other arrow (the arrow pointing right) button increases the value, as shown in the next step.

7) **With the Actions panel open, select the button that points *right* and attach this script:**

```
on(release){
  changeSlide(_root.currentSlide + 1);
}
```

This script is identical to the one in the previous step—with one exception: The parameter value passed to the changeSlide() function depends on how _root.currentSlide + 1 is evaluated. If currentSlide has a value of 0 when this button is pressed (after the movie begins playing), the changeSlide() function is sent a value of 1 (the result of adding 1 to the value of currentSlide, as shown). You'll remember that this value is evaluated by the if statement in the function, which, in in this case, since the number is between 0 and 2, allows the continued execution of the function, which will load the appropriate JPG, as described in Step 4. As the image is loading, the changeSlide() function also updates the value of currentSlide (in this case to 1) so that the arrow buttons we just scripted can act accordingly, based on this value, when they are subsequently pressed.

This button cannot navigate the slide show beyond the last image because once currentSlide has a value of 2, pressing this button again would send the changeSlide() function a value of 3 (which, you'll remember, the if statement in that function would analyze, then preventing the function from executing).

In tandem, these two buttons advance and rewind the slide show—though only within the limits described above.

8) Choose Control > Test Movie.

As soon as the movie begins playing, the image of a shark appears. In addition the **title** text field above the panel displays the text string "Shark." The upper-left corner of the image is placed at the registration point of the empty movie clip into which it was loaded.

Press the left-arrow button, and you'll see that nothing happens. Press the right-arrow button once and the next JPG image will load; press it again and another JPG will load. However, if you press this button a third time nothing will happen because you've reached the upper limit of how far this button can advance. The left button has a similar restriction, only in the opposite direction.

TIP *If you ever wish to remove a movie that's been loaded into an instance (so that the instance becomes empty), you can use the following syntax:*

```
unloadMovie("_root.nameOfInstance").
```

9) Close the test movie, and save the file as virtualaquarium3.fla.

This completes the exercise. We will build on this file in the following exercises.

TIP *If you wanted to add additional slides to this project, you would simply add the appropriate data to the* slides *array and place the JPG files in the directory. The movie would then accommodate the new images automatically. This means you can add hundreds of images without affecting the file size of the main movie.*

TIP *Because the images are external, you can easily bring them into a photo editor, update or change them, then resave them, and your changes will be reflected the next time the project is played.*

CREATING AN INTERACTIVE PLACEHOLDER

A placeholder is nothing more than a movie clip instance (empty or otherwise) into which external content can be loaded (also known as a target). Creating an *interactive* placeholder involves nothing more than attaching a script to the instance, which is triggered by an `onClipEvent` of some sort. The great thing about loading external content into an instance that has been scripted in such a way is that even though the instance's *content* will change, its scripted *functionality* can remain the same. Look at the following example:

```
onClipEvent(mouseDown){
  this._rotation += 30;
}
```

If you attach this script to an instance, each time the mouse is clicked, the instance will rotate 30 degrees. This instance can be thought of as an interactive placeholder, since any external movie or JPG that you load into it will also rotate when the mouse is pressed down; the only thing that changes is the instance's content.

One clip event designed expressly for loading external data (including variables and even movies) into instances is `onClipEvent(data)`. You can use this event when attaching a script to a placeholder, and it will be fired each time new variables or a new movie (or JPG) has finished loading into the instance—useful if you want an action to occur as soon as content has been loaded into the instance. While `onClipEvent(load)` will only fire once (when the instance first appears in a scene), `onClipEvent(data)` can fire numerous times, depending on how often variables or movies (considered data in this context) are loaded into it.

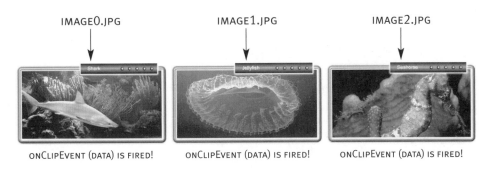

IMAGE0.JPG   IMAGE1.JPG   IMAGE2.JPG

onClipEvent (data) is fired!   onClipEvent (data) is fired!   onClipEvent (data) is fired!

There are numerous ways to create interactive placeholder movie clip instances with a minimum of scripting. Showing you how is what this exercise is all about.

1) Open virtualaquarium3.fla in the Lesson17/Assets folder.

This is the file we worked on in the previous exercise. In that exercise, we set our movie to dynamically load JPGs into the movie clip instance named **placeholder**. In this exercise, we'll attach ActionScript to that instance to make the loaded content draggable and to scale it 150 percent when the mouse is pressed down. That ActionScript will also ensure that when the mouse is let up, dragging will cease and the content will be scaled back to 100 percent. In the process of setting up this functionality, we'll use the black rectangle (a movie clip instance named **maskClip**) on the left of the stage as a dynamic mask.

Let's get started.

2) With the Actions panel open, select the *placeholder* movie clip instance and add the following script:

```
onClipEvent(load){
  thisX = _x;
  thisY = _y;
}
```

This script is executed the moment the **placeholder** movie clip instance is loaded. Its function is to set the value of two variables—thisX and thisY—to the *x* and *y* property values of the movie clip instance. The importance of these values will become evident in a moment.

> **TIP** *We could have easily opened the Property inspector, selected the instance, and copied the* x *and* y *values as shown there, and then set* thisX *and* thisY *accordingly, but this method is much more dynamic. It allows the values to automatically change if the instance is moved to a new point on the stage during development.*

3) With the *placeholder* movie clip instance still selected, add the following script just below the script you just added:

```
onClipEvent(mouseDown) {
  if (hitTest(_root._xmouse, _root._ymouse)){
    _root.maskClip._x = thisX;
    _root.maskClip._y = thisY;
    setMask(_root.maskClip);
    _xscale = 150;
    _yscale = 150;
    startDrag(this);
  }
}
```

This script is executed whenever the mouse is pressed down. First, an if statement determines whether the mouse is over the **placeholder** instance when pressed. If it is, the remaining actions will execute. In other words, because our JPG images are being loaded into this instance, these actions will only execute if the mouse is pressed down on top of the image.

The first two actions within the if statement dynamically position the black rectangle **maskClip** movie clip instance so that its *x* and *y* values equal thisX and thisY, respectively. This places the **maskClip** instance directly over the **placeholder** instance during this script's execution.

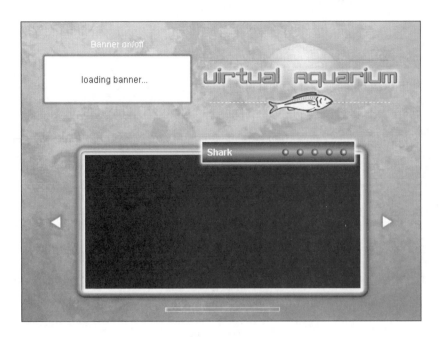

The next action dynamically sets the **maskClip** instance to mask the **placeholder** instance's content—necessary because the next two lines in the script scale its size by 150 percent. By masking **placeholder's** contents, those contents will appear to remain within the panel window even though it becomes larger.

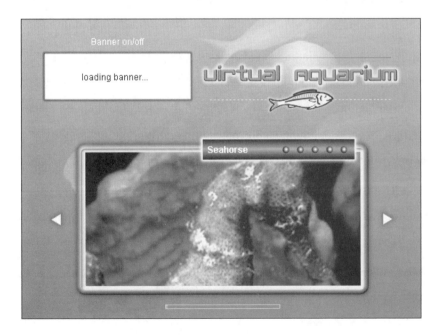

The last action makes the **placeholder** movie clip instance draggable.

4) With the *placeholder* movie clip instance still selected, add the following script just below the script you just added:

```
onClipEvent (mouseUp) {
  stopDrag();
  setMask(null);
  _xscale = 100;
  _yscale = 100;
  _x = thisX;
  _y = thisY;
}
```

This script—executed when the mouse button is released—simply reverses the actions that occur when the mouse is pressed: The first line stops the dragging process; the next removes the mask.

TIP *As shown, using* `null` *removes the mask effect completely.*

The next two actions scale the instance back to its original size. Because this instance was draggable, the last two actions perform the necessary task of resetting it to its original position.

5) Choose Control > Test Movie.

As soon as the movie begins to play, click and drag the image of the shark. When the mouse is pressed down, the image becomes larger and draggable, and the dynamic mask we set up takes effect. Release the mouse, and you'll see the **maskClip**. The reason for this is that when our script removed the masking effect, we didn't compensate for the fact that **maskClip** would become visible again as a normal clip. Obviously, this is not what we want. There is, however, an easy fix.

6) Return to the authoring environment. With the Actions panel open, select the *maskClip* instance and attach this script:

```
onClipEvent (load){
  _visible = false;
}
```

This makes the instance invisible as soon as it loads, and it remains this way because our movie doesn't contain an action to change it. Because the instance will be invisible, it won't interfere with viewing the images in the **placeholder** instance, even when the masking effect is disabled.

7) Choose Control > Test Movie.

Once again, as soon as the movie begins to play, click and drag on the image of the shark. With the mouse pressed down, the image becomes larger and draggable, and the dynamic mask we set up takes effect. Release the mouse, and the image will appear as it did originally. Not only that, but the **maskClip** no longer appears because it's invisible.

Using the right-arrow button, load in a new image. Click on that newly loaded image, and you'll find it has retained its original functionality. That's because the image's functionality resides not within the loaded asset but in the instance into which the asset is loaded. Thus, while the loaded content may change, the instance and its functionality remain the same.

8) Close the test movie, and save the file as virtualaquarium4.fla.

This completes this exercise. We'll continue to build on this file in the following exercises.

LOADING MOVIES INTO A LEVEL

Thus far, we've loaded external content into an existing movie clip instance. However, you can also load external movies and JPGs into *levels*. You can think of levels as layers of movies (SWFs) that exist within the Flash player window, all at the same time. For example, when you view an HTML page containing a Flash movie, a Flash player window is created and the initial movie (as identified in the `<object>` and `<embed>` tags) is loaded into the player. That movie is loaded into a *z-plane* (a term signifying depth) within the player window known as *Level 0*. You can load additional SWFs into higher levels in the player window.

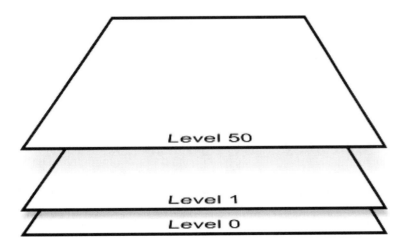

You do this by employing a variant of the `loadMovie()` action you've used up to now:

```
loadMovieNum("myExternalMovie.swf", 1);
```

There are two differences between this code and that used to load an external asset into a target/instance: First, the action is now named `loadMovieNum()` rather than `loadMovie()`. In addition, instead of identifying a *target* for the external asset, we've identified a *level number*. This action loads myExternalMovie.swf into Level 1 of the Flash player window.

It's important to keep in mind the following when loading a movie into a level:

- Only one SWF (or JPG) can occupy a level at any time.

- You don't need to load movies (or JPGs) into sequential levels. (For example, you can load a movie into Level 50 even if Levels 1 through 49 are empty.)

- The content of movies on higher levels appears above the content from levels below it. (In other words, the content of a movie on Level 10 will appear above all content on Levels 9 and lower.)

- The frame rate of the movie loaded into Level 0 takes precedence, dictating the rate at which all movies in the Flash player window will play. (For example, if the movie on Level 0 were set to play at 24 frames per second and an external movie, with a frame rate of 12 fps, is loaded into a target or level, the externally loaded movie's frame rate will be sped up to match that of the movie on Level 0.) Be sure to set similar frame rates when authoring your various movies; otherwise, you may get unexpected results in the final product.

- If you load a movie into Level 0, every level in the Flash Player will be automatically unloaded (removed), and Level 0 will be replaced with the new file.

In this exercise, we'll enable our project to randomly load banner movies into levels.

1) Open virtualaquarium4.fla in the Lesson17/Assets folder.

This is the file we worked on in the previous exercise. In this exercise, we'll add additional script to Frame 1. Because we'll be loading our banner movies into levels, as opposed to targets, you don't need to use any of the elements in the current scene to make the process work. A rectangular graphic (with an instance name of **bannerback**) has been added to the scene for design purposes.

Before going any farther, let's once again review the contents of the directory that contains our externally loaded assets.

2) Using your operating system's directory-exploring application, navigate to the Lesson17/Assets directory.

Locate the following movies:

- banner0.swf
- banner1.swf
- banner2.swf

Our project will be set up to randomly load one of these simple animated movies (each of which is 200 pixels W by 60 pixels H) into a level.

3) Return to Flash. With the Actions panel open, select Frame 1 of the Actions layer and add the following line of script just below where you created the `slides` array in the previous exercise:

```
banners = new Array("banner0.swf", "banner1.swf", "banner2.swf");
```

This creates a new array, named `banners`, which holds the paths to our external banner movies.

Now let's create a function that will randomly load one of these banner movies into our project.

4) Place the following function definition just below the `changeSlide()` function definition:

```
function randomBanner() {
  randomNumber = random (banners.length);
  loadMovieNum (banners[randomNumber], 1);
}
```

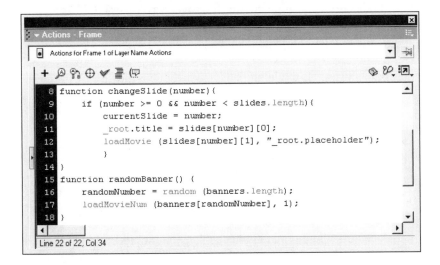

This creates a function named `randomBanner()` that works similarly to the `randomBackground()` function we set up in the first exercise in this lesson. Notice the slightly different name of the action that executes the loading function (`loadMovieNum()`), as well as the fact that we've indicated that it should load the movie into Level 1. Each time this function is called, a random banner is loaded into Level 1, replacing the one already there.

5) Place the following function call just below the `changeSlide()` function call:

```
randomBanner();
```

This function call is used to load the initial banner when the movie begins playing. Next, to make better use of the function, we'll use a `setInterval()` action to automatically call this function on a regular basis.

6) Place the following line of script just below the `randomBanner()` function call:

```
setInterval(randomBanner, 10000);
```

Using the `setInterval()` action, we've scripted the `randomBanner()` function to execute every 10,000 milliseconds (once every 10 seconds). This will provide our project with rotating banner functionality. You can use the `setInterval()` action to call any function or object method on a regular, timed basis.

7) Choose Control > Test Movie.

As soon as the movie begins to play, a random banner is loaded into the project. The main movie is loaded into Level 0 automatically, while the banner is set to load into Level 1—which means it's loaded above everything else in the project. If you replay the movie, chances are a different banner will load. As you will notice, however, there's a problem: The banner's position on the stage isn't correct; it should appear above the white rectangular box.

The reason for this is that the banner movie's top-left corner (its registration point) will, by default, load at a position of 0x and 0y in relation to the registration point of the movie on Level 0. In essence, the top-left corner of the loaded movie is automatically aligned to the top-left corner of the movie on Level 0. This is true of any movie loaded into any level.

However, because our banner movie is only 200W by 60H, a spacing discrepancy exists when it's loaded into a 550W by 400H movie. When the banner movie is loaded, it needs to be repositioned directly above the white rectangle on the stage—something we'll correct in the next exercise.

8) Close the test movie, and save the file as virtualaquarium5.fla.
This completes this exercise. We'll continue to build on this file in the following exercises.

CONTROLLING A MOVIE ON A LEVEL

You can control a movie loaded into a level from another timeline or from within itself. You'll remember from Lesson 3 that the target path to a movie loaded into a level is simply its level number. For example, if you've loaded a movie into Level 5, you would use the following syntax to make it rotate from any other timeline currently in the player window:

```
_level5._rotation = 45;
```

Pretty straightforward and simple.

It's also easy to place an action on Frame 1 of a loaded movie so that it does something immediately upon loading. We'll look at both approaches in the following exercise, in which we'll script our banner movies to reposition themselves correctly upon loading as well as create a banner On/Off button.

1) Open virtualaquarium5.fla in the Lesson17/Assets folder.

This is the file we worked on in the previous exercise. Take note of the white rectangle on the stage: This is a movie clip instance named **bannerBack**. The location of this instance's registration point (top left of the instance) will be pivotal in a script that repositions the banner movies when they're loaded into Level 1. Because this repositioning script will reside within the banner movies, we need to open the banner movie authoring files.

2) Choose File › Open. Navigate to the Lesson17/Assets folder, locate the file named banner0.fla, and open it in Flash.

This simple animated movie is made up of five layers, the top of which is named Actions. We'll place a two-line script on Frame 1 so that as soon as the banner movie is loaded, the script is executed.

3) With the Actions panel open, select Frame 1 of the Actions layer and add the following script:

```
_x = _level0.bannerBack._x;
_y = _level0.bannerBack._y;
```

These two lines of script set the *x* and *y* properties of this movie to match the *x* and *y* properties of the **bannerBack** movie clip instance on Level 0. This will cause the banner movie to load exactly on top of the **bannerBack** instance, even if it's eventually moved from its current location.

4) Add this same script to Frame 1 of the other banner movies (banner1.fla and banner2.fla). Then re-export them as banner0.swf, banner1.swf, and banner2.swf, respectively.

582

5) Return to virtualaquarium5.fla. Choose Control > Test Movie.

Once again, a random banner is loaded. However, this time it loads at the proper location. If you wait ten seconds, a different banner may load, also at the proper location in relation to **bannerBack**.

Since you can't attach an `onClipEvent()` to a movie loaded into a level, this is the best approach for triggering an action to occur as soon as the movie loads.

6) Close the test movie to return to the authoring file (virtualaquarium5.fla).

The banner movie loaded into Level 1 can easily be controlled from this movie as well. We will next script a button to demonstrate this.

7) With the Actions panel open, select the button with the text 'Banner On/Off' and add the following script:

```
on(release) {
  _level1._visible = !_level1._visible;
  bannerBack._visible = !bannerBack._visible;
}
```

This script creates a toggling functionality that makes both the banner movie loaded into Level 1 and the **bannerBack** movie clip instance either visible or invisible, depending on its current state. This syntax (use of the NOT (!) operator) provides a quick and easy way to reverse Boolean values of any kind.

8) Choose Control > Test Movie.

Press the On/Off button several times to test its functionality. Wait 10 seconds for the banner to change. The button will continue to work because it's set up to control the movie loaded into Level 1 rather than a particular banner movie.

9) Close the test movie. Save the file as virtualaquarium6.fla.

This completes the exercise. We'll continue to build on this file in the following exercises.

NOTE *Security issues can arise when loading files from different domains into a single Player window. There are a few restrictions to be aware of. For example, if a movie at www.derekfranklin.com/derekMovie.swf is being played, and it contains an action to load a movie located at www.electrotank.com/jobeMovie.swf into Level 5, these two movies initially will not be able to exchange data via ActionScript, since they were loaded from different domains. A permission setting for allowing movies loaded from different domain's to access each other's data can be used to override this restriction. In this scenario, if derekMovie.swf contains the setting (placed on Frame1): System.security.allowDomain("www.electrotank.com"), then jobeMovie.swf (loaded from electrotank.com) will have access to the data in derekMovie.swf. If jobeMovie.swf contains the setting: System.security.allowDomain("www.derekfranklin.com") then derekMovie.swf (loaded from derekfranklin.com) will have access to the data in jobeMovie.swf. This restriction does not exist for movies loaded from the same domain.*

Thus far, we've concentrated on loading and controlling graphical content. However, any good Flash developer knows that graphics are just a part of any great multimedia project. You also need sound. However, sound contributes significantly to file size, which means smart sound management is key. In the next two exercises, we'll show you how to use audio in your projects to your heart's content (well, almost)!

LOADING MP3S DYNAMICALLY

MP3s are everywhere these days—a popularity that can be attributed to the fact that they provide an acceptable way of delivering audio (especially music) over the Web in a low-bandwidth world. Although MP3s are much more compact than standard, noncompressed audio files, a single MP3 of any length (let alone several) can still balloon a movie's file size to an unacceptable level.

Flash, however, helps alleviate this problem by providing the ability to *dynamically* load MP3 files into movies. As you'll soon see, loading an external MP3 into our project is a bit different than loading an external movie or JPG—but almost as easy.

If you want to load an MP3 into Flash, the first thing you need to do is create a place where you can load it. This requires a Sound object:

```
myFavMP3 = new Sound();
```

Once you've created a Sound object, you simply use the loadSound() method to load an external MP3 into that object, as in following syntax:

```
myFavMP3.loadSound("mySong.mp3", true);
```

This loads the external MP3 file named mySong.mp3 into the myFavMP3 Sound object. Once the MP3 has been loaded, you can control volume, panning, and other characteristics (see Lesson 16, Scripting Sound). You'll notice that the loadSound() method has two parameters: The first one identifies the path to the external MP3, while the other determines whether the loaded file will be streamed (true) or instead considered an event sound (false). If this parameter is set to true, the externally loaded file will begin playing as soon as a sufficient amount has been downloaded. If set to false, the start() method must be invoked before the file will play:

```
myFavMP3.start();
```

NOTE *If the file is loaded as an event sound, it will not play (even if you invoke the start() method) until the complete file has been downloaded.*

In this exercise, we'll make it possible for each loaded image in the slide show to have an associated music track, which is loaded externally.

1) Open virtualaquarium6.fla in the Lesson17/Assets folder.

This is the file we worked on in the previous exercise. In this exercise, we'll simply add additional script to Frame 1.

Before going any further, let's once again review the contents of the directory that holds our externally loaded assets.

2) Navigate to the Lesson17/Assets directory.

Locate the following MP3 files and make a note of their names:

- music0.mp3
- music1.mp3
- music2.mp3

3) Return to Flash. With the Actions panel open, select Frame 1 of the Actions layer and modify the `slides` **array as shown:**

```
slides = new Array(["Shark", "image0.jpg", "music0.mp3"], ["Jellyfish",
"image1.jpg", "music1.mp3"], ["Seahorse", "image2.jpg", "music2.mp3"]);
```

Here, you'll see that the path/name of an MP3 file has been added to each element in the array.

Next, we'll alter the `changeSlide()` function (which we defined in an earlier exercise) to make use of this new data.

4) Add the following lines of script to the end of (but within) the *if* statement of the `changeSlide()` **function definition:**

```
slideSound.stop();
slideSound = new Sound();
slideSound.loadSound(slides[number][2], true);
```

You'll remember that the `changeSlide()` function is set up to load a new JPG image when called. The image that's loaded will depend on the number passed to the function when it's called. This number's value is evaluated and used to pull specific values out of the `slides` array. By adding the MP3 files' path names to the `slides` array and including the above three lines of script, we've extended the ability of this function so that when it's called and an image is loaded, the associated MP3 file will be loaded as well.

The first action stops the slideSound Sound object from playing—an action that's ignored the first time the function is called because the slideSound Sound object does not get created until the next line (since it's intended for use once a sound is playing and a new sound is loaded). This stop() action ensures that when a new sound is loaded into the slideSound Sound object, the old sound does not continue to be heard. This prevents one sound from "walking over" another.

The next line actually creates a new Sound object named slideSound. This object is simply recreated/reinitialized each time the changeSlide() function is called.

Using the loadSound() action, the next line loads the external MP3 into this Sound object. In the first parameter of this action, the value of number is evaluated to determine which MP3 file to load, as defined in the slides array. The second parameter indicates that the loaded file is set to stream; thus, the file will begin playing as soon as sufficient data has been downloaded.

Since we've just appended the way this function works, and we previously scripted a call to it, the sound should load and play as soon as the movie begins playing.

5) Choose Control > Test Movie.

As soon as the movie plays, the image in the panel is loaded and the associated music file is loaded and begins to play. If you advance the slide show by pressing the right-arrow button, not only does the image change, but a new sound file is loaded as well.

6) Close the test movie. Save the file as virtualaquarium7.fla.

This completes the exercise. We will continue to build on this file in the following exercises.

REACTING TO DYNAMICALLY LOADED MP3S

Want to trigger a set of actions to execute when a sound has finished playing? Want to know a sound's duration (play length) or current position (playback position)? Flash provides you with precisely this type of dynamic control when it comes to using loaded MP3s (or even internally attached sounds).

NOTE *Many of the ways sounds can be controlled dynamically were discussed in Lesson 16, Scripting for Sound.*

First, a brief explanation of how these actions work.

It's often useful to know when a sound will finish playing. Consider, for example, a presentation where the next screen of info should only be displayed once the voice-over has finished explaining the current screen. Or how about a music jukebox that automatically loads the next song once the current one has finished playing. You can easily achieve this type of functionality by using the `onSoundComplete` event handler. As is the case with other event handler methods, you can use two types of syntax, the first of which is as follows:

```
mySoundObject.onSoundComplete = function(){
  //actions go here…
}
```

Using this syntax, you would directly define a series of actions to be triggered when the event occurs. The second syntax looks like the following:

```
mySoundObject.onSoundComplete = mySoundFunction;
```

Using this syntax, you would define the name of the function that should be executed once the event occurs—useful if that function is employed elsewhere (that is, called from other sources in your movie) and you simply want to make a call to it when the event is triggered.

NOTE *A Sound object must exist in your movie before you can define an `onSoundComplete` event handler to it. If you delete or re-create the Sound object, you must redefine the `onSoundComplete` event. In other words, you can't attach an event to an object that doesn't exist, and once an object has been deleted or re-created, the attached event ceases to exist as well.*

NOTE *There is also an `onLoad` event handler that you can use in similar fashion to the `onSoundComplete` handler just described. Its purpose is to trigger a function when a loaded sound has finished loading. This event is only triggered if the loaded sound is set to load as an Event sound. Unfortunately, the beta version of the program we were using at the time of this writing produced unexpected results. Look for this event to function properly in the release version.*

A sound's duration is a property of any Sound object, representing the sound's length (in milliseconds). Accessing this property's value is accomplished in the following manner:

```
myVariable = mySoundObject.duration;
```

The above script sets the value of `myVariable` to the duration of the sound currently in the referenced Sound object. If the sound were 5.5 seconds long, the value of `myVariable` would be set to 5500 (1000 x 5.5). This property exists for loaded sounds as well as ones attached to the Sound object using `attachSound()`.

You can determine how far a sound has progressed in its playback by using the following syntax:

```
myVariable = mySoundObject.position;
```

If the sound in the referenced Sound object has been playing for three seconds, `myVariable` will be set to a value of 3000 (1000 x 3).

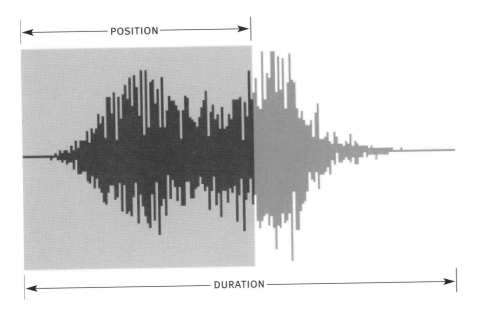

In this exercise, we'll use the `onSoundComplete` event to trigger a function. We'll also employ the `duration` and `position` properties of the Sound object to create a playback progress bar.

1) Open virtualaquarium7.fla in the Lesson17/Assets folder.

This is the file we worked on in the previous exercise. In this exercise we'll add additional script to Frame 1, as well as add a simple script to the **progress** movie clip instance (which is below the panel graphic).

2) With the Actions panel open, select Frame 1 of the Actions layer and add the following lines of script to the end of (but within) the *if* statement of the `changeSlide()` function definition:

```
slideSound.onSoundComplete = function(){
    changeSlide(currentSlide + 1);
}
```

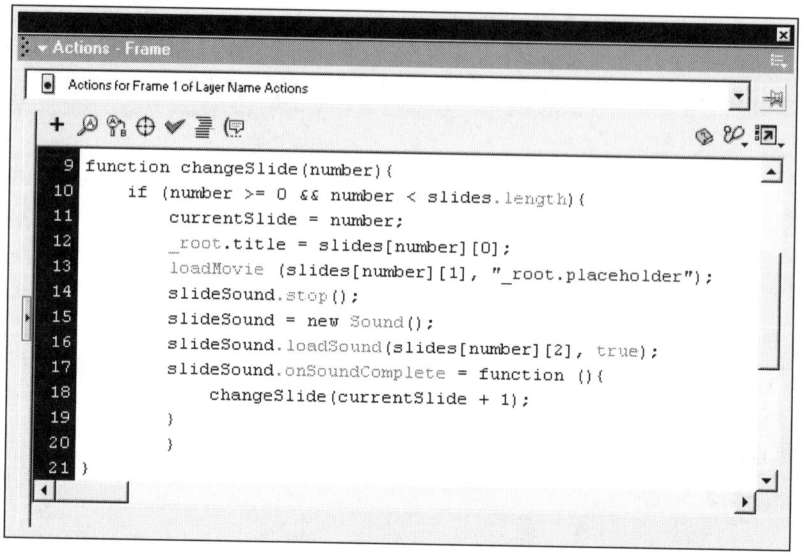

This defines what should occur when the sound loaded into the `slideSound` Sound object has finished playing. You'll see that a call is made to the `changeSlide()` function. This acts as an automatic advancing mechanism for the slide show: As soon as a sound has finished playing, the next image and sound are loaded.

Let's finish the exercise by scripting the playback progress bar. First, however, let's look at its structure.

3) Double-click the *progress* movie clip instance to edit it in place.

This movie clip is made up of three layers. We're most interested in the bottom layer, named bar, which contains a 100-frame tween. If you drag the playhead, you'll see that this tween is set up to emulate a progress bar with a range of 0 to 100 percent. In a moment, we'll add a script to move this timeline to the appropriate frame based on the percentage of the sound file that has played. In other words, if 47 percent of the sound file has played, this clip will be at Frame 47, showing the appropriate progress.

590

4) Return to the main timeline. With the Actions panel open, select the _progress_ movie clip instance and attach the following script:

```
onClipEvent(enterFrame){
  progressamount = Math.round(((_root.slideSound.position /
_root.slideSound.duration) * 100));
  gotoAndStop(progressAmount);
  if (progressAmount == 100){
    _visible = false;
  }else{
    _visible = true;
  }
}
```

By now, this script should be fairly familiar. Every `enterFrame` event, the value of `progressAmount` is updated to a percentage value between 0 and 100. This percentage value is determined by evaluating the current `position` and `duration` values of the `slideSound` Sound object, then rounding the result. This value is next used to move the instance's timeline to the appropriate frame, all of which emulates the functionality of a progress bar.

The `if/else` statement is used to make the progress bar invisible when `progressAmount` has a value of 100, as when the last image/sound has been shown/played. Anytime this value is less than 100 (whenever a sound is still playing), the progress bar will be visible.

5) Choose Control > Test Movie.

If you let the project play by itself, you'll see that once the first loaded sound finishes playing, the project automatically advances to the next image/sound, then repeats this process. Notice that the progress bar tracks the playback of the sound as well.

After the third image/sound has loaded and finished playing, the presentation stops and the progress bar disappears because there is no more content to load, as defined in the `slides` array. Only by pressing the left-arrow button can you bring the presentation to life again.

6) Close the test movie. Save the file as virtualaquarium8.fla.

This completes the exercise—and this lesson!

You've now created a fairly sophisticated project that loads external assets and can be easily scaled to include an almost limitless amount of external content. By loading content into a movie as it plays, you need never worry about huge files or stale content again.

This also marks the end of the book. Congratulations! You now have a very strong grasp of not only *what* ActionScript allows you to do with your projects, but more importantly, *how* to use it to implement fairly complex interactivity in your own unique projects.

Although we've covered a lot of ground in these seventeen lessons, you should continue to hone your skills as a scripter. ActionScript is a very extensive scripting language, therefore it is impossible for us to cover every use or possibility. This is where your creativity comes into play. As mentioned at the very beginning of the book, while most people might not see it as such, scripting is an art, where your task is to develop creative solutions for the task at hand. You now have a great foundation for doing so.

You'll continue on your own to learn powerful ways of accomplishing tasks using ActionScript, but it's also important to look at the code of scripters with a bit more experience than yourself. Doing so will give you insight to how those with years of scripting experience approach a task, and you'll learn many new tricks that you can use in your own work to make it more efficient and fun. That's the keyword, 'fun'! You'll find that the more you know how to use ActionScript, the more you'll enjoy doing things with it. So get out there and show the world what you can do.

WHAT YOU HAVE LEARNED

In this lesson, you have:

- Learned why and how external assets can enable you to deliver more dynamic projects (pages 556–560)

- Loaded a random external SWF into a target (pages 560–565)

- Created a scalable slide-show presentation using external JPGs (pages 565–572)

- Learned what an interactive placeholder is and how to use one in a project (pages 572–577)

- Created a rotating Flash banner system by loading external movies into a level (pages 577–580)

- Controlled a movie loaded into a level from within its own timeline as well as from another timeline (pages 581–584)

- Dynamically loaded MP3s into a project while it plays (pages 584–587)

- Created and used a function that automatically is called using the `onSoundComplete` event handler (pages 587–590)

- Scripted an MP3 playback progress bar using the `duration` and `position` properties of the Sound object (pages 590–592)

resources

DEREKFRANKLIN.COM

http://www.derekfranklin.com/

Description: derekfranklin.com is an evolving resource that's all about learning and using Flash creatively. Here you'll find unique information about Flash that goes beyond the run-of-the-mill Flash resources that you normally find on the Web. In addition, you'll find support for this book. Join the newsletter while you're there in order to learn new ideas and new ways to use Flash MX.

ELECTROTANK.COM

http://www.electrotank.com

Description: electrotank is not so much a site that teaches you how to use Flash, but one that shows you what can be accomplished with it. It has some amazing award-winning games that you can easily spend hours of time with. If you're into creating Flash games, this site will provide you with some great inspiration. It's also one of the most visited Flash sites on the Web.

FLASHKIT

http://www.flashkit.com

Description: Flashkit is the largest Flash resource site on the Internet. With thousands of source files and highly active user boards, Flash developers are sure to find help on anything Flash. One drawback of Flashkit is that it may have too many source files with no garbage control. While there are many great files, there are also many not-so-great ones, so finding what you want may take a while.

WE'RE HERE

http://www.were-here.com

Description: This site is very similar to Flashkit in the type of user support that it offers, but there are some differences. We're Here has hundreds of source files to offer but most people use this Web site for the great boards. If you are looking for specific FLA examples, you may be better off looking elsewhere, but if written help is what you need, then this is the place to be.

ULTRASHOCK

http://www.ultrashock.com

Description: Ultrashock provides an advanced level of source files, forums, games and cartoons, tutorials and more. What sets Ultrashock apart from other Flash resource sites is that it is geared toward the advanced programmer and each source file is screened for quality and uniqueness before it is offered to the public. If you are looking for help on advanced topics or just need a good example of an advanced FLA file, then this is the place to go. You won't have to spend hours sifting through garbage to find the treasures.

POCKETPCFLASH.NET

http://www.pocketpcflash.net/

Description: If you need help or information on developing Flash content for Pocket PC devices, then this is the place to go. PocketpcFlash.net provides tutorials, FAQs, and source files to help you get started.

MOTIONCULTURE

http://www.motionculture.org

Description: This resource site provides source files and user boards that cover many topics. MotionCulture is unique in that it provides resources on many non-Flash topics, such as HTML, CGI, and Photoshop. If you need help in more than one area of Flash design, then this may be a useful place for you.

MOOCK.ORG

http://www.moock.org/webdesign/flash/index.html

Description: Here you will find brilliant tutorials and learn some of the best programming practices. This site is not a one-stop shop for all of your Flash needs, but it will certainly meet a few needs more than any of the other resource sites can. For instance, you will find the best Flash detection script on the Internet on this site.

index

. (dot) syntax, 11–12, 20, 74
?: operator, 289–290
; (semicolon), 11, 313
-- operator, 268, 317
{ } (curly braces), 11, 13
- operator, 268
/ operator, 268
( ) (parentheses), 12, 126, 269
" " (quotation marks), 12, 266, 422
[ ] (square brackets), 255, 256
\ (backward-slash mark), 422
// (forward-slash marks), 12
!= operator, 286
% operator, 268
& operator, 338
&& operator, 286
* operator, 268
+ operator, 24, 267, 269
++ operator, 268, 316, 325
+= operator, 79
< operator, 24
= operator, 21, 24, 338
== operator, 286
> operator, 286
>= operator, 286
ll operator, 286
@ symbol, 409
_ (underscore), 125

A
absence detection, 55
absolute target paths, 86, 101, 107
absolute-value method, 271, 275
Access databases, 376
Accessibility object, 129
actions, 10, 310, 312
Actions panel, 3, 19, 128–129

ActionScript
  benefits of learning/using, 8
  dictionary, 76, 128
  elements, 8–13
  mixing with HTML, 424
  objects, 124 (*See also* objects)
  purpose of, 1
  resources, 594–595
Activation object, 184
addition operator, 267, 269, 326
AddUser.asp, 376
alarm clock. *See clock* movie clip
alphaAmount text field, 114–115
ampersand, 286, 338
AND operator, 286
animation tools, 8
application development tools, 336
Aquarium exercise, 556–557, 561–587
AquaServer, 384
arguments, passing, 152
arithmetic operators, 267–268
Array constructor, 129
Array object, 129, 244
arrays
  associative, 315
  copying contents between, 312
  creating, 129, 243–248, 332
  dynamically pulling values from, 259
  placing in objects, 178
  purpose of, 129
  setting values for, 267
  and shared objects, 358
  storing, 125
arrow movie clip, 77, 79
ASP pages, 339, 344, 345, 370, 376
Assets folder, 2
associative array, 315
attachMovie() method, 453–457, 458–462, 479

attributes, node, 369
audio clips, 526
Authoring object, 129
autoSize property, 429

B

backward-slash marks, 422
ball movie clip, 68–69, 71–72
Balloon exercise, 140–143
Banner exercise, 557, 578–584
barGraph movie clips, 351
base 10 numbers, 136
Basketball exercise, 524–525, 528–554
Best of 2001 exercise, 344–352
Boolean object, 129
Boolean values, 239, 266
borderColor property, 429
bottomScroll property, 430
bounce **Sound object**, 535, 536, 537
boundaries, 295–298, 530–535, 538–540, 544–545
braces. *See* curly braces
break action, 330–331, 334
bugs, 27, 28
bump movie clip, 42, 44
burglar movie clip, 57–67
Button object, 130
buttons
    assigning instance names to, 45–46
    changing hit area for, 46
    changing transparency of, 45
    continuous-feedback, 462–469
    event handler methods for, 75
    as part of timeline, 46
    timeline playback, 515–517
    treating movie clips as, 45, 46

C

cableBox movie clip, 167, 169
calls, function, 150, 154, 155, 168–170, 267
canvas movie clip, 472–475, 488
Capabilities object, 130
car movie clip, 77, 79, 81
Car Parts exercise, 77–82
card movie clip, 43–44
cascading style sheets, 437
CD, book's enclosed, 2
CFM, 339
CGI, 339
changeSlide() function, 570–571, 586
changeTemp() function, 276
Character Options dialog box, 251
Chat exercise, 366, 377–382, 386–394
child movies, 96–100, 118, 453
child nodes, 369
child objects, 179, 180

class definitions, 182–183, 186, 190, 192
classes, object
    contrasted with instances, 174
    creating, 182–187
    creating custom methods for, 198–203
    creating subclasses of, 192–198, 220
    defined, 127
    enhancing methods for, 211–216
    naming, 183
    registering, 220–234
clear() method, 489
clearContent() function, 491–492
Client/Server object, 129
clip events, 54–67
    descriptions of specific, 55–56
    exercise, 57–67
    purpose of, 54
    using inside *vs.* outside timelines, 92–93
    visual representation of, 56
clock movie clip, 505–506, 509, 512
Clown Hair exercise, 136–140
code, reusing, 150–151
code blocks, 13
collisions
    naming, 120, 165
    object, 306–308, 312
Color object, 126, 127, 130, 135–140
colors, randomly generating, 139
colors movie clip, 112–117
comments, 12
communication, timeline, 84–85, 86
comparison operators, 286
Completed folder, 2
composition, object, 197–198
computer
    identifying capabilities of, 130
    minimum system requirements, 5
computer-based interaction, 55
concatenation operator, 24, 268–269, 280
conditional logic, 282–309. *See also* if statements
    controlling flow of scripts with, 284–290
    defining boundaries with, 295–298
    detecting collisions with, 306–308
    operators used in, 286
    purpose of, 282–283
    reacting to multiple conditions with, 291–295
    reacting to user interaction with, 303–306
    turning scripts on/off with, 298–303
    validating data with, 399, 401
    variations on typical statements, 289–290
conditions
    defined, 282
    list of common, 290
    reacting to multiple, 291–295
    writing loop, 316–322

Confirm exercise, 420–427
Construct a Face exercise, 172, 175–234
constructor functions, 182, 192, 196, 438
constructors, 128, 135, 144
containers, 175, 179
continue action, 330
continuous-feedback buttons, 462–469
controller movie clip, 479–483, 483
conversions
    number, 127, 136
    temperature, 264, 271–276
Convert to Symbol window, 456
cookies, 339, 352
Core object, 128
createEmptyMovieClip() method, 457–458
createTextField() method, 427
credit card numbers, validating, 409
CSS, 437
cue ball. *See ball* movie clip
curly braces, 11, 13
current movie, targeting, 88–94
currentframe property, 519
custom classes, 182–187, 198–203, 220
custom messages, 24
custom methods, 198–203, 216–219
custom objects
    creating, 132, 174–175, 182–192
    and event handler methods, 75
    naming, 128

D

data
    defined, 10
    dynamic (*See* dynamic data)
    loading across domains, 340
    loading from external sources, 56, 338, 339–340
    manipulating, 264–265, 271–281
    retrieving from storage, 255–263
    sending/receiving, 336
    tracking, 14, 132
    types of, 266
    validating, 312, 396–418
data clip event, 56
data formats, 338–339
data sources, 14, 338, 339–340
data transfer, 338
date
    determining current, 497–502
    validating, 409
Date object, 130, 496, 497–498
decrement operator, 268, 317
depth, movie clip, 452–453, 479
derekfranklin.com, 594
developer resources, 594–595
dictionary, ActionScript, 76, 128

division operator, 268, 269
dot syntax, 11–12, 20, 74
_down frame label, 46
Dr. Frankenstein exercise, 192–198, 202–203
drag-and-drop behaviors, 484–489, 530–535
dragOut event, 37, 41, 43, 70
dragOver event, 37, 43
draw() function, 475
Drawing exercise, 472–476
drawing methods, 470–476
drop-down lists, 312, 317–322, 414
droptarget property, 484
duplicateMovieClip() method, 213–215, 450–453, 454, 479
duration property, 588, 591
dynamic content, 556
dynamic data, 236–263
    creating arrays, 243–248
    creating text fields, 248–254
    creating variables, 238–243
    retrieving, 255–263
    and SWF files, 236
    ways of using, 236
dynamic input, 448
dynamic objects, 77, 117
Dynamic Sounds folder, 549, 550
dynamic text, 248, 249, 251, 418–427
dynamically drawn lines, 470–472, 489–492

E

"effect" clips, 97
Electric Bill exercise, 6–7, 13–31
ElectroServer, 384
electrotank.com, 594
elements
    creating global references to, 118–120
    descriptions of, 8–13
    sharing among timelines, 117
else/else if statements, 23, 25, 287–288
email addresses, validating, 410–413
energy, giving objects, 55
enterFrame clip event, 55, 62–63, 71, 142, 462
equals sign, 21, 24, 286, 338
errors
    script, 27
    target path, 241
    validation, 401–403
escape sequence, 422–423
European Vacation slide show, 47–54
event handler methods, 73–82
    additional information on, 76
    and custom objects, 75
    and dynamically created objects, 77
    purpose of, 35, 73–74
    and target paths, 74
    using, 75–82

event handlers, 32–83
  choosing, 34
  for clip events, 54–67
  extending functionality of, 35, 73
  for frame events, 47–54
  for mouse events, 35–46
  purpose of, 32, 34
events
  "broadcasting" with listeners, 82
  defined, 9
  extending functionality of, 73
  orchestrating multiple, 68–73
exceptions, loop, 330–335
exercises. *See also* projects
  Aquarium, 556–557, 561–587
  Banner, 557, 578–584
  Basketball, 524–525, 528–554
  Best of 2001, 344–352
  Car Parts, 77–82
  Chat, 366, 377–382, 386–394
  Clown Hair, 136–140
  Confirmation Page, 420–427
  Construct a Face, 172, 175–234
  Dr. Frankenstein, 192–198, 202–203
  Drawing, 472–476
  Electric Bill, 7, 13–31
  Fingerprint Scanner, 37–45
  FlashWriter, 432–437
  Head, 172, 175–234
  Hot-Air Balloon, 140–143
  Login Register, 367, 377–382
  Mad Libs, 277–281
  Make My Day, 494, 498–513, 515–519
  My Journal, 336, 357–364
  News Flash, 236, 242–248, 252–63
  NotSoSoft, 396, 402–427
  Orchestrate Events, 68–73
  Person Object/Class, 175–192, 199–203
  Phone Book, 311, 330–335
  Picture Show, 310, 317–330
  Polling System, 344–352
  Preloader, 519–522
  Product Registration, 396, 402–420
  Rocket Launch, 282–283, 291–308
  Scrolling List, 458–469
  Self-Running Presentation, 47–54
  Slide Show, 47–54, 566–572
  Temperature Converter, 264, 271–276
  Therapy Chat, 366, 377–382, 386–394
  TV Remote Control, 154–170
  Virtual Aquarium, 556–557, 561–587
  Word Game, 277–281
  Word Processor, 145–149
  Yummi Cola, 556
Expert Mode, Actions panel, 19

expressions, 266–270, 326
eXtensible Markup Language. *See* XML
external assets, 556–593
  benefits of loading, 558–559, 592
  controlling on levels, 581–584
  and interactive placeholders, 572
  loading into levels, 577–581
  loading JPGs dynamically, 565–572
  loading movies into targets, 560–565
  loading MP3s dynamically, 584–587
  and preloaders, 564
  responding to MP3s, 587–591
  security considerations, 584
  types of, 556

F

Face exercise, 172, 175–234
false/true values, 71, 72, 127, 239, 266. *See also* conditional logic
fanClip **movie clip**, 78, 80
FAQs, 595
fast-forward button. *See* FF button
FF button, 515, 516, 517
Figleaf Software, 384
files
  JPG/JPEG, 560, 565–572, 577, 578
  lesson, 2–3
  MP3, 524, 560, 584–592
  SWF (*See* SWF files)
  text, 339
  XML, 338–339, 340
filled shapes, 476–479
Fingerprint Scanner exercise, 37–45
Flash
  as animation tool, 8
  as application development tool, 8, 336
  introductory book on, 3
  objects (*See* objects)
  resources, 2, 594–595
  and XML (*See* XML)
Flash Application Services, 352
Flash MX: Training from the Source, 3
Flash player, 356
Flashkit, 594
FlashWriter exercise, 432–437
flat fills, 476, 477
flip() method, 217
focusing, on fields, 79, 145
font property, 440
for . . in loop, 314–315
for loop, 313–314
formats, data, 338–339
formatting, dynamic text, 418–427
forward-slash marks, 12
fps, 513, 578

frame events, 34, 47–54
frame labels, 46, 57, 58
frames, 496, 519
frames per second, 513, 578
_framesloaded property, 519, 522
Frankenstein exercise, 192–198, 202–203
Franklin, Derek, 594
functions, 150–171
    calling, 150, 154, 155, 168–170, 267
    creating, 152–157
    defining, 155, 278
    and event handler methods, 74
    executing as functions *vs.* instances, 182
    passing arguments/parameters to, 152, 157–165
    purpose of, 150–151
    returning results from, 166–170
    using local variables in, 165–170, 201
    for validating data, 399–400

G

games, 594
GET method, 340–341, 349
getBytesLoaded() method, 522
getByteTotals() method, 522
getFontList() method, 442
getNewTextFormat() method, 440
getTextFormat() method, 440
getTimer() function, 496, 502–504, 506, 508, 513
global class definitions, 186
global elements, 118–120
global objects, 129, 140
gradient fills, 476, 477–479
greater-than (>) operator, 286

H

hair **movie clip**, 136–140
Hall, Branden, 384
hand **movie clip**, 39, 43
hard-coded text, 236
hardware. *See* computer
Hatfield **movie clips**, 89, 97–100, 102
Head exercise, 172, 175–234
hexadecimal numbers, 136
Hide Layer button, 59
hierarchy, timeline, 86–88
highlighting, text, 145, 148
highScoreList object, 356
hitAmount value, 69, 71–72
hitTest() method, 227, 484
Hot-Air Balloon exercise, 140–143
hScroll property, 430
HTML-formatted text, 249, 339, 387, 418–427
HTML tags, 368–369, 418, 437
hyperlinks, 424

I

icon **movie clip**, 483–487
icons **movie clip**, 223–225, 228, 230, 231
identifier names, 224, 228, 550
identities, multiple, 118
if/else if statements, 287
if/else statements, 288, 289
if statements
    and control of script's flow, 284–290
    and Electric Bill exercise, 23–24
    and mode values, 218
    and mouse movements, 64, 72
    nesting, 301
    and validation routines, 399–401, 405, 407
increment operator, 268, 316, 325
indentation, 12–13
indexOf() method, 144, 411
indicator **movie clip**, 47, 51
inequality operator, 286
info array, 332–333
infobar **movie clip**, 460–461
inheritance, object, 197–198, 212, 488
initialization, 47, 230–231, 257
input text, 248, 249, 250–251
inside clips, 92–93
instance-level properties, 188, 190–192
instance names
    assigning to buttons, 45–46
    assigning to movie clips, 101
    identifying text fields with, 18
instances
    attaching, 453–457, 458–462
    changing z-order of, 479–483
    contrasted with classes of objects, 174
    contrasted with global objects, 129, 140
    creating, 174, 182–187
    creating drag-and-drop, 484–489
    creating dynamically, 450–458
    creating empty, 457–458
    duplicating, 450–451
    removing, 489–492
    universal characteristics of, 187
instructions, receiving, 56
interactive placeholders, 572–577
interactivity
    and clip events, 55
    and conditional logic, 282–283, 303
    and event handlers, 34
    and Key objects, 140–143
    and multiple events, 68–73
    tools for creating, 8
isDown() method, 140
isNan() function, 28, 405

J

Java 2 Runtime Environment, 384
Java-based socket server, 384
JavaScript, 1
Journal exercise, 336, 357–364
JPG/JPEG files, 560, 565–572, 577, 578
JRE, 384
JSP, 339

K

key events, capturing, 140
Key object, 131, 140–143
keyboard, determining state of keys on, 131
keyboard-control events, 36
keyboard shortcuts, 55
keyDown clip event, 55, 67
keyPress event, 36, 44
keyUp clip event, 55, 67
keywords, 10

L

labels, frame, 46, 57, 58
Launch exercise. *See* Rocket Launch exercise
length property, 277, 328
less-than (<) operator, 24, 286
lessons
    files for, 2–3
    knowledge required for, 3
    list of, 1–2
    minimum system requirements, 5
letter index, 144
levels
    controlling movies on, 581–584
    loading movies into, 104–107, 577–581
    purpose of, 104
    targeting, 100, 104–117
libraries, sharing, 455
Library panel, 232, 549
lights movie clip, 59, 62, 64, 66
lines, dynamically drawn, 470–472
lineStyle() method, 470
lineTo() method, 471–472
linkage, 455–456
Linkage Properties dialog box, 224, 232, 550
listeners, 82
lists
    drop-down, 312, 317–322, 414
    scrolling, 462–469
load clip event, 55, 61–62, 64, 207
load() method, 339, 349
loadMovie() action, 86, 104, 560, 565–566
loadMovieNum() action, 560, 578
loadSound() action, 560, 585
loadVariables() method, 339, 344
LoadVars object, 75, 131, 339, 342–352

local variables, 165–166, 201
Logical AND/OR operators, 286
Login Register exercise, 367, 377–382
loop conditions, 316–322
loop exceptions, 330–335
loops, 310–335
    dynamic nature of, 312
    exiting from, 330–331, 334
    nested, 322–330
    and Sound objects, 552, 553
    types of, 313–315
    ways of using, 310, 312, 315
    writing conditions for, 316–322
lowercase. *See* toLowerCase() method

M

Macintosh system requirements, 5
Macromedia Flash. *See* Flash
Macromedia Press, 3
Mad Libs exercise, 277–281
main movie, targeting, 94–96
Make My Day exercise, 494, 498–513, 515–519
Math object, 131, 211–213, 271
Math.abs() method, 271, 275
Math.ceil() method, 271
mathematical operators, 267–268
Math.floor() method, 271
Math.round() method, 271, 274
Math.sqrt() method, 271
matrix object, 478
max() method, 212
maxhscroll property, 430
maxscroll property, 430–431
media assets. *See* external assets
message text field, 59
methods
    Color object, 126
    event handler, 73–82
        additional information on, 76
        and custom objects, 75
        and dynamically created objects, 77
        purpose of, 35, 73–74
        and target paths, 74
        using, 75–82
    MovieClip object, 126
    object, 126–127
        creating custom, 198–203, 216–219
        creating library of, 219
        enhancing built-in, 211–216
        purpose of, 126–127
        source of custom, 219
    Sound object, 126
    String object, 126, 268, 277–281
    Text Field object, 428
    TextFormat object, 441

Microsoft Access, 376
minus sign (-), 268
modulo operator, 268
Moock.org, 595
motion detection, 55
MotionCulture, 595
mouse events, 35–46
    attaching to movie clips, 42–46
    descriptions of specific, 35–37
    Flash 5 *vs.* Flash MX, 35, 45
    purpose of, 35
    using for fingerprint scanner, 37–45
Mouse object, 131
mouseDown clip event, 55, 66, 73–74, 475
mouseMove clip event, 55, 63–64, 72, 462, 475
mouseUp clip event, 55, 66
mouseXPosition, 62, 64–65
mouseYPosition, 62, 64–65
moveTo() method, 471, 472
movie clips. *See also* movies
    attaching mouse events to, 42–46
    attaching to timelines, 86, 453–457, 458–462
    changing depth of, 452–453, 479
    controlling color/transparency of, 112–117
    controlling playback speed of, 513–519
    creating dynamically, 450–458
    creating empty instances of, 457–458
    creating parent/child relationship between, 96–100, 118
    dragging and dropping, 484–489, 530–535
    duplicating, 213–215, 312, 450–453
    event handler methods for, 75
    initializing, 230–231
    naming, 101, 267
    registering to a class, 220–234
    removing, 489–490
    targeting, 101–103, 111–118
    treating as buttons, 45, 46
    z-sorting, 479–483
Movie object, 128
MovieClip object, 126, 127, 131
movies. *See also* movie clips
    controlling, 104–117
    controlling on levels, 581–584
    loading into levels, 104–107, 577–581
    loading into targets, 560–565
    targeting
      current, 88–94
      main, 94–96
      parent, 96–100
MP3 files, 524, 560, 584–592
multimedia assets. *See* external assets
multiple identities, 118
multiplication operator, 268, 269, 326
My Journal exercise, 336, 357–364
myKid **movie clip**, 103

N

naming
    classes, 183
    global elements, 119
    identifiers, 224, 228, 550
    movie clips, 101, 267
    nodes, 371
    object instances, 128
    object properties, 125
    objects, 128, 267
    sounds, 548, 550
    variables, 128, 165, 238, 258, 267
naming collisions, 120, 165
nested loops, 322–330
nested statements, 301, 465, 467
News Flash exercise, 236, 242–248, 252–63
nextFrame() method, 513
nextScene() action, 233
nodes, 369, 371
NotSoSoft exercise, 396, 402–427
null, 77, 576
Number() function, 22, 64, 132
Number object, 132
number values, 239, 240, 266
numbers
    base 10, 136
    converting, 127, 136
    generating random, 552, 563
    hexadecimal, 136
    manipulating, 271–276
    rounding, 271
    in text fields, 21–22
    treating strings as, 269
    validating, 416–418

O

object collisions, 306–308, 312
object composition, 197–198
object inheritance, 197–198, 212, 488
object methods. *See* methods
Object object, 132, 176, 182
object properties, 124–125, 175, 203–211, 243
objectives, course, 4
objects, 122–149, 172–235. *See also* specific objects
    characteristics of, 124, 125
    classes/types of, 127–134, 174, 182–187
    as containers, 175, 179
    creating custom, 128, 132, 138, 174–175, 182–192
    creating subclasses of, 192–198, 220
    detecting collisions between, 306–308
    exercises, 135–149, 175–234
    Flash's built-in, 124, 172, 174, 198, 211
    genetically programming, 187–192
    instances of *vs.* classes of, 174
    instances of *vs.* global, 129, 140

methods for (*See* methods)
modifying, 132, 138
naming, 128, 267
properties for, 124–125, 175, 203–211, 243
purpose of, 122, 124
restricting movement of, 295–298
shared, 339, 340, 352–364
as storage devices for data, 266
understanding mechanics of, 174–181
Objects book, 128–129
on (dragOut) event handler, 37, 41, 70
on (dragOver) event handler, 37, 43
on (enterFrame) event handler, 75
on (keyPress) event handler, 36, 44
on/off values, 71, 73, 239, 298. *See also* true/false
values
on (press) event handler, 21, 23, 35, 40, 69, 75
on (release) event handler, 9, 26, 35, 41, 53, 75
on (releaseOutside) event handler, 36, 43, 70
on (rollOut) event handler, 36, 40, 53–54
on (rollOver) event handler, 36, 39–40, 45, 53–54
onClipEvent event handler, 55–56, 74
onEnterFrame event handler, 77, 78, 80
onMouseDown event handler, 74, 82
onSoundComplete event handler, 75, 587–590
operators, 10, 267–269, 286
OR operator, 286
Orchestrate Events exercise, 68–73
outside clips, 92–93
_over frame label, 46

P

panning, 526, 542–548
parameters
    passing to functions, 152, 157–165
    separating with commas, 126
    settings for, 19
parent/child relationships, 96–100, 118, 179–181
parent movies, 96–100
parent objects, 179
parentheses, 12, 126, 269
parseInt() function, 136, 139
parsing, XML, 370, 371, 372–373
paths. *See* target paths
Person Object/Class exercise, 175–192, 199–203
Phone Book exercise, 311, 330–335
phone numbers, validating, 409
Picture Show exercise, 310, 317–330
pictures **movie clip**, 47–48, 52
placeholders, interactive, 572–577
planning process, 13–16
Play button, 515, 517
playback, controlling/tracking, 513–519, 548–554
plus sign (+), 24, 267, 269
PocketpcFlash.net, 595
Polling System exercise, 344–352

pool stick. *See stick* movie clip
position property, 591
POST method, 340–341
power, giving objects, 55
powerAmount **text field**, 72, 73
precedence, order of, 269–270, 326
Preloader exercise, 519–522
presence detection, 55
press event, 21, 23, 35, 40, 69
prevFrame() method, 513
Product Registration exercise, 396, 402–420
programming resources, 594–595
progress bar, 519, 523, 590–591
projects. *See also* exercises
    graphical elements/objects for, 1
    initializing, 47, 230–231
    planning, 13–16
    troubleshooting, 241
    using dynamic data in, 241 (*See also* dynamic data)
    using sound in, 526, 548 (*See also* Sound object)
    using time in, 494, 496–497
properties
    instance-level, 188, 190–192
    object, 124–125, 175, 203–211, 243
    prototype, 191
    text field, 20, 428–432
    TextFormat object, 440–441
    watching, 203–211
    XML object, 372–373
Property inspector, 249–251, 420
proto property, 197, 212, 223
prototype objects, 187–190, 197, 203, 223
prototype properties, 191

Q

quotation marks, 12, 266, 422

R

RAM, 5
random() function, 90, 213, 552
registerClass() method, 221–223, 228
registering classes, 220–234
Registration/Login exercise, 367, 377–382
relative target paths, 86–87, 104, 107
release event, 9, 26, 35, 41, 53
releaseOutside event, 36, 43, 70
remote **movie clip**, 154
removeMovieClip() method, 489, 490
resources, Flash, 2, 594–595
restrict property, 431
return action, 166–167
rewind controls, timeline, 515, 517
RGB values, 139
Rocket Launch exercise, 282–283, 291–308
rollOut event, 36, 40, 53–54, 54
rollOver event, 36, 39–40, 45, 53–54

root movie, 88, 94
root node, 369
root object, 132
_root target path, 95–96
_root timeline, 95, 101, 104
rotateClip() function, 496
round() method, 271
routines, validation, 398, 399–401
rubbing, 37

S

scanner **movie clip**, 37–45
script elements, 8–13
script errors, 27, 241
scripts
    controlling flow of, 284–290
    planning, 13–16
    server-side, 339
    testing, 27–31
    triggering, 15 (*See also* event handlers)
    turning on/off, 71, 73, 298–303
    using loops in, 310, 312 (*See also* loops)
    writing, 16–26
scroll property, 431
Scrolling List exercise, 458–469
security features/issues, 340, 584
Selection object, 132, 143–149
Self-Running Presentation exercise, 47–54
semicolon, 11, 313
sendAndLoad() method, 376, 379
sequences, validating, 409–413
server-side scripts, 339
setFocus() method, 145
setInterval() action, 496
setNewTextFormat() method, 440
setPan() method, 542
setRGB() method, 135–136
setTextFormat() method, 440
setVariable() action, 497
setVolume() method, 528, 535, 537
shapes, filled, 476–479
shared libraries, 455
shared objects, 339, 340, 352–364
shirt **movie clip**, 135
Show Layer button, 59
siren **movie clip**, 58, 67
skeletons, function, 152
slash marks, 12, 422
Slide Show exercises, 47–54, 566–572
snapping, 36, 42
socket servers, 5, 134, 340, 383–384
sound controls, 133, 524–525, 526. *See also* Sound object
Sound event handler, 75, 588–590

Sound object
    attaching to timeline, 526–527, 548–554
    as class of objects, 127
    controlling duration/length of, 588, 591
    controlling playback of, 548–554
    controlling volume of, 528, 535–542
    creating, 526–529
    methods, 126
    purpose of, 133
sources, data, 14, 338, 339–340
spacing, in code, 12–13, 371, 391
speedClip **movie clip**, 78, 80
square brackets ([ ]), 255, 256
square-root method, 271
stacking order, 452
standards, 366–367
startDrag() action, 534
State object, 133
static text, 248, 249–250
stick **movie clip**, 68, 70–71
stop() action, 49
Stop button, 515, 517
stopDrag() action, 534
storyboarding, 16
streaming technology, 519
String object. *See also* strings
    as class of objects, 127
    methods, 126, 268, 277–281
    purpose of, 133
    working with, 143–149
string operators, 268–269
string values, 239, 266, 269, 286
strings. *See also* String object
    concatenating, 268–269, 280
    creating, 133
    getting information about, 133
    manipulating, 268–269, 277–281
    validating, 403–408
style sheets, 437
subclasses, 192–198, 220
substr() method, 277, 279
subtraction operator, 268, 269
suffixes, object name, 128
swapDepths() method, 479
SWF files
    downloading, 519
    and dynamic data, 236
    and external assets, 558, 560, 561, 578
    loading into levels, 104
    and shared objects, 352
switch statements, 289
System object, 133
system requirements, 5

T

tabEnabled property, 431
tabIndex property, 431
tabStops property, 441
tags, HTML, 368–369, 418, 437
talk() method, 200–203
target paths, 84–121
  absolute *vs.* relative, 86–87
  checking for errors in, 241
  and event handler methods, 74
  exercises, 89–117
  and levels, 104
  loading external assets into, 560–561
  purpose of, 84–85, 86
  using this in, 43, 46, 88–89
target property, 441
targeting
  current movie, 88–94
  main movie, 94–96
  movie clip instances, 101–103
  movie clip instances on levels, 111–117
  movies on levels, 104–111
  parent movie, 96–100
  timelines, 88
telephone numbers, validating, 409
Television Remote Control exercise, 154–170
Temperature Converter exercise, 264, 271–276
ternary operator, 289–290
Test Movie command, 3, 27
text
  hard-coding, 236
  highlighting, 145, 148
  HTML-formatted, 249
  identifying as hyperlink, 424
  searching, 312
  types of, 248–249
Text Field object, 249, 427
text fields, 427–447
  adding/deleting text, 428–429
  applying TextFormat object to, 437
  configuring, 249
  creating, 144, 248–254, 427–437
  event handler methods, 75
  focusing on, 79, 145
  identifying, 18
  properties of, 20, 428–432
  removing, 428
  styling text in, 437–447
  treatment of numbers in, 21–22
text files, 339
text property, 20, 277
Text tool, 236, 248, 254
TextField object, 133
TextFormat object, 134, 437–447

textHeight property, 431
textWidth property, 432
Therapy Chat exercise, 366, 377–382, 386–394
this
  in class definition, 183–185
  in regular function, 200, 205
  in scaling script, 224
  in target path, 43, 46, 88–89, 256
time
  determining current, 497–502
  measuring passage of, 496, 502–513
timelines
  associating Sound objects with, 526–527
  attaching movie clips to, 86, 453–457
  buttons as part of, 46
  communicating between, 84–85, 86
  controlling, 101–103, 513–519
  hierarchical structure of, 86–88
  mouse X/Y positions on, 62, 64–65
  placing frame labels on, 46
  placing one inside another, 96–97, 179
  placing variables on, 179
  resizing, 96
  setting line style for, 470
  sharing dynamic elements among, 117
  targeting, 88
  using clip events inside *vs.* outside, 92–93
  using dynamic data in, 241
timer **movie clip**, 58, 63, 66
togglePower() function, 155, 157–159, 161
toLowerCase() method, 143, 277, 279
Tools panel, 249
toString() method, 139
_totalframes property, 519, 522
toUpperCase() method, 143, 201, 277, 279
trace action, 175–180, 182
Training from the Source books, 2, 3
transparency, 45, 112–117
triggers, 15, 73. *See also* event handlers
troubleshooting, 241
true/false values, 71, 72, 127, 129, 239, 266. *See also*
  conditional logic
tutorials, 594, 595
TV Remote Control exercise, 154–170
.txt files, 339
type property, 432

U

Ultrashock, 595
underscore, preceding property names with, 125
Unity socket server, 384
unload clip event, 55, 65–66
unwatch() method, 205
_up frame label, 46

uppercase. *See* toUpperCase() method
URL
  encoding, 371
  validating, 409
url property, 441
URL string format, 338, 339, 342
useHandCursor property, 45
UserLogin.asp, 376

V

Vacation slide show, 47–54
validation, 396–418
  handling errors identified by, 401–403
  against list of choices, 414–416
  of numbers, 416–418
  purpose of, 396–398
  role of conditional statements in, 401
  of sequences, 409–413
  steps in process, 398
  of strings, 403–408
validation points, 401, 404, 405
validation routines, 398, 399–401
values, variable, 144, 239, 267
variable property, 432
variables
  assigning string values to, 144
  copying, 453
  creating, 17, 118–120, 165–166, 238–243
  initializing, 257
  loading/sending, 342, 343
  naming, 128, 165, 238, 258, 267
  placing on timelines, 179
  referencing, 118–120
  setting values for, 267
  storing, 125
  toggling, 290
  types of values for, 239
  using local, 165–166, 201
Virtual Aquarium exercise, 556–557, 561–587
volume, sound, 28, 526, 535–542

W

warning action, 51
watch() method, 203–205, 209
watchCondition() function, 204, 205
weather array, 258–259
weather **movie clip,** 203–205
We're Here Web site, 595
wheel **movie clip,** 77, 79
wheelClip **movie clip,** 80
while loop, 313, 316–317, 319–323, 328, 332
white space, 13, 371, 391
Windows system requirements, 5
with statement, 433, 438, 443
Word Game exercise, 277–281
Word Processor exercise, 145–149

X

X/Y positions, mouse, 62, 64–65
XML, 366–395
  compared with HTML, 368–369
  documents, 369, 370
  event handler methods, 75
  files, 338–339, 340
  formatting, 371–372
  loading, 374
  nodes, 369
  parsing, 370, 371, 372–373
  purpose of, 366–367, 368
  sending, 374–375
  and socket servers, 340
  syntax for, 368–370
XML object, 134, 371–375
XML Socket event handler methods, 75
XMLSocket object, 5, 134, 385–394

Y

Yummi Cola exercise, 556

Z

z-sorting, 479–483
Zip codes, 144–145, 416–418

Macromedia Authorized Training—Get Trained, Get Certified

Get the skills to get ahead. Macromedia offers a mix of high quality training services to help you learn and master web design and development.

Instructor-Led Training

The Macromedia Authorized Training Partner (MATP) network is committed to the quality delivery of the Macromedia Authorized Curriculum. Every instructor is certified and meets specific training standards. For more information, visit **www.macromedia.com/go/mmtraining**

Online Training

Train at your own pace on a full set of Macromedia products and web technologies. Choose your skill level and work your way up through a variety of topics. For more detail, visit **www.macromedia.com/university**

SkillBuilding with ColdFusion® CD-ROM

An interactive, CD-ROM based, self-study training program designed to get new users up and running quickly and effectively with Macromedia ColdFusion. For more information, visit **www.macromedia.com/go/skillbuilding**

Macromedia Press

Expand your knowledge with books on Macromedia products for all skill levels. For more information, visit **www.macromedia.com/go/books**

Professional Certification

Set yourself apart and enhance your career. A Macromedia Professional Certification shows that you have the skills and training that employers, clients and peers respect. Certification exams are available in over 2,500 testing centers worldwide. For a complete list of exams, visit **www.macromedia.com/go/certification**

Macromedia Tech Support: http://www.macromedia.com/support

LICENSING AGREEMENT

The information in this book is for informational use only and is subject to change without notice. Macromedia, Inc., and Macromedia Press assume no responsibility for errors or inaccuracies that may appear in this book. The software described in the book is furnished under license and may be used or copied only in accordance with terms of the license.

The software files on the CD-ROM included here are copyrighted by Macromedia, Inc. You have the non-exclusive right to use these programs and files. You may use them on one computer at a time. You may not transfer the files from one computer to another over a network. You may transfer the files onto a single hard disk so long as you can prove ownership of the original CD-ROM.

You may not reverse engineer, decompile, or disassemble the software. You may not modify or translate the software or distribute copies of the software without the written consent of Macromedia, Inc.

Opening the disc package means you accept the licensing agreement. For installation instructions, see the ReadMe file on the CD-ROM.